Language and Culture

"What autobiographical writing does is to humanize authors, locate them in time and space, and invite critical engagement on the part of readers. . . . By writing in the first person and using the active voice, the authors in this volume establish a more equitable relationship between writer and reader, thus encouraging students to voice their own ideas and to actively engage in meaning-making. . . . As I prepare for my classes, I am challenged to find ways to validate the ethnic identities of students, but also to respond to their gendered identities, their socioeconomic histories, and their sexual orientations. I also strive to encourage students to engage critically with the written text, to take ownership of their ideas, and to claim their voices as members of our global profession. To this end, *Language and Culture: Reflective Narratives and the Emergence of Identity* will be essential reading in my classroom."

Bonny Norton, From the Foreword

This state-of-the-art exploration of language, culture, and identity is orchestrated through prominent scholars' and teachers' narratives, each weaving together three elements: a personal account based on one or more memorable or critical incidents that occurred in the course of learning or using a second or foreign language; an interpretation of the incidents highlighting their impact in terms of culture, identity, and language; the connections between the experiences and observations of the author and existing literature on language, culture, and identity.

What makes this book stand out is the way in which authors meld traditional "academic" approaches to inquiry with their own personalized voices. This opens a window on different ways of viewing and doing research in Applied Linguistics and TESOL. What gives the book its power is the compelling nature of the narratives themselves. Telling stories is a fundamental way of representing and making sense of the human condition. These stories unpack, in an accessible but rigorous fashion, complex socio-cultural constructs of culture, identity, the self and other, and reflexivity, and offer a way into these constructs for teachers, teachers in preparation, and neophyte researchers. Contributors from around the world give the book broad and international appeal.

David Nunan is Vice President for Academic Affairs at Anaheim University, California, Emeritus Professor at the University of Hong Kong, Professor in Education at the University of NSW, and Senior Academic Advisor to Global English Corporation in San Francisco.

Julie Choi is Teaching and Research Assistant in the Faculty of Arts and Social Sciences at the University of Technology, Sydney.

ESL & Applied Linguistics Professional Series
Eli Hinkel, Series Editor

Nunan/Choi, Eds. · *Language and Culture: Reflective Narratives and the Emergence of Identity*
Braine · *Nonnative Speaker English Teachers: Research, Pedagogy, and Professional Growth*
Burns · *Doing Action Research in English Language Teaching: A Guide for Practitioners*
Nation/Macalister · *Language Curriculum Design*
Birch · *The English Language Teacher and Global Civil Society*
Johnson · *Second Language Teacher Education: A Sociocultural Perspective*
Nation · *Teaching ESL/EFL Reading and Writing*
Nation/Newton · *Teaching ESL/EFL Listening and Speaking*
Kachru/Smith · *Cultures, Contexts, and World Englishes*
McKay/Bokhosrt-Heng · *International English in its Sociolinguistic Contexts: Towards a Socially Sensitive EIL Pedagogy*
Christison/Murray, Eds. · *Leadership in English Language Education: Theoretical Foundations and Practical Skills for Changing Times*
McCafferty/Stam, Eds. · *Gesture: Second Language Acquisition and Classroom Research*
Liu · *Idioms: Description, Comprehension, Acquisition, and Pedagogy*
Chapelle/Enright/Jamison, Eds. · *Building a Validity Argument for the Text of English as a Foreign Language™*
Kondo-Brown/Brown, Eds. · *Teaching Chinese, Japanese, and Korean Heritage Students: Curriculum Needs, Materials, and Assessments*
Youmans · *Chicano-Anglo Conversations: Truth, Honesty, and Politeness*
Birch · *English L2 Reading: Getting to the Bottom, Second Edition*
Luk/Lin · *Classroom Interactions as Cross-cultural Encounters: Native Speakers in EFL Lessons*
Levy/Stockwell · *CALL Dimensions: Issues and Options in Computer Assisted Language Learning*
Nero, Ed. · *Dialects, Englishes, Creoles, and Education*
Basturkmen · *Ideas and Options in English for Specific Purposes*
Kumaravadivelu · *Understanding Language Teaching: From Method to Postmethod*
McKay · *Researching Second Language Classrooms*
Egbert/Petrie, Eds. · *CALL Research Perspectives*
Canagarajah, Ed. · *Reclaiming the Local in Language Policy and Practice*
Adamson · *Language Minority Students in American Schools: An Education in English*
Fotos/Browne, Eds. · *New Perspectives on CALL for Second Language Classrooms*
Hinkel · *Teaching Academic ESL Writing: Practical Techniques in Vocabulary and Grammar*
Hinkel/Fotos, Eds. · *New Perspectives on Grammar Teaching in Second Language Classrooms*
Hinkel · *Second Language Writers' Text: Linguistic and Rhetorical Features*

Visit **www.routledge.com/education** for additional information on titles in the ESL & Applied Linguistics Professional Series

Language and Culture

Reflective Narratives and the Emergence of Identity

Edited by

David Nunan
University of Hong Kong

Julie Choi
University of Technology, Sydney

Routledge
Taylor & Francis Group
NEW YORK AND LONDON

First published 2010
by Routledge
270 Madison Avenue, New York, NY 10016

Simultaneously published in the UK
by Routledge
2 Park Square, Milton Park, Abingdon, Oxon OX14 4RN

Routledge is an imprint of the Taylor & Francis Group, an informa business

Typeset in Minion and Gill Sans by
Swales & Willis Ltd, Exeter, Devon

Library of Congress Cataloging in Publication Data
Language and culture : reflective narratives and the emergence of identity / edited by David Nunan, Julie Choi.
p. cm. – (ESL & applied linguistics professional series)
Includes bibliographical references and index. [etc.]
1. Language and languages. 2. Language and culture. 3. Multiculturalism.
I. Nunan, David. II. Choi, Julie.
P410.L36 2009
302.44–dc22 2009037281

ISBN 10: 0–415–87165–4 (hbk)
ISBN 10: 0–415–87166–2 (pbk)
ISBN 10: 0–203–85698–8 (ebk)

ISBN 13: 978–0–415–87165–5 (hbk)
ISBN 13: 978–0–415–87166–2 (pbk)
ISBN 13: 978–0–203–85698–7 (ebk)

To Soondely, Kevin, and Stella
In memory of Chloe
– Julie

To my co-editor
who was more than an equal partner in this venture
– David

Contents

Foreword

The manuscript for *Language and Culture: Reflective Narratives and the Emergence of Identity* arrived in my inbox on June 11, 2009, as I was in the midst of preparing to teach two summer courses at the University of British Columbia. One course, "Applied Linguistics for Language Teachers", is a core undergraduate course in our English Second Language program, and the second, "Language, Discourse, and Identity", is a graduate course I teach on a regular basis. This serendipitous arrival of the manuscript provided the ideal opportunity for me to reflect on the ways in which the themes in David Nunan and Julie Choi's edited volume might have relevance for two important audiences in the field of language education: aspiring language teachers on the one hand, and fledgling researchers on the other.

As I reflected on the possible impact of the manuscript on both student teachers and emerging researchers, my first observation was that the narrative genre chosen by Nunan and Choi not only makes the volume highly readable and enjoyable, but also serves three important functions at a more scholarly level. First, the autobiographical commentary helps to demystify well-known authors in the field, and gives students greater freedom to debate and critique the ideas presented. Many students come to class believing that the printed word has an absolute authority, and that the role of the student is to absorb and reproduce the ideas of authors on required reading lists. In my teaching, I strive to promote discussion on the ways in which ideas are generated, debated, and disseminated, and this volume will prove an excellent resource in this endeavor. What autobiographical writing does is to humanize authors, locate them in time and space, and invite critical engagement on the part of readers. Indeed, Allan Luke, perhaps tongue-in-cheek, goes so far as to invite readers to "feel free to rewrite" his words. Such an invitation represents both an exciting opportunity and a profound challenge to students.

The second point is related to the first: in adopting a narrative style, authors have written in the first person, and the voice of the writer is highly visible to the reader. Most of the texts that students read in the course of their studies are written in expository, third person style, and as Angel Lin has pointed out in earlier work (Lin, 2004), students frequently struggle to construct meaning from these disembodied texts. Scholars such as Fairclough (2003) and Janks (1997) remind us that texts written in the passive voice frequently conceal the agency of the writer, and reinforce inequitable relations of power between writers and readers. By writing in the first person and using the active voice, the authors in this volume establish a more equitable relationship between writer and reader, thus encouraging students to voice their own ideas and to actively engage in meaning-making. If students are to develop as both teachers and researchers, they need a safe space in which to enter into a productive debate with established research, and possibly challenge received wisdom. The authors in this volume have provided the safe haven necessary to promote self-reflection and critical analysis.

The third advantage of the autobiographical, narrative approach, as far as student learning is concerned, is the validation of past history and experience. One of the barriers I encounter in my teaching is that students frequently consider their own history and experience to be irrelevant to teaching and research. This perception is particularly common with students who have few material resources and a history of inequity. The authors in this volume take the opportunity to reflect on their own life histories, with particular reference to language learning, and convincingly demonstrate the centrality of personal experience in their professional lives. Mary Ann Christison, for example, describes how being told by a well-meaning teacher, at the tender age of 12, to "change the way you talk" led Christison to better understand the relationship between language and identity. What is reassuring, as Sumiko Taniguchi notes, is that adverse experiences can not only be analyzed and critiqued, but also transformed: "I kept thinking back and rewriting my AFS story", she says. Stein's (2008) research in the South African context serves a model for the ways in which the resources that students bring to the classroom can be re-appropriated and transformed in emancipatory ways.

While the genres of autobiography and narrative are particularly empowering for students, the authors in this volume raise a number of issues that are also highly relevant for experienced teachers and established scholars. Three issues, among many others, concern the identity of non-native language teachers, the relationship between theory and practice, and the distinction between culture and identity.

In recent years, there has been much interest in the role of the non-native teacher in language education, particularly in the field of English language teaching (Braine, 1999; Liu, 1999). This has led to debates on legitimacy in the field of language teaching, a topic of interest to a number of authors in this volume. Kimie Takahashi, for example, who learned English at school in Japan, describes how all writing and presentations at her two-year college had to be "checked and approved by native speaker teachers from the UK, US, Canada or Australia". This system, Takahashi argues, engendered the belief that it was the native speaker who was legitimate, and the non-native speaker who had "no authority". Of particular concern in the field is the effect of covert and overt forms of racism on language education (Kubota & Lin, 2006), and the association of the native English speaker with someone who is white. Eljee Javier, a native speaker of English of Filipino descent, describes in her chapter how her Chinese students were "confused" by her appearance, and assumed she could not be a native speaker because she looked "Chinese". It was only when Javier told the students that she was from Canada, that they (reluctantly) accepted her credentials. To support her arguments, she draws on Liu (1999), who noted that one of the participants in his research, a Ms. K, was seen by her students as a native speaker of English because she was white, despite having been born and raised in Denmark until the age of 10.

The relevance of theory to address these problems of practice is another important theme of great interest to teachers and researchers. For example, with respect to the legitimacy of non-native teachers, Julian Edge notes how he draws on Cook's (1999) research on multicompetence, and Pavlenko's (2003) research on the bilingual language teacher, to inform his practice. What Edge finds particularly powerful is the innovative pedagogy that Pavlenko uses, in which she encourages language teachers to re-imagine themselves as multicompetent and bilingual, rather than as deficient speakers of a second language. Stacey Holman Jones, another contributor to this volume, writes of the ways in which Foucault's (1988) theories of the panopticon and disciplinary power led to an enhanced understanding of women's visibility in contemporary society: "The air in the room changes. I am pulsing with recognition", she writes. Her visceral response to this theory is reminiscent of my own reaction to reading the post-structuralist theories of Christine Weedon (1997), while still a graduate student at the University of Toronto; her work on subjectivity was pivotal in my own evolving theories of identity as a site of struggle, changing across time and space, and reproduced in social interaction (Norton, 2000). There are multiple ways in which poststructuralist theories of identity are relevant for practice: if a student fails to thrive, the teacher is encouraged to consider what alternative identity positions might prove more productive for the learner, encouraging engagement from a position of power rather than powerlessness (Norton & Toohey, 2004).

This then brings me to the distinction between culture and identity, an issue raised by David Nunan, and of great interest to teachers and researchers alike. In the 1970s and 1980s, applied linguists tended to draw distinctions between social identity, which was seen to reference the relationship between the individual language learner and the larger social world (e.g., Gumperz, 1982), and cultural identity, which referenced the relationship between an individual and members of a particular ethnic group, who share a common history and language (e.g., Valdes, 1986). Today, as evidenced in this volume, distinctions between social and cultural identity have blurred, and identity is often framed as multiple and conflictual. Nevertheless, the remnants of more essentialist notions of identity, which frequently equate identity with culture, or ethnic identity, remain remarkably resilient. Thus Emi Otsuji, for example, expresses her embarrassment at assuming that students are from a particular country only because their family name sounds Chinese, or because they can speak Cantonese, and she seeks to address these problematic assumptions in her pedagogy: "I am trying to teach students that they should not stereotype Japan and that the relationship between language, nation state, cultural identity, and ethnicity is fluid", she writes. From a different perspective, Julie Choi's narrative, which represents a quest for connection to her Korean culture, is all too familiar to mobile students, teachers, and researchers in many parts of the world. Is it possible to embrace multiple identities, while simultaneously seeking a "home" and a place of belonging?

As I prepare for my summer classes, I am challenged to find ways to validate the ethnic identities of students, but also to respond to their gendered identities, their socioeconomic histories, and their sexual orientations. I will also strive to encourage students to engage critically with the written text, to take ownership of their ideas, and to claim their voices as members of our global profession. To this end, *Language and Culture: Reflective Narratives and the Emergence of Identity* will be essential reading in my classroom.

References

Braine, G. (1999). *Non-native educators in English language teaching.* London: Lawrence Erlbaum.

Cook, V. (1999). Going beyond the native speaker in language teaching. *TESOL Quarterly, 33*, 185–209.

Fairclough, N. (2003). *Analysing discourse: Textual analysis for social research.* London: Routledge.

Foucault, M. (1988). *Madness and civilization: A history of insanity in the age of reason* (R. Howard, Trans.). New York: Vintage.

Gumperz, J. (1982). *Language and social identity.* Cambridge, England: Cambridge University Press.

Janks, H. (1997). Critical discourse analysis as a research tool. *Discourse: Studies in the Cultural Politics of Education, 18* (3), 329–342.

Kubota, R., & Lin, A. (2006). Race and TESOL: Introduction to concepts and theories [Special issue]. *TESOL Quarterly, 40* (3), 471–493.

Lin, A. (2004). Introducing a critical pedagogical curriculum: A feminist reflexive account. In B. Norton & K. Toohey (Eds.), *Critical pedagogies and language learning* (pp. 271–290). New York: Cambridge University Press.

Liu, J. (1999). Non-native English speaking professionals in TESOL. *TESOL Quarterly, 33* (1), 85–102.

Norton, B. (2000). *Identity and language learning: Gender, ethnicity, and educational change.* Harlow, England: Longman/Pearson.

Norton, B., & Toohey, K. (Eds). (2004). *Critical pedagogies and language learning.* New York: Cambridge University Press.

Pavlenko, A. (2003). "I never knew I was a bilingual": Reimagining teacher identities in TESOL. In Y. Kanno & B. Norton (Guest Eds.), Imagined communities and educational possibilities. [Special issue]. *Journal of Language, Identity, and Education, 2* (4), 251–268.

Stein, P. (2008). *Multimodal pedagogies in diverse classrooms: Representation, rights and resources.* London and New York: Routledge.

Valdes, J. M. (1986). *Culture bound: Bridging the cultural gap in language teaching.* Cambridge, England: Cambridge University Press.

Weedon, C. (1997). *Feminist practice and poststructuralist theory* (2nd Edition). Oxford: Blackwell.

Bonny Norton
University of British Columbia, Canada
July, 2009

Preface

The contributions to this collection reflect an emerging perspective on language learning and use. The "traditional", product-oriented view, which still holds sway in many educational systems around the world, has it that language consists of a body of content, and the task for the learner is to internalize that content. According to this view, language is simply another subject on the school curriculum. In the 1970s, this view was challenged by a process-oriented view which sees language as a tool for communication. These views, while legitimate, are partial. As the contributions to this collection so powerfully attest, language is also a means for self definition and personal transformation.

In the course of crafting and making sense of our own narratives, as well as working with our contributors as they crafted and made sense of their own, our perspective on the three key constructs underlying the volume, language, culture, and identity, constantly metamorphosed. Writing thus became a vehicle for discovery and transformation, and we found ourselves living the question: how do I know what I think until I see what I write?

As the contributions began appearing in our in-boxes, we were delighted with the quality of the interpretive accounts, all of which contested the key constructs of culture, identity, and language. We were equally pleased with the ways in which the contributions illuminated the questions we had been contesting on the nature of research in terms of data, interpretation, and representation.

As we worked on the contributions, we were struck by the power of good stories, and these are all good stories. They give up their essence gradually. We were constantly reminded that good movies, novels, and songs present different faces on re-viewing, re-reading, and re-listening. As we re-read the personal narratives at the heart of each contribution, they showed a different face. This is partly because we were different the second and third time around, and the context in which we were reading had changed.

Stories in the book involve a range of languages, not just English. Learners developed a new sense of self through their new language. Each language has its own unique link to the culture with which it co-exists. Most importantly, there are ways of knowing and being that can only be expressed in particular languages. (Conversely, there are also things that *can't* be expressed.) Perceptions of the world are unique to each and every language, and learning that language makes those perceptions visible, and enables the second language speaker to express them.

This book is intended primarily for undergraduate and graduate students, researchers, and teachers. Given the accessibility of the contributions, we also hope the volume might find space on the bookshelf of the general reader who is interested in ways in which globalization is transforming our understanding of language, culture, and identity.

David Nunan and Julie Choi

Acknowledgments

We would like first and foremost to thank Eli Hinkel and Naomi Silverman for encouraging us to undertake this project in the first place, whose support for the project never wavered, and whose enthusiasm was infectious. Thanks also go to Meeta Pendharkar for her administrative and editorial support. We would also like to thank Rosemary Morlin and Richard Willis for their editorial guidance. Particular thanks to the anonymous reviewers of our original proposal who provided many insightful criticisms and suggestions.

We acknowledge and thank Akiko Muto for permission to reproduce her photographs in Michael Brennan's chapter, and Yasuhiro Yotsumoto for permission to reproduce the translated poem he wrote with Michael Brennan at the beginning of his chapter.

David Nunan and Julie Choi

Chapter 1

Language, Culture, and Identity

Framing the Issues

David Nunan
University of Hong Kong
Julie Choi
University of Technology, Sydney

Like many similar works, this collection began as a conversation. Well, to be honest, it was more an argument than a conversation. One night over drinks we began discussing new directions in research methodology. Julie had sent David a copy of Carolyn Ellis's "Final Negotiation," a compelling account of her life with a partner with a terminal disease. David, somewhat provocatively, asked, "Well, it's a wonderfully-written, moving account, but is it research?"

The ensuing "conversation" opened up a raft of questions and dilemmas. Many of these are well rehearsed in the literature on research methodology (see for example, Nunan & Bailey, 2009; van Lier, 1988, 1990). Questions we debated and discussed included:

What counts as legitimate data? Is meeting threats to reliability and validity a precondition for inquiry to count as "research?" Does the manner in which research is presented qualify or disqualify it as research? What is "academic" writing? Where is the boundary between fact and fiction? Are accounts based on introspection research or self-indulgence? These were all issues that came up time and again as we shaped the volume and began to solicit contributions to it.

When we issued invitations for contributions to this volume, we asked authors to include in their chapters three elements: a brief language learning history; one or two narrative events or critical incidents that occurred while learning or using language and that highlighted either some aspect of culture, identity, or language, or the interconnections between some or all of these constructs; and a commentary on the narratives. We were happy for contributors to either present the background, narratives and commentary separately, or to weave these elements together. For us, the resulting pieces can be characterized as "research."

Very early in the development of the collection we came head-to-head with the issue of academic style and personal voice. One reviewer of our initial proposal argued that the work needed to be "more academic." Another reviewer suggested we keep all of the narratives and commentaries separate. A colleague asked, "Aren't you freaking out about the use of 'I' in your research?"

The process of writing opens up questions and brings the writer face-to-face with the purpose and intention of the act of recording and interpreting narrative accounts. We and our co-authors set off in one direction and more often than not found ourselves in some place else. The act of writing thus became part of the act of inquiry. It became clear to us that *how* the story is told is as integral to the final product as *what* the story is about. The author's voice thus became an important motif in the evolution of the book. As we have noted elsewhere:

> By "voice" we are referring to the centrality of the human story to qualitative research in terms of *what* the story is and *how* the story is told. Stories touch the human heart as well as the mind. From time immemorial they have provided a vehicle for entertainment, but, more importantly in pre- and non-literature societies, for passing cultural knowledge from one generation to the next. In taking this stance, we believe that research methodology has to do with not just how the research is conceptualized and conducted, but how it is represented. We are aware of the ambiguity in the term "represent"; that it can be taken two ways—"to stand for" and "to re-present."
>
> (Nunan & Choi, forthcoming)

Whether we are monolinguals or multilinguals, experts or novices, we all come across and struggle with issues of how language and culture affect or influence our identity. (We note that the current literature identifies bi/multilinguals, not necessarily as someone with high levels of proficiency in two or more languages, but someone who functions in more than one language for purposes of communication. The term "plurilingualism" is also gaining currency to describe such individuals, whose numbers are on the increase with globalization and the international flow of peoples around the world.)

Micro Level Analysis as a Point of Departure

Initially we envisaged this as a "fun" project. We thought that producing a self report, then reflecting on it, analyzing it, and connecting it to the literature, if not easy, would not necessarily be difficult. How wrong we were! Many contributors, having embarked on the process, came back to us with comments on just how hard it was. Several had to confront the dilemma of self-disclosure, something they had never had to do in their regular academic writing. Others struggled with questions of whether the personal stories and their interpretations made sense, if the accounts were rigorous enough or would resonate with readers. One who was caught between two cultures told us that through the writing of her piece she finally knew where it was that she wanted to be buried. Most of our contributors sent their pieces to colleagues and personal acquaintances asking for guidance and feedback. Some also experimented with their stories in writing groups before they submitted a co-constructed final chapter. Most, if not all of the chapters, are thus a product of intertextuality, although ultimately individual authors made the final decision of what their stories meant to them. They were creating their own "truths." (This struggle to capture experienced "truths" in words reflects issues of voice and professionalism in Casanave and Schecter's 1997 edited collection.)

Despite all of the questions of what is or isn't academically acceptable, perhaps the chapters here are models for what senior and junior academics see as academically acceptable in terms of using personal narratives and theories for research purposes. Concepts of collaboration, reflexivity, personal narratives, storytelling, autoethnography, and writing life histories have been around for several decades but when they all come together and are examined in 5,000 words or less, a new genre emerges.

In addition to applied linguists, we invited contributions from writers in other fields: a well-known journalist and novelist, members of communications departments, etc. By looking outwards, we discovered that the conversations that we had begun having, and the questions and issues we were facing, were being confronted by individuals and groups from many different scholarly communities all over the world.

Defining and Differentiating Key Constructs

As the title suggests, the central constructs providing a scaffolding for the volume are *language, culture,* and *identity.* Another central concept is that of *reflexivity.* Many articles, and indeed whole books have grappled with the challenge of defining these constructs, and collectively, there are literally hundreds of definitions.

The three characterizations of "culture" we like are those by Kramsch (1998), Judd (2002), and Pennycook (1995). Judd (2002:10) suggests that "[c]ulture can be defined as the system of shared objects, activities and beliefs of a given group of people." Kramsch (1998:127) also emphasizes the notion of shared practice, suggesting that culture is "the membership in a discourse community that shares a common social space and history, and a common system of standards for perceiving, believing, evaluating, and acting." The contributions to this volume bear out the reality that as individuals we belong simultaneously to multiple cultures and sub-cultures. Pennycook sees culture "as the process by which people make sense of their lives, a process always involved in struggles over meaning and representation" (Pennycook, 1995: 47). Again, the reference to personal struggle within a larger social context resonates with numerous contributions to the collection.

"Identity is about belonging, about what you have in common with some people and what differentiates you from others" (Weeks, 1990: 88). Identity is therefore recognition of cultural belonging, which is internal to the individual, while culture is external. Identity is no longer seen as a unitary or ever stable construct. As Norton (forthcoming) has noted, and as our contributors attest in their narratives,

> [e]very time we speak, we are negotiating and renegotiating our sense of self in relation to the larger social world, and reorganizing that relationship across time and space. Our gender, race, class, ethnicity, sexual orientations, among other characteristics, are all implicated in this negotiation of identity.
>
> (p.2)

Such negotiation is interwoven with power, politics, ideologies and "interlocutors' views of their own and others' identities" (Pavlenko & Blackledge, 2004:1).

The metamorphic nature of the construct has become ever more apparent with globalization and the emergence of a globalized citizenry. We are witnessing the emergence of a more dynamic type of identity formation that confronts people with hybridized or cosmopolitan identities in the twenty-first century. As Delanty (2003:133) states,

> [s]trangeness has become more central to the self today, both in terms of a strangeness within the self and in the relationship between self and other. This experience of strangeness captures the essence of the postmodern sensibility, namely the feeling of insecurity, contingency and uncertainty both in the world and in the identity of the self.

In this current view of identity

> the capacity for autonomy is no longer held in check by rigid structures, such as class, gender, nation, ethnicity. The self can be invented in many ways. The contemporary understanding of the self is that of a social self formed in relations of difference rather than of unity and coherence.
>
> (p. 135)

In the narratives that follow, you will see this theme being played out time and time again.

Language is another construct that has resulted in hundreds, if not thousands of book-length treatments. (See for example, Nunan, 2007.) Kramsch argues that:

> Language is only one of many semiotic systems with which learners make sense of the world expressed in a different language. The acquisition of another language is not an act of disembodied cognition, but is the situated, spatially and temporally anchored, co-construction of meaning between teachers and learners who each carry with them their own history of experience with language and communication. Culture is not one worldview, shared by all the members of a national speech community; it is multifarious, changing, and, more often than not, conflictual.
>
> (Kramsch, 2004: 255)

Each of the contributions to this collection represents an exercise in reflexivity, reflexivity being "... the process of continually reflecting upon our interpretations of both our experience and the phenomena being studied so as to move beyond the partiality of our previous understandings and our investment in particular research outcomes" (Finlay, 2003:108). They also bear out Finlay's contention that

> When we narrate our experience (be it in an interview or when providing a reflexive account) we offer one version—an interpretation—which seems to work for that moment. Like an external observer, we have to reflect on the evidence and recognise the indexicality and non-conclusive nature of any of our understandings. "All reflection is situational . . . always subject to revision."
>
> (McCleary cited in Finlay, 2003: 110)

The pieces in this collection weave together learning histories, personal narratives, and theory. The words "theory" and "theorizing" get tossed around rather loosely in the literature. The following statement from Julian Edge, one of our contributors, comes closest to capturing our sense of the term and reflects what our contributors have done in situating their narratives within the research genres that intersect with the concerns, issues, and perspectives that emerge from the narratives.

> . . . what I mean by theory is an articulation of the best understanding thus far available to investigators as to why things are the way they are. This kind of formulation can exist at the level of a Nobel Prize winner, and at the level of a novice teacher. One tries to make a statement that accounts for the data as one understands them.
>
> (Edge, 2008: 653)

As we attempted to define key constructs, we came to question their separability. In other words, we became reflexive about our own area of inquiry. To what extent is it possible to separate culture and identity, language and culture, language and identity? In many texts, one is defined in terms of the other. Our own stance is that culture is an "outside the individual" construct, while identity is an "inside the individual" construct. Culture, as we have said, has to do with the artifacts, ways of doing, etc. shared by a group of people. Identity is the acceptance and internalization of the artifacts and ways of doing by a member of that group.

While reading and reviewing the contributions to the volume, we also came face-to-face with the "identity paradox." We all have multiple identities, and these can weld us together into cultures and subcultures separated by existential chasms. However, if we look beyond these chasms, we are all part of the human race, with similar aspirations and ideals.

In casual conversations with friends, colleagues, and even strangers, we found that "culture" and "identity" are pervasive but invisible until they are pointed out. Just as a fish is unaware of water until it is pulled from the ocean, the river or the stream, so most people are unaware of their culture or identity until they are confronted with other cultures and identities.

The Sapir-Whorf Hypothesis

As we worked on this collection, we were prompted to revisit the work of Edward Sapir and Benjamin Lee Whorf, two writers whose works would appear to be somewhat unfashionable at the present time.

> Sapir's great contribution to linguistic thought lies in his linking of language and culture. While all languages share certain universal characteristics, there are aspects of language that are culturally specific. According to Sapir, the language and culture into which one is born shape the way one thinks. They create mental "tracks" upon which our minds run. Sapir also argued that cultures sharing a language share a way of thinking, and that these ways of thinking constituted the psychology of the culture.
>
> (Nunan, 2007: 200)

Along with Sapir, Whorf formulated the notion that ability to make sense of the world is conditioned, if not determined, by the language that we speak. In his work as a fire-prevention officer for an insurance company, he was fascinated by the ways in which people constructed narrative accounts of their experiences of accidents caused by fires. These accounts said as much about the narrators and their cultural backgrounds as they did about the events themselves.

According to the strong version of the Sapir-Whorf hypothesis, we cannot see what we cannot name. Thus, according to the hypothesis, the Hopi Indians have no conception of time because the Hopi language has no tenses or time expressions. The notion that the way we talk conditions how we think, and, in fact, controls our perception of reality, has been hugely controversial. The linguistic determinism implicit in the Sapir-Whorf hypothesis has been largely discredited (are we really incapable of seeing puce if our language lacks a label for that particular color?), and is unfashionable these days. Nonetheless, it represents an important landmark in linguistic thought

(Nunan, 2007: 201). From numerous contributions to this collection, it would seem that it is not a matter of "can't see," but "can't say." In other words, it is not a matter of perception but of articulation.

Overview

Each contribution to this volume takes one or more critical incidents, and uses these to place language, culture, and identity under the lens. By critical incident we are referring to an event that stimulates the individual to restructure their understanding of the nexus between language, culture, and identity. There are many such incidents and events in an individual's journey but not all necessarily resonate with the learner at the time of the incident or on reflection upon it. In this volume all contributors were able to identify one or more critical incidents that helped them transform the language and culture within which they were functioning. Sub-themes such as voice, power, self, and other also emerge in the narratives and the theorizing that grows out of these narratives.

In Chapter 2, "Coat Hangers, Cowboys, and Communication Strategies: Seeking an Identity as a Proficient Foreign Language Learner," Kathi Bailey frames her efforts to learn Spanish, Korean, and French in terms of the tension between language as an academic subject to the studied and language as a tool for authentic communication. She recounts her struggle to use her Spanish and French to obtain common goods and services when she has a lower intermediate level of proficiency. She uses her experiences to explore the constructs of identity and investment.

David Block, who speaks English, Spanish, and Catalan, makes the case in Chapter 3, "Speaking *Romance-esque*," that speakers of one or more romance languages can communicate with each other using the different languages that they speak, rather than the language of their interlocutor. He calls the use of a range of romance languages for intercultural communication *Romance-esque* and suggests that the practice provides a useful antidote to the notion that English is the only vehicle for communicating on the global stage.

Each chapter in this collection illustrates, in its own way, the complex interplay between the key constructs of language, culture, and identity. Most authors choose to privilege one construct over the others, although all are represented in each piece in one way or another. In Michael Brennan's finely honed piece (Chapter 4, "空 Collaborating on Community, Sharing Experience, Troubling the Symbolic") culture finds its way to the foreground, although issues of language and identity also play a central part. All of the pieces in the collection are, by their nature, deeply personal; none so more than Brennan's which takes its departure from the death of that author's brother, and weaves through the narrative themes of mortality and loss.

Suresh Canagarajah, in Chapter 5, "Achieving Community," builds on two critical incidents with fellow Tamil Sri Lankans to challenge the construct of "community." On a visit to Canada, Canagarajah encounters a Tamil who denies knowledge of his native language. Assuming that Tamil immigrants do not want to identify with the Tamil community, Canagarajah learns not to initiate conversation in his native language with Canadian Tamils. Towards the end of his visit, however, a Canadian Tamil initiates a conversation with him in Tamil. Through these casual encounters, he is led to abandon his long-held assumption that "community" was monolithic and homogeneous. His experiences and insights resonate strongly with those of Choi in her interactions with Korean communities.

Language and power take center stage in Mark Cherry's contribution (Chapter 6, "Another Drink in Subanun"). Cherry recounts an incident at immigration in Denpasar in which he is clearly in the wrong, having inadvertently overstayed his visa. His provides a detailed analysis and interpretation of his brief interrogation by the immigration official, in which he chooses to use his less than perfect Indonesian rather than English. The encounter not only illustrates the interplay of language and power, but also dramatizes Dell Hymes's contention that effective communication requires much more than mastery of grammar and vocabulary, that central to the process is what we call "all that other stuff": knowledge of what to say, in what language, to what kinds of people in what kinds of situations (Hymes, 1962).

In Chapter 7, "Nonghao, I am a Shanghai Noenoe: How do I Claim my Shanghainese-ness?," Alice Chik deals directly with cultural identity. She outlines her struggle with the Shanghainese dialect, which her parents and extended family use at home, but not to her, and questions what it means to claim "Shanghaineseness." Her claim that "I feel more comfortable with the label of 'Shanghainese-Hongkonger.' I am more than Shanghainese and I am more than Hongkonger" resonates strongly with Choi's experience of "living on the hyphen" as a Korean-American. Chik grew up speaking Cantonese as her first language, eavesdropping on Shanghainese at home, and learning English at school. For her, personal identity is inextricably bound up with her languages and cultures.

In Chapter 8, "Living on the Hyphen," Julie Choi recounts a simple everyday life event that prompts her to reflect on several major critical incidents about language and culture from her past. These series of critical reflections of living in New York, Seoul, Beijing, and Tokyo as a Korean-American reflect on the variety of ways of how others' positioning of her and her agentic choices have influenced not only her decisions on when she chooses to reveal her Korean ethnicity but also what this hyphen means for cosmopolitans today. The title of the piece dramatizes the fact that there is not a Korean Julie and an American Julie, there is a Korean-American who inhabits a space that is defined by the hyphen, and whose identity is constantly morphing depending on the contexts in which she lives, and people with whom she interacts.

Mary Ann Christison orchestrates her contribution, Chapter 9, "Negotiating Multiple Language Identities," around critical incidents that demonstrate how she negotiates different language identities. The first incident is related to her struggle with dyslexia and the effect that this had on her identity, first as a child and later as an adult. The second concerns her initial encounters with Spanish as she befriended and interacted with children of Mexican farm workers and developed an identity as a foreign language learner. The final incidents lead to the formation of her identity as a bidialectal and ultimately called into question the allegiance she felt to her childhood community of practice.

The narrative at the heart of Martha Clark Cummings' chapter (Chapter 10, "Minna no Nihongo? Nai!") vividly illustrates a point that can be derived from the Sapir-Whorf hypothesis. Language does not prevent us from seeing; it prevents us from saying, a hard fact Cummings had to grapple with as she studied Japanese. She also articulates the sociocultural forces that interfered with her ability to shape a clear identity in Japanese.

In Chapter 11, "Elaborating the Monolingual Deficit," Julian Edge provides an eloquent account of "escaping monolingualism." His critical incident is almost identical to Nunan's (see below) albeit with a very different outcome. Through engaging in learning and using a number of languages, Edge is able to escape from his identity as a monolingal speaker of English, and embrace alternative identities. He makes the point that the escape act is not easy for someone born into a monolingual culture, demanding as it does an act of awareness-raising or imagination. His piece concludes with a timely reminder of the dangers of monolingualism.

One of the most potent and potentially divisive issues within language teaching pedagogy is that of the native versus non-native speaking teacher. In her chapter (Chapter 12, "The Foreign-ness of Native Speaking Teachers of Colour"), Eljee Javier, a Canadian-Filipino, recounts her experiences as a native speaking teacher of English who is also a visible ethnic minority. She argues that while the ostensible preference for native-speaking teachers is linguistic, there is an undercurrent of racism in the preference for White native speaking teachers. The chapter highlights the inter-relationship between assumptions about race and the native speaker, and the impact of these on the professional identity of native speaking teachers of color.

If the early language learning experiences of some of our contributors are anything to go by, their lives as language learners and linguists was kick started as young adults by the Berlitz organization to teach English in Spain. In Chapter 13, "Otra Estación—A First Spanish Lesson," Rod Ellis recounts his struggle to get from his native England to Santander in Spain without a single word of Spanish. His efforts to communicate illustrate several important principles and processes underlying early second language acquisition. First, the struggle to communicate, using language as a tool, is a very different process from memorizing grammatical paradigms and vocabulary for the purposes of passing exams. Second, using what we know, and deploying inductive reasoning can facilitate the acquisition process. In his case, Ellis used his schoolboy French to make sense of his Spanish speaking interlocutors. He later observed a native speaker of French who knew no Spanish and a native speaker of Spanish who knew no French communicating quite successfully using their respective language. This brings to mind and supports Block's call for the use of a range of romance languages for intercultural communication. Finally, Ellis' fear of communicative engagement and being made to look a fool underlies the threat to identity and a sense of self posed by early L2 engagement.

Bud Goodall, ethnographer, communication scholar, and author, implicitly challenges the notion that cross-cultural miscommunication only occurs across languages. In his chapter (Chapter 14, "Bewitched: A Microethnography of the Culture of Majick in Old Salem"), it is clear that a similar process occurs within languages. Goodall selects as his narrative a small but telling encounter with a "witch" in Salem, Massachusetts who runs a shop selling magic wands. As an opening narrative what could be more enticing as a means of encouraging the reader to read on? In his commentary, he contests the encounter against Michael Agar's (1994: 106) observation that in everyday conversation, "rich points" occur where cultural differences emerge from the discourse and you suddenly realize "you don't know what's going on." In attempting to negotiate through a "micro-exchange of languaculture" the interlocutors are building culture. Like other contributions to the collection, Goodall's piece provides unique insights into language, culture, and identity.

In Chapter 15, "Am I that Name?" Stacy Holman Jones takes us to the heart of issues of identity. "What is my identity?" she wants to know, and "What part does the act of naming play in identity formation?" Steve Marshall and Tim Mossman (see below) confront similar questions, although from a very different perspective—that of naming their bicultural children. This is a deeply moving, personal account of Holman Jones' struggle to make sense of herself, her life and the forces that shape her—in short, the search for identity. One senses that Holman Jones is comfortable with not knowing the answer to her question, comfortable with the process of becoming rather than the certainty of being.

Angel Lin provides, in Chapter 16, "English and Me: My Language Learning Journey," a detailed and insightful account of the struggle to learn English in the working class milieu of 1970s Hong Kong. In her piece, she describes writing to pen pals and of diary keeping as ways of providing opportunities for authentic communication. She reports that her diary was kept exclusively in English, that it provided a "third space" for her to record emotions and experiences that would not have been possible in Chinese.

> I felt that I could write my feelings more freely when I wrote in English—less inhibition and reservation—I seemed to have found a tool that gave me more freedom to express my innermost fears, worries, anger, conflicts or excitement, hopes, expectations, likes and dislikes (e.g., anger with parents or teachers, or a troubling quarrel with a friend at times) without constraint or inhibition—as if this foreign language had opened up a new, personal space . . .

In Chapter 17, "Adaptive Cultural Transformation: Quest for Dual Social Identities," Jun Liu traces his journey from boyhood in rural China during the Cultural Revolution to adulthood in the United States. His critical incident concerns an initial social encounter on first arriving in the United States. He uses his critical incident to explore the concept of "face," a critical aspect of Chinese culture and identity. The incident marked the beginning of Liu's Chinese identity loss in a totally new environment and the beginning of his adaptive cultural transformation, a transformation he explores in the rest of the chapter.

Allan Luke begins Chapter 18, "On this Writing: An Autotheoretic Account," with a disclaimer. He is not a writer, he claims. He then belies his own assertion by producing a very fine piece on the art and craft of writing. He attempts to capture the moment-by-moment reality of the creative act through a reflexive process that unwinds as he goes along. Luke makes a play for writing as craft rather than art. He ends rather playfully by stating that he has "no choice but to leave it to the reader to make of it what you may and if it ever gets to you, feel free to rewrite it."

Mike McCarthy's narrative (Chapter 19, "The *Festival* Incident") hinges on a single word he observed one of his students writing at the beginning of an essay. The topic was *If I ruled the world.* The student had written just one word: *Festival* and then hesitated, pen poised above the paper. McCarthy's cultural stereotyping and comparative lack of experience led him to ponder what on earth the connection was between his young Spanish-speaking student's predilection for festivals and the essay topic. We won't spoil the pun line by revealing what the student was really trying to say. However, a consideration of the student's error leads McCarthy into a fascinating excursion in speech processing, linguistic chunking, cultural identity, and the insights afforded by his later training in corpus linguistics.

Names are fundamental to who we are, how we construct our identities, and how our identities are constructed by others. In some cultures it is taboo to utter another person's first name, for to do so is to steal that other person's identity. In their joint contribution to this volume (Chapter 20, "Changing Identities in Japanese–English Bicultural Names: From Parents to Children"), Steve Marshall and Tim Mossman address the issue of name and naming in relation to their children. Both are married to Japanese women, and both have bicultural and bilingual children. The children have bicultural names. Both sets of parents chose names that were pronounceable to people from their respective cultures, meaningful to family tradition and ethos, containing appropriate Chinese characters for representing in Japanese, and that simply sounded right. While their intention was to give their children a bi-cultural grounding through binomial identification, they gave little consideration to the effect this would have on the children's daily lives and the processes of their identity formation. In the chapter, the implications of their binomial naming decision are explored, both from the parents' perspective, but more importantly from the children's.

Stephen Muecke orchestrates Chapter 21, "Berlin Babylon" around his encounters with German in the course of teaching a semester in Berlin. In his piece, he picks up the themes of language, myth, and storytelling, and views them through the lens of the writer for whom the distinction between fiction and non-fiction is more ostensible than real. The resulting contribution to the volume is challenging, refreshing, and unique. When we invited Muecke to contribute to the volume, we knew to expect something different. We were not disappointed.

In Chapter 22, "Changing Stripes—Chameleon or Tiger?," Denise Murray provides an entertaining account of her career as a language teacher in various parts of the world. She recounts several incidents that revolve around the theme of language variety. Murray talks about the discrimination she suffered in Europe as a result of her regional accent (Australian), and decided to challenge this discrimination by developing a British accent. Some years later, she moved to the United States, and was yet again required to change her accent (although this time she resisted the requirement!). Murray's piece illustrates the powerful assumptions that people have based solely on accent. It also shows the ways in which accent and identity play out in different contexts and situations. Murray concludes her piece by explaining why it was that she changed her variety of English so completely in Britain that she was assumed to be British and yet, after almost three decades of living in the US, she has a blended variety that is neither Australian nor American. "The answer lies in the rather opaque title I gave this chapter. In some situations, I'm a chameleon; in others, like the tiger, I can't and don't change my stripes. I prefer to be different."

As Cynthia Nelson explains in Chapter 23, "Vanishing Acts," her joy at becoming a second language teacher contrasted sharply with the alienation she felt as a foreign language learner. She vividly recounts three unsettling moments—two from Spanish language classes that she took in the United States, and one (relayed to her by a German acquaintance) from an ESL class in that country. In her narratives and commentary, she shows how students can become disengaged when teachers act in ways that deny, dismiss, or constrain the spectrum of sexual identity options that exists in the classroom and beyond. The chapter's ending makes it clear that there is still some way to go before language education is widely understood to be a multi-sexual space.

In Chapter 24, "Dog Rice and Cultural Dissonance," David Nunan takes a seemingly trivial transactional encounter: buying rice in a Bangkok market, and unpacks the complex linguistic and cultural assumptions that made the encounter problematic. This chapter illustrates the ways in which these assumptions can have a powerful impact on the effectiveness of interpersonal and transactional encounters and underlines a central motif of the volume: that effective communication requires much more than mastering the phonological, lexical, and grammatical subsystems of the language.

In her contribution to this collection (Chapter 25, "'Where Am I From': Performative and 'Metro' Perspectives of Origin"), Emi Otsuji interrogates the construct of origin. At the beginning of her narrative, she admits to having experienced a lifelong ambivalent and unstable sense of origin. Within her, she says, the sense of connection and alienation co-exist and yet compete against each other. What, she asks, is the implication of this as it relates to the definition and the constitution of the notion of "origin"? Her critical incident revolves around a question that many of us find difficult to answer "Where are you from?" Having been born in the United States, and having lived in many different countries, Otsuji's immediate reaction is to reply, "Well, I don't really know." Speculating on her narrative, she argues that identity, culture, origin, and even language itself are fluid rather than fixed entities. She concludes that "'Where I am from' to me is not pre-given but is an ambivalent, transgressive and dynamic discursive construct that manifests itself through repeated acts."

Several contributions to the collection take their point of departure from food. There's Nunan and dog rice in Thailand. And then, in Chapter 26, "Sweating Cheese and Thinking Otherwise," there's Alastair Pennycook and cheese in Hunan. The cheese, blue, sweating in the Hunan heat, sits on the refectory dining table like an alien from another world. The cheese is a gift from a visitor from the West, a well-intentioned foreigner who imagines that the expatriates teaching in Hunan must miss television, chocolate, music, salad, strawberries, wine . . . and cheese. The cook, a master at preparing vegetables, frog, dog, all with chilli, approaches the plate of cheese with suspicion, tastes and rejects. Pennycook invests the cheese with identity. There's a time and place for blue cheese but the food hall at a provincial university in Hunan is definitely not one of them. Pennycook uses the cheese anecdote to explore a far heftier theme: that of otherness. Pennycook's observation that "If we consider seriously the difficulty of engaging with the Other, of the incommensurabilities of cultural difference, what then can it mean to assume the double distinction of both knowing the other and knowing the others' reading of oneself? This a moment not only of otherness, but of double otherness." An observation that calls to mind the multiple "othernesses" in the Nunan piece.

Interestingly, no such admission was forthcoming from Kimie Takahashi, despite the fact that the title of her chapter (Chapter 27, "Multilingual Couple Talk: Romance, Identity and the Political Economy of Language") and the story that followed, were about as personal as it was possible to be in a collection such as this. We wondered what our editor, Naomi Silverman, would think as we read the opening to Takahashi's piece: "English was the language spoken by my first object of romantic infatuation . . ." Reading on, we were not disappointed. Although the initial object of infatuation faded, another took its place, and the chapter turns out, in part at least, to be a touching love story. In terms of the themes of this collection, it bears witness to Ingrid Piller's contention that in cross-cultural couplehood, identity is not a matter of labels and categories, but rather an "act of doing" in which private talk is informed "by wider public discourses such as gender, nationality, immigration and international marriage."

Sumiko Taniguchi explores, in Chapter 28, "Transforming Identities In and Through Narrative," the relationship between narrative and identity, and highlights the transformative potential of narrative for personal identities. Her story begins with a scene at an Australian rock concert, where she finds herself a visible minority. This experience reminds her of her first sojourn in America in her teens. Her account illustrates the ways in which her first overseas experience as a high school exchange student has been told and re-told over the years in different times and places. As a consequence of re-storying and re-interpreting her experience, her identities have been constantly under revision. She concludes that the significance of re-storying past experience is one of the contributions of narrative to an understanding of her own trajectory as a language learner/user.

As we indicated earlier in this framing chapter, when we set out to put this collection together, we thought that it would be a relatively "easy write" for our contributors. What could be more straightforward than selecting an anecdote, lending it a personal voice, and then tying it into the literature on culture, identity, and language? In fact, many of our contributors found crafting their stories extremely challenging. As first drafts drifted into our inboxes, they were more often than not accompanied by messages on just how difficult the writing process had been. Self-revelation, it seemed, led down pathways that had rarely been traversed in public.

Nury Vittachi has a rich language background. He has traveled and worked extensively around Asia as a lecturer in creativity, a novelist, and a journalist. He draws on this background in his chapter (Chapter 29, "A Short Course in Globalese"). The thesis he offers is that people are traveling and communicating as never before and that the language of communication is English. However, it is rarely a form of standard English. Rather it is a mixed-code language using elements from a variety of sources that, in the Asian region, might include English vocabulary, Chinese grammar, and emerging terms from technology and commerce. He argues that this is leading to the emergence of a new language for which he coins the term *Globalese*. Vittachi draws on a rich database of anecdotes to support his case. He notes that in his extensive travels through Asia, from Laos, to Taipei, to Vietnam, to Kerala, this stripped down and transformed variety of English is used, not just between local and English-speaking travelers, but between any two people who do not speak a common language. His piece in part echoes Block's contribution based on communication in Europe between speakers of different Romance languages. Same problem—somewhat different solution.

Issues that emerged from these contributions include: the Self and Other, cultural stereotypes, reflexivity, the separability of language, culture and identity, different styles of presentation, and the tension between creative and academic writing.

In writing this introduction, we shuttled back and forth between the original contributions and the summaries we made of them. As we did this, we were constantly struck by the richness of the contributions and the poverty of our interpretive summaries. How does one capture the richness of each entry in a paragraph? The answer eludes us. That said, the opportunity to summarize and to provide our own interpretive gloss on each piece was a rewarding one. Hopefully, what we have done here is to provide signposts to the treasures ahead.

References

Agar, M. (1994). *Language shock: Understanding the culture of conversation.* New York: William Morrow/Quill.

Casanave, C., & Schecter, S. (Eds.). (1997). *On becoming a language educator: Personal essays on professional development.* Mahwah, NJ: Lawrence Erlbaum Associates.

Coghlan, D., & Bramnick, T. (2005). *Doing action research in your own organization* (2nd Edition). London: Sage Publications.
Delanty, G. (2003). *Community.* London: Routledge.
Edge, J. (2008). Interested theory and theorising as goal. *TESOL Quarterly* 42/4, 653–654.
Finlay, L. (2003). Through the looking glass: Intersubjectivity and hermeneutic reflection. In L. Finlay & B. Gough (Eds.), *Reflexivity: A practical guide for researchers in health and social sciences.* Oxford: Blackwell Science.
Finlay, L., & Gough, B. (Eds.). (2003). *Reflexivity: A practical guide for researchers in health and social sciences.* London: Blackwell.
Hymes, D. (1962). The ethnography of speaking. In T. Gladwin & W. C. Sturtevant (Eds.), *Anthropology and human behaviour.* Washington, D.C.: Anthropology Society of Washington.
Judd, E. (2002). *Cross-cultural communication: An ESL training module.* Chicago: Board of Education of the City of Chicago.
Kramsch, C. (1998). *Language and culture.* Oxford: Oxford University Press.
Kramsch, C. (2004). Language, thought, and culture. In A. Davies & C. Elder (Eds.), *The handbook of applied linguistics.* Malden: Blackwell Publishing.
Merleau-Ponty, M. (1964). *Signs.* (R. C. McCleary, Trans.). Evanston, Illinois: Northwestern University Press.
Norton, B. (forthcoming). Language and identity. In N. Hornberger & S. McKay (Eds.), *Sociolinguistics and language education.* Clevedon, UK: Multilingual Matters.
Nunan, D. (2007). *What is this thing called language?* London: Palgrave/Macmillan.
Nunan D., & Bailey, K.M. (2009). *Exploring second language classroom research.* Boston, MA: Heinle.
Nunan, D., & Choi, J. (2010). *Language and culture: Reflective narratives and the emergence of identity.* New York: Routledge.
Nunan, D., & Choi, J. (forthcoming). Shifting sands: The evolving story of "voice" in qualitative research. In E. Hinkel (Ed.), *Handbook of research in second language teaching and learning.* Volume II. New York: Routledge.
Pavlenko, A., & Blackledge, A. (2004). *Negotiation of identities in multilingual contexts.* Clevedon: Multilingual Matters.
Pennycook, A. (1995). English in the world/the world in English. In J. Tollefson (Ed.), *Power and inequality in language education* (pp. 34–58). Cambridge: Cambridge University Press.
van Lier, L. (1988). *The classroom and the language learner: Ethnography and second language classroom research.* London: Longman.
van Lier, L. (1990). Ethnography: Bandaid, bandwagon or contraband? In C. Brumfit and R. Mitchell (Eds.), *Research in the language classroom.* London: Modern English Publications.
Weeks, J. (1990). The value of difference. In J. Rutherford (Ed.), *Identity: Community, Culture, Difference.* London: Lawrence & Wishart.

Chapter 2

Coat Hangers, Cowboys, and Communication Strategies

Seeking an Identity as a Proficient Foreign Language Learner

Kathleen M. Bailey
Monterey Institute of International Studies

Autobiographical Statement

I grew up on a flower ranch in rural Southern California about an hour north of the Mexican border, where my family raised gladioli and birds of paradise. My father was the ranch foreman. I can remember him driving a plow behind Pete, the plow horse. Pete was eventually retired to a sunny corral when we bought a gas-powered rototiller, but my father still walked behind the noisy machine, pushing it forcefully between the rows of plants to till the soil. My mother worked in the greenhouse, supervising the small seedlings until they were ready for transplanting in the fields.

Most of the people who worked on the ranch with us were Mexican—the men weeding and cutting the flowers, the women sorting them and packing them tightly in ten-gallon tins for shipment to the commercial flower market in Los Angeles. My siblings and I were surrounded by the sounds of Spanish from the time we could walk. I remember, before I went to kindergarten, taking my bologna sandwich outside at lunch time, to sit on the ground with the workers, where they would tip over a rusted ten-gallon tin shipping can, and build a fire in it to warm their tortillas, the air redolent with the scent of *frijoles* and eucalyptus. Our neighbors were the Cruzes. I played in the dirt with their dog and watched in horrified fascination as Mrs. Cruz routinely beheaded the chickens roaming free in their yard.

Under those circumstances, I should have learned Spanish easily from the workers and my neighbors. But there were invisible social barriers more powerful than our physical proximity, and like other Anglo children in our school district, I started to learn Spanish as a foreign language in junior high school. After two years of grammar exercises and vocabulary lists, I was bored with Spanish and switched to Latin in high school, because it would surely be helpful if I decided to become a doctor or a nun. (No, I'm not Catholic, and yes, you may laugh.) Studying Latin consisted of textbook exercises, translating texts into English, learning the cases, and taking vocabulary quizzes. There was never an expectation that we would speak the language. At best, the Latin classes gave me word-attack skills and a certain amount of meta-language that would be useful in the future for taking standardized tests.

After two years of Latin (the most offered in our school), I started Spanish again—literally. It was back to beginning Spanish. After two more years of grammar exercises and vocabulary lists, I went off to college and enrolled in a curriculum that didn't require any foreign language courses. Later, I transferred to the University of Arizona and was placed in second-semester Spanish. I don't remember much about the teachers or the courses, but I do remember my response to the required weekly sessions in the language lab. It was dead boring and I felt like "Big Brother" was watching me. Our endless repetitions were monitored from the main control panel by the teacher, a disembodied voice that suddenly intruded in our earphones to correct pronunciation problems and grammar gaffs.

Eventually, I transferred again and finally I graduated from the University of California at Santa Barbara as an English major. Doing so required that I complete Spanish 5—a course in Spanish literature. Although I didn't know the term at the time, this course was taught through content-based instruction. We were expected to learn about both the target language and the literature we studied. I enjoyed the literature, but I was never better than a "B" student.

A few years later I lived in Korea for ten months, the wife of a US serviceman stationed there. We rented an upstairs room in a Korean home in Uijongbu, looking out over the rice fields and on to the mountains beyond. That year, after six weeks of evening classes, two hours a week, I became a fluent (but highly inaccurate) speaker of the Korean-English pidgin of Korean taxi drivers and the local "business girls" by interacting with my neighbors and the people in the village. My neighbors were amused that an American woman would try to learn Korean. They eagerly taught me the vocabulary I needed to survive, and I used concrete nouns and present tense verb forms on a daily basis. Sadly, upon returning to the US, I no longer practiced speaking Korean and have since forgotten nearly everything I ever knew.

Six months after returning to the US, I entered the TESL MA Program at UCLA, which required two semesters of language study. I enrolled in beginning French, but arrived at school two weeks late due to family commitments. To my great horror, the beginning French course was taught with the direct method, and many of my classmates were false beginners who already had some knowledge of French grammar and vocabulary. We were actually expected to speak French! *Mon Dieu!* When the teacher called on me to answer a question in French during my first day in class, I opened my mouth and Korean words fell out. I felt the sweat trickle down my ribs and the other students gawked at me as if I were speaking in tongues.

Eventually I completed the two required terms of beginning French. I never had a genuine conversation in French or used the language for any authentic communicative purpose. Three years later I undertook a French reading course and then engaged a private tutor to help me prepare for the French translation exam required by my PhD program.

Five years later, after taking a job at the Monterey Institute, I was able to audit an intermediate Spanish class for a semester. The teacher was young, enthusiastic, flexible and smart. The syllabus was grammar-based, but we spent most of the class time talking, trying to use the required grammar structures in conversation. Two years after that, I enrolled in an intermediate Spanish course at the local community college: more grammar exercises, vocabulary lists, and required weekly sessions in the hated language laboratory.

Do we see a pattern here?

Narrative of a (Repeated) Critical Incident

As a teacher educator, I have given courses, workshops, and conference presentations in some Spanish-speaking countries, including visits to Argentina, Costa Rica, Guatemala, Mexico, Peru, Uruguay, and Spain. While traveling in those countries, I have had many occasions to use Spanish, but the grammar exercises and vocabulary quizzes of the past have not been particularly helpful in Latin America or Spain. I recall some grammar rules dimly, as things that I *should* be able to remember. But, time and again, the need to communicate in Spanish would force me to "notice the gap" (Schmidt & Frota, 1986, p. 310) between what I wanted to say and what I could say. Here is an example.

Unpacking in a hotel, I needed more coat hangers, but I didn't know the Spanish word. I asked the hotel maid, "¿Cómo se dice la cosa dónde ponemos nuestra ropa?" (What do we call the thing where we put our clothes?) She responded, "Guardaropa." Now anyone who knows even a modicum of Spanish or other romance languages will recognize the cognate of *wardrobe*. But being intent on getting unpacked and getting my message across, I told her, "Pues, necesito cinco más guardaropas, por favor." (Well, I need five more wardrobes, please.) When she looked at me quite startled, I realized that I had said something wrong. I went to the wardrobe and showed her a coat hanger. "Esta cosa—¿cómo se dice?" I asked her. "Ah—gancho," she said. "Okay," I responded. "Necesito cinco más ganchos, por favor." Mission accomplished.

In another country, sometime later, faced with the same dilemma, I couldn't remember the word for coat hanger, but I knew better than to ask for five more wardrobes. This time, with a coat hanger in hand, I asked the hotel maid, "¿Cómo se llama esta cosa?" "¡Percha!" she told me. That didn't seem quite right, but it made sense: A coat hanger is something on which clothes can perch. I asked her for *cinco más perchas* and got what I needed.

Yet again, in another country, coat hanger in hand, I asked the maid, "¿Cómo se llama esta cosa?" She smiled and told me, "Es una sercha." *Sercha*? How could that be? The word rang no mental bells whatsoever, though it did seem to rhyme with something I'd heard somewhere. Perhaps I was misremembering. Nevertheless, I got what I needed and unpacked.

Another year, another country, another hotel. At the reception desk as I checked in, I anticipated my usual dilemma and asked the English-speaking clerk, "What is the Spanish word for coat hanger?" He said, "Gancho." *Gancho*? *Gancho*? I'd heard that word before. I tried to picture it in my mind so I could remember it and use it at need. But for a visual learner, auditory memory is a weak ally. I should have written *gancho* on the palm of my hand. When the hotel maid came by, I confidently asked her for "cinco más gauchos, por favor." Her startled face told me clearly that, once again, I'd said the wrong thing. But think about it! After all a "u" is nothing but an upside down "n," and for a slightly dyslectic left-handed, lower-intermediate Spanish speaker, the mistake is surely understandable! (Of course, the hotel maid was probably not accustomed to having guests ask for five more Argentine cowboys, when previously there had not been even one in the room.)

Clearly communication strategies are not isomorphic with learning strategies, though they may contribute to learning if there is something about their use that makes the conversational breakdown or repair memorable. The story of my efforts to get coat hangers (and to learn the blasted word[s] for *coat hangers*) clearly illustrates the power (and the peril) of communication strategies. But I am not daunted. As I write these words, I am in a hotel in Denver, Colorado, where I have learned (or at least written down) the Spanish words for *sheets* (*sábanas*) and *shower cap* (*gorra*)—the latter obtained by asking for *un sombrero de baño.*

Commentary

What can we learn from this narrative, and what does any of it have to do with identity? Here I will adopt Norton's (1997) definition of identity as "how people understand their relationship to the world, how that relationship is constructed across time and space, and how people understand their possibilities for the future" (p. 410). There are five ways to view identity, according to Wenger (1998, p. 149):

- Identity as *negotiated experience.* We define who we are by the ways we experience our selves through participation as well as by the ways we and others reify ourselves.
- Identity as *community membership.* We define who we are by the familiar and the unfamiliar.
- Identity as *learning trajectory.* We define who we are by where we have been and where we are going.
- Identity as *nexus of multimembership.* We define who we are by the ways we reconcile our various forms of membership into one identity.
- Identity as *a relation between the local and the global.* We define who we are by negotiating local ways of belonging to broader constellations and of manifesting broader styles and discourses.

We will return to these conceptions of identity after briefly considering language learners' attempts to communicate in the target language.

Norton (1997) asks, "Under what conditions do language learners speak? How can we encourage language learners to become more communicatively competent? How can we facilitate interaction between language learners and target language speakers?" (p. 410). Using communication strategies can help both foreign and second language learners get their points across in the target language and understand what others are trying to say to them. Efforts to keep communicating may also show the interlocutor that the learner is trying to sustain a conversation. These efforts, in turn, may encourage the interlocutor to be supportive and to pitch his utterances to the apparent proficiency level of the language learner. Thus a connection between identity and communication strategies is the idea that identity is not "a fixed, invariant attribute in the 'mind' of the individual learner. Rather, identity is theorized as a contingent process involving dialectic relations between learners and the various worlds and experiences they inhabit and which act on them" (Ricento, 2005, p. 895). Using communication strategies is one way that I can negotiate the "various worlds" in which I find myself working. Furthermore, I may seem more or less proficient in Spanish, depending on the support provided by my interlocutor at any given time.

My attempts to request coat hangers (rather than cowboys) are examples of *transactional language,* i.e., "language that is used to obtain goods and services" (Nunan, 2007, p. 219). My attempts to get coat hangers without knowing the Spanish word exemplify the use of *communicative strategies.* Such strategies are generally described as the attempts of a language learner (or the joint attempts of the learner and her interlocutor) to achieve some sort of desired understanding in a context where the language learner's linguistic competence is insufficient to convey her point readily or to understand others' ideas in the target language. Communication strategies have been discussed in the speech of both second language learners (see, e.g., Labarca & Khanji, 1988; Tarone, 1980, 1981) and foreign language learners (e.g., Dörnyei, 1995; Houston, 2006; Nakatani, 2005).

In the speech act of requesting, the speaker asks the hearer to provide something, whether that something be information, help, directions, or coat hangers. The desired perlocutionary force of the request can only be conveyed to the hearer if the speaker is able to name or describe the object or service she requires, or to identify it in some other way (e.g., by pointing or gesturing). When the speaker lacks some key knowledge—in this case, the name of the desired object—she can give up entirely—an option known as *message abandonment* (Tarone, 1981), or she can resort to her first language and hope that her interlocutor will understand the request. As an alternative, she can use communication strategies and continue in the target language. But this choice can be risky. When I inadvertently asked the hotel maids for five wardrobes and five cowboys, I was revealing myself to be a less-than-competent speaker of Spanish, because

> Every time language learners speak, they are not only exchanging information with their interlocutors; they are also constantly organizing and reorganizing who they are and how they relate to the social world. They are, in other words, engaged in identity construction and negotiation.
>
> (Norton, 1997, p. 410)

My efforts to use communication strategies—indeed to speak Spanish at all when I could pretend to be entirely monolingual—consistently expose me to risk and possible ridicule. (*Gracias a Dios* that most of the Spanish speakers I've encountered are too polite to laugh out loud or make fun of my efforts.) My attempts to speak Spanish repeatedly identify me as a lower-intermediate learner. Please note that here I am using *to identify* as a transitive verb with the person as the object: X identifies Y as Z. (My lack of vocabulary identifies me as non-proficient.) And yet, in the recent literature on identity and language acquisition, *to identify* (*with* or *as*) is often used as a verb in which the grammatical subject is the actor, the agent, as in "Julie identifies with a community of educated multilingual people" (see Tabouret-Keller, 1997, for further discussion of transitive and intransitive uses of *to identify*).

The identities of L2 learners "are deeply connected to their status as members of distinct but interrelated communities in which bilingualism (as opposed to monolingualism) is the norm" (Ricento, 2005, p. 906). The community with which I identify most strongly is that of international language educators—people who teach other people languages, who train teachers to carry out that role, and who often travel to other countries in their work. These are people who conduct research on how bilingualism and foreign language proficiency can be attained. And yet, I myself am not bilingual. I am not even an advanced speaker of my most proficient non-L1 language. My limited Spanish proficiency prohibits me from claiming full membership status in the multilingual professional community to which I aspire. Golfers have a saying about someone who talks a good game but doesn't play well: "He talks the talk, but he doesn't walk the walk." When it comes to applied linguistics and teacher education, I do just fine, thank you. But when it comes to being bilingual, I literally cannot even "talk the talk."

Indeed, I fear that I shall go to my grave as a lower-intermediate learner of Spanish. In fact, if I were diagnosed with a fatal illness and told I had two months to live, I'd probably enroll in an intensive Spanish course in an immersion environment, perhaps overlooking the bay at Zihuatanejo, surrounded by bougainvillea and iguanas, in a last-ditch effort to gain control over the subjunctive, and to sort out *por* and *para* (the two forms of *for* in Spanish) before meeting St. Peter at *las puertas de cielo*. Of course, when I arrive there, St. Peter will probably ask me for the password in Spanish, rather like the Gileadites asking the Ephraimites, in the Book of Judges, to say the word *Shibboleth*. (Apparently the Ephraimites could not pronounce *sh-* properly, and would say *Sibboleth* instead—a pronunciation error which literally caused heads to roll.) I expect I will be unsure about whether to use the *tú* form or the *usted* form when I respond to St. Peter's question.

Yet I still hope that I will learn Spanish well someday. I see myself carrying on witty conversations, conveying my sense of humor and my intellect in Spanish, rather than sounding like a clumsy tourist whose accent improves slightly after a second margarita. I do not believe my interlanguage has fossilized. Instead, I choose to think of it as gelatinized, because every time I spend a few days speaking Spanish, I feel my grammar changing and my lexicon growing. I believe (or *hope*?) that if I were to really invest in learning Spanish, I could in fact become a better Spanish speaker. I am heartened by the idea that "we conceive of identities as long-term, living relations between persons and their place and participation in communities of practice" (Wenger, 1998, p. 53).

But wait. There have been successes—notably when I am with a monolingual speaker of my target language and a monolingual speaker of my native language who is relying on me to get things done. I spent five days in Lima, Peru, conversing entirely in Spanish on behalf of a friend (who lived in Spain but claims his Spanish is not as strong as mine) and our driver, Señor Bonilla, who says he speaks no English. (I am not so sure about either man's claim, but I appreciate their gallantry.)

While working in Puebla, Mexico for a week, I helped to negotiate taxi destinations and meals for myself and a colleague who is proficient in French but not in Spanish. One extraordinary evening we spent together at a Swiss restaurant, which started with me trying to recall if the proper request for a glass of wine was *un vaso de vino* or *una copa de vino*—a muttered utterance which the waiter (a born teacher if there ever was one) happened to overhear. Business was slow, so he brought fourteen different types of glasses to our table (all empty) and proceeded to give us a Spanish-for-drinking-purposes lesson, naming every single glass with what I can only infer were the Spanish equivalents of *snifter, tumbler, martini glass, highball glass, champagne flute, shot glass*, and so on.

One night in Rosario, Argentina, my sister and her husband (a native Argentine) took my dad, my brother and me to a local club where the people dance country folk dances to a live band. My sister is more Argentine than American now and she speaks Spanish brilliantly. (Her English is Spanish-accented.) My dad and my brother speak classroom Spanish, and I am somewhere in the middle. For me, trying to acknowledge the gracious welcome of the dancers and organizers in Spanish was excruciating: I didn't want to embarrass my sister or her husband with my ungrammatical efforts, but I did wish to communicate with the hosts and the dancers, who were surprised and delighted to have tourists visit their local club. I am sure I embarrassed my sister, but not trying to communicate would have been worse.

Sometimes we don't have a choice: communication becomes essential. One day my sweetheart, Les, and I took a trip on a tourist catamaran out of Puerta Vallarta, Mexico (Bailey, 1991, pp. 169–171). We stopped to go snorkeling about two hours south of the city. The water was very choppy and *el capitán* insisted that we wear life vests—probably a good safety precaution, but a near fatal mistake as it turned out. A jellyfish got caught inside Les's life vest and we couldn't get it out. The poisonous tentacles were smashed against his back as we tried for three or four minutes (or was it hours?) to undo the sodden canvas ties of the life vest, while treading water in the choppy seas. Eventually we got the life vest off and swam back to the catamaran, where Les doubled over as the pain moved into his lower back. The big catamaran could not put in to shore on that rocky coast, so we hailed some fishermen in a small boat, who kindly took us ashore. I asked the people on the beach where we could find a doctor. No, they said, there was no doctor in the village. We had to go back to Puerto Vallarta.

I begged a boy standing nearby to run ahead and get a taxi for us. As we clambered up the beach, the boy ran ahead, flagged down a cab, and then ran back to guide us to the taxi. We collapsed in the back seat and I told the driver—"*¡Al hospital!*" Did we want the big hospital or the little hospital, the driver asked. We wanted the first hospital as fast as possible, I replied.

When we arrived at the small hospital, Les hobbled into the waiting room, doubled over in pain; the doctor took us in immediately. She and I negotiated in Spanish what had happened, whether Les had any drug allergies or was taking any medications, and where the pain was located. She gave him antihistamines and painkillers intravenously, and then she turned to me, took one look at my swollen hands, and repeated her questions. I too was dosed with painkillers and antihistamines. We both lived through this nightmarish experience and I expect the gracious people we encountered that day would have tried to help us even without my poor attempts at Spanish for first aid purposes. But later Les told me he was really glad I could speak Spanish. (Faith is a wonderful thing, and ignorance continues to be bliss.)

Perhaps my most surprising success (albeit less dramatic) as a foreign language speaker was spending a day traveling between Rouen, France and the beaches of Normandy, also with Les, who spoke no French, and our driver, who said he spoke no English. We spent seven hours together, going to and from various historic sites, having lunch at a café in Ste-Mère Église, and returning to Rouen. During that trip, using my extremely limited French, we learned about the driver's family, his business, the history of the region, the local people's views of Americans, racism in France, the economy, and a range of local products. Not bad for someone who'd never carried on a genuine conversation in French before that day. I'm sure my French was execrable, but *Mon Dieu*! I understood the driver most of the time and he seemed to understand me.

Let us return to Wenger's (1998, p. 149) ideas about the five ways to view identity:

- "Identity as *negotiated experience*. We define who we are by the ways we experience our selves through participation as well as by the ways we and others reify ourselves" (ibid.). Okay, I may not be the world's most accurate Spanish speaker, but I try, and most people are willing to negotiate meaning. By and large, my attempts to communicate in Spanish have encouraged me to keep trying, and the use of communication strategies enables me to do so. I experience myself as someone who works at speaking Spanish, and trying to remember new words.
- "Identity as *community membership*. We define who we are by the familiar and the unfamiliar" (ibid.). The familiar involves speaking English, my L1, but in my home community it also includes people, particularly my students and colleagues, who constantly communicate in their second language—most of them much more

successfully than I do. The unfamiliar arises every time I must speak Spanish or French—particularly when I am partly responsible for someone else who does not. But I have hope that the unfamiliar can become more familiar.

- "Identity as *learning trajectory.* We define who we are by where we have been and where we are going" (ibid.). Where I have been is in numerous foreign language classes, over many years, some of which were more effective than others. Where I am going is to continue learning Spanish, both by traveling and by self study. (Lately, I've taken to watching my favorite movies in Spanish.)
- "Identity as *nexus of multimembership.* We define who we are by the ways we reconcile our various forms of membership into one identity" (ibid.). I am trying to reconcile my identity as an international educator and applied linguist who promotes multilingualism with my identity as a lower-intermediate learner of Spanish as a foreign language. The cognitive dissonance between these two selves is so jarring that I feel compelled to improve my Spanish, and regularly try to communicate, when I am in a Spanish-speaking country, in spite of the difficulties involved. A problem in terms of my language acquisition, however, is that *regularly* is not the same as *frequently.* Most of the time, I have no need to use my target languages. I remain, alas, a foreign language learner.
- "Identity as *a relation between the local and the global.* We define who we are by negotiating local ways of belonging to broader constellations and of manifesting broader styles and discourses" (ibid.). Locally, in my home environment, I am a competent and respected professional. Globally, I want to be more than a tourist with broken Spanish; I want to engage in those "broader styles and discourses" (ibid.).

I am heartened by the idea that "human beings are characterized both by continuous personal identity and by discontinuous personal diversity" (Davies & Harré, 1990, p. 46). Likewise, "there seems to be a tension between the multiplicity of selves as expressed in discursive practices and the fact that across those discursive practices a relatively stable selfhood exists" (Harré & van Langenhove, 1990, p. 61). In fact, "one and the same person is now this and now that" (ibid.). If these three statements are true, then perhaps I can be both a competent language teacher, applied linguist, and teacher educator, on the one hand, as well as a semi-competent L2 user. There. I've said it. I've come out of the *guardaropa* as a non-proficient foreign language learner.

Concluding Remarks

It seems to me that much of the literature on identity and language acquisition deals with second language learners, such as immigrants and refugees—people who must cope with everyday living in a language not quite their own. What then is the place of the identity construct in *foreign* language learning?

Norton (1997) says that "identity relates to desire—the desire for recognition, the desire for affiliation, and the desire for security and safety" (p. 410). But another important issue is *investment,* which Norton (1997) defines as "the socially and historically constructed relationship of learners to the target language and their sometimes ambivalent desire to learn and practice it" (p. 411). I have the desire to learn, but as a foreign language learner, I must invest much more time and effort to get the input, interaction and practice opportunities I need in order to improve. Perhaps I will make a serious effort at time management, rethink my priorities, and actually enroll in another Spanish class someday.

Fortunately,

> at any given time, a person's identity is a heterogeneous set made up of all the names or identities, given to and taken up by her. But in a lifelong process, identity is endlessly created anew, according to very various social constraints (historical, institutional, economic, etc.), social interactions, encounters, and wishes that may happen to be very subjective and unique.
>
> (Tabouret-Keller, 1997, p. 316)

References

Bailey, K. M. (1998). *Learning about language assessment: Dilemmas, decisions, and directions.* Boston: Heinle & Heinle.

Davies, B., & Harré, R. (1990). Positioning: The discursive production of selves. *Journal for the Theory of Social Behaviour, 20* (1), 43–63.

Dörnyei, Z. (1995). On the teachability of communication strategies. *TESOL Quarterly, 29* (1), 55–85.

Harré, R., & van Lagenhove, L. (1999). The dynamics of social episodes. In R. Harré & L. van Lagenhove (Eds.), *Positioning theory: Moral contexts of intentional action* (pp. 1–13). Oxford: Blackwell Publishing.

Houston, T. (2006). Communication strategies in the foreign language classroom. *Applied Language Learning, 16* (1), 65–82.

Labarca, A., & Khanji, R. (1998). On communication strategies in second language research: A critique, a revision, and some (non-)implications for the classroom. *Studies in Second Language Acquisition, 8* (1), 68–79.

Nakatani, Y. (2005). The effects of awareness-raising training on oral communication strategy use. *Modern Language Journal, 89* (1), 76–91.

Norton, B. (1997). Language, identity, and the ownership of English. *TESOL Quarterly, 31* (3), 409–429.

Nunan, D. (2007). *What is this thing called language?* Houndmills, Basingtoke, Hampshire, UK: Palgrave.

Ricento, T. (2005). Considerations of identity in L2 learning. In E. Hinkel (Ed.), *Handbook of research in second language teaching and learning* (pp. 895–910). Mahwah, NJ: Erlbaum.

Schmidt, R. W., & Frota, S. N. (1986). Developing basic conversational ability in a second language: A case study of an adult learner of Portuguese. In R. R. Day (Ed.), *Talking to learn: Conversation in second language acquisition* (pp. 237–326). Rowley, MA: Newbury House.

Tabouret-Keller, A. (1997). Language and identity. In F. Coulmas (Ed.), *The handbook of sociolinguistics* (pp. 315–326). Oxford: Blackwell Publishers Ltd.

Tarone, E. (1980). Communication strategies, foreigner talk and repair in interlanguage. *Language Learning, 30,* 417–431.

Tarone, E. (1981). Some thoughts on the notion of "communication strategy." *TESOL Quarterly, 15,* 285–295.

Wenger, E. (1998). *Communities of practice: Learning, meaning, and identity.* Cambridge: Cambridge University Press.

Chapter 3

Speaking *Romance-esque*

David Block
University of London

Autobiographical Statement: Languages in my Life

Notwithstanding extensive contact with African American English throughout my childhood and adolescent years and some contact with Spanish when I attended a junior high school with a significant Hispanic population, by the time I left the US at the age of 22, I was for all intents and purposes classifiable as a monolingual English speaker. The most significant and critical language learning experiences in my life coincided with a short stay of four months in Paris in Autumn 1978, during which I activated some of the French that I had learned during two semesters of study in my last year at university, and, more importantly, a very long stay of 18 years in Barcelona. I arrived in Barcelona in December 1978 with a rudimentary knowledge of Spanish, mainly acquired during four semesters of university study. I say rudimentary because while I could do simple things like ask for a morning *café con leche* (coffee with milk), I would get tripped up when asked if I wanted the milk in my coffee *caliente o natural* (hot or lukewarm) or if I desired anything else, such as *una pasta* (a pastry). Aware of my deficiencies, I immediately applied a great deal of effort to improving my skills in Spanish, utilizing many of the self-directed language learning strategies I was later to learn about when I began to read applied linguistics books (e.g. Wenden & Rubin, 1987). For example, prior to social encounters with unknown individuals (e.g. buying food in a market, making enquiries about utilities, asking for directions), I would attempt to anticipate what would be said, ensuring that I would both understand and be able to produce key lexical items when I was actually engaged in conversation. As a result of my efforts, by the time I had been in Barcelona for six months I was reading Spanish language novels and conversing confidently and freely.

However, in conversations with the local people I was meeting and becoming friends with, I soon noticed a pattern emerging. Many of them were speakers of a language called Catalan, and they tended to use this language when speaking to each other. Meanwhile, upon registering my presence, they would switch to Spanish to talk to 'the foreigner' in their midst. I remember that I found this phenomenon both interesting and disconcerting. And given my emerging desire to remain in Barcelona permanently and my concomitant desire to 'integrate', that is to be accepted as an insider by the people I was meeting, I soon made a conscious switch in my linguistic allegiances from Spanish to Catalan. As a result, by the time I had been living in Barcelona for two years, I had become what I would call a Catalan-preferent speaker in the complex bilingual milieu of Barcelona in the 1980s. This meant that in a variety of service encounters, I would begin all conversations in Catalan and only switch to Spanish if it became apparent that my interlocutor did not speak Catalan. As years went by, I applied the same Catalan-first policy in encounters with new acquaintances, such that by the time I had been in Barcelona for several years, most of my personal relationships were mediated by Catalan and not Spanish.

At present, after some 13 years in London, I retain Catalan as the language that I speak with my wife and any other Catalan speakers with whom I come into contact. Meanwhile, Spanish is a language that I use with a handful of friends in London as well as with non-Catalan speakers when I am in Barcelona and Spain in general. In addition, both languages have at times served me well in recent years when I have travelled to different parts of the world, as I will now explain.

Narrative

In November 1994, I travelled to Rome to attend a language teaching conference. Once inside a taxi that would take me from Fiumicino Airport to my hotel in Rome's city centre, I participated in the following exchange with the taxi driver:

DB = David Block; TD = Taxi Driver
DB: <very slowly> Jo no parlo Italià però parlo Català. Jo parlaré Català.
TD: Io non parlo Catalano.
DB: No, no. <very slowly with hand gestures> Jo parlaré Català i vostè parlarà Italià. Val?
TD: OK io parlo italiano . . .

DB: <very slowly> I don't speak Italian but I speak Catalan. I will speak Catalan.
TD: I don't speak Catalan.
DB: No, no. <very slowly with hand gestures> I will speak Catalan and you will speak Italian. OK?
TD: OK I'll speak Italian . . .

There then ensued a thirty-minute conversation during which I only spoke in Catalan and the driver only spoke in Italian. During this conversation, we both spoke very slowly and we understood each other well enough to communicate. I recall that there was very little need for repair or repetition.

Fast-forward some 13 years to late May and early June 2007, and I find myself in Brazil for 12 days to give a talk at a conference and to lead seminars at two universities. I have never studied Portuguese and I don't speak it, but on two or three occasions, I have been involved in conversations, much like the one with the Roman taxi driver, that is, conversations in which I spoke Catalan or Spanish and my interlocutor spoke Portuguese. So what should I do while in Brazil? My first instinct is to speak in Spanish or Catalan and ask my interlocutors to speak to me in Portuguese. However, there are two problems with this strategy. First, I will in many cases be in contact with people who teach English for a living and who certainly speak the language well enough to maintain a conversation. I certainly do not want to offend people in this group by somehow suggesting that I think that their English is not good enough for a conversation with me. Second, I am wary of a certain fatigue and irritation among Brazilians when they have to deal with visitors who assume that they speak Spanish because their country is located in South America. I am very aware of this phenomenon, having had it explained to me in numerous conversations over the years with Brazilians complaining about outsider ignorance of their linguistic history.

In the end, during my stay in Brazil I used English for most of my contacts with people at the two universities and the conference. However, at times in these environments, and certainly when I was away from them (e.g. in a hotel or in a market), I found that if I just spoke Spanish, with no preamble about why I was doing so, people tended to go along with my intention that they should understand me and then reply in Portuguese. And on two occasions in hotels, when I put the choice to staff at the reception desk – *no falo português mais falo espanhol e inglês* (I don't speak Portuguese but I speak Spanish and English) – I was pleasantly surprised to find that they chose Spanish. Of course, in one case, my interlocutor actually did speak Spanish so this was, in effect, just a conversation involving two Spanish speakers. However, in several other exchanges I did manage to speak in Spanish, and in some cases Catalan, while my interlocutors spoke in Portuguese. On one occasion, I spoke Catalan for an hour with a Portuguese language teacher who, by her own estimation, spoke very little English. As she found the issue of mutual comprehensibility interesting for professional and personal reasons (she had taught Portuguese to a good number of Spanish speakers and she had family in Barcelona), the conversation became an act of reflexivity as it was about what we were doing linguistically, that is communicating while using two different languages.

In November 2007, I spent several days in Florence, again to give a talk at a conference and once again I engaged in conversations during which I spoke in Catalan or Spanish to Italian speakers. In one instance, I explained my theories about the mutual ineligibility of Romance languages to a fellow conference participant, an Italian sociolinguist. We then went on to have a Catalan/Italian conversation about the state of Italian politics, during which time there were no significant breakdowns in mutual comprehensibility. Thus, there was the occasional need to repeat a phrase, but on the whole we managed to converse at a fairly even and brisk pace.

Away from the conference setting, there were several other similar conversations with strangers, which I often initiated without announcing my intentions. On one occasion, I asked a woman in a clothing shop to help me select a tie to go with a shirt that I was going to buy. We talked for several minutes about various possibilities, neither one of us drawing attention to the fact that we were, in effect, speaking two different languages. Afterwards, I wondered what she must have thought. Perhaps she thought that I was the speaker of a particularly bizarre variety of Italian. Or perhaps she recognised that I was speaking another Romance language that she was able to understand well enough to continue the conversation.

Commentary

What I find interesting in my experiences is the idea that speakers of one or more Romance languages can communicate with each other using the different languages that they speak, but crucially not the language of their interlocutor. My discussion here is limited to four languages – Catalan, Spanish, Italian and Portuguese. However, I would venture that the rules of mutual intelligibility apply to all of the Romance languages within the current nation-state borders of Spain (e.g. Galician, Valencian, Asturian and Aragonese, in addition to Catalan and Spanish) and Italy (e.g. Neapolitan, Sardinian, and Sicilian, in addition to Italian), but perhaps that they apply less so when speakers of these languages come in contact with Romanian, French or any other Romance languages spoken inside the nation-state borders of France (with the exception of Corsican), Belgium and Switzerland, and vice versa. However, there clearly is much scope for research based on what, in effect, is an empirical question.

To put a name to my experiences, I introduce the notion of all-purpose plurilingual speakers of *Romance-esque.* These individuals speak one or more Romance languages and this linguistic capital allows them to communicate well in contexts where other Romance languages are the predominant means of communication. In some cases, a great deal of code mixing takes place and this creates the effect of a hybrid language (e.g. in the case of Spanish and Portuguese mixing, one might be said to be speaking *Portuñol*). Alternatively, as the cases I have cited above show, each speaker in a conversation sticks to his/her own language. In such cases, each speaker acts as what some would call a 'passive bilingual', that is 'someone [who] may be able to understand a certain L2 but not speak it' (Meyers-Scotton, 2006, p. 44). In taking this line of action, the individual engages in what has been termed 'receptive bilingualism' (Leopold, 1939–49, as cited in Mackey, 2004) or 'semicommunication' (Haugen, 1966, as cited in Gooskens, 2007). However, following Charlotte Gooskens, here I prefer to use the term 'reciprocal bilingualism' to describe such processes. In reciprocal bilingualism, each speaker speaks a different language but mutual comprehensibility is achieved and maintained. As Gooskens explains:

> [S]ome genetically related languages are so similar to each other in terms of grammar, vocabulary and pronunciation that speakers of one language can understand the other language without prior instructions. Speakers of such languages are able to communicate with each other without a lingua franca or without one speaker using the language of the other.
>
> (Gooskens, 2007, p. 445)

In her research, Gooskens has explored how related language clusters, in particular Scandinavian languages – Danish, Norwegian and Swedish – and West Germanic languages – Dutch, Frisian and Afrikaans, can be grouped together by their mutual intelligibility and how individuals often do take the option of speaking their own language when interacting with speakers of related languages. She explores the mutual intelligibility of the above-cited languages in two triads across dimensions such as phonetic distance and lexical distance. Among other things, she confirms commonly accepted views about how mutual intelligibility works, for example how it is often asymmetrical. Thus, speakers of Swedish report low mutual intelligibility with Danish, while speakers of the latter report having fewer problems with Swedish speakers. Gooskens attempts to explain such difference in terms of linguist-produced accounts of how the different languages being used are structured (phonetically, lexically, syntactically, morphologically and so on). However, in taking this exclusively linguistic tack, she does not address all kinds of attitudinal and identity related factors which might provide more speaker-centred understandings of why people report what they report in this type of research. For example, surely the intertwined histories of Scandinavian nation-states shape both attitudes and self positionings when Swedish speakers are asked about Danish speakers and Norwegian speakers are asked about Swedish speakers, and so on. And, returning to my examples, there are no doubt differences in, for example, Portuguese-Spanish dyads, as regards how speakers of these two languages would report mutual comprehensibility. Anecdotal evidence leads me to expect Portuguese speakers, on the whole, to claim greater mutual comprehensibility with Spanish speakers than Spanish speakers with Portuguese speakers.

I see an interest in reciprocal bilingualism articulating with the already established and ongoing interest among sociolinguists in code switching (see Gardner Chloros, 2009 for a recent overview). Thus, over the past several decades there has been much research on phenomena such as morphological, syntactic, phonological and lexical shifting, both in inter-language contacts (often according to a view of language behaviour in terms of multiple monolingualisms) and intra-language contacts (more about styling or register variation). In the case at hand, one point of interest is the relative integrity of the languages being used, a point that I alluded to previously when I mentioned *Portuñol*. If I examine whether in my own experiences I have used exclusively Catalan or exclusively Spanish when talking to an Italian or Portuguese speaking interlocutor, I find that I have tended to be loyal to the notion of purity in my practices, opting for one language or the other at a time. This language ideology, according to which languages exist as separate entities in pure forms, is to a great extent a product of my particular socialisation into the two languages as part of my own personal Barcelona history. My formative years as bilingual took place in the late 1970s and 1980s, during which time I coincided with a certain reconstruction of Catalan in both institutional and social environments (see Strubell, 1996, for an account). Nevertheless, I might deviate from this one-language-at-a-time norm. Thus, when talking to an Italian speaker, I might consider that while the Spanish verb for call, *llamar*, is similar to the Italian verb *chiamare*, the Catalan equivalent, *trucar*, is not. Meanwhile, the Catalan verb for 'eat' is *menjar*, similar to *mangiare* in Italian, while *comer*, the verb in Spanish, seems more distant. Two questions worthy of research, which arise from my ruminations, are: (1) Across a multitude of such emergent communicative events, what do speakers do? and (2) Do speakers stick to one language at a time or do they strategically engage in a code mixing based on their intuitions about similarity and difference?

The use of *Romance-esque* is also an interesting line of inquiry for future sociolinguistic research because it involves languages other than English, and thus is a welcome counterweight to the well-documented phenomenon of English as an international language or *lingua franca*. Although not always acknowledged by authors writing within the general area of World Englishes, all too often there seems to be a kind of working assumption that English is, effectively, the only game in town. Thus, Florian Coulmas (2005, p. 225, as cited in McKay & Bokhorst-Heng, 2008, p. 8) argues that the current dominant status of English is due to the 'fact' that it is, among other things,

> the dominant language of the world's military power; allocated (co-)official status in a third of the world's countries; spoken by the very rich and very poor; used across a wide range of ethnicities and nationalities . . . [and] involved in more language-contact situations than any other.

While I do not doubt that what Coulmas says is, on the whole, an accurate assessment of the global extension of English and the intensiveness of the contact that people around the world have with it, I am concerned at how a certain preoccupation with English often travels with the view of other languages in multilingual settings as relatively useless. As a result, in my experiences of using Spanish and Catalan with Italian and Portuguese speakers in Italy and Brazil respectively, I have very self-consciously resisted the notion that the international academic, independently of whether or not he/she speaks languages other than English, is expected to use English in all service, professional and social encounters (or what Coulmas calls 'language contact situations').

In addition, just as the *lingua franca* use of English is so often seen metaphorically as a means of lifting speakers out of local contexts and up to global contexts, so too the use of *Romance-esque* may be seen to confer on speakers of Romance languages the status of global communicators, that is, individuals who are able to communicate competently with others while engaging in activities on the global stage. However, more importantly, by protecting the individual's right to speak in a language in which he/she feels competent, this type of conversation serves to validate all speakers equally, something which does not and indeed cannot happen when English as a *lingua franca* is used. I say this because despite the laudable work of scholars such as House, Jenkins and Seidlhofer, who have acted as advocates for non-native speakers of English worldwide in their research over the past decade, dominant language ideologies with regard to the relative value of different accents and styles of speech persist as a kind of sociological/anthropological fact of life. This notion was always so central to Pierre Bourdieu's work over the years (e.g. Bourdieu, 1984, 1991) and is integral to the more recent work by Jan Blommaert (2005, 2008), who states succinctly that '*differences* in the use of language are quickly, and quite systematically, translated into *inequalities* between speakers' (Blommaert, 2005, p. 71).

With practices such as reciprocal bilingualism, matters are different. For example, both the Roman taxi driver and the woman in the clothes shop in Florence emerged as my linguistic equals in conversations in which they used Italian and I used Catalan. By contrast, had I forced English on them, an action based on the premise that it is after all the *lingua franca par excellence*, I would very likely have set up unequal encounters during which one interlocutor (not me) struggled with the code in which the conversation took place. My point is that in emergent transnational and plurilingual communication events involving *Romance-esque*, both speakers manage to negotiate the subject position of legitimised interlocutor (Bourdieu, 1991), that is someone who is ratified, in the act of speaking, as worthy of respect, attention and trust. By contrast, speaking English, or any other language in which one's linguistic, communicative and semiotic competence is limited, leaves considerably less margin for self positioning as someone with whom others can feel at ease in a conversation.

A final interesting aspect of my focus here on uses of *Romance-esque* as the mediator of reciprocal bilingualism is the way that it reminds us of the need for micro-level research on language practices occurring locally and 'on the ground'. Such research is necessary as a counter to accepting certain views without question, such as the idea that there is always a need for a single language of communication (based on the metaphor of languages as borders which preclude mutual intelligibly) and above all, the notion that English is the only game in town as regards language practices in extra-local/global contexts. An interesting challenge to such widely held views would be to follow up my anecdotal ruminations in this short chapter with empirical research into some of the questions arising from them. Doing so would, in effect, be an attempt to understand emergent transnational and plurilingual communication practices as what Clifford Geertz (1983) calls *experience near* (i.e. the story as lived by participants), as opposed to *experience far* (the story as lived by researchers). The uses of *Romance-esque* are, to my mind, a good example of how participants in the *experience near* can surprise researchers living the *experience far* and move them towards seeing the multi-levelled world of plurilingual communication practices in new and different ways.

References

Blommaert, J. (2005). *Discourse.* Cambridge: Cambridge University Press.

Blommaert, J. (2008). *Grassroots Literacies.* London: Routledge.

Bourdieu, P. (1984). *Distinction: A Social Critique of the Judgement of Taste.* London: Routledge.

Bourdieu, P. (1991). *Language and Symbolic Power.* Oxford: Polity.

Coulmas, F. (2005). *Sociolinguistics: The Study of Speakers' Choices.* Cambridge: Cambridge University Press.

Gardner-Chloros, P. (2009). *Code-switching: An Introduction.* Cambridge: Cambridge University Press.

Geertz, C. (1983). *Local Knowledge: Further Essays in Interpretive Anthropology.* New York: Basic Books.

Gooskens, C. (2007). The contribution of linguistic factors to the intelligibility of closely related languages. *Journal of Multilingual and Multicultural Development*, 28, 445–467.

Haugen, E. (1966). Semicommunication. The language gap in Scandinavia. *Sociological Inquiry*, 36, 280–297.

Leopold, W. B. (1939–49). *Speech Development in a Bilingual Child*, 4 volumes. Chicago: Northwestern University Press.

McKay, S., & Bokhorst-Heng, W. B. (2008). *International English in Its Sociolinguistic Contexts.* London: Routledge.

Mackey, W. (2004). Bilingualism in North America. In T. K. Bhatia & W. C. Ritchie (Eds.), *The Handbook of Bilingualism* (pp. 607–641). Oxford: Blackwell.

Meyers-Scotton, C. (2006). *Multiple Voices: An Introduction to Bilingualism.* Oxford: Blackwell.

Strubell, M. (1996). Language planning and classroom practice in Catalonia. *Journal of Multilingual & Multicultural Development*, 17, 262–275.

Wenden, A., & Rubin, J. (Eds.) (1987). *Learner Strategies in Language Learning.* Englewood Cliffs, NJ: Prentice Hall International.

Chapter 4

空 Collaborating on Community, Sharing Experience, Troubling the Symbolic

Michael Brennan
Faculty of Policy Studies, Chuo University

Old house

In the same dream, he is back,
we are sitting on a crate
in the house under the house.
I touch the bricks, the pillars

rising up to the support beams.
Someone is walking about
up above, calmly, not pacing,
simply moving about the room

going from one thing to the next.
The footsteps are like a conversation.
We listen to them, first going this way,
then that, as if they are gathering things

from the various parts of the room.
I touch the thick white grout
joining bricks together, feel it
rough against fingers.

It's an old house, we lived here.
Neither of us are talking.
We sit listening to the footsteps
wandering about above.

(Old house)

同じ夢の続き、兄が戻ってきている
ぼくらは木箱に腰かけている
家の下にあるもうひとつの家のなかで
ぼくは手をふれる

煉瓦や梁を支える柱に
誰かが落ち着いた足どりで
上の家を歩きまわっている
なにかを手にとり、部屋をよこぎって

また別の物を手にとって
足音は会話に似ている
ぼくらは耳を澄ます、最初はあっちの方へ
それからこっちへ、部屋のあちこちから

物を集めてまわっているみたいだ
ぼくは手をふれる
煉瓦を繋ぎあわせている
白い漆喰に、そのざらざらを
指先に感じる

ここは古い家だ、ぼくらは昔ここに住んでいた
ふたりとも黙ったまま座っている
上の家を歩きまわる足音に
耳を澄まして

Autobiographical Statement

My language learning experiences have been generally haphazard and more outside the classroom than in. In seventh grade we had to learn lists of Greek and Latin roots and in eighth grade I started to learn Latin, following the adventures of Quintus Caecilius Lucundus, his family and slaves in Pompeii. By year ten I had managed to rise to the third worst student in the form and happily exited into French about the time Caecilius freed his slave Clemens for saving him from the conflagration in Pompeii, and sadly just before we moved onto the first passages of Ovid. I studied French for four years at high school and one year at university. French appealed to me largely due to the teachers, who were relaxed and friendly and would sometimes take us out of boarding school to see films, such as Michele Deville's *La Lectrice* and Jean-Paul Rappeneau's *Cyrano de Bergerac*. We'd then have coffee and discuss the film (fortunately never in French), which for a seventeen-year-old with literary leanings was almost as seductive as Miou-Miou reading Baudelaire aloud.

I went onto a year of French at university, where I was a middling student with good teachers. I stopped studying French then to devote myself to English literature studies, though I kept reading French novels and poetry on and off for pleasure. I ended up doing a PhD on the influence of French symbolism on an Australian poet, and so spent two periods in Paris reading through the letters and essays of Mallarmé and the essays of Maurice Blanchot under the not unromantic green-shaded lamps of the Salon du Livre in the old Bibliothèque Nationale Richelieu with its great domed roof, or in the long hall of the Bibliothèque St Genevieve at the Sorbonne. As for spoken French, I had the happy fortune to be befriended by a French student who was friends with the German journalism student who lived down the hall in the other shoebox in the rundown attic of an apartment block on the rue du Bac. Stephanie and Judith would take me out with their friends, and later to Stephanie's family home near Chantilly, and let me first listen to the rounds of conversation until I was exhausted from trying to catch what was going on and then slowly bit-by-bit make my way into their common language, dragging my *accent du kangourou* along. I became friends with her cousins after a motorbike trip to Normandy, where my *habitus* was sorely tested by a breakfast of very runny and very strong smelling cheese, and so had the good and unusual fortune to be befriended by a group of Parisians.

When I turned up in Japan several years later, after living for times in Prague, Berlin and London, I became friends with a Korean professor married to a French sinologist turned French language professor, both fluent in Japanese. Soonhee did her undergraduate study in Seoul in Korean, her masters in France in French, and her doctorate in Japan in Japanese. She is to me the exemplar of how we should be as language-animals. Through that friendship my French improved, while my Japanese never really got going. Since being in Japan on and off over the last five years, I've studied the language in various ways and have reached a level where I have friends who I only talk to in Japanese as they refuse to speak in English out of a certain shyness and probable amusement from watching me fumble through a sentence like a student of the Grand Academy of Lagado. I am years away from fluency in conversation and probably decades away from the ability to read Japanese in the way I'd like to be able, but happy enough waiting for the day the polite compliments about my Japanese give way to actual comprehension. Still, having *worked* as a poet for the last ten years, I have a reasonable sense of how slippery or polysemous words can be, and how communication often unfolds elsewhere than simply in language. Much of my work in poetry has been responsive to "foreign" language poetry—though perhaps poetry as a whole might constitute a foreign language to many readers these days—and an effort to write into that space I believe exists without the symbolic and the imaginary, what Lacan named *the real.*

Narrative

In 2006, while undertaking a writer's residency at the Cité Internationale des Arts in Paris I met Japanese installation artist Akiko Muto. We befriended each other and through various conversations broken between her English and my Japanese we discovered we had both lost a brother suddenly years before and gone through the long process of mourning. Akiko's brother had died in his teens from heart failure through heat exhaustion, and my brother had died in his mid-thirties from a heart attack caused by undiagnosed heart disease. Despite the cultural and linguistic differences, it appeared that there was a great deal in common in how we saw mourning and death and how it had affected our respective practices of writing and installation art, and more simply lives. We decided to work on a collaboration and while it seemed likely that it would be related to our brothers in some way, we had no set ideas. The collaboration was itself a form through which our friendship would evolve and through which we might understand each other's relationships to art, communication and identity.

Following our initial decision to collaborate, we did not really have any immediate idea beyond I'd write a sequence of poems and Akiko would do a series of paintings or sculpture which could then be photographed and put into a book together. Who would respond to who was not something we discussed. As it turned out, our discussion lead to a burst of writing in which I decided to look at the time immediately after my brother's death closely, *head-on* as it were, rather than shy around the edges of it, as I had in an earlier poem published in my first collection *The Imageless World*. I wanted to write an elegy but one that would not simply be about my experience but the experience of my family, and our inability fully to know the other's grief even though that grief was itself shared. Over a period of three to four days I wrote a sequence of twelve poems. As I started writing, I knew that I wanted to adopt a simple, almost child-like form of expression akin to that used in the Japanese poet Shuntaro Tanikawa's collection *Naked* and the Australian poet Robert Adamson's collection *Where I Come From*. I wanted a very clear, at times naive voice, in which to approach the images that formed the basic narrative of the sequence. That said, I also wanted to incorporate something of the German poet Paul Celan's structuring of language, image and meaning, and actually found my start into the sequence through his poem "Flower." So, starting from a conversation with a Japanese installation artist in the Jardin du Luxembourg, I took reference points from a Japanese, an Australian and a German poet, and then set out to try and communicate in the language that left me an experience I had largely only approached through dreams over the six years intervening between the time in Paris and my brother's death.

Once I had the first draft finished, I took them to Akiko and suggested they might form a start to our collaboration. She read through them alone and when I returned seemed positive about the poems. Her response suggested something centred on an emotional resonance in the images and ellipses of the poems rather than a response to narrative, language, voice or tone. Over the subsequent month or so, her atelier started to fill with small sculptures of images that were both familiar and strange to me, recognizable but in a differing form to the images in my mind at the time of writing. In many ways, her work was not a re-working of the poems but Akiko's production or communication of a space *parallel* to the space the poems attempted to map out, the space of mourning and memory, the space left by a brother's death and so the changed space the family occupied in the aftermath. In her work, Akiko was very conscious of the inter-relation and interplay of our respective "materials," language for me and for her clay, paint, wood, metal, then finally photography and light. She commented,

> I imagined the place *someone* and the brother are living, in different places, separate like layers, very close but not touching, unable to touch. I think I wanted to overlap the images, the surface of the book (the pages) and the wall. I thought it was interesting, Michael used language but in the book it too is a surface. When we read the poem, we can catch a lot of images and we can go somewhere else though all we start with is surface. We can go somewhere because we can use imagination.

This space, close but not touching, unable to touch, captures a sense of how I understand the living's relationship with the dead, much as the relationship between the real and the symbolic, being-in-the world and being-in-language. It is also resonant with how I understood Akiko's grief and my own, mourning more generally.

Akiko produced seven works in all, five sculptures and two paintings, none of which are simply illustrative of the poems but with them form their own language, or sign system. Later when I asked Akiko whether she was responding to the poems or her experience, she told me,

> It's yes and no. While I was prompted to imagine things after reading the poems, I used my own experiences and memories. I read the book and the poems and I imagined a lot of things. Such as scenery from Japan, images from where I was born, such as Chiba, places I've been to when I was a child when I traveled with my family in Tochigi, Gunma, Chiba and Ibaraki. I always think and use imagination from my childhood memories in my art. Like patchwork. I saw flat land, planes, sky and one flower in a field. And after that I saw lots of walls, the walls of my house, walls from Kyoto, walls from my university. I can't decide the place.

This place, this elsewhere, opened by the poems and by her memories, neither one being privileged, is the centre of the collaboration as far as I can see. It is neither Akiko's nor mine, nor does it exist beyond the act of communication we were engaging in. It is a point of convergence. Akiko was able to identify with images from the poems and communicate through the sculptures and paintings an exacting and minute intricacy, almost a childlike clarity, layers to memory and mourning that were her own, or that in 空 were shared, the act of communication becoming a form of communion.

Subsequently, I contacted a Japanese poet, Yasuhiro Yotsumoto, to see if he would translate the poems into Japanese, which with his usual generosity he agreed to. From the outset Yasuhiro was asked to feel free to approach the poems as he saw fit and to "make them his," so that the resulting book was a collaboration authored by the three of us equally, wherein identity was not so much related to authorship as identification with the shared space of the work. Yasuhiro noted that in the translations,

> First, I read them through, over and over, raising many questions but resisting the temptation to answer them. On this level, the approach is not intellectual but rather sensitivity/texture-oriented. This was followed by a line-by-line, word-by-word cross-examination with the author, addressing to any point of ambiguity. The subsequent correspondence with the author did not necessarily clarify those points

Figure 4.1 Akiko Muto, *The flower blooms* (2006)

19.4x18x8.8cm wood, aluminium, paint

but rather identified critical knots in the poems which remained mysteries even to the author himself.

Yasuhiro continued:

> The voice and the tone of it are the most critical elements in this translation. In the Japanese language, the voice and the tone of a written text are largely determined by the selection of "I," as there are more than a dozen kinds of "I" depending upon the gender, social and cultural background, age, etc. In the end, I have chosen "boku," a common pronoun for a relatively young man with informal and private nuance. I have also used, here and there, certain post-positional particles at the end of the sentences (such as ". . . dayo" or ". . . nanosa") to give a personal and intimate tone, a linguistic device available to Japanese but not to the original English. Overall, I tried to reproduce the voice of a younger brother, now grown-up but still the younger one in the family, through my Japanese.
>
> The images in these poems are very strong . . . these are the poems driven by the images more than anything. Some images, like the "emptiness" in the first poem, was difficult for me to grasp at first and the direct Q&A with the author was helpful. But in most cases, the images speak loud and clear to me. In the translations, I tried to keep my Japanese as visual and as concrete as in the original.
>
> I found the language simple and unpretentious but ambiguous and rich in association. It is the language of poetry, and, in that regard, universal regardless of the languages. We explored this universe of *Sky was sky* together through a number of email correspondences, trying to understand each other as well as the poems themselves. I think it went very well, because, when I finally met the author, I did not feel like meeting him for the first time at all.

Interesting to me is Yasuhiro's development of "boku" in the poems, where he was able to embed an aspect of the narrative (the place of "boku" in the family, the speaker's youth) through grammar alone, in a way alien to English. While writing the poems, and while writing poetry generally, the persona of the "I" is always elusive to me, not really a construction of autobiography (though obviously personal experience offers one dynamic to the writing of the "I"), but more often a construction of tensions between experience (personal and of reading), the images evolving and the confines of lexical choices and grammar. Ideally, for me, the "I" is impersonal, suggesting the tensions between language, experience and circumstance through which we construct ourselves and are constructed, as well as hopefully offering glimmers of being-in-the-world along the way. By creating the "boku" figure, Yasuhiro's poems press the speaker of the poems more closely into a specific narrative.

Of particular interest to me as a writer was the emerging relation between my English, Akiko's images and Yasuhiro's Japanese, wherein one is not subordinated to the others but are given in the book as a whole, as interdependent and interwoven. Not simply does this seem a good example of transcultural flow (Pennycook, 2007) but in some ways presents an opening of discrete sign systems, as much as discrete subjectivities, into a shared system of communication and exchange, albeit one premised on difference and at times the enclosure of the familiar within the foreign. This estrangement, which from my perspective in the text is strongest in terms of Yasuhiro's translations, forces me to approach the work I wrote in English through the unfamiliar, perhaps alienating, sign systems of Japanese and visual art, disrupting my habitual relations to language, identity and experience, widening both the social practice and social field. Due to the content of poems themselves, it is hard not to sense a resonance within this disruption not dissimilar to the overwhelming disruption experienced through mourning wherein a form of *metanoia*, "a transformation of one's whole vision of the social world" (Bourdieu & Waquant 1992, p. 251) is effected.

Commentary

> . . . we have three axes whose specificity and whose interconnections have to be analyzed: the axis of knowledge, the axis of power, the axis of ethics . . . How are we constituted as subjects of our own knowledge? How are we constituted as subjects who exercise or submit to power relations? How are we constituted as moral subjects of our own actions?
>
> (Foucault, quoted in Fairclough, 2003, p.28)

空 was premised on a shared sense of grief between Akiko and myself, and also, no doubt, on our burgeoning friendship. It is worth noting that the collaboration was more a work of excitement and joy than some kind of sorrowful meandering and shared self-pity. We were excited to see the connections being created, even though (as Yasuhiro noted) the meanings were not always clear. In many ways, meaning was the last thing on our minds though, rather sharing experience. That said, in our discussions, we were aware that the shared understanding of grief was not a sharing of the loss itself. Interestingly, Yasuhiro also noted that through the translations he was responding to the loss of his mother. At the level of event there is a commonality but at the identificational level there is a degree of difference. The discourse is created through the dialectical tension between the event and identificational meanings of the text. Put in terms of Bourdieu's *habitus*, the "embodied dispositions" arrived at through socialization and experience are disrupted by the negativity of death/mourning, questioning *habitus* at its most basic levels and forcing the individual to reconsider the structures which underpin their embodied disposition. The text of 空 exteriorizes this process. The text forces a kind of disembodiment of dispositions through the convergence of sign systems into a hybrid and unfamiliar sign system. In this, the text in some way mimics or at least suggests the experience of mourning itself, as the work of mourning, especially that first instance when someone immediate to us, loved, dies renders much of our former knowledge meaningless, and demands we find new words, new structures, through which to constitute a sense of the world, or else accept new meanings unfolding within the sign system we previously thought we understood and had mastered.

Through the convergence of sign systems and the multipolarity of the events each author draws from, the text opens up as a social practice wherein the individual's ability to constitute themselves as a subject of knowledge unfolds in relation to the knowledge of others, and where the commonality of the experience (of mourning) opens out to a reconstitution of knowledge and power as something shared. In a more straightforward way, perhaps one of the critical knots that Yasuhiro noted in our discussions was the double nature of the term 空 itself and the way it enacts this play of negativity in the text. Yasuhiro explained:

> The title of the book, *Sky was sky*, was translated into Japanese as 空は空 , which can be read either as "sora wa sora" or "sora wa ku." The former means the same as the original English title, because sora = the sky. The latter means the sky was "ku" in the sense of the Buddhism term. It can be translated as emptiness or nothingness, but this emptiness is far from empty, but rather filled and charged with emptiness. The title poem does talk about both the sky and an emptiness. Further more, this emptiness fills "me" complete. Shortly after translating this book, I have gotten very much interested in the concept of "ku" and started to read a lot about it. I feel as if I owe some "ku" to this book and the author.

Akiko had mentioned this doubleness of the kanji 空 back in Paris after reading the first drafts of the poems, and it was in response to that, and our shared joy in the word(s) itself, that I then revised the poems, further emphasizing aspects of the doubleness, not least in the choice of title for the sequence as a whole. The sky—with its mysterious doubleness, its immensity and omnipresence coupled with its emptiness and impermanence—has long signified just this sense of "ku" to me. It was a revelation to find that the kanji in Japanese contains and offers this doubleness as a given.

In terms of Foucault's first axis of knowledge, the knowledge from which I began the poems was at some level related to self-knowledge (or its lack), but through the collaboration was given to me anew as shared. The images are familiar but strange and not as I imagined, Akiko's works carrying layers of signification alien to the images I wrote into the poems, while Yasuhiro's poems are withheld from me by my own lack of literacy in Japanese, making what was my experience no longer accessible, far from *my* own. Akiko's wall of bricks, the floorboards, the door permanently open, the flower turning on itself, are familiar but not inscribed in the text I wrote, much as the symbolic value of each could still be further unfolded for me by Akiko a year on after the book was published. Meaning arrived as shared, polysemous, a symbiotic layering of Akiko's sense of the image *within*, *across*, or *over* my own. A word here, or a gathering of recognizable kanji there in Yasuhiro's poems, recalled to me some part of the poems I wrote, the elemental parts 空 ("sky"), 空 ("earth"), 石 ("stone"), 木 ("wood"), perhaps even 兄 ("brother") which in terms of the poems becomes elemental, coupled with the omnipresent flashes of 空 ("emptiness"), made visible but unreadable, unpronounceable to me but for the kanji disembodied from the sentences, the presence of these *things* disembodied by the symbols, English and Japanese. Similarly, the music of Yasuhiro's poems is utterly strange to me when I've asked a friend to read them to me, the rhythms of the poems charting out different subjectivities, voices, though within those differences they offer the same basic narratives. Below the narratives, once again, is the convergence of differing events forming the sign system itself (the death of Yasuhiro's mother; the death of Akiko's brother; my brother's death; the weight, embodiment offered in Akiko's images; the dissonance of the Japanese and English texts; the friendships evolving through the collaboration; the imagined reader). The deeply personal experience of mourning was returned in the collaboration as dispossessing but in an affirming way. It was not individual but something shared, weighed up by others, voiced, inscribed or encrypted by others through their experience and as their experience, and so no longer

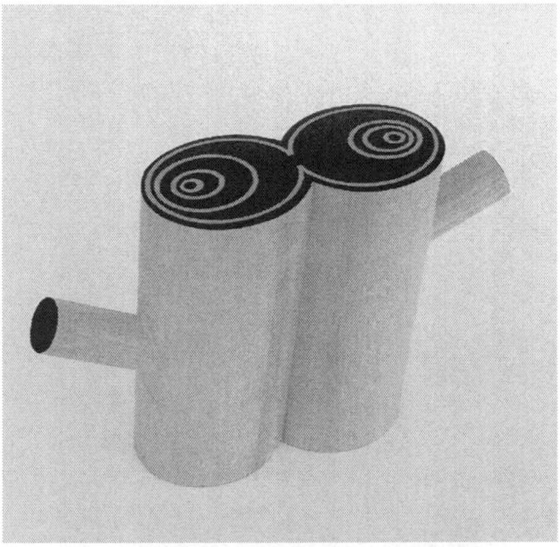

Figure 4.2 Akiko Muto, *Two ways* (2006)

19.3x6x12.8cm wood, paint

Figure 4.3 Akiko Muto, *The night* (2007)

53x503cm acrylic on paper

centered on a suffering self, on identity and the failure of self-knowledge before death, but an experience of loss shared in a community, given to each other, where we are subject not simply to our knowledge but the knowledge of others, where through that knowledge, that estrangement, self-knowledge unfolds and with it perhaps an ethics.

"Power is not something that is acquired, seized, or shared, something that one holds on to or allows to slip away; power is exercised from innumerable points" (Foucault, 1978, p. 94). Such is the case in 空. By working in collaboration, the text itself produces the power relations from "innumerable points." This problematizes the symbolic content of the text in as far as the diffusion of power among the texts and the contributors diffuses the "personal" or "biographical" content being represented. As such, the text's emphasis is not simply communication of "representational meanings" of a single author, nor the internalization of Action, Representation and Identification (Fairclough, 2003, pp. 27–29) in a single author text, but the externalization of such dialectical work through collaborative textual practice, opening analysis up to multiple (polyvalent) readings as the text's symbolic function is extended through the diffusion of power in textual practice between the contributors and through the accumulation of social practices the text incorporates.

Fairclough (2003) defines social practices as an articulation of action and interaction, social relations, persons (beliefs, attitudes, etc.), the material world and discourse (p. 25). He notes the interrelation and interdependency of discourse and social practice, saying "each in a sense contains or internalizes the other." In 空 this interrelation and interdependency rather than being a condition uncovered through analysis is the condition of the text as social event; its semiotic value exceeds its symbolic value, bringing into question and problematizing social structures (languages), social practices (orders of discourse) and social events (the text itself). While social events are "causally" shaped by networks of social practices (in this instance, the use of elegy for example, the theories of translation, the tradition of *ekphrastic* art), the dialectical relation of the social event and the practices forming it become heightened in the reading of the text, and compounded by the positioning of the reader premised on their cultural capital (their ability to read English, Japanese, visual images; their familiarity with genres of elegy, abstract expressionism, minimalism, bricolage, installation art, translation practice).

More pointedly, the text as social event externalizes spaces where readers as well as the contributors have limited access or are excluded through their accumulated cultural capital (whether it be a lack of fluency in English or Japanese, or a lack of familiarity with the cultural capital underlying the texts themselves). For my part, the Japanese texts create a space of exclusion, so that I am forced to face the unfamiliarity and resistance of the semiotic (the experience of mourning) as the symbolic itself (language, in this instance Japanese). This is not simply about a lack of embodied cultural capital (in terms of Japanese language proficiency) as can be seen when considering the similar resistance effected by the visual elements of the sign system created. Akiko's commentary on her works made this point apparent, as images familiar from the poems took on layers of signification. This was apparent for example in the image of sky, which is a sculptured patchwork of shades of blue over planes cast at different angles. Akiko noted:

> The colour of the sky is always changing, so I changed the colour and angle. I wondered what is the colour of sky really. *Yoru no sora wa kuraikedo honto wa kum*

> *ga aru dakedo taiyo no hikari ga ataranai kara watashi wa miru koto ga dekinai. Shi no imagi wa wakaranai kedo*. . . I think night is more close to death than day. When my brother died, night was so hard for me. Day I can live and walk and talk with my friends, but at night I'm alone, I can think about my brother. The light patches are clouds at night, or grey sky. I think the night sky can be grey. It is all night sky. At different times. It is also like a patchwork.

This intersection of subjectivities, illuminated by the places where the sign systems, or by expansion social fields, we were each attuned to merged or resisted or added layers of signification, is precisely the sense of communion the collaboration has left me with. Akiko's sky and the sky in the poems are close but never exactly touching though never separate either. They are the same image, the same symbol, with a similar referent, but at the point that referent is placed in terms of a subjectivity, it shifts and refracts, taking on other dimensions. Interestingly, even while Akiko and Yasuhiro both note that I wrote the originating text for the collaboration, the resulting text is largely seen as impersonal by the three of us, more originating in the book itself than one of us. Yasuhiro says, "To me, the author of this book is without doubt Michael Brennan. To a Japanese reader who does not read English, though, he or she might get the impression that it be the book itself who owns those words and images." Similarly Akiko refers to an impersonal speaker (a "someone"), neither her nor me nor Yasuhiro, and the impersonal dead, neither hers nor mine nor Yasuhiro's.

So what's the point? Luke (1996) argues for an "approach to literacy which reframes the text not as a genre but as a *social strategy* historically located in a network of power relations in particular institutional sites and cultural fields" (p. 333). In part, the textual production being considered here is an example of such a "social strategy," not simply in the reading of the text but its very production. In this form of literacy, "social identities and power relations . . . would become primary objects of analysis, critique and study" (Luke, 1996, p. 333). In the situation where "power is utterly sociologically contingent" this reworking of literacy can be applied not simply to pedagogy but to textual practice more broadly, and indeed is an aspect of literary and artistic practices generally, not simply avant-garde efforts of the nineteenth and twentieth centuries which transgressed, collapsed or combined genre boundaries. This is not in any way to refute Luke's demands, but rather to emphasize with him the need of a self-reflexive examination on the part of those who produce, critique and teach texts to consider the "social and cultural consequences" of their approach wherein such practices run the risk of "renaturalizing" texts to established power bases in the ruling ideology/discourse.

Foucault asks: "How are we constituted as subjects of our own knowledge? How are we constituted as subjects who exercise or submit to power relations? How are we constituted as moral subjects of our own actions?" These are fundamental questions to view language and power through. In the context of 空, they stimulate the question how are we constituted as subjects of our own knowledge when the knowledge is outside our knowing, beyond the power of the symbolic to represent, as is the case with death, if not with mourning? What I've been hoping for in this commentary is to sketch out an ethics of difference wherein we become subjects of our own knowledge through the knowledge of others; where we neither exercise nor submit to power but are an aspect of the evolution of power, not agency but trajectory within a community; where we are constituted as moral subjects when our actions bespeak an openness to difference and a cohabitation within discourse, an openness to the otherness and negativity of experience and its polyvalence as experience shared in community. This does not constitute the erasure of meaning. Each of the events operating within the text are real to us as far as memory and the sign systems governing it allow. There is history, not simply interpretation; presence not simply re-presentation. But meaning here is constituted as active and participatory, open to refutation or better yet broadening, connection, convergence, so that even the most personal might become shared, not contingent on the authority (or delusion) of self-knowledge but contiguous with knowledge beyond the self, that places self-knowledge in question. Through the defiance of social fields and practices, 空 presents an instance of transcultural flow, where self-knowledge or identity begins within relation to the other; where literacy or language fail, giving the symbolic up to the semiotic; where culture as much as cultural capital, and the privileges or limitations it affords, give way to community. Theory aside, I think Yasuhiro summarized 空 best:

> I like to think that the collaboration has built up a three dimensional structure into which readers are invited to enter. I hope it should serve as a virtual pyramid: in the middle of it, one sits alone for his or her own mourning and meditation.

References

Adamson, Robert. (1979). *Where I Come From.* Sydney: Big Smoke Books.

Bourdieu, P. (1992). *An Invitation to Reflexive Sociology* (L. Wacquant, Trans.). Cambridge: Polity.

Bourdieu, P., & Wacquant, L. (1992*). An Invitation to Reflexive Sociology.* Chicago: The University of Chicago Press.

Fairclough, N. (2003). *Analysing Discourse: Textual Analysis for Social Research.* London: Routledge.

Foucault, M. (1977). *Power/Knowledge: Selected Interviews and Other Writings 1972–1977* (Ed. Colin Gordon). New York: Pantheon.

Foucault, M. (1978). *The History of Sexuality. Vol I: An Introduction* (R. Hurley, Trans.). New York: Random House.

Janks, H. (1997). "Critical discourse analysis as a research tool," *Discourse Studies in the Cultural Politics of Education*, vol.18, issue 3, pp. 329–342.

Kristeva, J. (1984). *Revolution in Poetic Language* (Margaret Waller, Trans.). New York: Columbia University Press.

Luke, A. (1996). "Genres of power? Literacy education and the production of capital," in *Literacy in Society*, R. Hassan and G. Williams, Eds. Longman, London, pp. 308–338.

Pennycook, A. (2007). *Global Englishes and Transcultural Flows.* London and New York: Routledge.

Tanikawa, Shuntaro. (1996). *Naked* (William I. Elliot and Kazuo Kawamura, Trans.). Berkeley, California: Stone Bridge Press.

Chapter 5

Achieving Community

Suresh Canagarajah
Pennsylvania State University

I had driven the previous day to Toronto to do a survey on language maintenance in the Sri Lankan Tamil community. The first morning there, before visiting some of my subjects, I thought I should wash my vehicle (an SUV) so that my status-conscious community members wouldn't disapprove of me. As I drove into a carwash, I encountered a young attendant who appeared to be a Sri Lankan Tamil. (It is we Tamils who can make out a Sri Lankan Tamil from the dizzying array of brown-skinned people in Toronto—i.e., Indians, Pakistanis, and Bangladeshis, not to mention other tan non-South Asians in the city.) Coming from a small town in New Jersey, where there are no Sri Lankan Tamils around, I was glad to meet someone with whom I could now talk Tamil. As the attendant was getting ready to hose-wash the front of my SUV and let it into the carwash, I thought of alerting him to the fact that my vehicle had extra heavy dirt from highway driving. So I told him:

> "aNNai, mun pakkattai koncam kuuTa kaLuvi viTunkoo. kanakka uuttai irukku." ("Big brother, wash the front side a bit more. There's a lot of dirt there.")
>
> He said, "What?" in English. I repeated my request in English this time.
>
> He replied gruffly: "We can't guarantee that all the dirt will go away."

I thought I had made a mistake in assuming he was Tamil. I looked at him more carefully and found that he had an identification badge on him. I found that his name was "Muthiah"—a Tamil name. I was so eager to bond with my countryman that I phrased my second request to him also in Tamil: "aNNai, antenna-vai kaLatturataa?" ("Big brother, should I take down the antenna?") He replied in English: "We are not responsible for any part that might break." I wondered if his reply meant that he had understood my question this time. But, then, the intelligibility could also be attributed to the English borrowing I had used: "antenna."

The incident left me puzzled. When I drove out of the carwash, I asked myself: Why would someone refuse to bond with a fellow community member? Why would one refuse to reciprocate a friendly gesture from his compatriot? I had even used an honorific aNNai (big brother) to someone who was clearly younger than me. I felt rebuffed.

It was later, during my conversations with friends and acquaintances in Toronto, that I heard that claiming to not know Tamil language was a phenomenon commonly observed in the city (and in other diaspora settlements such as London or Sydney). But my acquaintances were themselves puzzled by this behavior. A seventy-year-old community elder, Mani, observed in Tamil: "Those who came thirty years back haven't forgotten their Tamil. Those who have come lately, those who came about fifteen years back, are saying they have forgotten all their Tamil, that they don't know how to speak Tamil." However, the director of the local Tamil cultural organization, Bala, offered an explanation for this behavior, considering it as mere pretense. Using Sri Lankan English, he said:

> I don't know why, why, what's the reason. I can't believe it. I can't believe it, . . . but our people are very *quickly* forgetting their language . . . maybe our Sri Lankan caste system. Caste system, because most of the people here in Canada, affected by the caste system. . . . Here they feel the freedom. So they didn't want to bother about the culture and tradition. Because they are affected by the culture, no? . . . English gives them the freedom. . . . Freedom and a sophisticated life and sophistication and status . . . . They reach the status very quickly, no? By money, by money, by money. Easy money, easy money. That also one of the reasons they are pretending.

Bala's suggestion that status differences might have something to do with this unusual behavior has some merit. In Sri Lanka, access to English is restricted to those from privileged backgrounds. Though English is supposed to be taught in primary and secondary schools, there aren't enough teachers for all the schools. Eventually, only the private schools and some urban public schools have the teachers with adequate training to teach English. As a result, members of the lower caste and class groups do not have access to English. Even the few who manage to study the language through their own limited resources are discriminated by the privileged groups. Treating their "educated" Sri Lankan English as the norm, the privileged folks would identify some phonological and syntactical features of the less educated to label theirs as "non-standard" Sri Lankan English.[1] (In fact, the unusual article usage, question tags, and clipped sentences of Bala are some markers of non-standard Sri Lankan English. Interestingly, I had started the interview with Bala in Tamil, but he insisted on speaking in English.) However, when the less privileged folks migrate to the West, they have greater access to English. In addition to attending the compulsory free classes in English for migrants, they are also able to pick up English from everyday contexts of social use. This proficiency in English gives the previously disadvantaged access to new material resources, identity positions, and social possibilities.

But is it not enough to speak English? Should one also pretend that he or she doesn't know Tamil? It does appear that one has to discard Tamil to lay claim to these new identities. As Bala suggests, Tamil language is loaded with caste associations. When people of two different castes speak in Tamil, they have to choose lexical items and personal address forms that suit their caste level. Furthermore, a conversation in Tamil between two non-acquaintances leads to prying personal questions about one's background. A conventional conversation opener is: "unkaTai uur etu?" ("What's your village?"). Through the area of residency in Sri Lanka, one can locate the other's caste identity. Therefore, it is not enough to speak English; one must also dissociate oneself from Tamil. To lay claim to the new identities more effectively, one must cut oneself off from the old identities associated with Tamil language and culture.

Now let's turn to elder Mani's observation. Why is it that people who migrated thirty years ago don't claim to have forgotten Tamil, and those who migrated recently do? There is a status difference between the people who migrated from Sri Lanka at different periods. Those who came in the 1960s, before the ethnic conflict there intensified, came for professional reasons or higher education. Those who migrated after the 1983 militarization of the conflict belong to a more diverse group. Many of them are undocumented, and claimed refugee status after entering the country. They are less educated and hold unskilled jobs. This difference is also reflected in the settlement patterns. The earlier migrants have moved to the suburbs (such as Scarborough or Ajax or Mississauga), while the latter live in the high rises in the inner city. In my survey on language choice, the majority of people in the inner city stated that they speak only English at home, encouraged their children to learn English and ignore Tamil, and felt that Tamil lacked usefulness for their life in Canada. Those in the suburbs, especially those who had migrated before 1983, had more positive things to say about Tamil language and its usefulness. Though their children didn't always speak Tamil, they affirmed the importance of the language. It appeared that the latter wanted to claim solidarity with the Tamil language and community. The former wanted to dissociate themselves from the language and community that had once discriminated against them. There was also the practical reason that the less privileged groups had to make use of the new opportunities and catch up on English proficiency to make up for what they had lost for generations in Sri Lanka. They also wanted their children to learn English as soon as possible.

The observations by Mani and Bala helped me understand why the carwash attendant had failed to reciprocate in Tamil with me. I later recollected that he was wearing dark glasses on a gloomy December morning in Toronto. He obviously wanted to mask his identity. My use of the honorific Annai wasn't enough to neutralize the many sources of inequality in the encounter. Perched high on my seat in an imposing SUV with an American license plate, I was literally looking down at him standing humbly with his mop and hose. There is some stigma attached to unskilled labor in the Tamil community. The situation was too unequal for him to enjoy community. Besides, the use of Tamil will also bring up other details of caste and regional inequalities associated with the language. Therefore, the best option for the attendant was to pretend not to know Tamil. With the community affiliation taken off, we are both compelled to conduct this interaction as any other impersonal service encounter—i.e., between strangers.

Against Community

The realization that certain segments of the Tamil community may not like to enjoy community oneness in diaspora contexts was surprising to me. It was even more surprising in the context of resistance to ethnic discrimination, activism for language rights, and militant struggle for self-determination that had led to the dispersal of my community in the first place. This community, bound together by its common aspirations, was itself riven by internal differences and conflicts. And I had to come to the diaspora to realize all this. These tensions were certainly already there in Sri Lanka, but I hadn't had the eyes to see them. As a member of the English-educated group in Sri Lanka, I hadn't realized how others in my community were disadvantaged by lack of access to that language. Perhaps because the Tamil community in Sri Lanka was tightly structured around a certain hierarchy of values and distribution of resources for such a long time, we had taken them for granted for generations, and focused on developing a unity by "naturalizing" the differences. When those assumptions are disturbed in a new locale, and the previous social stratification is thrown into disarray, the subtle tensions in our community had begun to open up deep fissures. The "community" now seems non-existent. We all enter into a frenzied race to define ourselves according to the new resources and values in the new habitation.

But who would doubt community bonds? I grapple with the idea that community may not be always desirable for everyone. It comes to me as a shock that community can be repressive. It is not only I who hunger for community for the understandable reason that as I missed the companionship of my fellow Tamils in bland New Jersey. It appears that sober-minded social scientists also assume community as a positive experience and the foundation for all other constructs they analyze. For example, the role of community in providing a rationale for language norms, linguistic rights, and identity claims has been a basic assumption in sociolinguistics. In general, community comes loaded with notions of cohesion, unity, boundedness, sharednesss, meaningful relationships, commitment, reciprocity, harmony and bonds that are durative over time. Raymond Williams observes: "What is most important, perhaps, is that unlike all other terms of social organization (*state, nation, society*, etc.) [community] seems never to be used unfavourably . . ." (1976, p. 76; emphasis in original). Such positive connotations prevent linguists and social scientists from addressing both the problems and new possibilities in community formation. Can we theorize language, communication, and identity without resorting to a bounded community—or by reimagining group life to accommodate conflict, mobility, and diversity?

The Pleasures and Benefits of Anonymity

If Tamils in Toronto are pretending that they don't know Tamil and are distancing themselves from the Tamil community, what community are they joining? Does their use of English, often a variety that approximates the locally dominant forms, indicate that they prefer to join the Anglo-Canadian community? I found from my conversations that Tamils were keenly aware of the limits of mobility. They didn't romanticize agency and freedom. They knew that they couldn't join any community at will or adopt any new identity. To begin with, their skin marked them as Asiatic and prevented them from passing as Anglo-Canadian. The reality of racism was also in their minds. A young Tamil woman in London put it well when she said:

> No matter what, when you are in UK, they call you Paki. They are not going to ever accept you as British. No matter how much, how noble, or whatever they are, the Queen is never going to take *you* in for a tea or anything. No matter how high you get in your life. Because all you have is your skin.

So what are these Tamils achieving through this pretense? On one level, it appears as if they are simply constructing a relative anonymity. By saying that they don't speak Tamil, they are telling other Tamils (and perhaps other communities) not to assume that they belong to the Tamil community and apply any stereotypes one associates with that identity. What community do they belong to? That's left to one's imagination. Because of their physiognomy, they could belong to Indian, Pakistani, Bangladeshi, East Asian Caribbean, Polynesian, Mediterranean, Malaysian, Singaporean, or South African Indian communities, depending on one's pigmentation level. In other words, they are leaving open their community belonging and identity.

In some cases, certain Tamils might take this desired anonymity further and literally cut themselves off from other Tamils. Many are known to use English even for domestic communication and adopt an Anglicized lifestyle in their private life. They might adopt diversified social networks, aligning with other migrant communities and even the dominant Anglo community, leaving their community affiliation fluid. Through this strategy, they gain the nimbleness and openness to join any community or construct any identity.

Whatever the practical alternatives for these underprivileged Tamils, the benefits of anonymity are clear. They are basically telling their fellow Tamils and others not to bring associations and categories related to the Tamil community (such as lower/upper caste, educated/uneducated, recent/early immigrant) into the conversation or interaction, but negotiate with them on equal terms. In fact, by loosening the connections with ethnic community and distancing themselves from identity categories based on their native community, these subjects are asking others to focus more on situational identities that are more relevant to the contexts of interaction (i.e., teacher/student, citizen/official, client/service provider etc.). More importantly, they are keeping open the possibility of joining other social networks and adopting more diverse identities.

It seems that through their pretense, the underprivileged Tamils are constructing a *floating identity.* I use this term analogous to *floating signs* in cultural studies. These are signs that are relatively empty of content, but gain diverse meanings in relation to their changing contexts. But, then, signs are always of that nature. It is we who have permanently fixed the meaning of signs in ways that are advantageous to one group or the other. The same applies to identity. The Tamils who dissociate themselves from Tamil are simply reminding everyone that identity is a floating signifier.

Is it really important for everyone to belong to a stable and durable community? Would some people benefit more from not belonging to any permanent community affiliation? And I am not talking about misanthropes here! The people I am considering here desire engagement with people—but with more diverse communities, with more options for life opportunities, and a broader range of subject positions. Now that scholars have started to talk about transnational, imagined, and virtual communities, we have to also consider the possibility of *liminal communities.* Perhaps more people than we know occupy these nebulous in-between social positions that give them the nimbleness to shuttle between identities and communities.

Reconfiguring Community

Despite the advantages of anonymity, or floating identities, there are certain contexts where Tamilness cannot be masked or denied. When I meet someone in a temple, a Tamil grocery store, a wedding or birthday party of a Tamil acquaintance, or a Tamil cultural event (such as a dance, music, drama performance), the context defines us as Tamils who have come to that gathering because we understand the Tamil language and share certain other cultural affinities and affiliations. What happens to the choice of language in such contexts?

There is no need to pretend that one doesn't know Tamil in such contexts. However, status differences are negotiated through different varieties of English. The difference is that traditional bilinguals from Sri Lanka come with a variety of English that is prestigious in the home country—educated Sri Lankan English (see Kandiah, 1979)—while the previously disadvantaged have mastered Canadian English. Traditional bilinguals (like me) who migrated with a prior proficiency in Sri Lankan English find it difficult to adopt a new variety in the new lands of habitation, especially late in life. However, those who learn English after migration (Shall we call them "nouveau bilinguals" without the sarcasm behind "nouveau riche"?) learn the locally dominant Canadian variety successfully. Not only do they have the advantage of learning it in local educational contexts from local teachers, but also gain much reinforcement from everyday contexts of socialization. The locally dominant variety of English serves as a symbolic capital in the new land of settlement for those previously disadvantaged in Sri Lanka.

So, what happens when I greet a nouveau bilingual in Tamil in a Sri Lankan dance festival? He will respond in Canadian English. Thereafter, I am forced to stick to Tamil or shift to Sri Lankan English. As he continues speaking in Canadian English, his accent will rub into me the following: that I am not socialized into the Canadian community; that I am probably "fresh off the boat"; that I don't have class; and that I am socially inept. However, that's not the end of the story. In most cases, I'll be correct in guessing that the speaker is not a traditional bilingual from Sri Lanka. That would imply economic and class differences as well. Traditional bilinguals will be professionals with advanced education; nouveau bilinguals will be in unskilled or semiskilled labor. From this difference derive other language differences beyond accent (and other surface level markers). Though their accent is Sri Lankan, traditional bilinguals will have a larger vocabulary range (especially those relating to expert registers in different fields), more complex syntactic proficiency, and familiarity with diverse professional and institutional discourses. To use Basil Bernstein's well-known terms here, traditional bilinguals are armed with the expanded code, while nouveau bilinguals possess a restricted code. If the traditional bilinguals want to, they can bring up some of these complex registers and discourses to disadvantage the new bilinguals and expose their less educated status. However, the success of either party to enforce their valuations on the variety chosen will depend on diverse contextual factors. In the evening dance event, the traditional bilingual's attempt to initiate a conversation on Habermas will appear forced and irrelevant. On the other hand, if a nouveau bilingual meets me in my university office, he will look powerless despite his Canadian accent. I will unleash a barrage of literary terms and linguistic constructs that will stun him into silence. Is it accent or register that will define power and status? That needs to be negotiated in context.

Consider the interaction with the carwash attendant now. Though he had feigned lack of knowledge of Tamil in the first turn, he changed his strategy to showing comprehension of my second question in Tamil in the second turn. It is possible that he observed me looking at his identification tag and realized he couldn't pull off a non-Tamil identity successfully. Therefore, in his second turn, he appealed to a different form of prestige. In response to my Sri Lankan English, he adopts a variety that approximates Canadian English. In terms of language, then, he has the upper hand. He conveys to me that I am "fresh off the boat." However, he stands there with his mop and hose, while I am perched on an SUV. There is a slight inequality in our positions as client and service provider. Still, however, my SUV doesn't have to mean that I am from a different class. He may have an SUV as well. My vocation is also not clear in that context. In this situation, his attempt to define status according to accent alone might be quite successful.

It was clear from my conversations in Toronto that members of the community are becoming very conscious of the power differences deriving from the different varieties of English. Thiru, a journalist in a Tamil newspaper, who lacks higher education and comes from a traditionally Tamil-dominant family in Sri Lanka, was full of glee at the prospect of status reversal. He told me in Tamil (with some code mixing, highlighted in italics): "Educated families . . . they are the folks who are struggling hard. I know that because they can't understand the *Canadian accent.* They face a problem of dignity here, that we might think they don't know *English.*" What the formerly less privileged members of the community are doing through these "accent wars" is not just redefining their own status in the community. They are going further to reconstruct the community stratification according to new norms and values. Now that they are outside Sri Lanka, they are asking whether status shouldn't be defined according to different variables and categories. In this sense, they are reconfiguring the Tamil community according to new values, resources and norms.

Shuttling Between Communities

At the end of my three-month stay in Toronto, I packed up my survey responses and went to the gas station to fill my tank before driving back home. I saw a Tamil gas service attendant behind the counter. By this time, I had stopped opening conversations in Tamil even when I saw someone with an identification tag that suggested a Tamil name. I had learnt my lesson well—I knew that language choice and community allegiance cannot be assumed. So, I used English to talk to the attendant whose badge said his name was "Kanthan." I said, "I am on pump five." He said, "Ten sixty." When I took the cash out, I mistook a quarter for a dollar coin. When the attendant looked at me for more money, I didn't understand what more was needed. Then he said in Tamil, "aNNai, itu irpaccaintu catam" ("Big brother, this is twenty five cents"). I gave him the dollar required. Then he uttered the good old conversation starter, "unkaTai uur etu" ("What is your village?"). He proffered his information unasked. (Yes, we had caste differences.) Then we went on to talk about mutual friends in our hometown Jaffna, and other details about the schools we had studied in, and the way we had migrated—all in Tamil on a quiet Sunday afternoon when few people were around in that gas station.

I was surprised by this experience of community when I had least expected it. It threw into confusion all the variables and categories I had carefully worked out as to why or when someone will feign lack of proficiency in Tamil. Perhaps there were good reasons why the gas station attendant had used Tamil despite the social differences between us. The fact that I had seemed to fumble because of my lack of knowledge of Canadian currency was a neutralizer of inequalities. The attendant could take the upper hand and help me out. Perhaps he was himself looking for an opportunity to use Tamil after a boring day behind the counter, using only English with his customers. Whatever the reason, this was a rare and welcome experience of community.

I now think the beauty of community is when it is *achieved* in this manner. Community "happens." It happens in the most unexpected moments and transforms the relationship between strangers. It temporarily suspends social categories and hierarchies to connect people. Community magically reconstructs the context from impersonal to intimate in a rare moment through an unexpected word or gesture. Looking back on my whole field trip, I can recollect many occasions when community happened in these unexpected ways on rare occasions. It was not only with Tamils that I established community in this manner. In many cases, I enjoyed community with other ethnic groups through English or, sometimes, without any common language at all. I think of: the night when I was stranded in downtown because my usual route was closed for construction work, and two drunken "punk" Anglo teenagers showed me an alternate route to get back home; when I foolishly walked into a toilet in a public park where a drug transaction was taking place, and the two black men who walked toward me menacingly let me go when they heard my best impressions of African American English ("I be your home boy") in an attempt to put them at ease; when I got the attention of a police officer when an elderly Chinese couple were mugged, and they could thank me only in Chinese (which I perfectly understood though I was hearing the language for the first time). When community is taken for granted because of some purported social or linguistic features that are shared, it loses its value. More importantly, social hierarchies and status differences suppress the "experience" of bonding and unity. If community is not given but achieved, it is constantly constructed and reconstructed through the language choice and negotiation strategies of individuals. It is probably this that migration scholar Papastergiadis meant when he said "communities are not just dominated by rigid structures and fixed boundaries but are like a 'happening'" (2000, p. 200).

Underprivileged Tamils don't dislike community. They are keeping their options open to shuttle between communities and construct bonding groups as suits their needs, interests, and situations. Rather than letting conventional forms of identities and values restrict their mobility and creativity, they are forming communities on their own initiative and on their own terms. Rather than letting predefined expectations of who they are to dictate their community, they are enjoying the freedom to shuttle across social groups and domains and reconstruct both themselves and their communities. Some of the stories I heard in Toronto now make better sense. Children who leave Tamil homes dressed one way, pull out other "hip" clothing from their backpack, and change in their bathroom before school starts in order to bond with others in their shared teen culture; some teenagers hang out mostly with South Asians as they share many concerns and struggles together and enjoy a pan-Asian community; families in the inner city told me that they enjoyed wonderful relationships with the Black families in their neighborhood as "they understand what it means to be discriminated"; some Christian families said they meet for weekly home group meetings with the Anglo members of their church for deep and meaningful fellowship. These are the new possibilities for Tamils when they move out of their traditional homeland and the restrictions that come with it. Rather than be chosen by a community, they choose their communities.

To quote Papastergiadis again:

> We need to explode the myth of pure and autonomous communities, reject the earlier mechanistic and territorial models of community and present new perspectives on the concepts of space and time which can address the dynamic flows that make community life.
>
> (2000, 200)

He calls this a "processual view of community." I call this the "shuttling" model of community (Canagarajah, 2006). We need better metaphors to describe this kind of community formation. On further thoughts, we might have to abandon the term "community" itself as it still gives the impression of something bounded and static. Papastergiadis prefers the term "cluster" in order to accommodate the fluid and changing identity of people groupings, almost as in a kaleidoscope.

It is ironic that I had to wait till the end of my survey research to understand something that should have guided my research from the beginning. My casual language interactions taught me things that challenged my research assumptions. In my survey questions, I had treated the Tamil "community" as monolithic and homogeneous in my effort to understand the implications of language maintenance for its continuity in diaspora settings. My casual interactions outside the research context taught me that the community life and language choice of my compatriots were more complex than I had assumed. Perhaps I should have queried the multiple expressions of Tamils' community life rather than holding it static to serve as the rationale for my research. Blommaert (2005) argues for an approach that "will show how a wide variety of widely used concepts—culture, ethnic group, language community, society, nation—can be reconceived and reconceptualized as analytical tools. When starting from a semiotic point of departure, such concepts are empirical, that is, they cannot be used a priori any more" (p. 204). It is time now to question and reformulate this staple of linguistic scholarship—community.

Note

1 See Parakrama 1995 for more on these differences.

References

Blommaert, J. (2005). *Discourse: A critical introduction.* Cambridge, UK: Cambridge University Press.

Canagarajah, A. S. (2006). Toward a writing pedagogy of shuttling between languages: Learning from multilingual writers. *College English 68*, 589–604.

Kandiah, T. (1979). Disinherited Englishes: The case of Lankan English. *Navasilu 3*, 75–89.

Papastergiadis, N. (2000). *The turbulence of migration.* Cambridge, UK: Polity Press.

Parakrama, A. (1995). *De-hegemonizing language standards.* Basingstoke: Macmillan.

Williams, R. (1976). *Key words.* New York: Oxford.

Chapter 6

Another Drink in Subanun[1]

Mark Cherry
University of Technology, Sydney

I'm a poor language learner. That's not modesty; that's fact. I speak English and not much else. Granted I can bow, mumble and gesture in a variety of countries, but does that really count?

Growing up in Canada, my first encounter with learning another language was when my bilingual mother enrolled me in a French kindergarten not far from our home. Fantasies of me fluently conversing with my French grandmother seemed to dance in the background of her decision. Grandmamma couldn't speak much English and our sporadic phone conversations were very limited. They always started with her singsong laughing greeting '*Bonjour mon petit*' to which I'd been drilled to reply '*Bonjour Grandmamma*'. This greeting stage was followed up by '*Ça va?*' to which I would reply '*Bien*'. We were talking but we never spoke meaningfully. As a result I was lukewarm with the French Kindergarten idea. This didn't really matter because when you were a kid in my family, you ate what was on your plate. Any resistance was met by my mother's standard response, 'I'm not running a cafeteria here'. In my mind, food and school had a lot in common.

I wound up going to that kindergarten. I wish I could say I have strong memories of my struggles and victories with French language acquisition, but the truth is I don't. I do, however, remember how I felt after wetting my pants once. Suffice to say I found the social context with its rules, routines and repercussions more memorable than anything connected with language. I learnt a lot at kindergarten but only a fraction of it seemed to be much help with my phone calls to Grandmamma.

Years later and I was in Australia, enrolling in first form at a boy's high school. Language learning was once again on the menu – three terms, three languages and a choice to be made about one of them for 2nd year. This was a different kind of language learning and light years away from the immersion approach used in my kindergarten. Ducking teacher wrath was a highly strategic exercise. Failure to do so meant a trip to see the Deputy Headmaster. Once in his timber-panelled sanctum, six lashes from his stout cane was almost inevitable. I kept my head down most of the time at St Francis Xavier's School for Boys. Even so I have vivid memories of my hands stinging for hours after slight miscalculations of what was appropriate behaviour in class.

Latin was abstract, an interminable series of singsong lessons, drilling and conjugating in what turned out to be a strangely reassuring cadence. German, on the other hand, was not reassuring. I couldn't make the unfamiliar sounds and this together with Fraulein's obsession with uncontextualized vocabulary lists led me to be quite unimpressed with its overall utility. Besides, the only German people I'd ever come across were on TV and they were usually portrayed as two-dimensional and very much 'other'. They didn't seem to be my kind of crowd.

But during the third term, French popped up again and things were different. Monsieur Hocking was firmly at the helm. He was an impressive character. Magnificent hair, receding and swept back, a prominent brow and always a crisp white shirt that smelled strongly of Gaulloise. When he spoke he used quick, measured gestures like an orchestra conductor. He would stride into the room using French exclusively; and I was totally engaged. Brandishing our class reader *Louis En Vacances* like a holy text, he had us reading (often without much comprehension) from Day One. Fixing us with his steely gaze, his questions demanded answers in French. My acquired get-out-of-jail card for frequent states of incomprehension was: drop gaze, contrite stance and a rehearsed, if mumbled, *Je ne comprends pas, Monsieur.* In that class the key to avoiding a trip to the office and all it entailed was understanding what was required and then producing it. It sure was different from German.

Partly due to the theatricality of Monsieur Hocking's classes and partly due to rekindled memories of kindergarten, I passed French. But it was all to no avail. Puberty kicked in hot and strong about then and I dumped foreign languages in favour of Technical Drawing. It promised fewer problems than verb conjugations.

A few years went by and I found myself kicking around Sri Lanka and India. Using little more than a developing nose for social context, I managed to slip in and out of situations that seemed to trip up other multilingual travellers. All I had going for me was a neatly tied *lungi*,[2] a little respect, and the knowledge that my left hand was the one that never touched the food. The importance of the eating etiquette was underlined the day a Dutch tourist unwittingly insulted a restaurateur by eating with both hands. His intermediate Hindi was of no use for what transpired. Nothing was said but he did develop severe stomach pains after a second helping of rice and curry.

While living in Osaka I found that to best teach, work, shop and socialize meant to decode context first, find words second. And even though I was still a lousy language learner, I managed to acquire some of the social cheat-keys that help foreigners get by in Japan. I did learn a few greetings and how to order in a restaurant, but more important than the spoken word was learning how to force my way onto a crowded train (avoid eye contact) and how to offer and accept a business card in the correct way. A valued lesson was discovering that for me it was better to remain silent than emulate the other *Gaijin*[3] who learnt Japanese from their girlfriends. Apparently these guys sounded like teenage girls, and were a laughing-stock to anyone in the know.

Denpasar 2007

The line is getting shorter. Up ahead, the immigration officer is the only thing between me and a flight home. My visa is expired and this is a bad thing. Playing at the edge of my nervousness are flashes of that scene in Oliver Stone's *Midnight Express* (1978) when drug smuggler Billy Hayes is arrested at the airport. In the film, just before he gets busted, Hayes is chewing gum, his sunglasses hiding eye sockets dank with sweat. I lick my lips and exhale slowly; glad I'm not wearing Ray Bans.

I laugh in spite of myself – what an imagination! I haven't done anything wrong; I'm not smuggling, nor anything like it. But I had booked a flight one day later than I should have and because of this I am worried. There's no denying that I am in breach of the law; and in Indonesia, transgressions, real or imagined, can have serious consequences.

It's no wonder that the unfolding Denpasar situation was worrying me. Years previously I'd flown from London into the United States of a newly elected Ronald Reagan. With months of Covent Garden night clubs under my belt, I stood out from the American kids on their way home from weekends in Prague. I'd swaggered off the plane, cockily brushing off the importance of a chat at US Immigration and things went badly. As I sat in an interview room waiting for someone to come talk to me, I had time to reflect. I was genuinely confused. Despite the fact that I'd been involved in an event carried out in my first language, I was in trouble. I'd misunderstood the situation, underestimated the gravity of official scrutiny and was about to pay the price. From that time onwards, I've been wary of immigration checks.

The queue is moving again; I try to slow down my breathing, to block out images of Schapelle Corby,[4] uniformed guards, and newspaper headlines. I tuck in my shirt and compose my body language.

Nevertheless as much as I try not to think of it, Westerners being detained in Indonesia is not a rare phenomenon. Sukarno's use of incarceration, and later Soeharto's, springs to mind – understandable, as a latter-day response to centuries of colonial repression (May, 1978).

Around me, I can hear English being spoken but it's a burdened English, burdened by history. English may be the lingua franca of international travel but the English(es) heard at airports around the world is a polyphonic and multi-textured thing. Here in Denpasar, speakers of English as an Additional Language put their identities under pressure as they exchange information in order to have their passports stamped.

People in airports don't always represent themselves as confidently as they might. One reason relates to the 'reduced personality' syndrome (Harder, 1980), which can be unwittingly projected by the non-native speaker of English. Indeed, Harder asserts, that from an interactional point of view, such a speaker may come across as 'a coarse and primitive character'. This may explain some of the tremendous tension one feels in airports. In any case, differing varieties of English jostle and co-exist in a world where English always equals Western; and because of this no encounter in English can ever be free of its complex history (Pennycook, 1994).

I start to put together a plan. Whatever I say has to be in Bahasa Indonesia. As Wajnryb (2009) says, whole languages carry their own bundle of connotations, a large part of which is shaped by the immediate context of action. I pick over my meagre stockpile. A few greetings, mostly casual, a few forms of address and a few phrases and common forms (I could say 'excuse me' and 'sorry'). Not really enough to talk my way out of a jam. Up ahead a tourist with a Cockney accent is arguing futilely about something or other. He is steered toward a nearby office. I imagine it's because of an issue like mine. I reach for a stick of gum, think better of it and settle for a wipe of the brow. I've got a big scene coming up and although I'm not Billy Hayes, I've got a feeling it'll be a series of close-ups.

Night Int: Ngurah Rai International Airport Denpasar Bali

The airport is crowded. Long lines of tourists, many dressed very casually. Hand luggage fills the immigration hall. There is no customs check on departure at this airport. The sound of English, German and Japanese can be heard clearly. I'm dressed conservatively. To the side of the hall one-way windows hint at the private world of Indonesian interview rooms. When my turn comes I approach the immigration officer.

ME
(dropping gaze and offering passport)
Salamat Malam Pak (Good evening Sir)

IMMIGRATION OFFICER
(officiously)
Malam

The IMMIGRATION OFFICER flicks through the passport once, then goes through it again slowly soaking up the multiple Indonesian entries and exits. He occasionally flicks a hard look at ME.

ME
(clearing throat slightly and deliberately hesitating)
Permisi Pak (excuse me Sir), *Maaf* (sorry).

IMMIGRATION OFFICER
(quizzical look)
Apa? (what?)

ME
Mungkin (maybe)
(more deliberate hesitation)
Visa problem.

The SOUNDS of the airport drop several decibels and the situation seems to teeter with infinite possibilities. Venetian blinds in a nearby immigration interview room snap shut audibly as a protesting GERMAN WOMAN is led into the office.

IMMIGRATION OFFICER
(with stony gaze)
Mmmmmm

ME
(dropped gaze, speaking hesitantly)
Permisi Pak

The IMMIGRATION OFFICER allows the discomfort to extend. Nothing is said.

IMMIGRATION OFFICER
(a long pause and then in perfect English)
You must be more careful on your next visit.
(he stamps the passport with a loud bang)

ME
(respectfully)
Terima Kasi Banyak Pak (thank you very much Sir)

Relieved I walk past the immigration checkpoint and head towards the departure lounge.

How is it that a tourist could pass through immigration in such a way? How could an opportunity for penalty be passed up in a country that's been called one of the world's most corrupt? Even though the government has made solid attempts to combat *corrupsi,* bribery remains endemic.

Despite this mystery, if my Denpasar encounter were to be assessed for its filmic potential, it may well fail the interest test. After all, it certainly lacks the drama of *Midnight Express.*

Let's explore this further. The reason that *Midnight Express* works so well in film may be because it beautifully conforms to Hollywood script doctor David Mamet's three rules: Who wants what from whom? What happens if they don't get it? Why now?

Certainly Mamet's questions as applied to my encounter at Denpasar can explain what happened in narrative terms. I wanted to pass through Immigration without penalty or delay. If I didn't get what I wanted, I'd have to pay a fine or be forced to negotiate a bribe, or both. The temporal circumstance has to do with my imminent flight.

However, in the absence of overt, explicit drama in the *Midnight Express* sense, the explanatory power of Mamet's paradigm only goes so far. To truly appreciate what meanings were contained in the encounter, the textual surface needs to be probed surgically. An alternative analysis reveals that the apparently smooth communication event was actually a fraught encounter that at any time could have split off into any one of a number of possible pathways, any of which may have had serious consequences. The fact that it cannot be explained with reference to Saville Troike's seminal ethnographic approach in which 'observed behaviour is [seen] as a manifestation of a deeper set of codes and rules' (1982: 109).

Another way to understand the event is to strip the encounter back to the bare utterances. Because although an eavesdropper may have heard our conversation as normal, natural and wrinkle-free, such an assessment would be blind to the cross-cultural currents and contextual eddies that lurked just below the surface. Examining the encounter, turn by turn, exposes – or at least, allows for an interpretation of – what was going on at each point. What decisions were made? What possible options were rejected, and how, turn by turn, the Indonesian gate-keeper came to the conclusion that I should be waved through to the departure lounge?

1	Me	*Selamat Malam Pak* (Good evening Sir)
2	Immigration Officer	*Malam* (Evening)
3	Me	*Permisi Pak* (excuse me sir), *Maaf* (sorry)
4	Immigration Officer	*Apa?* (what?)
5	Me	*Mungkin* (maybe). Visa problem
6	Immigration Officer	Mmmmm
7	Me	*Permisi Pak*
8	Immigration Officer	You must be more careful on your next visit
9	Me	*Terima Kasi Banyak Pak* (thank you very much Sir)

While standing in line, before the conversation commenced, I was aware of trouble ahead. I knew I had violated the law: leaving one day beyond my visa expiry date was a situation that attracted penalty. If I suggested a monetary gift and it didn't go well, I could land myself in hot water. The one-day-beyond-visa-expiry, minimal as crimes go, was nonetheless happening in a country that was both overtly hard on immigration statutes and covertly big on corruption.

This meant any encounter with officialdom would be starkly asymmetrical. All power resided with the uniformed man with the stamp in his hand (Fairclough, 1989). I knew that any sense of Western entitlement would go down poorly. I was a foreigner on foreign ground, who knew little language and not much of the culture, save the implications of my relative helplessness in the situation that was about to unfold. I had to play by local rules and I knew it.

In Turn 1, the greeting is ultra-polite, ultra-deferential and carried out in formal Indonesian. This was not a display of L2 fluency; more a recognition of the need for me to defer to authority with all respect shown. In Brown and Levinson's (1978) terms, I needed to exercise 'negative politeness' to demonstrate my awareness of how my 'visa problem' represented an imposition on Indonesian officialdom. My opening gambit set the linguistic terrain up as consciously unequal. It established from the outset that I was making an effort to show deference.

The official's clipped reply in Turn 2 signals an acceptance of this dynamic. His response bypassed any pretence at politeness and in doing so consolidated the inequality that was to feature strongly in the ensuing conversation.

Turn 3 is the confirmation of what my body language had flagged from the outset. There was a problem; I was to blame; I was asking for leave and at the same time preparing to apologize. At this point, despite the obvious crudeness of my language choices, it was clear that I was choosing to reinforce his authority by highlighting my own powerlessness. The use of English from this point on would not have had this effect, nor served my purpose. Granted, the medium of English would better have allowed me to explain the circumstances of my status but I would have forfeited the implied admission of guilt and remorse.

In Turn 4, the officer shoots back at me with a probing interrogative. There is no politeness offered or intended. In fact, it is the opposite: he's being rude. He has my passport in his hands. He already knows the issue that we are heading towards; and because of my stammering ineptitude with the language, he equally knows that I will be unable to account for myself adequately in Indonesian. Yet he chooses to keep the game going in Indonesian, knowing he will not get the answers that the situation requires him to seek.

In Turn 5, I offer *Mungkin*, a word I half-know to mean 'maybe'. In this exchange, the idea of 'maybe' is actually intended to mean 'more likely than probably'. This type of modality allows for the digestion of the subsequent offering of 'visa problem'. Although the words 'visa problem' are imported English words, they work well in Indonesian, albeit in a more nuanced way. In the context of Indonesia, any reference to a 'problem' is best understood as an allusion to something that can/could/should/might be able to be fixed. To understand the elasticity of this notion is to realize that in Indonesia, nearly everything can be fixed. It's often just a question of creating the logistical and political will. So, in what seems to be a superficially naïve collection of poorly collocated ideas, my raw beginner's Indonesian operates as an embryonic plea for leniency: a kind of dog-whistle (Fear, 2007), coded specifically for my interlocutor and no other. 'A dog-whistle is ambiguous' (Fear, 2007, p.5), but in context the deal I put forward is clear, namely I'd pay for my sins through self-debasement and humility.

When the dialogue reaches the juncture of Turn 6, the officer slows the conversation down from the pace he imposed in Turn 4. In doing so, he creates a space for me to enter into a phase of justification and rationalization. However, this offer, this quiet place in our exchange, is an 'enough rope' situation. I'm being offered the opportunity to hang myself by reneging on my unmitigated guilty plea. For me, at this point, to blame someone else, reject responsibility or mount a case for a misunderstanding, would be a big mistake: it would mean I'd missed the subtle cues that indicate he values the cultural contrition implied in a Westerner admitting fault. Despite the fact that our conversation is being carried out in tourist-friendly Bali, there is deep bruising in post-colonial Indonesia and at some level my Mea Culpa works.

Turn 7 signals that I recognize and admit I have no excuse to offer. *Permisi Pak* is a simple reiteration of Turn 3. This second 'Excuse me, Sir' unequivocally transfers any vestige of cultural status I may have had to the government official. In doing so, it alludes to my request, made to him the strong-and-powerful one, to show mercy to me, the weak-and-remorseful one.

With the smooth switch from Indonesian to English, in Turn 8 the Immigration Officer demonstrates that our conversation could easily have been conducted in English. By moving back to the lingua franca, the tension of our special little 'interactional cruce' (Candlin, 1987) dissipates, replaced by the demeanour of brisk international discourse.

In Turn 9, I thank the officer in formal Indonesian. Although I might have expressed gratitude in English, to finish on this note would have been to reinvest myself as a Westerner and subtly mock the favour I had been granted. This was the last thing I wanted to do. It had been an intense little dance but in the end he had been generous and graceful.

Epilogue

Situations like the airport interlude convince me of the importance of the social dimension of any communication event. Without the cultural keys, doors can remain stubbornly locked.

Anthropologist C.O. Frake crystallizes this view with his advice for the (hypothetical) Stranger trying to get by outside his language community – specifically, trying to buy a drink in Subanun.

> Our Stranger requires more than a grammar and a lexicon; he needs what Hymes (1962) has called an ethnography of speaking: a specification of what kind of things to say in what message forms to what kind of people in what kinds of situations.
>
> (1972, p. 87)

Frake's research strikes a chord with me. And though I'm no better with languages now than I was as a child, I feel justified, when travelling, in prioritizing social practice over phrase books.

To conclude again with Frake: 'To ask appropriately for a drink in Subanun, it is not enough to know how to construct a grammatical utterance. . . . Rendering such an utterance might elicit praise for one's fluency . . . but it probably would not get you a drink' (1972: 87).

Nor in my case, an exit permit.

Notes

1 The Subanun are indigenous agriculturalists from the Zamboanga Peninsula of the Philippines.
2 A piece of material used as a sarong in India, Burma and Sri Lanka.
3 The Japanese word used to refer to foreigners, aliens, non-Japanese.

4 In 2004 Australian Schapelle Corby was arrested at Denpasar Airport for drug smuggling. The case received widespread attention in both Indonesia and Australia.

References

Brown, P. & Levinson, S. (1978), *Politeness: Some universals in language usage.* New York/Sydney: Cambridge University Press.

Candlin, C.N. (1987), Explaining moments of conflict in discourse. In R. Steele & T. Threadgold (Eds.), *Language topics.* Amsterdam/Philadelphia: John Benjamins Publishing Co.

Fairclough, N. (1989), *Language and power.* Harlow/New York: Longman.

Fear, J. (2007, September), *Under the radar: Dog-whistle politics in Australia.* Discussion Paper 96, Canberra: The Australia Institute.

Frake, C.O. (1972), How to ask for a Drink in Subanun. In Pier Paolo Giglioli (Ed.), *Language and social context.* Harmondsworth, Middlesex: Penguin Books.

Harder, P. (1980), Discourse as self-expression – on the reduced personality of the second-language learner. *Applied Linguistics,* Vol. 1, No. 3, pp. 262–270.

May, B. (1978), *The Indonesian tragedy.* London/Boston: Routledge & Kegan Paul.

Pennycook, A. (1994), *The cultural politics of English as an international language.* London/New York: Longman.

Saville-Troike, M. (1982), *The ethnography of communication: An introduction.* Oxford: Basil Blackwell.

Wajnryb, R. (2009). The language of luxury. *'Words', Spectrum, The Sydney Morning Herald.*

Chapter 7

Nonghao, I am a Shanghai Noenoe

How do I Claim my Shanghaineseness?

Alice Chik
City University of Hong Kong

Am I a Shanghai *noenoe*?

I grew up speaking Cantonese and eavesdropping on Shanghainese at home, and learning English at school. My personal identity is tied intimately with my languages and cultures. Growing up in Hong Kong, Cantonese is my first language. I was encouraged to learn and speak English well. My relationship with Shanghainese has always been a difficult one: I can understand but can not speak the dialect. I have to admit that I have not put in enough effort to learn my ancestral dialect. But my frustration with Shanghainese is also a product of the language and cultural policies of the time. In this chapter, I will revisit my linguistic upbringing in light of the discourses on Hong Kong identities, language and cultural policies, both officially and academically.

My parents were immigrants from Shanghai, arriving at Hong Kong in the 1950s without a word of Cantonese. As native speakers of Shanghainese, a Northern Wu Chinese dialect, my parents soon realized that Cantonese, a southern Yue Chinese dialect, was the language of survival in Hong Kong. Their stories were similar to many of the Chinese immigrants of their generation: speaking accented Cantonese, socializing in Shanghainese-speaking communities and marrying a Shanghainese-speaking partner (Kuah & Wong, 2001; Lin, 2002a; Sinn, 2003). For me, together with English, Cantonese was the usual language at home. Like many other second generation migrant children, though we were not encouraged to learn our ancestral dialect, we grew up in an extended social network of our ancestral dialect speakers (Kouh & Wong, 2001; Ma, 2001).

At school, however, there was always a little box in our student handbooks where our parents had to fill in our "Ancestral Home" (籍貫). It was through the word in this little box, Shanghai, that I found myself to be different. Others had Chaozhou, Foshan, Shantou . . . etc. We were no longer "Cantonese," as signified by our shared language, or "Hongkonger" (香港人), our shared cultural identity. We now belonged to smaller groups divided by geographical locality of our ancestors. I also found that being Shanghainese meant I am *not* Cantonese. The issue of identity was further complicated by linguistic differences. Classmates, especially those living with their grandparents, had family members speaking their own "ancestral" dialect at home. I am Shanghainese, because it said so in my student handbook, even though I spoke Cantonese from birth. However, this was perhaps where the institutional recognition stopped: only spoken Cantonese, written Modern Standard Chinese and English were used in school. Regional sub-ethnicity and linguistic variations were nothing more than paper trails.

For a long time, being a Shanghainese descendent primarily meant I preferred the cuisine and knew some phrases in Shanghainese. My parents speak Shanghainese to each other at home and to our relatives at gatherings, but not to us. Shanghainese is their language, not mine. I am happier communicating in Cantonese and English.

After the implementation of the Open Door policy in China, my parents took me to Shanghai to visit my paternal grandmother in 1983. My grandmother decided to stay in China when my father came to Hong Kong, so I had never met her before. My father seldom talked about her, and having been married in Hong Kong, even my mother had not met her. My grandmother only spoke Shanghainese and at that time, I was too young to understand her. I also met a lot of relatives who were just strangers speaking in a strange language. They were not like *my* Shanghainese-speaking relatives in Hong Kong, whom I have known my whole life. At my grandmother's house, I did not need to speak to get anything. At the hotel, I used English to get my Coca-Cola at the counter. When I stepped out of the hotel, people whispered "foreign child" (外國小囡, *ngakoh xioanoe*[1]). Tourism in China in 1983 was a novelty, so we were constantly surrounded outside our hotel. There was also a lot of hair pulling, face touching and clothes groping by strangers. Like many city dwellers, I spent my entire life avoiding unnecessary physical contact with strangers. Though my mother assured me that these people were just curious and meant us no harm, nonetheless, the physical contact was shocking and threatening. I came to think of Shanghai as a foreign city where people don't behave in the same ways as Hongkongers. I also developed a separate distinction about my "Shanghaineseness": being a Shanghainese in Hong Kong is alright because I am sharing that identity safely with my extended family. Being a Shanghainese in Shanghai, and sharing it with strangers, was too abstract!

Over the years, I did not quite learn to speak Shanghainese from my extended family. However, my listening comprehension was fairly good as I could usually follow any conversation in Shanghainese during family gatherings. My problem was speaking the dialect. Whenever I made a good attempt, this was how it always ended, "Miss Thirteen Dot (a silly girl), what are you talking about?" (十三點, 儂講啥閒話? *sha sai di, nung kong sa hewo*?). So, my extended family continued to gossip in Shanghainese while I replied in Cantonese. All children were pretty much treated in the same way, and this form of bidialectal switching is a standard practice in my extended family. None of the younger generation learned any Shanghainese beyond restaurant ordering phrases, but everyone is pretty good at eavesdropping on the family gossip. This is very much the status of Shanghainese in my life: reserved for family gossip and secrets, but it really has no place in other aspects of my life. I framed my linguistic identity through Cantonese and English. I am a Cantonese- and English-speaking Hongkonger who just knows some Shanghainese. Over the years, I felt guilty that I could not speak Shanghainese. Several half-hearted attempts with self-directed learning materials were made, but I didn't get beyond the end of CD 1 in most cases, leaving me feeling I was not a true Shanghainese *noenoe* (囡囡 daughter).

Strangely, it was in Austin, Texas that I rediscovered my Shanghainese linguistic identity. With a booming Asian population, Asian (and predominantly Hong Kong) films were shown at midnight on Saturdays at a local cinema. On one such night, I saw Wong Kar Wai's *Days of Being Wild*, and I was delightfully surprised by the star appearance of Rebecca Pan (潘迪華). In the film, Pan plays a Shanghainese-speaking part as Leslie Cheung's adopted mother. I found myself crying during the film and yearning for her screen appearance: simply for her Shanghainese and her Shanghainese-accented

Cantonese. It was then I realized that I was homesick not only for Hong Kong, but also for the Shanghainese part of my Hong Kong world. Did I truly turn Shanghainese at that moment? Is there a linguistic connection? Yet, what does it mean to claim one's "ancestry"? Is it even legitimate to claim one's ancestry in Hong Kong when I don't even speak my ancestral dialect? These were the questions occupying my mind during my last visit to Shanghai, where I encountered language and culture that was both familiar and strange.

Am I Entitled to be Shanghainese?

It was almost twenty years later that I revisited my "ancestral" city again, with an English-speaking companion, during the Christmas of 2006. The arrival at the hotel was not smooth as my Putonghua was rusty and the hotel staff were not very happy speaking English to a Hong Kong Chinese. While we were negotiating over certain surcharges in broken Putonghua and English, the staff started complaining to each other in Shanghainese.

Porter: What was the problem? Why is it so slow? (做啥拉？為啥家慢？*Zu sa la? Wei za ga men?*)

Desk Staff: They did not want to pay. She comes from Hong Kong, so why is she speaking in English? Can't she understand? (伊拉勿要付鈔票。伊是香港人，講啥英文，伊聽勿懂？*Yilah veh fu zho piu. Yi zi Xiangkong ning, kong sa yingveng hewo? Yi ting ve dong?*)

Porter: She is sharing a room with a foreigner? (伊拉外國人兩家人一間房間？*Yilah ngakoh ning liang jia ning yeh ga fang ga?*)

Desk Staff: She is a troublesome woman. Why is she fussing over this small thing? She is annoying (伊嘎女人哪能家麻煩家討厭？*Yi ga niu-ning nan eng ga mu feng ga tau yi?*)

Like my parents, the staff were using Shanghainese as their private language because they thought they would not be understood. The two carried on like that while we were waiting and listening. At the beginning, I found it amusing that I could eavesdrop on their complaints in Shanghainese. But soon, I was annoyed. When I travel, I do not expect the hotel staff to comment on my private life, at least not in my face. From a Hongkonger's perspective, this was both unprofessional and inappropriate in a business setting. After fifteen minutes of waiting and listening to their complaints and gossiping, I finally told both of them that I could understand their Shanghainese perfectly and it was not polite to do so in front of the guests. Unfortunately, I did it in English. The porter just stared at me and walked off the other way, without as much a *tevechi* (對勿起 sorry). The other desk staff gave me a contemptuous look. In the end, we were taken to our room by an unhappy-looking porter.

On the next morning, we wanted to go to the Temple of the Town God (城隍廟 *Chong Huang Miau*). It was a term that I knew very well, and I was quite confident that I could say it correctly.

Taxi Driver: Where do you want to go? (儂去哪？*Nong qi na?*)

Alice: Go to Temple of the Town God (去城隍廟. *Qi Chong Huang Miau.*)

Taxi Driver: Where? (啥地方？*Sa difong?*)

Alice: Driver, go to Temple of the Town God (司機，去城隍廟. *Zhi ji, Qi Chong Huang Miau.*)

Taxi Driver (turned to the porter): What? Can you say the place? (哪能? 儂講講看啥地方. ? *Naneng, nung kong kong khoe sa geh difong*?)

Porter: Master, nowhere special, just the Temple of the Town God. She can't say it clearly. (師傅, 勿啥地方, 城隍廟. 伊講勿清爽. *Shi fu, veh sa difong, Chong Huang Miau la. Yi kong va ching zhong.*)

I reflected upon this experience, while sulking (and complaining) all the way to the temple. I also noticed that I used the wrong addressing term. I addressed the taxi driver as "Driver," instead of "Master," which is the customary term used in China for drivers. Still, that should not have stopped him from understanding my pronunciation of "The Temple of the Town God." The porter, with whom we already met on the previous night, knew that I could understand him perfectly but he still had to comment on my linguistic ability. I was bewildered by the behavior of these "Shanghainese" people. I felt as clueless as the night when my American housemates were having a round of "Are you Ginger or are you Mary Ann?" (it took me a while to work out that these were characters from an old TV show, *Gilligan's Island*). Even though there was a linguistic connection, everything else was unfamiliar. The notion that I am a "Shanghainese" was no longer on the table. I felt that I was rejected, and at the same time, I could not identify with them. When I got out of the taxi, I was just another tourist in a busy city, not someone returning to her ancestral home. My search for an "imagined" heritage identity would not be found in the city of Shanghai itself. My understanding of the language did not help me in any particular way. I couldn't quite speak the language and I couldn't get the vocabulary right. Is there a space for Hong Kong people to search for their identity through their ancestral dialects?

Identities of Hong Kong People: Historical, Cultural, Ethnic and National

About 6 million Hongkongers, 90.8 percent of the population (6.6 million), claim to speak Cantonese as their usual language (Hong Kong Census and Statistics Department, 2007). Geographically located in the south of the Guangdong province, the number may not be surprising, but it is an increase from 79 percent in 1961. Hong Kong has been, and still is, an immigrant society. The population of Hong Kong only stood at about 254,400 in 1898, which increased with the influx of Chinese immigrants during periods of political turmoil: 368,986 in 1901, 878,947 in 1931, 2.3 million by the end of 1954 and finally at about 6.8 million in 2006. It is reasonable to assume that these immigrants would have come from different parts of China, thus bringing with them regional heritage and linguistic practices. Since Chinese was given the official language status in Hong Kong in 1974, Cantonese had been the unofficial lingua franca of Hong Kong. Though Cantonese has been viewed as the low language of everyday culture and Modern Standard Chinese as the high language for use in education and formal contexts, Cantonese has become the de facto vehicle for the hybridized Hong Kong cultural identity construction, with English and Putonghua trailing behind (Hyland, 1997; Joseph, 2000, 2004; Ma, 2001; Mathews et al., 2008; Snow, 2004; Vickers, 2005). After the sovereignty handover, only the term "Chinese Language" (中文) is used in the Basic Law (Article 9), thus downplaying the discrepancy between written and spoken variation in Chinese. Yet the Chief Executive Tung Chee Hwa, in his 2001 Policy Address, promoted "Bi-literacy and Tri-lingualism" (兩文三語) to encourage all Hong

Kong citizens to have written literacy in Chinese and English, and spoken fluency in Cantonese, Putonghua and English. This language policy had essentially elevated Cantonese to an official status, which is unprecedented for a Chinese dialect (Erbaugh, 1995). At the same time, the government is also assuming that all ethnic Chinese in Hong Kong *should* speak Cantonese.

Cantonese is currently the dominant Chinese dialect in Hong Kong, but it is the result of a converging linguistic pattern over the last few decades. In the 1961 census, the Cantonese-speaking portion then was only 79 percent, with another 15.5 percent speaking other southern Chinese dialects (Hakka, Hoklo and Sze Yap) and 2.65 percent speaking Shanghainese as their usual language. There was not only greater diversity in dialect use, the different dialect groups also tended to congregate and live in different parts of Hong Kong: Shanghainese concentrated in Hong Kong Island and Tsim Sha Tsui while the Hakka lived in the New Territories. The residential preferences of different dialect groups reflected the heterogeneous and sub-ethnic identities of the Chinese diasporas (Lin, 2002a; 2002b). These diversities are further substantiated by the establishment of regional associations (*huiguans* 會館, or *tongxianghui* 同鄉會). The more commonly used term, *tongxianghui*, which literally meant an association for people from the same ancestral home village or city, is an illustrative example. In these *huiguans*, immigrants seek social, financial and emotional support from their own speech community (Sinn, 1997). The listing of all regional Chinese *huiguans* in the territory dating from the early twentieth century shows that Chinese immigrants had always been preferred staying within their own speech community (Sinn, 2003). This is something I experienced directly. Though my parents are not active members of their *huiguan*, I grew up going to our Shanghainese *huiguan* for dinner on special occasions. In the Shanghainese *huiguan*, one hears more Shanghainese than Cantonese as the waiters always address the customers in Shanghainese and only Shanghainese cuisine is served. It used to be that no Cantonese would dare to enter a Shanghainese *huiguan* for dinner (unless invited by Shanghainese friends), just as a Shanghainese would not enter the Chaozhou *huiguan* uninvited. In reviewing the ethnicity structure of Hong Kong up to the late 1970s, Guildin (1997) coined "Cantonese chauvinism" to suggest the binary opposition of the Chinese ethnicity in Hong Kong: Cantonese and non-Cantonese. Ethnic Chinese who do not speak pitch-perfect Cantonese will be considered as "outsiders" and marginalized (Guldin, 1997; Ma, 1999). It was only in the 1970s, when the younger generation of Hong Kong grew up in a relatively homogeneous education system and society that regional differences started to disappear (Sinn, 1997). Hong Kong born descendents of non-Cantonese origins seldom master any degree of fluency in their own ancestral dialects (Kuah & Wong, 2001).

The dialectal convergence did not arise simply because of the educational and language policies. Government policies on cultural heritage also attributed to this convergence. The funding of educational projects and the setting up of the Culture and Heritage Commission provided only skewed perspectives. First, only educational projects dealing with 'local indigenous' culture were funded (Education Department, 1996). Second, the Cultural and Heritage Commission (2003) claims that "Hong Kong owes its cultural roots to the 'Lingnan' (south of the ridges) tradition, as manifested by popular art forms such as Cantonese opera and films that flourished from the 1840s to the 1950s/1960s" (p.3, 1.10). This "indigenous" culture, though privileged by government funding and support, is not, and cannot be, the "common heritage" for an immigrant society (Cheung, 2003). The claim that Cantonese operas and films were popular is only partially true. First, Cantonese operas were performed in Cantonese only from the early 1920s onwards, replacing Guilin stage *guanhua* (桂林舞臺官話), which is a Guangxi variation of Mandarin (Yung, 1989). Second, the majority of blockbuster films in the late 1950s and 1960s were made in Mandarin by the Shaw Brothers Studio and MP & GI studio (Ma, 2001; Snow, 2004; Yu, 1997). There were also films made in Chaozhou and Fujian dialects (Yu, 1997). Third, before the late 1970s, all best-selling Hong Kong singers recorded and performed almost exclusively in English and Mandarin. Hong Kong popular music was not sung in Cantonese before the mid-1970s (Benson & Chik, 2008). The official promotion of a Cantonese-only, and thus presumably "Hong Kong," cultural heritage was in contradiction to the historical and cultural development of the city.

The change of sovereignty in 1997 shifted the exploration of a Hong Kong identity into a political discourse: Hong Kong Chinese or Chinese Hong Kong. Academics suggest that the binary opposition between the finer division of being Hongkongers or Chinese, rather than any other sub-ethnic or linguistic variations, is the major site of struggle in identity construction (see for example Ma & Fung, 2007; Mathews et al., 2008; Pennington, 1998). The binary opposition presupposes a homogeneous Cantonese-speaking identity of the ethnic Hong Kong population struggling against the Putonghua-speaking Mainland Chinese population. It is also assumed that linguistic variations in ancestral dialects do not influence or add to individuals' choices of identity formation. When the conceptualization of a linguistic identity is limited to Cantonese-only, regardless of sub-ethnic diversities, the access to a fuller cultural identity profiling of the Hong Kong people is severely compromised. The milieu for identity construction of ethnic Chinese in Hong Kong is thus simplified to the homogeneity of a Cantonese-speaking community with an "indigenous local" culture, and a Chinese national identity with a global economic outlook.

Conclusion: A Small Story in the Backdrop of Historical Change

Gunn (1982: p.8) views autobiography not as "the private act of a self writing" but as "the cultural act of a self reading." Through autobiography, we come to know not only the "authentic" subject of the writer, but also the world that the subject inhabits and inhabited, both historically and culturally. In the predominantly Cantonese-speaking Hong Kong, my personal struggle with my Shanghainese heritage goes beyond the linguistic challenge. My two visits to Shanghai also brought out the cultural differences between two communities. As a child on the first trip, I had difficulty accepting a Shanghainese grandmother and relatives that I had never met. I was also shocked by the differences in accepted social convention as manifested in the physical contact with strangers. As an adult on the second trip, I was shocked by the lack of professionalism of the hotel staff. Shanghai as a city was very remote from my imagination. Shanghainese were also very different from my own Shanghainese-speaking family in Hong Kong. Over the years, many of my cousins from Shanghai migrated to other parts of the world and we had also met outside Shanghai, but we never bonded as family. They could be somewhere in Europe or Japan, but they remained Shanghainese. As a grown-up, I began to see our differences, not in dialects, but in our socio-cultural and historical upbringing.

What I perhaps have misunderstood about my struggle with the linguistic learning of Shanghainese was actually a struggle to locate my Hongkonger identity. If given only a binary choice of Hong Kong-Chinese or Chinese-Hong Kong, I would no doubt choose the former. I was first a Hongkonger, and then had to learn to become a Chinese. Yet this term does not fully articulate my sense of national identity: within the community of Hong Kong Cantonese speakers, I am also of Shanghainese heritage. My Shanghainese heritage is both linguistic and social. With only decent proficiency level in listening, I am only tip-toeing in the world of Shanghainese culture. My upbringing reflected the socio-historical and political development of Hong Kong. We were brought up in the extended social network of dialect speakers, but we were all baptized into Cantonese chauvinism. We watched Cantonese-language TV programs which mocked everyone who speaks non-standard Hong Kong Cantonese. We perfected our Hong Kong Cantonese but never developed a decent proficiency level in our ancestral dialects. Even our government thought we were all Cantonese speakers. UNESCO listed language as an intangible heritage, but it is not cherished in Hong Kong. We are officially all "Cantonese-speakers."

I eventually met Ms Rebecca Pan (who plays the Shanghainese-speaking part in *Days of Being Wild*) in 2007 and told her my anecdote of the film. She just laughed and said, "Shanghainese is magical, isn't it?" She was right. Shanghainese is magical because it is the connection to my ancestral home. My "ancestral home" is not the city of Shanghai, but my Shanghainese part of Hong Kong. Do I need to claim my Shanghaineseness? Should I be hiring a Shanghainese dialect tutor? I may never be able to get the pronunciation right. In the end, it probably does not even matter. I am more comfortable speaking in Cantonese and English. I am still a Shanghai *noenoe* in Hong Kong.

Note

1 I found it difficult to find an authoritative source for the Romanization of Shanghainese. The only authoritative dictionary available is Qian et al. (2007). However, the vocabulary is presented in IPA phonetics. I followed the IPA pronunciation and Romanization used in some of the more readily available language textbooks. These sources include: Qian (2002) and Tang (2005).

References

Basic Law (2008). *Chapter 1: General principles.* Retrieved January 20, 2009, from http://www.basiclaw.gov.hk/en/basiclawtext/chapter_1.html.

Benson, P., & Chik, A. (2008). *Hong Kong pop history.* Retrieved January 20, 2009, from http://home.ied.edu.hk/~hkpop/music/hkpophistory.html.

Cheung, S. C. H. (2003). Remembering through space: The politics of heritage in Hong Kong. *International Journal of Heritage Studies,* 9(1), 7–26.

Culture and Heritage Commission. (2003). *Policy Recommendation Report.* Hong Kong: Culture and Heritage Commission Secretariat.

Education Department. (1996). *Heritage-related activities in schools.* Hong Kong: Education Department.

Erbaugh, M. S. (1995). Southern Chinese dialects as a medium for reconciliation within Greater China. *Language in Society,* 24(1), 79–94.

Guldin, G. E. (1997). Hong Kong ethnicity of folk models and change. In G. Evans & M. Tam (Eds.), *Hong Kong: The anthropology of a Chinese metropolis* (pp. 25–50). Surrey, UK: Curzon.

Gunn, J. (1982). *Autobiography: Towards a poetic of experience.* Philadelphia: University of Pennsylvania Press.

Hong Kong Census and Statistics Department (2007). *2006 Population by-census: Summary reports.* Retrieved December 15, 2008, from http://www.bycensus2006.gov.hk/FileManager/EN/Content_962/06bc_summary_results.pdf.

Hyland, K. (1997). Language attitudes at the handover: Communication and identity in 1997 Hong Kong. *English World-Wide,* 18(2), 191–210.

Joseph, J. E. (2000). The tao of identity in heteroglossic Hong Kong. *International Journal of Sociology of Language,* 143(1), 15–31.

Joseph, J. E. (2004). *Language and identity: National, ethnic, religious.* Hampshire, UK: Palgrave Macmillan.

Kuah, K. E., & Wong, S. L. (2001). Dialect and territory-based associations: Cultural and identity brokers in Hong Kong. In P. T. Lee (Ed.), *Hong Kong reintegrating with China: Political, cultural and social dimensions* (pp. 203–217). Hong Kong: Hong Kong University Press.

Lin, G. C. S. (2002a). Hong Kong and the globalisation of the Chinese diaspora: A geographical perspective. *Asia Pacific Viewpoint,* 43(1), 63–91.

Lin, G. C. S. (2002b). Transnationalism and the geography of (sub)ethnicity in Hong Kong. *Urban Geography,* 23(1), 57–84.

Ma, E. K. W. (1999). *Culture, politics, and television in Hong Kong.* London: Routledge.

Ma, E. K. W. (2001). Peripheral vision: Chinese Cultural Studies in Hong Kong. In T. Miller (Ed.), *A companion to Cultural Studies* (pp. 259–274). Malden, MA: Blackwell.

Ma, E. K. W., & Fung, A. Y. H. (2007). Negotiating local and national identifications: Hong Kong identity surveys 1996–2006. *Asian Journal of Communication,* 17(2), 172–185.

Mathews, G., Ma, E. K. W., & Lui, T. L. (2008). *Hong Kong, China: Learning to belong to a nation.* London: Routledge.

Pennington, M. C. (Ed.). (1998). *Language in Hong Kong at century's end.* Hong Kong: Hong Kong University Press.

Qian, N. (2002). *Learn Shanghainese with me* (in Chinese). Shanghai: Shanghai jiao yu chu ban she. 錢乃榮著 (2002). 跟我學上海話. 上海：上海教育出版社. .

Qian, N., Xu, B., & Tang, Z. (2007). *Shanghainese Dictionary* (in Chinese). Shanghai: Shanghai ci shu chu ban she. 錢乃榮，許寶華，湯珍珠編著 (2007). 上海話大詞典. 上海：上海辭.

Sinn, E. (1997). Xin Xi Guxiang: A study of regional associations as a bonding mechanism in the Chinese diaspora. The Hong Kong experience. *Modern Asian Studies,* 31(2), 375–397.

Sinn, E. (2003). A history of regional associations in pre-war Hong Kong. In D. Faure (Ed.), *Hong Kong: A reader in social history* (pp. 121–156). Hong Kong: Oxford University Press.

Snow, D. B. (2004). *Cantonese as written language: The growth of a written Chinese vernacular.* Hong Kong: Hong Kong University Press.

Tang, Z. (2005). *Travel with Shanghainese* (in Chinese). Hong Kong: Zhonghua shu ju. 湯志祥 著 (2005). 上海話旅遊通. 香港:中華書局(香港)有限公司. .

Vickers, E. (2005). *In search of an identity: The politics of History as a school subject in Hong Kong, 1960s–2005.* Hong Kong: Comparative Education Research Centre, The University of Hong Kong.

Yu, M. W. (1997). *80 Years of Hong Kong Films* (Rev. Ed. in Chinese). Hong Kong: Regional Council. 余慕雲著 (1997). *香港電影八十年*. 香港:香港區域市政局修訂.

Yung, B. (1989). *Cantonese opera: Performance as creative process.* Cambridge: Cambridge University Press.

Chapter 8

Living on the Hyphen

Julie Choi
University of Technology, Sydney

"How do you get the glass table so clean?" I ask Sophia, my cleaner, who is a South Korean immigrant living in Sydney.

"You need to use . . . some kind of . . . sponge. Mmm . . . no, like some cleaning material . . . No . . ."

"You mean like a cloth?" I interrupt.

"Yes, yes, like cross [cloth]. Mmm . . . bery [very] soft cross."

"Some kind of special fabric?"

"Special? Mmm . . . yes . . . sha . . . sham . . . Mmm . . . I don't know what you say English . . . I show you . . ." and she goes to get it.

Daniel, my (Celtic) Australian partner wonders why I don't just speak to her in Korean and get it over with. I detect a sense of irritation on his part thinking it is rude of me to hide my ability to speak Korean thereby forcing her to speak in English. I've been reluctant to reveal my Korean identity to her which has to do largely with my awareness of the Korean ways of behaving towards elders in Korea, the performance I have to put on when I speak in Korean, and the awkwardness of handing her money at the end of her job (which I give to her later in an envelope only to receive the response "no need envelope next time"). But there is no time to explain all this to Daniel because Sophia comes back with a soft beige piece of cloth, which Daniel tells us is called a *chamois*.

Being a Korean-American-Chinese-Japanese (-Australian?)

When people ask me where I'm from, I hesitatingly say "the US." I know they are curious about my ethnicity because of my Asian appearance so I quickly add "I'm Korean-American." Growing up as a child in New York as a second generation Korean-American didn't seem confusing but issues of identity were always present (see other studies on Korean-Americans in Hinton, 1999; Palmer, 2007; Park et al., 2003; and other second generation groups in Brettell, 2006; Louie, 2006).

In Seoul, where I lived for a year attending junior high school, my *gyopo* [Korean living abroad] status allowed me to see how Korean-Americans were received in Korea. Korean TV shows had *gyopo* actors portraying us as having funny accents and mockingly imitated the way we used *Konglish* [a mixture of Korean and English]. Looking back, it is strange for me to think this tiny observation had such an impact on the way I have subsquently felt about speaking Konglish. From then on, the act of speaking, having a native-like pronunciation in Korean, and fluency became crucial but also intimidating. I intuitively assumed people would think speaking Konglish would make me look unintelligent and a cultural misfit. Going back to New York for a year after the year in Seoul, I felt out of place not quite sure any more if I saw myself as "Korean" or "Korean-American."[1]

Later in Beijing, where I went to high school and university for seven years, I wasn't accepted as a "real Korean" because of my American citizenship but again, because of my Asian appearance, I was also not a "real American." Living in a Korean community, I tried desperately to fit in as a Korean. Perhaps the pre-defined cultural aspects of what it meant to behave like a Korean (i.e. calling people who were older either *uhn-ni* [older sister] or *oppa* [older brother], using two hands to pour drinks to elders, looking away when drinking alcohol in the presence of an elder, not eating until the eldest person had started or eating slowly so that I didn't finish first etc.) were exaggerated in my mind but it was important to me that I performed what I believed was "Korean" like a Korean. Many years later though, I received a letter from a Korean friend from university saying "people distanced you because they didn't know who you were" (Choi, 2006:38). I wasn't surprised. Even I felt awkward around myself back in those days. Though I learned Chinese intensively in school, apart from my arguments with cab drivers, my life was predominantly centered around South Korean and ethnic Korean communities in China.

I had quite the opposite experience in Japan. I learned to speak Japanese far better than my Korean or Chinese could ever probably be. Living in an area where there weren't any foreigners and being able to teach English to Japanese students, I felt liberated from the "Korean" expectations and cultural constraints. It seemed to me I wasn't seen as Korean because I spoke English and was born in America, which was to my advantage considering the political struggles that stemmed from our historical past. At the same time, I was lucky I lived in Japan at a time when it was "cool" to be *positioned* as Korean thanks to *Hanryu*, the rise of Korean popular culture in Asia (see Shim, 2006). It was also beneficial I wasn't seen as "American" either, which is typically thought of as being "white," considering George Bush's disapproval ratings in Japan and the invasion of Iraq in 2003.

In Sydney, where I am currently located, I am unpacking these past experiences of the languages and cultures I have acquired in order to understand how they have shaped and continue to shape my identity. Here, I am first positioned as Japanese apparently because of my low nose, makeup and the Japanese *bento* [Japanese lunch box] I carry. "I'm Korean-American" to me, is just a label. It doesn't mean I feel especially close to other Korean-Americans, or "at home" in a Korean-American neighborhood in the US nor do I assume other second generation Korean-Americans have the same experiences I have. In fact I have to think about what questionnaires mean by Korean, Chinese, Japanese, American, Asian or Western when I am required to tick the box I fall into. In the short excerpts that follow, I use my diary to reflect on a variety of ways of how others' positioning of me and my agentic choices influence how and when my Korean ethnicity is revealed.

Pre-positionings

June 14, 1998 while visiting a wealthy Korean friend's house in Korea, Tae-woo introduces me to his 15-year-old Korean niece who has started studying English in Boston

Tae-woo: (in Korean) This is my friend. She's visiting from China.
Na Young: (whispers loudly to Tae-woo in Korean) She's a *joseonjok* [ethnic Korean from China]?!
Julie: (in English) Actually, I'm Korean-American.
Na Young: (in Korean) Oh *gyopo*, so your Korean must be bad (dismisses me and talks to Tae-woo about her golf lessons).

Joseonjok, the ethnic Koreans who migrated to China between 1850 and1945 to escape famine and Japanese invasion, worked illegally in South Korea "mostly in '3-D' (dirty, difficult, and dangerous) positions, which average Korean people avoid" (Bergsten & Choi, 2003:116). Aware of their social status in the South Korean context and the class ideologies embedded within the South Korean society, I felt she "put me down just because she comes from a wealthy family. I can't stand this class bullshit in Korea" (personal diary entry).

On the other hand, I used my awareness of the power the English language had in South Korea to assert my own identity. Though they were unspoken, there was an agreement of the ideologies and stereotypes of what it meant to be from a wealthy family, from China, to be a *joseonjok*, a Korean-American, a *gyopo* or Korean between us, which shaped and pre-determined our positions.[2] As Pavlenko and Blackledge (2004:1) assert, "language choice and attitudes are inseparable from political arrangements, relations of power, language ideologies, and interlocutors' views of their own and others' identities."

Located Positionings

May 14, 2009 eating Korean food with Daniel

Daniel: (fumbling with the meat on the lettuce as we eat *bulgogi* [barbecued beef])
Julie: In Korea, *we* wrap it like this.

March 28, 2003 cooking with a Korean friend

Julie: (making kimbab [Korean rolls])
Korean friend: (in Korean) *We* do it like this.

Outside the Korean context, I naturally situate myself as a Korean emphasizing that I am a member of a collective "we" even though my Korean friend's usage of "we" automatically positions me as an outsider. There is an eagerness to teach me about certain rituals and the proper Korean ways of doing them. Despite the fact that I have been to Korea at least once a year for the last 20 years of my life, lived in Korea for a year, cook Korean food, watch Korean dramas, read and write in Korean, since I was not born or raised in Korea it seems I will always be a foreigner. Who gets to be the "expert" seems to relate strongly to where one was born and raised.

Positioning as Choice

June 18, 2002 while working in Japan during the Korea vs. Italy World Cup match

Japanese colleague: (casually says to me in Japanese) Since you're Japanese, you won't mind me saying that it would be an embarassment on Italy's part if they didn't win.

Julie: (in Japanese) Mmm . . . I guess not (only to find myself bothered by it all day then go home later and write "I hope Korea wins!").

To Seiji, I am *both* Korean *and* American and these labels are all backdrops to which he is sensitive to and curious about. Sensitive because of the 35-year history of Japanese occupancy in Korea but curious because what he sees in the foreground is someone who is fond of Japan, eager to speak the language fluently and become a member of the culture. My enthusiasm to acculturate to *his* culture allows him to speak freely. In situations where an outsider is eager to become a member of the Other's culture, it may seem the highest compliment one could receive from a native is to also be recognized as a fellow native. But does it mean I must trade in my Korean ethnicity if I am *to be honored* of holding the title of being called Japanese? Can I indeed "be" a Japanese? If so, the statement "since you're Japanese" does not seem to be necessary. Is there a difference between developing a Japanese identity or be able to *do* Japanese and to actually claim oneself to *be* Japanese? In the midst of thinking about being Japanese or Korean, where did my "American" side disappear to?

May (2001:39) states, "there is an obvious degree of overstatement in the situational view of ethnicity . . . where postmodernist commentators reject any forms of 'rooted' identity based on ethnicity, nationality and (one has to assume) language." While I want both to be and not to be Japanese, Seiji's comment and my irritation throughout the day and desire for Korea to win was a reminder that I do not want to be stripped of my Korean ethnicity nor do others allow me to reject certain "rooted" identities. Was there a sense of patriotism on my part because of my ethnic affiliation? Did I feel a need to defend Korea because he (who was Japanese) had spoken of Korea unfavorably even though I knew he did not have ill intentions? These real-time moments pass by so quickly I have no time to wonder what would have happened if situations were posed differently. If the match had been between Japan and Korea, would he have said the same thing? If the match was between Italy and Japan, could I have made the same comment? If I am defensive will that make me look "too" Korean? I do not fear being different or disagreeable but at the same time, I am careful of how my Korean-American hyphen chooses and responds to the various subtleties of everyday situations and interactions in which it is set in.

Positioning as Negotiation

May 4, 2009 having a conversation with Emma, a South Korean exchange student in Sydney who is two years older than me

Emma: How come you don't speak Korean with me?

Julie: I don't want to have to think so hard about what I'm going to say and then worry about how I'm going to be perceived.Why don't *you* speak it to me?

Emma: Because I don't want to be an *uhn-ni* [sister]. But why do you speak Japanese with your Japanese friends?

English is not a *neutral* language for us but acts as a "third space" where "the meaning and symbols of culture have no primordial unity or fixity," a place where we both negotiate the creation of a space we are building together (Bhabha, 1994:37). She is aware of the dynamics at work in a relationship where one is older than the other when speaking in Korean and how this might inhibit a close friendship from being able to develop organically rather than mechanically. Perhaps for her, if we were the same age, speaking Korean would not be an issue. For me, it is more complex as speaking English in this context is about breaking free from my past experiences of having to struggle to feel that I "fit in." Japanese also comes with cultural norms but I feel freer knowing that I am not bound to certain cultural expectations since I am not Japanese. A part of me partially rejects and resists the cultural baggage that comes along with the Korean language but at the same time that same part of me also admires those restrictions and the way they are expressed in the Korean language. My ambivalence also has to do with the lack of fluency and language deterioration. Aside from speaking about the mundane issues with my family or conversational Korean, I would not be able to discuss, for instance, my research or teaching, which is also something I *am* able to do in Japanese.

Emma says I am more conservative than most other Koreans she knows. We have concluded this has to do with my fragmented experiences with various overseas Korean communities comprised of immigrants who may be seen as having what Krupinski (1984) calls the "broken clock syndrome": a condition whereby migrant memories become fossilized in a particular time period. Even though we mix Korean here and there, we both feel free from the cultural chains we bring individually to our friendship. She asks me for help related to things in English and I seek her thoughts on Korea and ask her if my interpretations are strange. Though it is only our little world, *we* work the cultures we bring to our meetings, *we* define what we can or cannot say and we drink soju the way *we* please. In this "*in-between* space – that carries the burden of the meaning of culture . . . we may elude the politics of polarity and emerge as the others of our selves" (Bhabha, 1994:38–39).

Korea

After seven years in Tokyo, I missed nosy Mrs. Kim, a chatterbox *ajumma* who lived next door to us.[3] I missed the closeness of calling someone *uhn-ni* or *oppa* [sister or brother]. I longed to eat *ddukbokgi* [spicy rice cakes] on the streets and go to a *pojangmacha* [street stalls] in the winter to have *soju* [rice distilled alcohol] late at night. On the other hand, the absence of Korea deludes me into thinking that because I am sentimental about these things, I accept and am fond of the way things are done in Korea. In my yearly trips back, I immediately become irritated with *ajummas* who race for subway seats. I don't call anyone *uhn-ni* or *oppa* unless they are relatives or family. I don't eat *ddukbokgi* on the streets and I can't be bothered to go to *pojangmachas* late at night or watch Korean dramas. Even in the midst of "hybridity and the rise of Korean popular culture," some aspects of the culture seem so backward and rigid. Still, the rigidity is precisely also what I like about the Korean culture. Korea for me is a sentimental home or to put it in Hannerz's (1996:110) words "a privileged site of nostalgia." It is one that I appreciate, identify with and protect but at the same time am not "radically committed to the unique ingredients and peculiar tendencies of the group . . ." (Simmel, 1950:402).

The Hyphen

The current trend in postmodernist theories of identity focuses on identity as multiple, shifting, constructed and continuously reconstructed where aspects of "rooted" identities based on ethnicity are often rejected (May, 2001). In this autoethnographic journey, I recounted a simple everyday life event that prompted me to reflect on several major critical incidents about language and culture from my past. These series of reflections of living in New York, Seoul, Beijing, Tokyo and Sydney as a Korean-American reflected on a variety of ways my Korean ethnic identity appears according to the contexts, others' positioning of me and my agentic choices.

In Giampapa's (2001) study on Italian-Canadians, her participant describes the hyphen as a "symbolic role where 'losing the hyphen' represents for Diana not only a loss of outward expressions and avenues of Italian Canadian culture (language, radio, television), but also a loss of an important aspect of her identity" (p.203). The hyphen I describe here gets me out of conflicting situations, acts as an insider and outsider, bears the weight of social and political predispositions, presents the possibility of the range of choices available to me and creates a new space as I continue a conflicting relationship with my rooted and future cultural affiliations. The hyphen reminds me that the way others perceive or position me is out of my control but their positioning of me helps me to become more conscious of what I would or would not like to take on as I continue to negotiate my identity. It is a misperception to think that the hyphen is only "a term that implies a dual identity, an ethnocultural one, and evokes questions and debates regarding which side of the hyphen the person belongs to" (Sharobeem, 2003). Today, it goes beyond cultural groups and is a source of new possibilities through the constant searching and interpreting of one's own interpretations and reflections. Transgressive theories (Pennycook, 2004) and other terminologies such as *glocalization* (Robertson, 1995), *trans-migrant* (Fouron & Glick Schiller, 2001), *cosmopolitanism* (Hannerz, 1996) and *metroethnic* (Maher, 2005) are increasingly being used to describe destabilized, fluid, blended identities that "desire to go beyond, to think otherwise, to transcend the boundaries of the modern" (Pennycook, 2004:41). Following Pennycook's notion of *transgressive theory*, the hyphen for me is "about desire, alterity and freedom . . . it demands a continuous and simultaneous questioning of how we come to be as we are, how such limits have been imposed historically, and how we can start to think and act beyond them" (pp. 42–43).

While the explosion of research around language and identity over the past decade is needless to say very important, self-examination through "critical incidents" (Nunan & Choi, forthcoming) and reflection is crucial in finding and understanding the "selves [that] account for our identity" (Weigart & Gecas, 2003:268). In this process, diaries act as a powerful tool and space where hyphenated individuals can reflect and construct a deeper understanding of the role their rooted ethnicities play as they continuously reconstruct their identities.

Notes

1 Here I refer to "Korean" as someone who was born in South Korea with South Korean citizenship, "Korean-American" as someone who was born in the US with Korean ethnicity.
2 This reflection must also acknowledge my own prejudice back then that by acknowledging she has "put me down," I too saw the ethnic Chinese as inferior to not only South Koreans but also to Korean-Americans as my response "Actually, I'm Korean-American" can also be interpreted as a politicized act of identity.
3 A term used to address an adult female individual of married age. The stereotypical "ajumma" image is that of a short, stocky, tough old woman with permed hair, who races to get a seat on the subway.

References

Bergstein, F., & Choi, I. (2003). *The Korean Diaspora in the World Economy.* Washington: Peterson Institute.
Bhabha, H. (1994). *The Location of Culture.* London: Routledge.
Brettell, C. (2006). Introduction: Global spaces/local places: Transnationalism, diaspora, and the meaning of home. *Identities, 13*(3), 327–334.
Choi, J. (2006). A narrative analysis of second language acquisition and identity formation. Unpublished thesis, Anaheim University, Anaheim, California.
Fouron, G., & Glick Schiller, N. (2001). The generation of identity: Redefining the second generation within a transnational social field. In H. Corero-Guzman, R. Smith & R. Grosfogiel (Eds.), *Migration, Transnationalization, and Race in a Changing New York* (pp. 58–86). Philadelphia: Temple University Press.
Giampapa, F. (2001). Hyphenated identities: Italian-Canadian youth and the negotiation of ethnic identities in Toronto. *International Journal of Bilingualism, 5*(3), 279–315.
Hannerz, U. (1996). *Transnational Connections: Culture, People, Places.* London: Routledge.
Hinton, L. (1999). Involuntary language loss among immigrants: Asian American linguistic autobiographies. *Georgetown University Roundtable on Languages and Linguistics,* (99) (pp. 203–254). Washington, DC: Georgetown University Press.
Krupinski, J. (1984). Changing patterns of migration to Australia and their influence on the health of migrants. *Social Science and Medicine, 18,* 927–937.
Louie, V. (2006). Growing up ethnic in transnational worlds: Identities among second-generation Chinese and Dominicans. *Identities, 13*(3), 363–394.
Maher, J.C. (2006). Metroethnicity, language and the principle of cool. *International Journal of the Sociology of Language,* 25, 83–102.
May, S. (2001). *Language and Minority Rights.* Harlow: Pearson Education.
Nunan, D., & Choi, J. (2010). *Language and Culture: Reflective Narratives and the Emergence of Identity.* New York: Routledge.
Palmer, J. D. (2007). Who is the authentic Korean American? Korean-born Korean American high school students' negotiations of ascribed and achieved identities. *Journal of Language, Identity, and Education,* 6(4), 277–298.
Park, C., Goodwin, A., & Lee, S. (Eds.). (2003). *Asian-American Identities, Families, and Schooling.* Charlotte, NC: Information Age Publishing.
Pavlenko, A., & Blackledge, A. (2004). *Negotiation of Identities in Multilingual Contexts.* Clevedon: Multilingual Matters.

Pennycook, A. (2004). *Global Englishes.* New York: Routledge.
Robertson, R. (1995). Glocalization: Time-Space and Homogeneity-Heterogeneity. In M. Featherstone, S. Lash & R. Robertson (Eds.), *Global Modernities.* London: Sage Publications.
Sharobeem, H. (2003). The hyphenated identity and the question of belonging: A study of Samia Serageldin's *The Cairo House. Studies in the Humanities 30*(1–2), 60–83.
Shim, D. (2006). Hybridity and the rise of Korean popular culture in Asia. *Media, Culture and Society, 28*(1), 25–44.
Simmel, G. (1950). *The Sociology of George Simmel* (K. Wolff, Trans.). New York: The Free Press.
Weigart, A., & Gecas, V. (2003). Self. In L. Reynolds & N. Herman-Kinney (Eds.), *Handbook of Symbolic Interactionism* (pp. 267–288). Lanham, MD: Altamira Press.

Chapter 9

Negotiating Multiple Language Identities

Mary Ann Christison
University of Utah

Autobiographical Background

I grew up in a rural community in the western part of the United States and attended a small, six-room elementary school that included three classrooms, a small gym, a lunchroom, and two bathrooms. There were a total of 52 students in six grades. I was acquainted with a small circle of children and adults because we seldom traveled to "town" or spent time interacting with people outside of our community.

In rural communities, such as the one in which I grew up, people rely on each other to make their lives work. No one in my community had much money in terms of cash flow, so families traded services. For example, my father was a skilled welder—a trade he had learned during his stint in the U.S. Army during World War II. When the neighbors' farm machines broke down, my father would repair them in return for services the neighbors could provide for us. This kind of exchange of services created interdependence among families that contributed to the solidarity of the community, our strong sense of a shared identity, and the pride that most of us felt about our common backgrounds and cultural heritage.

If you have been a city dweller for most of your life, it might be hard to understand the attraction many people have to rural life. Because we had no access to restaurants, clubs, movie theaters, shopping malls, concerts, museums, or television, it may seem to an outsider that we lead boring and unfulfilled lives. However, as children we believed we lived rich and rewarding lives filled with wonderful adventures that included bikes, pets, homemade rafts, and fishing boats. We had favorite swimming holes, tree houses, huts, hiking trails, and acres of wide-open spaces to explore.

The people I interacted with in my community all spoke my native language of English. Little did I know at the time that the spoken language of my childhood community was different in many ways from the English spoken elsewhere in the United States. At that time, I simply took it for granted that I could communicate successfully with anyone who spoke English and that my version of the English language would be widely accepted. As a child, I had not yet had any experiences to the contrary.

I had a very hard time with school in the beginning. By the end of second grade, my parents considered holding me back because I still had not learned to read. I was good at memorizing, so it took almost two years for my teacher and my parents to discover that I couldn't read. There were a couple of reasons for the difficulties I experienced in acquiring literacy skills. First of all, I simply could not figure out the literacy code like the other children in my class; nothing seemed to make sense. My difficulties were compounded by the fact that I was sick a great deal and had missed more days of school than I was able to attend. My parents worried about the social stigma associated with holding me back in school, so my mother agreed to work with me at home over the summer before I entered third grade. My mother worked with me on recognizing and writing the letters of the alphabet out of sequence. I remember the day I finally figured out the code. I realized that what I saw when I wrote the letters was different from what my mom was seeing. Of course, I didn't actually know what my mother was seeing, but I learned how I had to write the letters to get her approval. I didn't share this knowledge with anyone, not even my mother, because I felt that I was doing something wrong. Much later in life, I learned that I was dyslexic, but this was not something that anyone was aware of at the time. Fortunately for me I loved school and loved learning, so after I figured out how to break the literacy code and my health improved, I did well in my studies.

I did not possess keen language awareness skills in my early days, but I was keenly interested in language. As teenagers, my friends and I were able to acquire almost native-like fluency in both Pig Latin[1] and Double Dutch[2]—two invented languages that require high levels of phonological awareness, especially phonemic awareness. We were motivated to acquire advanced levels of expertise in these languages in order to carry on private conversations and keep secrets from our younger brothers, whom we considered to be unfortunate appendages to our social lives.

At this point in my life, I did not see language as representing how I understood myself, my history, or my social surroundings. These understandings came to me much later through incidents that ultimately changed the way I saw myself in relationship to language and would lay the groundwork for the career choices that I would ultimately make.

Narratives of Critical Incidents

There are different ways in which identity can be framed, such as social identity, sociocultural identity, voice, cultural identity, and ethnic identity (Norton, 1997). To this list of identities, I add language identity and suggest by way of the critical incidents presented below that language identity is complex and multidimensional and that most of us negotiate multiple language identity throughout our lives.

Native Language Critical Incidents

The summer that I turned 12 years old was a pivotal one for me. My parents allowed me to attend a summer camp sponsored by the local farmer's organization. The camp was for young women between the ages of 12 to 17. One of my mother's friends agreed to be our chaperone, and my parents somehow found the money to let me go. Although the camp was only about 50 miles away, it was a huge event for me and was the first time that I had been away on a trip without my family. We were housed in a canyon resort comprised of small, rustic cabins, a swimming pool, tennis courts, a softball field, picnic areas, pool tables, and a small café. I stayed in a cabin with three of my best friends. The total group consisted of about 35 young women. It did not take long for the boys in the neighboring town to learn that we were there. One afternoon, just before dinner, we were seated on the front steps of our cabin when some of the local boys came by to talk to us. They asked us what we were doing there. Naturally, we told them we were attending a summer camp called Farmer's Union Camp. The word *farmer* in my native dialect was pronounced like the word *former*, so, of course, the young men did not understand what we were saying. The question was asked and answered a second time, and still there was no comprehension. Finally, I spelled the word for them. "F – A – R – M – E – R – S," I replied. When the young men finally figured out what we were saying, they all began to laugh. "Where are you from?" they taunted, "Hicksville, USA? Were you *barn* in a *born* as well?" They laughed and laughed and walked away from us. I remember not quite understanding what had happened in the exchange, but I knew that whatever it was, I did not like it. I knew the boys were making fun of us, and I felt embarrassed. I had no idea what we had said to elicit this reaction. Everything sounded normal to my friends and me.

At the end of the summer, I began junior high school with about 450 other students. It was a huge adjustment from my small elementary school of 52 students in six grades. Trying to make new friends and adjusting to different teachers was a frightening experience for me. I was quiet and shy, making friends was not easy, and I had few classes with old friends from my community. In order to make up for my dismal social life, I studied constantly and received high marks in all of my subjects. One day in ninth grade, one of my teachers took me aside and said, "I think you're an excellent student with considerable potential, so I am telling you this for your own good. If you want to get an education, do well in high school, and do something with your life, you must change the way you talk. Do you understand what I am saying?" Of course, I didn't truly understand what he was saying, but I knew it was not good. At that time, I truly had no idea what made my language so different from many of my peers. Once again, I felt as if I had done something wrong, and it was absolutely the worst emotional feeling I had ever had. Even though I am quite certain this teacher meant well, I was devastated. There was a big knot in my stomach, and I had a lump in my throat.

Foreign Language Critical Incident

As a young girl, I was wild about horses and lived for the after school and weekend horse rides with my two best friends. We each had our own horses. My friend, Susan, rode a gentle little horse called Lady, and she was true to her name—always gentle and well behaved. Louise rode a brown and white pinto pony. He knew he was gorgeous, and he could run like the wind. My horse was an old and ornery beast that always had the upper hand in our relationship. He would stop abruptly during a gallop or run, flinging me forward over his head, and landing me abruptly to the ground. During the course of my childhood I had more sprained ankles, wrists, and fingers than I care to remember. Saddling a horse is difficult and time consuming when you are a rather small person. Saddles are cumbersome and heavy with some unmanageable pieces; consequently, we all learned to ride without saddles by tightening our legs around the horse's sides and sometimes holding on to the lower part of the horse's mane—a part of the mane that had been left for that purpose when the horses' manes were clipped. I relied heavily on this feature because I was the least competent rider, and my horse was the least well behaved. Although Susan and I had similar skills as riders, her horse was the best behaved. Louise's skill as a horsewoman was in another category altogether. She had begun riding when she was very young, so no matter what her horse did or didn't do, she never fell off and seemed to stick like glue to the horse's back.

One summer day the three of us went for a late afternoon horse ride. We were riding in an empty field next to an old abandoned house that Louise's family owned. Migrant workers and their families lived in the house during the summer months. As we rode by the house, four or five children came out to watch us and began calling to us in a language that I, for one, did not understand. I think Louise had met the children before and recognized the oldest boy. The children were from Mexico and were staying in the old house because their parents had been hired to work in the sugar beet fields for Louise's father. We were curious about the children, so we rode our horses in their direction. We spent quite a bit of time trying to talk with them, and I remember it was fun learning the Spanish words and phrases that came up naturally in our attempts to communicate—horse *(caballo),* friends *(amigos),* brother *(hermano),* sister *(hermana), ride* (montar), parents *(padres),* What is your name? *(¿Cómo te llamas?),* How old are you? *(¿Cuántos años tienes?).* I enjoyed pointing, talking, laughing and trying to communicate with these new friends; it was like a game. The oldest boy wanted to ride Louise's horse and kept asking her again and again in Spanish *Por favor, quisiera montar su caballo. ¿Está bién?* and mimed the riding of a horse. Louise finally got off her horse in order to let him ride. Instead of taking a leg up from one of us in order to get on the horse, he moved behind the horse about 30 feet, started running, and magically vaulted onto the horse from behind. Once he was on the horse, it took off on a dead run. The pony's mane was flying, and the young man rode in complete harmony with the horse; they looked as if they were one. Even after all of these years, this memory has stayed strong in my mind. In my dreams I had always wanted to ride in this way, so I was deeply moved by his skill as a horseman. I remember wanting to ask him how he had learned to ride like that before I realized I couldn't; we did not share a common language. I am certain that my desire to study a foreign language in secondary school, stemmed from this early experience with young Spanish speakers, as if speaking Spanish would somehow make me a better horsewoman or help me fulfill the dream related to horses.

Commentary

The use of language to construct identity (Adger, 1998; Bucholtz, 1999; Fordham, 1998; and Toohey, 2000) is a topic that has been of keen interest to me for more than two decades, and it is a topic that concerns a growing number of scholars in bilingual and second language education (Johnson, 2000; Morales, 2002, Norton, 1997; Pierce, 1995; and Zentalla, 2002). Language and identity are not fixed notions (Pierce, 1995), so it is possible not only for language to change over time but for identity to change as well. We use language to communicate ideas and to represent ourselves in relation to others with whom we interact. How we represent ourselves to others is dynamic; consequently, most of us are in the process of negotiating multiple language identities throughout our lives. The events that I have shared above have a common thread—they center on language and they represent the bases for the formation of my language identity as a bidialectal, as a dyslexic, and as a foreign language learner. Because language is a complicated tension between both internal and external interpretations of identity, these different identities have created certain conflicts for me that I detail in my commentary below.

Negotiating Identity as a Bidialectal

Bidialectal is a term commonly used to refer to individuals who have acquired a second dialect. *Bidialectalism* comes from the term *bilingualism,* where it is assumed that a speaker can use two languages in nonpracticed conversational exchanges. The linguistic variation inherent in bidialectalism is a tool we use to "construct ourselves as social beings, to signal who we are and who we are not and cannot be" (Lippi-Green, 1997, pp. 234–235). Researchers interested in bidialectalism investigate the linguistic and sociolinguistic constraints on linguistic variation that govern bidialectal speakers.

I define bidialectals (also called *bidis*) as individuals who are accepted by and interact with more than one community of practice. A community of practice is a group of individuals "whose joint engagement in some activity or enterprise is sufficiently intensive to give rise over time to a repertoire of shared practices" (Eckert & McConnell-Ginet, 1999). These shared practices include linguistic practices that are thought to be appropriate within the community, but may not be viewed positively outside of the community itself. For example, the linguistic practices of my own community were marked or stigmatized in many different ways, particularly phonologically and syntactically. For example, in some words the vowels /a/ and /o/ are switched such as in the words *barn/born, farm/form,* and *star/store.* Some vowels were laxed as in the words *mail, pin,* and *pool,* pronounced [mɛl], [pɛn], and [pəl]. In addition, some vowels are not laxed when they normally would be, such as in the word *egg,* pronounced [eig] not [ɛg]. The word *don't* is used with third person singular as in *He don't know or She don't care.* The use of the word *ain't* with double negatives is common as in *He don't know nothing* or *He ain't got none.*

Because language is the "way individuals situate themselves in relationship to others, the way they group themselves, the powers they claim for themselves, and the powers they stipulate to others" (Lippi-Green, 1997), it is the primary way in which individuals demonstrate their membership in and allegiance to a community. Reciprocal linguistic forms used within a community also create solidarity within a group, and this solidarity is important for the survival of the community. Although I did not realize it at the time, my decision to acquire a second dialect was one that would change the solidarity of my relationships and separate me in many ways from my childhood community of practice.

From the moment I consciously began my journey to acquire a second dialect, I had to think about everything I said all of the time. Even after I consciously understood what features of my native dialect I wanted to change, implementing these changes was not easy. Maintaining consistent change over time was exhausting and required constant vigilance on my part. Sometimes I opted not to speak at all because if I let my guard down for even a moment, it seemed as if features of my native dialect would surface sporadically, sometimes causing me great embarrassment during academic lectures in my classes or in giving conference papers and presentations. I could not consciously shift dialects at will, as is commonly implied in the literature on language variation and change (e.g., Biber & Finegan, 1994; Coupland, 1980; Giles & Coupland, 1991; Labov, 1972).

Over time, I have been able to change my spoken language in order to pursue my professional and academic goals, but this change has not been without its costs. In hindsight, I have always felt conflicted over my choice to acquire a second dialect. By embracing a new dialect, I lost much of the intimate connection I once had to my childhood community of practice. In addition, I have never been able to move back and forth with ease between the dialect of my childhood and the one I acquired as an adult. Although I have accepted the consequences of this decision for the work that I wanted to do, I still feel the internal pull towards an identity that no longer exists for me. To my childhood community, I am now an outsider.

Negotiating my Identity as Dyslexic

Dyslexia is a learning disability that is defined as a condition in which, for no independent reasons, such as lack of intelligence or education, someone has a serious difficulty with written language, particularly reading (Matthews, 1997). In my own case, the difficulty also extended to writing. Although I have read this definition on numerous occasions, and reassured myself intellectually that being dyslexic is independent of intelligence or education and that it is related to how the brain processes written and spoken language, it does not always feel as if this definition is true for me. I was not diagnosed as dyslexic until I was an adult, so I did not have the benefit of specialized instruction to assist me in learning to read and write. I had to figure it out on my own. As a result, I see learning to read and write within a time frame that only momentarily slowed down my educational progress.

In trying to analyze my personal experience with dyslexia, I have often reflected on how I broke the code and began my journey towards literacy. Until recently, I had always thought that breaking the code was related solely to difficulties with visual processing—the fact that I saw letters on the printed page different from other children. Of course, I still experience difficulties with visual processing when I am writing freehand and not using a computer. Although the visual processing component of literacy caused me difficulty in writing, I don't think it was at the root of the difficulties with reading. The bigger part of my own dyslexia has been connected to difficulties in phonological processing and my ability to perceive sounds in spoken language. To this day, I have difficulty with various components of phonological processing, such as understanding words that are irregular and verbalizing the names of letters in spelling.

I have two identities as a dyslexic—a child identity and an adult identity, and they are both very different from each other. The child identity wants to hide the disability from others and finds it difficult to talk about the condition. The adult identity is fascinated with how the brain processes information in dyslexic individuals and enjoys talking about the condition, reading research on dyslexia, and discussing issues with colleagues. In addition, the adult identity can easily admit to having this condition and can discuss how the disability manifests itself in personal literacy related behaviors. Even as an adult, I am constantly negotiating between these two identities, and the fluidity of movement is determined by a complex set of factors in my own environment, factors that also include my comfort level, as well as personal and professional relationships.

Negotiating my Identity as a Foreign Language Learner

From the time that I had my first experience in Spanish with the Mexican migrant children when I was 11 years old, I looked forward to the day when I could study Spanish in school. I was highly motivated by my first positive experiences with the language. Unfortunately, the opportunity to study a foreign language in school did not avail itself until I was in high school, and the foreign language class that I took was very different from what I thought it would be. In retrospect, I am not exactly certain what I thought a foreign language class would be like; I guess I thought it would be like the interactions I had experienced with the migrant children. I thought we might talk with the teacher as I had with the Mexican children; however, the class was traditionally audiolingual in nature. We participated in drills and memorized dialogs. I was extremely good at memorizing the dialogs and grammatical paradigms for the drills and was one of the best students in the class; consequently, I initially developed a positive image of myself as a foreign language learner. In class, we never actually used Spanish in communicative activities that required us to produce and comprehend nonpracticed language. This positive image, however, was short lived. I was on a blind date during my junior year in high school with a young man who had just returned from a two-year mission for his church in Chile. My friend told him that I spoke Spanish, but I was humiliated when he initiated a conversation with me that I could neither comprehend nor respond to. My self-image as a good foreign language learner quickly vanished. Very little of what I did and did well in my foreign language class seemed to translate to the use of Spanish in real life situations. Since that time, I have had numerous experiences traveling and working in Spanish-speaking countries. I can easily read newspapers and periodicals, write personal letters and cards to friends and professional colleagues, and do quite well in speaking to and comprehending individuals who are strangers, such as hotel and restaurant personnel and taxi drivers. In addition, I feel successful in communicating with individuals who do not speak English as well as I speak Spanish. Nevertheless, in all of these negotiations, I still struggle with my self-image as a foreign language learner, and I have transferred this negative image to other languages I have studied. No amount of positive reinforcement, such as compliments on my pronunciation or grammatical accuracy, seems to change my identity as a foreign language learner. When I meet strangers at various functions and am asked what it is I do for a living, I still feel inclined to lie and resist telling strangers that I am a linguist because the most common question lay people ask of linguists is "How many languages do you speak?"

Concluding remarks

Experiences with language play a central role in a person's individuality. We use language to create an impression of ourselves, and it is an important way in which we communicate our identity to others both within and outside of our social group. Language and identity are responsive to external and internal changes over time; consequently, most of us are negotiating language identity throughout our lives. Until I was asked to write this chapter on language and identity, I was not aware of the complex nature of language identity or the fact that most of us have what Saville-Troike (1989) referred to over two decades ago as one's "repertoire of social identities."

Notes

1 *Pig Latin* is based on alterations of the English. In order to make the Pig Latin form of an English word, the initial consonant sound (or in some instances the consonant cluster) is transposed to the end of the word and an */ey/* is affixed (Ex: horse would be orse-hey). According to Wikipedia, the reference to Latin is a deliberate misnomer and is used to refer to a language that is a strange and foreign-sounding language.

2 Similar to Pig Latin, *Double Dutch,* is based on alterations of English as well. In order to make the Double Dutch form of an English word, /ai/ + /b/ sounds are added after the first consonant (Ex: Double Dutch would be Dibouble Dibutch).

References

Adger, C.T. (1998). Register shifting with dialect resources in instructional discourse. In S. Hoyle & C.T. Adger (Eds.), *Kids Talk: Strategic Language Use in Later Childhood* (pp. 151–169). New York: Oxford University Press.

Biber, D., & Finegan, E. (Eds.) (1994). *Sociolinguistic Perspectives on Register.* New York: Oxford University Press.

Bucholtz, M. (1999). "Why be normal?": Language and identity practices in a community of nerd girls. *Language in Society,* 28(2), 203–225.

Coupland, N. (1980). Style-shifting in a Cardiff work-setting. *Language in Society,* 9, 1–12.

Eckert, P., & McConnell-Ginet, S. (1999). New generalizations and explanations in language and gender research. *Language in Society,* 28(2), 185–201.

Fordham, S. (1998). Speaking standard English from nine to three: Language as guerilla warfare at Capital High. In S. Hoyle & C.T. Adger (Eds.), *Kids Talk: Strategic Language Use in Later Childhood* (pp. 205–216). New York: Oxford University Press.

Giles, H., & Coupland, J. (1991). *The Contexts of Accommodation: Dimensions of Applied Sociolinguistics.* Cambridge: Cambridge University Press.

Johnson, F. L. (2000). *Speaking Culturally: Language Diversity in the United States.* Thousand Oaks, CA: Sage Publications.

Labov, W. (1972). *Sociolinguistics Patterns.* Philadelphia: University of Pennsylvania Press.

Lippi-Green, R. (1997). *English with an Accent* (p. 31). New York: Routledge.

Matthews, P. (1997). *The Concise Oxford Dictionary of Linguistics.* New York: Oxford University Press, Inc.

Morales, E. (2002). *Living in Spanglish: A Search for Latino Identity in America.* New York: St. Martin's Press.

Norton, B. (1997). Language, identity, and the ownership of English. *TESOL Quarterly,* 31, (3), 409–429.

Pierce, B. N. (1995). Social identity, investment, and language learning. *TESOL Quarterly,* 29, (1), 9–31.

Saville-Troike, M. (1989). *The Ethnography of Communication,* p. 30, 2nd ed. Cambridge, MA: Blackwell Publishing.

Toohey, K. (2000). *Learning English at School: Identity, Social Relations and Classroom Practice.* Clevedon: Multilingual Matters.

Zentella, A.C. (2002). Latin languages and identities. In M.A. Suárez-Orozco & M.M. Páez (Eds.), *Latinos: Remaking American* (pp. 321–338). Berkeley: University of California Press.

Chapter 10

Minna no Nihongo? Nai!

Martha Clark Cummings
Kingsborough Community College

Finding My Voice in French

I grew up in Glen Ridge, New Jersey, a town infamous for its sexism, racism, and xenophobia. I never heard anyone speak any language other than English until the day I walked into my French One class at age 14 and the teacher greeted us with a hearty, "*Bonjour*!" This seems implausible to me now. We were only 17 miles from New York City. Today, of course, the area has evolved, and I have become a world traveler.

I can still remember the first French dialogue we were told to memorize for homework. "*J'entre dans la salle de classe. Je regarde autour de moi. Je vois les élèves et le professeur. Je dis 'bonjour' au professeur. Je prends ma place.*" Little did I know that one day I would find my place—and a new identity—in French.

I brought my book home that night and asked my father for help reviewing it for the next day. I turned to my father whenever I had difficulties with school. He was the person who could solve any problem, explain any difficult concept, and coach me to meet any challenge at school. And yet, when I presented him with this dialogue, he was at a loss. He didn't know French! Why had he encouraged me to study something he didn't know himself? My view of my father as the authority on everything was shaken. And by studying French, I was embarking on a journey my parents had never taken. Many years later, as I became fluent, it was through French that I developed an identity far from the critical range of my parents' surefire aim.

My French teacher—an overweight middle-aged man with a thick moustache named Mr. Moskowitz—told us his technique. He listened to French audiotapes over and over again, for hours, in order to understand and imitate the voices. But we 14-year-olds could not picture ourselves doing this. Mr. Moskowitz's attempts to share his enthusiasm only alienated us further. None of us wanted to emulate *him*. He brought us photographs and postcards of France and menus from French restaurants, all of which we sneered at contemptuously.

I continued taking French; studying a second language was required. But I didn't begin to embrace French as "my" language until after high school graduation. That summer my parents sent me to France to get me away from Virginia, my high school sweetheart—hoping to divert me from another identity I was about to forge. I stayed with a family in a small town near Biarritz. This family seemed so magical to me, so loving, so different from my own family. And of course, life around the French dinner table is *enchanté*. My mother was the type who would serve a teaspoonful of peas then, with the ice cubes in her bourbon clinking, get mad when I asked for seconds. My father used dinner as an excuse to pontificate. But this family was generous and fun to be with in a way I'd never experienced. Even the *grandmère* teaching me to put my bread on the table, not on the plate, did not try to shame me for what I didn't know as my own parents would have done. I wanted to live with them forever. The French language took on a new meaning. It was not just some language a heavy-set man who spat when he got really excited wanted me to learn so he could grade my papers. It was not words in a textbook to decode with a dictionary. It was a haven, a place I could escape to and become someone else. In French, I could express myself without worrying about my parents' criticisms or judgments or laughter or neglect or disregard.

In college, I majored in French and spent my senior year abroad at a French college. Afterwards, I lived in Paris, on and off, for four years. When I moved to New York, my French came in handy at an import/export company on Canal Street. I lived with my French girlfriend on Jones Street in the Village for another four years. Janine—fortunately for me—decided learning English wasn't really necessary, so we spoke only French together. By then, my French was good enough for me to be part of her circle of French friends. My life during those years was led so entirely in another language that to this day, it is difficult for me to think or speak about that time in English. *C'était dans une autre vie.* And I was someone else.

So yes, I am fluent in French and I also went on to learn Spanish pretty well, but I can't say learning these languages was easy. Although I struggled to learn French and Spanish, during the struggle it seemed like something I could achieve. Of course, I am still anxious about certain things in French, and in Spanish, too. I have never had the native-like confidence in gender, for example. Is it: *le table, la table, le fauteuil, la fauteuil*? Common household words I would never have to think about had I grown up speaking French. I still make mistakes in Spanish, too. But overall, I can say that before I began to study Japanese, I was, by dint of exertion, effort, motivation, will-power, determination, and total immersion, a fairly successful language learner. So I approached the learning of Japanese with the knowledge that I had become fluent in two other languages. Surely I could do it again.

Voiceless in Japanese

In the summer of 2000, I was on leave from my job and living in the countryside in central Wyoming. I had just finished writing a novel, and I was trying to decide what to do next when I got a phone call from the Tokyo campus of Teachers College Columbia University. They needed someone to teach TESOL Classroom Practices that summer. Several people had suggested I might be available. The conditions sounded ideal—the salary and per diem were appropriately hefty—and I needed a change of pace. After saying yes, a slow, insidious sense of dread crept over me. Not only had I just agreed to go to a very large, very hot city in the peak of the summer to teach in Shinjuku, one of the most crowded neighborhoods in the world, but I only knew three Japanese expressions: *konnichi wa; ohaiyo gozaimasu; sayonara.* Hello, good morning, goodbye. I had not yet tried to master "please" and "thank you." I told myself not to worry. Lots of friends and graduate students who had traveled to Japan had reported that the biggest impediment to learning Japanese in Japan was that most Japanese people are so eager to practice their English, you never get to try. So that summer, my adventures in (not) learning Japanese began.

Unlike my first experience overseas in France, where by learning to speak French I was welcomed into a loving French family and over time, speaking French gave me a new identity, in Japan there was more than a complicated language to learn. Japan was a world I would never join, a door that kept sliding shut in my face, a table I could sit around with others, yet not be able to find room for my feet in the tiny space underneath, let alone room to express myself or take on a new identity. During my first summer in Tokyo—this year will be my tenth—I learned this lesson immediately.

One requirement of the program at Teachers College was each day the class met, the professors had to have lunch with a group of the students, mainly Japanese high school English teachers. I admit, my social skills are limited and I find switching roles and contexts particularly difficult when I'm with strangers, so I had prepared a list of questions to fall back on. One question involved a friendly woman my partner and I had nicknamed "Pony Tail Gal" from her hairstyle. I saw her at a convenience store almost every day when I stopped in on my way back to my room at the International House. She smiled in such a friendly way I wished I could learn to say, "Hi again," or "Nice to see you again," or "How are you tonight?" or, jokingly, "I'm back!" as I might have said at a deli I frequented in New York City. As soon as we had ordered lunch—they had to order for me because I could not read the menu and it was not one of the ones with photos of dishes an illiterate can point at—there was the first awkward silence. I said, "I have a question about Japanese." Then I explained the situation. An even more uncomfortable silence ensued. Then my students began whispering to each other in Japanese. Finally, the oldest one among them gently explained, "You can't say any of those things. They are simply not said."

"But she's young," I protested. "I'm foreign. Maybe she's foreign, too."

Another uncomfortable silence was followed by more whispering.

"You are a professor," another student told me. Apparently it was her turn to break the bad news. "You can say, '*Atsui desu ne.*'"

"What does that mean?" I asked.

When the giggling subsided—they were amused that I didn't even know how to talk about the weather—she said, "It's a hot day, isn't it?"

"But that's not even related to what I want to say."

"In this situation, to this person, in a store, this is what is said by people of your stature: Doctors, professors, high-ranking executives."

My stature. This word foreshadowed what was to come.

Two years later, in the spring of 2002, I moved to Aizu-Wakamatsu to teach full time at a Japanese university. My loved one had a fellowship in Tokyo, and we brought everything we owned, even our two cats. Naively, I assumed my life in Japanese was about to begin. When I lived there, everything would be different from when I had visited. I imagined my American colleagues spoke and understood Japanese, as well as read and understood at least the two syllabaries, and soon I would, too. I quickly learned how wrong I was. My colleagues, some of whom had been there for over a decade, had learned to navigate the small city where we lived, but they knew it as residents of the City of the Illiterates. When they talked about places, or tried to explain where to go, it was as if they were speaking in a kind of code.

"Do you mean the place with the dancing pig on the window?" one would say, trying to identify a restaurant where ordering was easy.

"No, no. Next door. The giraffes."

At the University of Aizu, my colleagues and I were coddled, protected, and kept apart in a fortress-like university planted on the outskirts of the city surrounded by rice fields. We were housed in cell-block-like faculty apartments at the top of a very steep hill even further out of town. Not only was this an inconvenient location, in winter it was often treacherous to descend. Our jobs required us to be in our offices from 9 to 5, whether classes were in session or not. Every memo and email message was translated into English. Each time we went to town for business—to open a bank account or make travel arrangements, sometimes even to find things at the store—there was an interpreter ready to accompany us. It turned out that the only *gaijin* (the word for foreigner which means, literally, outsider) who had learned Japanese had learned it before arriving in Aizu-Wakamatsu. We were part of a system where our sole purpose at this university was to dispense the English language. Almost like the ubiquitous vending machines—*jidoohanbaiki*, a word I still feel inordinately proud to remember. Feed money, out comes what you want. But often, the students wanted no part of this scheme.

Despite all of these barriers, I tried to learn. I watched Japanese TV, straining to understand even one word, I studied the books that were available in the library—*Japanese for Busy People* and *Minna no Nihongo* (Everyone's Japanese). I tried to practice *hiragana* by reading children's books, cheered on by the cute animals, but found it impossible to tell where one word began and the next one ended. Whenever I could, I went downtown to walk up and down the streets or sit in a coffee shop. I swam at the local pool. I went to the farmers' market. And I listened. But I understood nothing. Why not? After all, because interacting was too stressful, I had learned French and Spanish mostly by eavesdropping. But what was I supposed to do if I listened and understood nothing? Within the sounds swirling around me, I could not even pick out a word.

In the meantime, I made several attempts at formal study. The university offered a course for beginners that met for 90 minutes once a week. When I asked why so little, the translator explained that ten years earlier, when the university opened, they offered classes to the faculty for three hours a day, five days a week, but no one came. I attended the 90-minute class dutifully. The International Center in town offered another course for beginners for 90 minutes a week, and I went to that one, too. Still, out in the community, while I could make myself understood if my requests were simple enough, I understood nothing that was said to me.

Finally, I hired a former student, Naomi, to tutor me. She was able to understand most of what I was saying and because she had mastered English, she seemed a good candidate. She came to my office for an hour, three times a week. These tutoring sessions continued for a couple of months, but they were hindered by sociolinguistic and social psychological problems I had never imagined possible.

First of all, I had been Naomi's teacher and she found this very inhibiting. Then, whenever I asked her, in English, how to say something in Japanese, her answer was always, "It depends." It depends on the context and the other person. She would sit across the table from me, paralyzed with the anguish of trying to explain to her professor. I wanted to know how to ask the office ladies about their weekend as opposed to how to ask a Japanese professor or my students or a Japanese friend—should I ever be lucky enough to make one. It depends. It depends. I suggested that she teach me all the forms, and then I would use the appropriate one in the appropriate situation.

We began with the scenario of inviting someone to go to the movies. First, Naomi informed me that if I used the formal level of speech I was being taught in my classes, it meant I was not close enough friends with the person to consider inviting him/her to the movies. Then she began a lengthy explanation in English and Japanese and finally told me three possible ways to suggest going to the movies.

Polite: *Eiga o mimasen ka?*
To a friend: *Eiga mini ikanai?* Or: *Eiga mini ikkoo?*

I had never heard anyone use the casual form. Or if I had, it had been one of the countless times I did not understand. As Naomi explained all this to me, I felt as if I were waking up from a dream.

"Wait a minute!" I said. "Are you saying that *everything* I have learned to say so far, I could not say to a friend?"

She lowered her eyes.

"Not just to a friend," she said. "Not to any ordinary person. Your students. The people who run small stores. The rice farmers. Not anyone."

Aha! I'd been so busy struggling to say and understand anything—busy trying to learn the two "easy" syllabary (compared to kanji) and cope with daily life in a country where I could not read and a culture where some days everything was the opposite of how I expected it to be—that I'd missed this crucial point.

"Teach me how to speak to ordinary people," I said, fighting back tears.

"I can't," she said. "You are a professor. I was your student."

So there I was, stranded on my academic island, being taught to speak in a way that was only appropriate when talking to the President of the University or a bank teller. Maybe to buy a stamp at the post office. I was not really learning Japanese! Almost no one spoke the way I was being taught. No wonder I couldn't eavesdrop. No wonder learning Japanese was so frustrating.

The Literature Explains It

As I try to interpret my experience, I am fully aware of Pavlenko's (2007) admonishment: "... the act of narration unalterably transforms its subject and any further interpretations interpret the telling and not the event in question"(p.168). Yet I am someone who tells stories. I do so to understand what happened. I try to keep in mind her suggestion that we consider

> macro-level–historic, political, economic, cultural circumstances of production. The local or micro-level should attend to the context of the interview . . . and thus to the influence of language choice, audience, setting, modality, narrative functions, interactional concerns, and power relations on ways in which speakers and writers verbalize their experiences.
>
> (p.175)

OK. The big picture. And yes, I'm a sociolinguist. Yes, I'm a language teacher. Yes, I understand all this. But it's hard to take a professorial stance given that I spent four years struggling to speak a level of Japanese I couldn't really use in my everyday life in Japan.

Kubota (2002) eloquently explains the concerns at the macro level by saying, "... teaching Japanese as L2 has tended to focus on the essentialized forms of Japanese language and culture, trying to converge learners' behaviours toward an ideal norm" (p. 24). If only I had read this when I lived there! She goes on to say,

> Japanese culture is presented uncritically as consisting of predetermined facts that are imagined rather than lived and reproduced in textbooks, teaching, and teacher

> training . . . Not only is Japanese culture essentialized but also Japanese language. For instance, the taken-for-granted view that the Japanese are conscious about the social hierarchy and gender roles endorses the pedagogical practice that presents the normative use of honorifics (polite registers).
>
> (p.25)

As for the role of Japanese teachers, she explains that

> teaching Japanese to speakers of other languages tends to converge towards cultural and linguistic norms that highlight distinct Japaneseness while failing to recognize the diversity and dynamic nature of language and culture . . . these converging tendencies simultaneously alienate learners from discovering how to function effectively in real social contexts. In other words, while the fixed norm expects learners to assimilate into an imagined, ideal Japanese society, it also prevents them from becoming accepted members of the mainstream Japanese society.
>
> (p. 26)

This lack of "real social contexts" reminds me of the lessons where we pretended to invite each other for tea, pretending to visit a friend's home, all in a language no one would speak to a friend, and it explains what I had been up against and why I could not learn Japanese the way I'd learned my other languages.

While the sociocultural forces were at work hindering my progress in Japanese, on a more personal level, another battle was going on. I was unable to shape a clear identity in Japanese, a process described by Brooke (1991) as ". . . dynamic interactions between the individual and the social groups surrounding that individual . . ." I had no social groups to be part of let alone that could be ". . . formed through the negotiations in which individuals work out their own stances toward those expectations" (p.16).

When I shaped my identity in my own culture and in France, I relied heavily on what Goffman calls "underlife." Brooke (1991) describes this as

> a normal feature of social interaction: whenever individuals are cast into a social role by a social organization (as teacher or student, as boss or employee) they are likely to exhibit behavior which shows there is more to them than the role suggests. Such behavior demonstrates that, even though they may fulfill their role obligations, people are far more complicated and hold other values and play other roles in other contexts. Thus, within any social interaction, role behavior and underlife behavior consistently occur. Underlife allows individuals a means of asserting their uniqueness while also complying with social demands.
>
> (p.57)

Yes, in Japan I had my role as a professor, but I was also someone who wanted to make little jokes with the office ladies or greet the young people at the convenience store counter and make small talk. My professor status as well as the formal language I had learned to use kept me an outsider just as much as my foreign, *gaijin*, identity did.

On that day when I had my first lunch with my Japanese students and was told that the way I wanted to interact with Pony Tail Gal was not done, I had an inkling that "underlife" was not going to be an option for me in Japan. Yet, I didn't realize how my outsider status was so firmly held within the very nature of the language I was learning.

As a consequence, the longer I stayed in Japan, the more I felt my identity was slipping away. Granger (2004) explains that "... the self, the identity, can also be silent, unexpressed, and even—at least temporarily—lost" (p.7). I became so discouraged, my Japanese language learning ground to a halt.

Remarkably, about a year after the incident with my student, Naomi, I decided to try again. I found a way to learn Japanese that I could tolerate. My partner had taken a free demo lesson in Tokyo and reported that she'd found *the* method for us. Her teacher in Tokyo introduced me to Shioya-san, a woman in a neighboring town who was using the Kumon Method to teach English to Japanese children. Shioya-san was different from my other teachers who were mostly wives of professors. She ran a liquor store and loved to listen to Stevie Wonder. And she was willing to let me come to her little studio and sit at the table with the children to learn Japanese. Twice a week, for two or three hours in the afternoon, I slipped out of the university and drove to Inawashiro. The children were welcoming and kind. They gathered around me and helped me with my lessons and I helped them with theirs. Most importantly, my life at Kumon was a secret. I never told anyone at the university that I was doing this. And I didn't tell anyone in Inawashiro that I was a professor.

Now that I can speak Japanese like a five-year-old child, I've discovered most Japanese people I meet find this either hilarious or charming. And after all, children can holler, "I'm back" whenever they feel like it. So I do this now, too. And because I never, ever mention that I am a professor, I have slowly come to find there is a place for me at the table after all. And Japan is a wonderful place to be a beloved child.

Acknowledgment

Thank you to Lisa Vice, who patiently and meticulously edited this chapter, asking helpful and trenchant questions along the way. I alone am responsible for whatever is still wrong with it. Thank you, too, to my colleague, Natasha Lvovich, who discussed this chapter and its issues with me at length, giving me an idea about what to write next.

References

Brooke, R.E. (1991). *Writing and sense of self.* Urbana, IL: NCTE.

Granger, C. (2004). *Silence in second language learning: A psychoanalytic reading.* Tonawanda, NY: Multilingual Matters.

Kramsch, C. & Whiteside, A. (2008). Language ecology in multilingual settings: Toward a theory of symbolic competence. *Applied Linguistics 29*, 645–671.

Kramsch, C., Francine A. Ness, & Wan Shun Eva Lam (2000). Authenticity and authorship in the computer-mediated acquisition of second language literacy. *Language Learning and Technology, 4 (2)*, 78–104.

Kubota, R. (2002). The impact of globalization on language teaching in Japan. In D. Block & D. Cameron (eds.) *Globalization and language teaching.* New York: Routledge.

Pavlenko, A. (2007). Autobiographic narratives as data in Applied Linguistics. *Applied Linguistics 28,* 163–188.

Chapter 11

Elaborating the Monolingual Deficit

Julian Edge
University of Manchester

Background

I was born into the manual working class of the industrial English Midlands in the aftermath of the Second World War. This time and place offered me a small historical window of social mobility, based on a now outmoded respect for education, that has allowed me to build a way of life very different from that of my parents without ever feeling that I have left the long historical tradition of working class development (Thompson, 1968) that I share with them.

Entry into secondary school at that time was selective, according to performance on an examination called the eleven-plus. Having passed that examination, I became the first member of my extended family, and the only member of my friendship group, to go to what was called a Grammar School, a school at which the emphasis would be on academic subjects, rather than on vocational training.

One element of our education that was addressed immediately was our use of English. For some of us, our colloquial language included dialect remnants such as the occasional use of 'thee' and a second-person singular form of *can you* that probably began as a notional *canst thou* and emerged in our actual speech as /kɛst/. Such forms were strictly forbidden. Elocution classes also set out to establish, for example, the idea that the vowel sounds in *put* and *putt*, or in *plum pudding* were actually different. This was not easy for teacher or students, and while I did learn to tell the difference, I have never learnt to produce it without pausing and applying a very conscious effort.

I tell this part of the story in order to index my own experience of the requirement to master an *elaborated code* (Bernstein, 1971), as I would later come to call it, in order to be able to understand and deal with concepts and processes from beyond my known context in those concepts and processes' own terms, and thus proceed with my education. This seemed perfectly natural at the time – a perception that I now recognise as a nice demonstration of the exercise of power that one does not perceive as such, but rather as the natural consequence of the way things are. What also seemed quite obvious to me, and for this I am very grateful indeed, was that I felt no superiority/inferiority involved in the relationship between my restricted and elaborated codes. I learnt how to talk about poetry and I learnt how to talk about chemistry, but neither way of talking was of any use when standing behind the Boothen End goal with my dad on a Saturday afternoon in order to support Stoke City's football team, exchange pleasantries with visiting supporters, or evaluate the achievements of the referee. In later life, these concepts of hegemony, of appropriacy and of respect for the language that one comes from would prove extremely important in professional terms, but my story does not go there yet.

As far as traditional 'languages' are concerned, the context was monolithically monolingual and in it I was taught French. At family gatherings, I would be requested to, 'Say something in French', and had to put up with the wonder and merriment that greeted my attempts to recall sentences from the chapter of the text book that we had most recently studied. In our second year of French, when I was twelve, there was a school trip to France. As this was expensive, and as we had no family experience of 'abroad', apart from my father's time in the army, about which he did not speak, and as we saw no apparent usefulness in such an excursion, I was among those who did not sign up. I remember a teacher giving a 'dos and don'ts' talk to the class before the trip. At one point he told us that if we went into a public toilet, we might find that there was a woman in there. We should not make a fuss, but simply 'go about our business' as usual. To a class of twelve year old British boys, this was both hilarious and unimaginably risqué. [*I wonder why that French word comes out now?*] What has struck me much more forcibly in the meantime, however, is that no matter how much I came to learn about the three unities of classical French drama, the fin-de-siècle symbolism of Verlaine and the influence of existentialism in the novels of Camus, I think that that piece of information about public toilets was the only insight that my six years of school French gave me into contemporary French society.

However, I was 'good at French', in school terms, albeit only in the same way that I also got good marks in Physics and Chemistry, my second-best O-level grade. Understanding 'going to university' as meaning having to do another three years of whatever it was one was best at in school, and in the sure knowledge that another three years of the study of French as I knew it would cause my brain to fall out, I determined not to go to university at all. My Latin teacher, Louis Sassi, still a friend as I write, sat me down in the school library, banged onto the table a bigger book than I think I had ever seen and said,

> OK, Edge, you go through that and if there's nothing there worthy of your continuing interest, then don't go to bloody university!

It was an alphabetical guide to university courses available in Britain. I got as far as Arabic. It wasn't a language degree as such, but it included language and it covered the history and geography and anthropology of the Middle East. They had me with, 'Merhaba'.

Critical Incident

When I walked into the staff room of the Men's Teacher Training College, Amman, Jordan, one morning in 1970, only Professor Mustafa Ali Ibrahim was there, and he had his back to me as he searched through his briefcase. I greeted in the normal fashion, a formulaic, three-part exchange involving reference to peace, god and good health on both sides. I sat down and started to sort out my own papers. After a minute or so, I noticed that Mustafa was looking round the room in a puzzled fashion. I looked at him and shook my head, to mean, 'What's up?'

> 'Was that you?' he asked, in English.
>
> 'Was what me?'

'Who just said, "Al-salaamu alaikum," and all that?'

'Ain't nobody else here,' I replied, becoming a little embarrassed.

'I wouldn't have thought it. That was really good. When I saw you, I thought someone else must have come in and gone out again.'

'I only said, "Good morning."'

'Yes, but it sounded right.'

'Well, thank you.'

In the Arab world, in my experience, it doesn't take a lot for a person's communicative efforts to be warmly appreciated. And in the Anglo world, I acknowledge, it doesn't take much for us to start feeling good about our achievements, no matter how small. Of course, it mattered that he couldn't see me (see Nunan, this volume), but *when* he couldn't see me, for that brief, but complete exchange, I had been there, in the zone, where it counts: not *that* me, not the slightly gormless English youth doing voluntary service – whatever that meant – still me, but another me. I had been momentarily transformed. I loved it. And now, when I reflect . . .

Interpretation

In one sense, of course, Mustafa was absolutely correct: someone had come in and gone out again. The person to whom he spoke in English was not and could not be the person with whom he had exchanged those greetings in Arabic. If it had been *that* me who had greeted him, then rather than perhaps picking up some unusual sonorities in my pronunciation and delivery of the phrases and writing them off subconsciously as a difference of dialect, he would have heard mistakes. For a few ridiculously satisfying moments, however, I had shaken off the identity of a speaker who made mistakes, and become simply a speaker of Arabic with my own voice. I had lost one identity and gained a different one. I had become a 'credible insider' who came into the room and left before Mustafa turned round – a short life, perhaps, but a tremendously satisfying one!

Beyond that, I confess, I have never succeeded in living in Arabic as I sometimes live in German (a later development, a significantly different critical incident and very definitely another story), but I have lived on several occasions on the border of Arabic as the foreigner who could (unexpectedly) make things happen, whether the issue at hand was educational, commercial or social, and that was also always a good feeling. I don't say that I scored the best deal down at the canal-side café in Alexandria on those warm summer nights, but I never got burnt. This role as potential 'broker' (Wenger, 1998) between communities is as attractive an identity in its way as the identity of credible insider. It also has the added attraction of being more easily sustainable.

Furthermore, since I left the Arab world, now over thirty years hence, Arabic has sometimes accorded me the identity of something like a 'legitimated visitor', a guest who has not only a valid passport, but also an appropriate visa. In 2008, for example, I was invited to give a talk in Dubai and decided to make a few opening comments in Arabic as a way of showing respect for my hosts and my context, and also, it must be admitted, to stake a claim to be not only that most oxymoronic of creatures, the foreign expert. Having prepared what I wanted to say, I asked a doctoral candidate in our department, Mariam Attia, to listen to me. In an immensely supportive way, she gave me some appropriate opening phrases that I had not known, checked that what she had understood was indeed what I wanted to say, corrected a few errors of pronunciation and left the rest alone, warts and all. When I returned, I told her that the talk had gone well and that the Arabic introduction had been very well received. She e-mailed back:

> I am pleased that your talk went well, yet not surprised. In fact, it was not only a beautiful start and a nice gesture in a host country that speaks Arabic, but also a sign of your understanding of and appreciation for elements of reciprocal friendliness deeply imbedded in the culture and symbolised in the well-known Quranic verse: '*and when you are greeted with a greeting, greet with a better than it or return it*' (4:86). This is why the traditional response to, '*assalamu alaikum*', is, '*wa alaikum assalam*', and yet better with the additional, '*wa rahmatullahi wa barakaatuhu*'. I read that the word '*greeting*' in Arabic (*tahiyya*) comes from the same root as the word '*life*' (*hayah*), possibly due to the profound impact that reciprocal gestures of peace and kindness have on the wellbeing of human communities. Of course, greetings do not have to be in words, but can be actions too.
>
> So, here they invite you to deliver a talk (which is their '*assalamu alaikum*'), and to their surprise you not only respond by giving the talk (your '*wa alaikum assalam*') but also make the effort to start it in Arabic (which is the extra '*wa rahmatullahi wa barakaatuhu*').

While this commentary speaks much more of Mariam's grace and sensitivity than of my own intercultural sophistication, the point that I really want to make here is that my feeling of having established a slightly different identity-as-speaker was not merely a subjective idiosyncrasy.

> [*As I work on this interpretation, I notice not only that I have already evoked more incidents than the 'critical' one with which I began, but that yet more are circling this emergent text and demanding to be let in. It is less the case that I have an incident as an example of a theoretical understanding, and more the case that I need to let the incidents assemble in order to understand what kind of a theorisation will make sense of them.*]

With regard to what I have called brokering, for example, the process sometimes releases one completely from one's birth-related identity. The memory of translating a notice in Spanish for monolingual French tourists in Andalusia brings back an exhilarating sensation of having been freed entirely (albeit again briefly) from my identity as a speaker of English. And as a legitimated visitor to Germany, the experience of beating back the (perhaps justifiably) stereotypical expectation that as I am English, one has to speak English to me brings frequent satisfaction. And then comes a very powerful memory of taking part in one of a series of meetings in Paris called the Triangle Seminars (Edge, 1994). In these seminars, the working assumption was that all participants would have sufficient communicative ability in French, German and English to allow each individual to speak in the language of his or her choice. In my case, I gave my presentation in English, took questions in any of the three languages and responded in English, sometimes by first checking in English that I had understood the question. The experience of extended linguistic interaction not based on the use of a single, common language was novel to me and also strangely liberating. Each one of us was, at least, released from the limitations of saying only what we could, and allowed to say what we meant. I seemed to intuit a sense of belonging to a human community of far greater potential than I had hitherto known, where I was, despite my asymmetrical levels of linguistic ability, a credible insider.

These fragmentary experiences, which I had never brought together before writing this piece, are perhaps emblematic of the slow, monolingual process of learning experientially the deep truth of the metaphorical observation that the world is not named once and then translated. To some, the obviousness of this state of affairs is a birthright. To me, in its various manifestations, it has been a continuing revelation. This revelation, moreover, has changed me from ever being able (or wanting to be) just English, with views based only on that particular perspective. This may, again, sound like a small thing, or an obvious one, but it has, since 1969, felt like something special to me, just as it used to irk my mother to hear me talk about 'the English', and not about 'us'.

The escape from a monolingual perspective is not easy for those born into it. Indeed, it might always demand an act of awareness-raising or imagination, no matter what one's linguistic inheritance. The entrenched hegemony of the monolingual perspective is apparent in the discourse of 'first' and 'second' language acquisition and of 'native' and 'non-native' speakers. It becomes even more blatant when one realises the impossibility of going to the library to consult such urgently needed volumes as: *Monolingualism*, or *Monolingual Education*, or *Monolingualism in Development: Language, Literacy and Cognition*, or *The Monolingual Family: A Handbook for Parents.* I am not aware of any learned journal articles earnestly urging that we must not be trapped into accepting a deficit model of monolingualism. There appears to be no highly politicised debate as to whether we should adopt a mainstreaming or withdrawal approach to the problems of the monolingual child.

There is, moreover, an additional consideration to grapple with when the monolingual language is English. Both Brumfit (2006) and Kumaravedivelu (2006) foresee a globalised future in which, at least for the short to medium term, English will have a dominant role. Kumaravedivelu (ibid. 16) sees in this the self-indulgence of power, where 'native speakers of English will have the luxury of remaining monolingual while all others will have to learn their language'. From a different perspective, Brumfit (ibid. 46) sees this outcome as his most pessimistic (but also most likely) scenario, in which native speakers of the major English dialects assume their right to use that language for all local, regional and international purposes, thus becoming, 'the only educated monolinguals in the world'.

Writing in the context of the US-led invasion of Iraq and President Bush II's 'war on terror', Brumfit (ibid.) captures the bleakness of this scenario in all its parochial myopia when he writes:

> Perhaps current international politics is already acting out the beginnings of such a pessimistic prediction.
>
> *[At this point in my telling, I realise that the increasing sense of tension that I feel is caused not so much by the number of incidents that have pushed their way into this*

text, but rather by the increasing number of identities that are clamouring to be expressed. Among them, I recognise the born monolingual who wants to talk about his partial escape from this psycho-social ghetto; then there is the sociolinguist who recognises that being monolingual in English has particular significance in the contemporary world, then the ESOL professional who has positions on the cultural politics of TESOL, but also the teacher educator who recognises that any sense of reflexivity in his work demands that he unpack all of the above and their mutually shaping effects on each other. In what follows, I attempt to discipline this unruly crew by returning to my critical incident.]

First of all, why did this specific moment come back to me so immediately and insistently, as it certainly did, when I was invited to identify a critical incident? This is a pressing question, as I feel a distinct dissonance with regard to the concept of the credible insider as I described it there, and the argument that I now put to my English language students along the lines of,

> *'Why get upset about having a Greek accent? You are Greek. What's wrong with that?'*

On the one hand, I acknowledge and respect the desire to become someone else, to be that person who entered the room when Mustafa was not looking. Beyond that fleeting moment, however, my conviction is that the important issue is not so much a question of *how well* I perform when I speak against a standard of who I am not, but of who I speak *as*. The *credible insider*, the *broker*, or the *legitimated visitor* are all identities that I can inhabit with regard to the communities in which I live and to which I aspire. It is in this sense, as a teacher, that I want to help learners of English empower themselves by claiming ownership of a shared international language without feeling that that ownership is diminished if they also demonstrate their backgrounds.

And further, I want to be a part of the experience whereby people not only learn another language in the limited sense of learning another code into which they can translate their given world, but in the sense whereby they exceed this fundamentally monolingual world view and develop an elaborated code that allows them to understand and deal with concepts and processes from beyond their known context in those concepts and processes' own terms.

> *[Is this simply a playing out of my own autobiography? I must be sure to listen very carefully here to what learners tell me, because a one-size-fits-all response based on extrapolations from my own very different experience is unlikely to be satisfactory.]*

If I see a way ahead, at the time of writing, in this search to learn through reflection on one's own experience while not being limited by it, that way lies in further work with Cook's (1999) concept of multicompetence, especially as taken up by Pavlenko (2003:262), who writes, 'that people who know more than one language have a distinct compound state of mind, not equivalent to two monolingual states, and can be considered legitimate L2 users'. Pavlenko reports on research that invited teachers of English who had learnt the language consciously to stop categorising themselves as inadequate users of English when compared to native speakers of the major dialects of the language, and to begin imaginatively to construct the community of multi-competent teachers of English to which they already belonged. An important part of this re-imagining relates to the acceptance of the idea that one does not have to be born into bilingualism, but one can learn to be a member of this community. She continues (ibid. 266):

> In this case, reimagining themselves as multicompetent and bilingual allowed some students not only to view themselves positively, but also to transmit those views to others and to engage in active attempts to reshape the surrounding contexts.

I see the potential of these ideas for teacher education and engage with them in my work as teacher educator. Equally relevant, however, to the concerns of this chapter is that I also see a community to which I myself can aspire to belong, as I work to elaborate my monolingual inheritance through conscious effort with regard to intercultural communication.

And then, as I imagine myself into this community, further consequences follow for my work as a TESOL professional. First, to the usual parameters of accuracy, fluency and appropriacy that we use to guide our students' learning, we need to add that of flexibility: the capacity to communicate with others whose formulation and use of English differ from our own. Second, for those of us who grew up in English, we need to exemplify in our own behaviour the realisation that such flexibility is demanded first and foremost from *us* if we are to contribute most positively to global communication via English(es). In this, I rejoin Pavlenko, when she writes (ibid. 266) that:

> . . . marginalization within the profession will continue unless those who use the target language as their first join the process of critical reflection on language ideologies and linguistic theories that inform our practices.

It is in this vein that I offer the above reflection, with only the careful caveat that I do not strictly view my first language as the actual target language of my students. As I make my way of languaging my life, writing this chapter has helped me understand better some of the connections that operate around me and within me as a whole-person-who-teaches (Edge, 1996).

Of one thing, I feel relatively sure: the monolingual vision will not see humankind through in good shape. In doleful harmony with Brumfit's comment above on the outcomes of educated monolingualism in terms of current international politics, I hear a line from Cohen (1992), illuminated in the glare of white phosphorous:

I've seen the future, brother; it is murder.

Acknowledgements

My sincere thanks to my colleagues, Susan Brown, Richard Fay, Gary Motteram, Diane Slaouti and Juup Stelma for their clarification, critique and collaboration on an earlier draft of this chapter, and to Donna Butorac for introducing me to Pavlenko's work on *imagined communities.*

References

Bernstein, B. (1971). *Class, codes and control* (Vol. 1). London: Paladin.

Brumfit, C. (2006). What, then, must we do? Or who gets hurt when we speak, write and teach? In J. Edge (Ed.), *(Re)Locating TESOL in an age of empire* (pp. 27–48). Basingstoke: Macmillan Palgrave.

Cohen, L. (1992). The future. On *The future.* Sony Music: Columbia. Leonard Cohen Stranger Music Inc.

Cook, V. (1999). Going beyond the native speaker in language teaching. *TESOL Quarterly, 33,* 185–209.

Edge, J. (1994). Empowerment: Principles and procedures in teacher education. In R. Budd, D. Arnsdorf & P. Chaix (Eds.), *Triangle XII: The European dimension in pre- and in-service language teacher development: New directions* (pp. 113–134). Paris: Didier Erudition.

Edge, J. (1996). Cross-cultural paradoxes in a profession of values. *TESOL Quarterly 30,* 9–30.

Kumaravadivelu, B. (2006). Dangerous liaison: Globalisation, empire and TESOL. In J. Edge (Ed.), *(Re)Locating TESOL in an age of empire* (pp. 1–26). Basingstoke: Palgrave Macmillan.

Pavlenko, A. (2003). 'I never knew I was a bilingual': Reimagining teacher identities in TESOL. *Journal of Language, Identity and Education 2,* 251–268.

Thompson, E. (1968). *The making of the English working class.* Harmondsworth: Penguin.

Wenger, E. (1998). *Communities of practice: Learning, meaning and identity.* Cambridge: Cambridge University Press.

Chapter 12

The Foreign-ness of Native Speaking Teachers of Colour

Eljee Javier
Manchester Metropolitan University

Background

I'm a Canadian-Filipino. By this description I am both Canadian and Filipino. But how is this combination really defined? I've been asking myself that question for the past 30 years and still haven't arrived at a satisfactory answer. My parents emigrated from the Philippines in 1976 and three years later I became the first child from both sides of the family to have been born abroad. This was important as I would be the first of the family to have grown up being influenced by two different cultures.

My parents had a strong influence in my cultural upbringing. From an early age I was taught the 'rules' of how to conduct myself in Filipino society. However, my parents also wanted their daughter to be a 'full' Canadian and insisted that I grew up speaking only English as a way to integrate into Canadian society with more ease. I wasn't encouraged to learn Tagalog (Philippine national dialect) or Ilocano (my mother's dialect) for fear that it would be a hindrance to my development as a Canadian. As such, I was expected to participate in learning Canada's second official language: French. From the age of 5 to 14 I learnt French formally at school. I eventually stopped learning French not only because it was no longer compulsory but also because I didn't see any use for it in my future. Parallel to this decision was my own choice to forgo attempts at learning my parents' dialects due to the fact that in many ways I didn't feel Filipino enough to do so.

Ironically in university some of my courses involved studying various dead languages, such as Latin, Ancient Greek and Aramaic. These I relished as they didn't have a stake in my own identity. I could study these languages free of any further implication they would have had on me.

Upon finishing university I travelled to China to teach English. During my time in China I was often mistaken for a local teacher because of my Filipino background. In this context I discovered that my students had certain pre-conceptions of what an English language teacher embodies. Whenever I walked into a classroom to start a brand new course, my initial appearance would often be met with a mixture of surprise and disappointment, and sometimes with anger. At the time I couldn't understand what my students were saying to each other but it was clear from their facial expressions that they didn't feel comfortable with me as their teacher. From the outset it became apparent that the majority of students assumed that a native speaker would not only be from Canada (or the UK, USA or Australia), but that they would also be White. This was a huge eye-opener for me because I hadn't thought that my ethnicity would be an issue, much less a liability. For a while I felt extremely frustrated at my situation because I couldn't find an easy way to cope, let alone find a solution. In many ways I also felt isolated. My colleagues were very supportive and encouraged me along the way, yet they didn't share the same anxieties as I did simply because they didn't look like a local.

One of the ways I used to address the issue was first to expect the mixed reactions of my students whenever I started a new class. In doing so I was better able to prepare myself both emotionally and practically for the challenge of, essentially, proving my credentials as their English language teacher. Therefore, part of my routine, when starting a brand new class, was to launch into a mini-monologue about myself. I would usually share some anecdote about my life in Canada and present it at a normal speaking rate in order to demonstrate that I was a native speaker of English. As soon as I finished my students immediately became more willing and open to the idea of accepting me as their English teacher. In a way, it was my attempt to 'attack first' by establishing who I am before any questions were raised.

Ironically, I took to studying Chinese as a way to 'blend in' to the world outside the classroom. In many ways I was granted an insiders' view as people would carry on with whatever they were doing when I entered the scene. However, as soon as I spoke Chinese my charade was up and their behaviour changed. This was frustrating for me as I wasn't quite sure what was expected of me. I look like I should speak Chinese, but I don't. They were often confused as my outside appearance didn't fit into their idea of a 'foreigner'.

The following narrative is a description of a singular event that serves to highlight the issues surrounding native speakers of colour. In the section after the narrative I try to make sense of the incident in terms of the theme of this collection: language and culture with a particular focus on the formation of native speaking teachers of colour.

Narrative

It was toward the end of the 15 minute break and I was back inside the classroom erasing the whiteboard in preparation for the next session. I had been in the country for nearly nine months and, at the time, considered myself rather conversant in Chinese. I was able to travel independently around the city, go shopping and read basic Chinese characters. However, I made it a point not to let my students know that I understood the language as I found that their assumptions about my lack of Chinese language ability helped to distance myself from my students.

This was only the third lesson that I'd had with this group of students, during which I would often have a few late-comers joining the class for the first time. Consequently they would miss the pre-prepared speech I so often gave at the beginning of each course and, upon arrival, were confused with my appearance. Usually, during these instances I would let the other students inform their classmates about me. It took the pressure off me to try to validate my position as their teacher, which was a relief in many ways. I eavesdropped on their conversation, which took place in Chinese, and this usually went along the lines of:

New Student: I thought our teacher was a native speaker!
Current Student: She is a native speaker.
New Student: *(pause)* But she looks Chinese!
Current Student: She's not! She's Canadian.

At the time I wasn't really aware of the implications that this conversation had, other than feeling that I'd rather let my students defend my right to be there at the front of the classroom than repeating my speech over again. On this particular day, though, I remember one of the new students approached me with the following question (in English):

New Student: So, you're not Chinese?
Me: No, not at all!
New Student: Your family is Chinese?
Me: No, none of them are Chinese. Both my parents are from the Philippines.
New Student: But your English is so good!
Me: Well, I'm a native speaker.
New Student: Of course.

At this point I could tell she wasn't convinced of my English credentials. I felt myself grow increasingly frustrated and I found myself defensively saying the following:

'I'm from Canada.'

Suddenly the light seemed to go on. Her face lit up in a smile and she thanked me for my time before sitting down, obviously pleased with the news. I had told previous classes that I was from Canada but this was the first time that I had used that fact as a deliberate way of validating myself as a native speaker.

Commentary

My narrative highlights various wide-ranging issues that I will briefly focus on in this article. Moreover, the issues are complex and raise further implications. First, it is evident that there persists a preference for native speakers over non-native speakers. Moreover there are assumptions made which contribute to the confusion over native speakers of colour.

The first is the perception that there is a standard of English that exists from which all other varieties of English(es) are measured against. This notion is derived from Krachu's model of concentric circles (in Quirk & Widdowson 1985, p. 16) where the countries in the inner circle (i.e. Canada, the USA, United Kingdom) are considered 'norm-providing' countries and therefore assumed to possess a standard of English, which are seen primarily as British and American varieties. Phillipson (1992) further describes the perception in terms of being a source from which the notion of a standard arises, types of English which come from 'norm-providing' countries that Krachu (1985) identifies. Medgyes (1999) sees this perception as an idealization in the industry that stems from various assumptions made of the rules and norms which certain people attempt to adhere to (p.7).

The perception that there is a Standard English remains widely accepted and has further implications for the language user. The native speaker is perceived to have arrived at the 'standard' of English, not only characterized by the phonological aspects of accent but also having the capacity to produce fluent and spontaneous discourse (Medgyes 1992, p.12). Hence, native speakers are 'potentially more accomplished users than non-native speakers' (ibid.) and are therefore more proficient users (Leung, Harris & Rampton 1997). One of the first questions my Chinese students always asked was if I was a native speaker of English. This was important to them as they had come specifically to this school to be taught by a native speaker. They had a preference for a native speaking teacher because they wanted to improve their pronunciation and, in order to do so, needed a native speaker as a model. This subsequently leads to the belief that since native speakers are more competent in the language, they are expected to be more competent teachers (Medgyes 1992; Liu 1999). My students, like countless others, aspired to a native-like competency and pronunciation which they believe is best achieved through a native speaking teacher.

The next issue that was raised by my students was defining the identity of a native speaking teacher. The standard pronunciation of 'norm-providing' countries is also extended to an un-stated racial standard of the native speaker. Amin's (in Braine (ed.) 1999) and Liu's (1999) research revealed that learners, by being associated with 'norm-providing' countries, racially define native speakers as White. For the purposes of this chapter I use the label 'White' to denote individuals of Caucasian/Anglo-Saxon descent. The invisible power relations that exist in the labels of native and non-native speaker reinforce the idea of a linguistic and racial standard. For my students, my appearance didn't match with their assumptions of what a native speaker entailed. My exterior labelled me as a member of the local community and therefore I was assumed to behave and operate within the same social norms as the local community. In the first conversation, the new student questioned the claim that I was a native speaker by stating '**But** she looks Chinese!' In doing so, she implied that since I look Chinese, I must also speak the language and therefore cannot be a native speaker of English. The second conversation echoes the sentiments previously expressed, '**But** your English is so good!' In both these instances there underlies the assumption that a native speaker of English cannot be Chinese.

Or, conversely, a native speaker is assumed to be a foreigner to the host country and, by assumption, would not look Chinese. The bias was not confined to the expectation of a native speaking teacher but a specific expectation for a White native speaking teacher. This expectation is echoed by other visible ethnic minorities (VEM) who are native English speaking teachers (NEST). The personal account of Romney (2006), who is African-American, describes her struggles with being regarded as a non-American and thus labelled as a non-native speaker on the basis that her outward appearance does not conform to the 'standard' of the native speaking teacher. In contrast, Liu's (1999, p. 97) research revealed that one of his participants, Ms. K, was seen by her students as a native speaker of English because she was White, despite the fact that she was born and raised in Denmark and moved to the US at the age of 10.

Thus, myself and others like me are a categorical problem in the field of ELT: I am a visible ethnic minority (VEM) who is also a native English speaker (NES). For the sake of clarity, I define a visible ethnic minority as an individual who is non-White. Assumptions made of native English speakers are connected to an assumption made of the countries that English is associated with, namely the 'norm-providing' countries such as the USA, United Kingdom and Canada. A VEM-NES, by virtue of their mixed backgrounds, does not necessarily conform to the assumptions made by others and therefore poses a categorical problem.

In light of the various linguistic and cultural beliefs that contribute to the definition of a 'standard' native speaker, I found that I turned to using my 'foreign-ness' as a way to validate my native speaking status. The first conversation ended with my current student's reply: 'She's not [Chinese]! She's Canadian!' In emphasizing this fact my student defined me as a foreigner and therefore not Chinese as a way to establish that

I am a native speaker. This was necessary as the new student, at the time, was not convinced that I was a native speaker because I didn't conform to her expectation of what a native speaker entailed. Alternatively, my students did not associate a native speaker with a Chinese background but they did associate a native speaker with having a Canadian background.

In the above example, the native speaker is someone not from the host country (i.e. China) but from abroad, more specifically, from 'norm-providing' countries. Furthermore a native speaker is assumed to be a foreigner to the host country and by assumption would not look similar to the local people. It is a general stereotype but a commonly held one. Native speakers are racially classed as White, which is associated with the idea of 'foreign-ness'. This fact demonstrates the invisible power relations in the labels of native and non-native speakers (Liu 1999, p. 97), in that it is not really a linguistic categorization but socially constructed identities based on cultural assumptions on who conforms to the preconceived notions of the native speaker (Brutt-Griffler & Samimy, 1999, p. 422). By emphasizing my foreign-ness ('I'm a Canadian!'), I detached myself from the status of being considered non-White ('But she looks Chinese!'), which was at odds with the commonly held notion of a native speaker, and became elevated to the status of being considered a foreigner. In doing so, I was closer to being accepted as a native speaker than before.

Despite the obvious hierarchy of native and non-native speaking teachers, there is a less obvious hierarchy of native speaking teachers. This hierarchy is a social construct that places individuals who are White native English speakers over their coloured counterparts. These preferences are most evident in hiring practices worldwide, where putting a White face on a school's marketing material would boost the school's image. It is important to note that although these assumptions prevail, they are not so deeply entrenched as to reject the VEM-NEST entirely. In my own narrative, once my student learnt that I was from Canada, she was pleased and became more accepting of the idea that I was a native speaker but, more importantly, she was more open to the idea of accepting me as her teacher. I was treated as the exception to the commonly held stereotype and, as a result, was generally regarded as a native speaker.

For the moment it seems that the status of the VEM-NEST is not regarded as the same status as a White native speaker, yet not quite as low as a non-native speaker. This is the paradox I, and others like me, are faced with. I have to, in part, accept the system in which I work, realizing that I will be categorized no matter what I say or do. Yet, in asserting my foreign-ness as a way of validating my native speaking status, I uphold the very system that I am fighting against. Do I choose to align myself with the native speaker 'camp' in order to bolster my own status as a native speaker of colour while, at the same time, negating the legitimacy of non-native speaking teachers (of all colours)? Is there a way to go beyond the distinctions in order to distinguish English language teachers in their own right, native/non-native, coloured or otherwise?

My own experiences are not isolated instances but are a reflection of the discrimination that is prevalent in the TESOL industry. In my own research, I have encountered other individuals with similar backgrounds to myself with their own experiences. However I believe it isn't enough to informally 'rant' about these problems but there needs to be a more defined push into creating an open discussion about race and race related issues. Amin, Kubota and Lin are among the number of academics who have highlighted the growing need for further research in order to properly theorize race within the educational sector as a way to begin dealing with some of the difficult and awkward questions. If the industry believes that there isn't a 'standard' of English, how can this be marketed so that the wider community accepts this? Can a 'non-standard' of English exist? Can a VEM-NES teacher be accepted at 'face value'? I would like to one day feel free to teach without having to justify myself but for now, being a 'foreigner' is the best attempt at a practical solution, however flawed.

References

Amin, N. (1999). Minority women teaching of ESL: Negotiating White English. In G. Braine (ed.). *Non-native educators in English language teaching.* (pp. 93–104). London: Lawrence Erlbaum Associate Publishers.

Brutt-Griffler, J. & Samimy, K. (1999). Revising the colonial in the postcolonial: Critical praxis for non-native, English speaking teachers in a TESOL programme. *TESOL Quarterly*, 33 (3), 413–431.

Krachu, B. (1985). Standards, codification and sociolinguistic realism: The English language in the outer circle. In R. Quirk & H. Widdowson (eds.). *English in the world – teaching and learning the language and literatures.* (pp. 11 – 34). Cambridge: Cambridge University Press.

Kubota, R. & Lin, A. (2006). Race and TESOL: Introduction to concepts and theories. *TESOL Quarterly*, 40(3), 471–493.

Leung, C., Harris, R. & Rampton, B. (1997). The idealized native speaker, reified ethnicities and classroom realities. *TESOL Quarterly*, 31(3), 543–560.

Liu, J. (1999). Non native English speaking professionals in TESOL. *TESOL Quarterly*, 33 (1), 85–102.

Medgyes, P. (1992). Native or non-native: Who's worth more? *ELT Journal*, 46 (4), 340–349.

Phillipson, R. (1992). *Linguistic imperialism.* Oxford: Oxford University Press.

Quirk, R. & Widdowson, H. (eds.) (1985). *English in the world: Teaching and learning the language and literatures.* Cambridge: Cambridge University Press.

Romney, M. (2006). Not a real American: A reluctant ambassador. In A. Curtis & M. Romney (eds.). *Colour, race and English language teaching: Shades of meaning.* (pp. 149–160). New Jersey: Lawrence Erlbaum Associates Publishers.

Chapter 13

Otra Estación – A First Spanish Lesson

Rod Ellis
University of Auckland

Off to Spain

It is May 1965 and my university days are over. I have only two things in mind. One is to earn some money doing a holiday job and the other is to find some way of escaping the grey skies of England and living abroad. I achieve the first by getting a job as a waiter in a five star hotel in Frinton-on-Sea, an upper class seaside resort on the east coast of England. I achieve the second by securing a position as a teacher in a new Berlitz school that has recently opened up in Torrelavega, a small town in Cantabria, Spain. My experiences in the hotel are quite eventful but it is my Spanish adventure that I want to write about. It is in Spain where I first really experienced what it is to be a language learner.

The first point to make clear is that I do not know a single word of Spanish as I set off for Spain. I don't even know the Spanish word for 'no'! I do know some 'schoolboy' French and German, mainly grammar, but with minimal communicative ability. I have no prior experience of learning a language 'naturalistically' in a context where the language is a part of my daily life. In fact, I have very limited experience of trying to communicate with anybody who is not a native speaker of English.

The journey to Spain takes me to Dover, across the Channel and on to Paris. From there I board an overnight train to San Sebastián – a rather beautiful town just across the border from France. My Spanish adventure starts in San Sebastián. I need to get a train that will take me to Santander, a seaside resort some two hundred plus miles down the coast. This is where I am due to be met by the owner of the Berlitz School who will train me and then send me to Torrelavega.

Armed with a bundle of pesetas, I disembark from the Paris train and advance on the ticket booth at the station and ask for a ticket to 'SAN – TAN- DER', pronouncing the word as if it were an English word. I am greeted by a stream of Spanish that is totally incomprehensible and – no ticket!! I retreat to my suitcase and sit on it wondering what to do next. There is nothing else for it – I shall have to try again. Once more I advance on the ticket booth and again request a ticket to SAN-TAN-DER. Once again I receive a stream of Spanish that is gibberish to me – and no ticket. So once again I retreat to my suitcase to ponder my next course of action. A Spanish policeman eyes me suspiciously as he might an anti-Franco agitator. At this point, a man approaches me. He gestures violently in a direction away from the station and says 'Santander – otra estación'. I look blank. He repeats his gesture and says again 'Santander – otra estación'. This time the penny drops. Drawing on my schoolboy French I work out that 'otra' is the same as 'autre' and drawing on the close similarity between 'estación' and 'station'

I finally grasp that he is telling me I need to go to another station if I want to go to Santander. I also observe his pronunciation of 'Santander'.

I notice a taxi driver puffing on a cigarette (probably a 'Celtas' – a cheap brand I later indulged in) while he lounges against the boot of his car. I approach him warily wondering how I am going to explain that I need to get him to take me to the station where I can buy a ticket to Santander. I say one word – 'Santander', this time approximating more closely the Spanish pronunciation. It is sufficient. He takes my suitcase, opens the boot and pushes it inside. I get in the taxi and we are off. I watch the metre anxiously, fearing my bundle of pesetas will deplete rapidly and dangerously. But in a few minutes he deposits me at 'otra estación'. I head off to the ticket office and ask for a ticket to 'Santander' only once again to be faced with a stream of incomprehensible Spanish except this time I do recognize a single word in the stream – 'no'. This time, however, a ticket is pushed at me and I hear the word 'Bilbao'. I slowly put two and two together and work out that I can only buy a ticket as far as Bilbao, the next city down the coast. I hand over the pesetas (rapidly thinning) and pocket the ticket. The next task is to find out what time the train leaves – 'When train leave?' I say in pidgin English. More incomprehensible Spanish follows. But then he pushes a timetable at me. I inspect it and discover that I have just missed the morning train and that the next train is in the afternoon. I confirm this by pointing at the pm departure time and the ticket seller nods and says what sounds like 'porlatathe'. I have six hours to wait. I sit in the small waiting room and observe Spain. Or rather I note with interest that every other person seems to be a policeman of some kind or another.

Finally, it is time to board the train to Bilbao. I sit in a crowded third class carriage surrounded by Basque men all of whom are wearing the same kind of black beret. I smile and am smiled at. I desperately try to avoid being talked to so I don't have to face up to the embarrassment of my total failure to understand.

The train chugs through mountains stopping at every little station. The distance is not much more than 100 km but it takes three hours. Eventually I arrive in Bilbao and head immediately to the ticket kiosk. 'Santander' I say, remembering how to pronounce the word. A stream of Spanish follows and again I hear the word 'no'. 'Otra estación?' I say. 'Sí, sí, sí' the man says nodding furiously. I look for a taxi, throw my suitcase in and jump in. 'Santander' I say and we are off immediately bumping down street after street of drab industrial buildings that makes me think of Dickens's Victorian London. I anxiously watch the meter ticking away. But soon we are at the otra estación and I pay off the taxi driver and drag myself and my suitcase to the ticket office. 'Santander' I say, feeling more pleased with my pronunciation with each attempt. The man points at a train on a nearby platform obviously on the point of departing and gestures for me to hurry to board it. I abandon all thought of buying a ticket and rush towards the train. I throw my suitcase through an open door and clamber after it just as the train starts to pull out of the estación.

One hundred kilometres and three hours later I am in Santander. I have arrived six hours later than expected but the English owner of the local Berlitz school is there waiting for me to escort me to my pension. I am starving. The landlady pushes a bowl of bean soup in front of me and I gobble it down even though I don't like beans. 'Se gusta?' she asks. 'Se gusta?' I smile and nod. 'Yes, gusta, gusta', I say. Then, miming tiredness I say 'Very tired'. 'Si cansado, muy cansado' she says. 'Si, muy cansado' I repeat.

And so my first day in Spain comes to an end. Not bad, I think. I managed. I learnt a few words of Spanish. Feeling rather pleased with myself, I fall into a deep sleep.

Discussion

Prior to my arrival in Spain my only experience of learning a foreign language was in the classroom where the focus was on grammar and translating sentences from English into French or German. I had had no experience of actually trying to communicate in a foreign language. My period in Spain exposed me to situations in which I had no choice but to try to communicate with whatever resources I had at my disposal. Looking back at this period now I can see that my own experience mirrored that of countless other learners who learnt a new language by struggling to communicate in it – as I would subsequently document in the books on second language acquisition I started to write some twenty years later.

What then does my first experience of naturalistic language learning tell us about the nature of learning a language? The first thing is perhaps the most important. You do not need any grammar to get started. I knew nothing about Spanish grammar and yet I was able to communicate and through communicating learn a few words and expressions. The early stages of naturalistic acquisition are, in fact, agrammatical. The European Science Foundation investigated the acquisition of L2 Dutch, English, French, German, and Swedish by adult migrants (Klein and Perdue 1997). They found that all these learners in all of these languages went though an initial period that they labelled the 'pre-basic variety', which was characterized by the use of very simple noun phrases with no verbs and no grammar. At this stage the learners' attempts to use the language were heavily 'scaffolded' and context-dependent (i.e. utterances were constructed over more than one turn and relied extensively on situational support to achieve meaning). In time, the pre-basic variety gives way to the basic variety. At this stage verbs begin to appear in the learners' speech but with no attempt to mark them for tense or aspect. This stage is still essentially agrammatical. It is not until the 'post-basic variety', where finite verbal organization finally appears and grammar starts to emerge. It is clear that I was just at the beginning of the pre-basic variety for Spanish. My total output in day one consisted of 'Santander', 'otra estación', 'gusta' and 'muy cansado'. Not a verb in sight. And every single word 'borrowed' from the preceding discourse.

There are a number of other key aspects of early L2 acquisition that my first day's experience with Spanish illustrates. One is the importance of making use of what you already know. I didn't know any Spanish but I did know some French and I did know quite a lot of Latinate English words. It was this that helped me to get started. I would never have been able to work out that 'otraestación') meant 'other station' if I had not been able to make the link between 'otra' and 'autre' and 'estación' and 'station'. There is plenty of evidence in the L2 acquisition literature to point to the importance of 'positive transfer' from one's first language or another second language. Sjöholm (1976), for example, reported that Swedish learners of L2 English do better in vocabulary learning than Finnish learners, Swedish being closer than Finnish to English and thus possessing many more cognates. Later in my stay in Spain I saw for myself how useful a knowledge of French was when I observed a French and a Spanish friend conversing in a mixture of the two languages and, apparently, achieving full comprehension. But I also saw how cognates can sometimes get you into trouble when I tried using the word 'cosmopolita' with my Spanish landlady only to be met with a look of total puzzlement. This is in fact a Spanish word but not one that my landlady knew! Still, without my French and the advantage of some English/ Spanish cognates I might never have made it to Santander!

A problem that every beginner language learner faces is how to segment the stream of L2 speech into words. Until the learner can do this no learning is possible. So how does it happen? When I first heard 'otraestación' I heard it as a continuous stream, not as two words. It took several repetitions before I was able to apply my knowledge of French and English and work out that it was 'otra + estación'. Only then was I able to understand. Repetition is enormously important for language learning. It allows time for the language learner to apply the conscious, controlled processing of the input that it initially necessary. It facilitates segmentation. Pica (1992) has also shown how repetition, in the context of negotiating for meaning, helps learners to segment the stream of speech. She gives this example of a learner negotiating 'buvdaplate' with a native speaker interlocutor:

NS: with a small pat of butter on it and above the plate
NNS: hm hmm what is buvdaplate?
NS: above
NNS: above the plate
NS: yeah

(Pica 1992: 225)

Here the native speaker's repetition of the single key word 'above' was enough to help the learner segment the phrase. Similarly, repetition and context helped me understand my landlady at the end of a long and tiring day – 'gusta' and 'cansado' were two of my earliest Spanish words.

My first day's experience of learning Spanish illustrates two other points that figure in the literature on early L2 acquisition. One is the sheer fear that beginner learners experience about being swamped by the language, not being able to understand a word and looking a fool. This is exactly how I felt as I sat in the crowded railway carriage surrounded by strange men in berets. Communication apprehension is a well documented phenomenon of language learning (see Gardner and Smythe 1975) and it is not just something that classroom learners experience. It is a very real for naturalistic learners too. This is surely why some learners – and not just children but adults as well – opt for a 'silent period'. But as Krashen (1981) pointed out this does not mean that no learning is taking place providing, of course, that the silent learners are attending to and understanding the language. Sitting in that railway carriage I was silent and I was attending. However, I don't recall learning anything.

What really helped me to learn a few Spanish words that first day was communicative need. I needed to understand what was being said to me or else I would never have got to Santander. I needed to make myself understood. So I needed to be able to say 'Santander' with a pronunciation that could be understood. I needed to work out what 'otraestación' meant. I needed to be able to say 'otra estación' to check that I really did have to get myself to a different station in Bilbao. We are talking here about a particular kind of motivation – the motivation that derives from the need of achieving a communicative goal and the satisfaction that arises from succeeding in doing so. Current theories of motivation talk about the role that the L2 plays in your 'ideal self' or 'ought-to-self' (Dornyei 2005) but this is not what got me started on learning Spanish. Of course these other kinds of motivation may subsequently become very important, especially for classroom learners. But on day one in Spain I was motivated to communicate to survive.

Evelyn Hatch (1978) seems to me to have got it right when she said many years ago 'One learns how to do conversations, one learns how to interact verbally, and out of this interaction syntactic structures are developed' (p. 404). In a very simple way that was what I was doing that first day in Spain back in 1965.

Concluding Comments

It is often said that teachers' beliefs about teaching are formed in large part by their previous experiences of being taught and trying to learn a language. My experiences of language learning Spanish have definitely had an impact on my beliefs about how to teach a language. I was only in Spain for three months but I remember more of my Spanish than my French and German which I studied respectively for four and six years in secondary school and which I passed examinations in with high grades. My Spanish was learnt through communicating (although I did eventually get hold of a Spanish grammar to try to get some grounding in the grammar of the language). Spanish for me was not just an object to be analysed and studied but a tool for living. It seems to me that unless we find ways to teach a language that can produce adequate copies of the kind of experiences I had with Spanish we cannot expect students to learn how to use it as a tool for living. This is the challenge that faces the classroom teacher. It is one of several reasons why I have become an advocate of task-based teaching (see Ellis 2003) – as a way (perhaps the best way) of creating communicative need inside the classroom.

References

Dörnyei, Z. 2005. *The Psychology of the Language Learner: Individual Differences in Second Language Acquisition.* Mahwah, NJ: Lawrence Erlbaum.

Ellis, R. 2003. *Task-based Language Learning and Teaching.* Oxford: Oxford University Press.

Gardner, R. and P. Smythe. 1975. 'Second language acquisition: A social psychological approach'. *Research Bulletin* 332. Department of Psychology, University of Western Ontario, Canada.

Hatch, E. 1978b. 'Discourse analysis and second language acquisition' in E. Hatch (ed.). *Second Language Acquisition.* Rowley, MA: Newbury House.

Klein, W. and C. Perdue. 1997. 'The basic variety (or: Couldn't natural languages be much simpler?)'. *Second Language Research* 13: 301–48.

Krashen, S. 1981. *Second Language Acquisition and Second Language Learning.* Oxford: Pergamon.

Pica, T. 1992. 'The textual outcomes of native speaker–non-native speaker negotiation: What do they reveal about second language learning' in C. Kramsch and S. McConnell-Ginet (eds.). *Text and Context: Cross-disciplinary Perspectives on Language Study.* Lexington, MA: D.C. Heath and Company.

Sjöholm, K. 1976. 'A comparison of the test results in grammar and vocabulary between Finnish- and Swedish-speaking applicants for English' in H. Ringbom and R. Palmberg (eds.). *Errors Made by Finns and Swedish-speaking Finns in the Learning of English.* Åbo, Finland: Department of English, Åbo Akademi. ERIC Report ED 122628.

Chapter 14

Bewitched

A Microethnography of the Culture of Majick in Old Salem

Bud Goodall
Arizona State University

I pause before *The Broom Closet* out of language curiosity and because this is a self-proclaimed "witches shop" in Old Salem Village, Massachusetts, USA,[1] legendary and infamous home to witches both real and imagined, to witch trials real and reenacted,[2] now a postmodern historical site[3] constructed out of a past that never was quite as culturally dressed up and commercially successful as it is now. So I open the door.

During its infamous past, Salem was policed by George Corwin—a thieving money-and-land hungry High Sheriff of Essex County—and, because the church chose its leaders, governed by a corrupt religious zealot named John Hathorne.[4] It was also a village populated by politically frightened and rhetorically inflamed Puritans who, between February 1692 and May 1693 saw 150 people arrested, tortured, and imprisoned after being accused of practicing witchcraft or entering into a pact with the Devil.[5] Eventually, Hathorne and Corwin saw to the hanging of 14 women and 5 men,[6] mostly on the testimony of children who were, according to contemporary explanations, either acting out to gain attention or who were the innocent victims of hallucinations caused by eating rye bread made from grain infected by the fungus *Claviceps purpurea* (the mold from which LSD is derived). The townspeople, cowed by fear and motivated by some combination of greed, jealousy, and religious conviction, contributed to the mass hysteria by supporting the trials, the hangings, and the stoning, as well as by offering testimony against their accused neighbors.

But all that was over three centuries ago. Today, at least at street level, the witch trials are little more than a convenient rhetorical inducement designed to appeal to the interest tourists often have in the happy confluence of history, spectacle, theatre, and commerce.

Once inside the shop, with images of Puritans and witches dancing in my head, I approach a display of wands. These are the prized, hand-made, J. K. Rowling-endorsed Alivan wands,[7] and there are many of them to choose from. As I stand admiring the collection, I am approached by a woman who I take it runs the shop.

"So," I ask, "does the wand choose the wizard or does the wizard choose the wand?" I smile.

She doesn't return my smile. Probably she's heard this line (from Harry Potter) many times before. "*I* choose the wand," she says.

I regard her anew. She is a petite woman, probably in her late 20s or early 30s, dressed in jeans and a black sweater. She exudes an air of seriousness, not play. Perhaps my reference to the Harry Potter line was in some way offensive or bothersome to her.

"I'm a witch," she says, simply.

It's not every day a fellow like me hears a statement like that. Without thinking much about it I reply, "And I'm a wizard."

One eyebrow arches. "Wiccan," she says.

"Rhetorician," I reply, solemnly. "Ph.D. from Penn State years ago, but casting rhetorical spells and narrative enchantments ever since." I smile. "These days I'm an ethnographer."

There is a long pause between us. This scene could play either way. Both of us, I think, sense that.

"Allow me to help *you* choose your wand," she says, moving between me and the display case.

"Certainly," I reply.

She selects a redwood model and explains that it contains the "essence of a unicorn mane hair."

I nod appreciatively. Why not, right?

"Redwood is known to be extremely useful for protection spells as well as to help obtain focus and discipline," she says. Handing me the wand, she continues: "The user of this wand will find complete serenity in the most chaotic of situations."[8]

Was she mocking me? Probably. Or perhaps it was just advanced salesmanship. Or witchery. Hard to say.

We conclude the purchase without more dialogue. I watch as she carefully wraps the redwood wand into an attractive blue velvet satchel and places the satchel into a well-crafted blue box, complete with its "certificate of authenticity." I pay with a Visa. For no good reason, I sign it "Sir Harold, Wizard of Phoenix."

She doesn't notice. Kind of makes a nonverbal point of it.

I realize, only later, that in fact the witch—not me, not the wizard—chose my wand! Clearly, I think to myself, I was bewitched.

* * *

Michael Agar (1994) suggests that "rich points" occur in everyday conversation when differences in cultures emerge from ordinary language use and you suddenly realize "you don't know what's going on" (1994, p. 106).

When this happens—and Agar says it happens all the time—there are various possible responses, ranging from ignoring it to reading it as a sign that the speaker is deficient in some way, or

> you can wonder—wonder why you don't understand, wonder if some other languaculture isn't in play, wonder if how you thought the world worked isn't just one variation on countless themes. If you wonder, at that moment and later as well, you've taken on culture, not as something that "those people" have, but rather as a space between you and them, one that you're involved in as well, one that can be overcome.
>
> (1994, p. 106)

When my Wiccan salesperson said, "I am a witch," I understood the words she spoke but realized that I did not understand their meaning in her world. Similarly, my reply to her "and I am a wizard," complete with the key words following it—Ph.D., rhetorical spells, narrative enchantments, ethnographer—probably provided a similar, yet distinctively different (and probably gendered) rich point for her. For both of us, that micro-exchange of languaculture opened up a space for us to build "new knowledge born of personal experience, a new awareness, a new connection between you and them (sic) that can take any number of shapes. You are building *culture*" (1994, p. 107).

It is also true that our brief conversation—our exchange of languacultures—is laced with gendered issues of rhetorical power, authority, and control. The utterance "I am a witch" is clearly a statement of gendered authority (hers is a witch shop, after all), but it is also an exertion of power aimed at controlling the situation and narrative. My response is a playful attempt to counter her authority with resources of my own—the advanced degree, the terms drawn from magic (e.g., "spells," "enchantments"), and my professional status (i.e., "ethnographer"). Taken together, these terms constitute a newly shared culture, but one defined and delineated by cultural and gendered differences.

Her statement "*I* choose the wand," coupled with her seemingly clerk-like "Allow me to help *you* choose your wand," followed by her successful selection of a wand for my purchase is a clever inversion of our constructed status positions, whereby the person, as Kenneth Burke (1989) expresses it, once "down" is by symbolic action transfigured into a one "up" position of power. In short, rhetorically and practically I am the one "bewitched" into doing her bidding while—and perhaps because—I content myself with the business of maintaining the illusion that I am, in fact, as a wizard not only equal to her status as a witch, but moreover that I am making the purchase decision for myself. Which didn't happen. Nor did I recognize that it didn't happen until later, when, as Agar puts it, I was left "wonder[ing] if how you thought the world worked isn't just one variation on countless themes" (1994, p. 106).

Notes

1 http://www.salem.org/
2 For a quick and historically accurate account, see: http://en.wikipedia.org/wiki/Salem_witch_trials
3 The town of Salem celebrates its witch history in the recreated Salem village. It also hires college students to populate the streets in period costumes and pays actors to perform street theatre reenactments of the arrest of supposed witches. Daily reenactments of the witch trials are also available. Salem is an example of Jean Baudrillard's concept of "simulacra," particularly as it is represented in his book, *America* (1988).
4 Grandfather of Nathaniel Hawthorne, who inserted the "w" into the family name as penance for the witch trials.
5 Generally this "pact" meant signing their name into the Devil's book.
6 Five children who were also accused of consorting with the Devil died in prison. Corwin also stoned to death two dogs for being in league with the Devil and one 80-year-old man named Giles Corey. The elderly man, however, placed a curse "on the blood" of the High Sheriff and all who would come after him to that office. To date, every High Sheriff of Essex County has died in office from a heart ailment or blood disease (see http://www.hauntedsalem.com/hauntinghistory/gilescorey.html).
7 http://www.alivans.com/?gclid=COX6y9uF15UCFSAUagodhyPNXA
8 As it turns out, that is precisely the language contained on the Alivan website to describe this particular wand.

References

Agar, M. (1994). *Language shock: Understanding the culture of conversation.* New York: William Morrow/Quill.

Baudrillard, J. (1988). *America.* London: Verso.

Burke, K. (1989). *On symbols and society.* Chicago: University of Chicago Press.

Chapter 15

Am I that Name?

Stacy Holman Jones
University of South Florida

Autobiographical Statement: Waiting to Know

As an undergraduate, I didn't know who I wanted to be, who I wanted to become. True to form (or was it content?), I was an Interdisciplinary Studies major. This designation—this name—was a placeholder for the undecided, the emergent, the *possible* (and not, as I assured my parents, a flimsy legitimizing discourse that covered over underachievement, failure, and lack of choice). This name was a space of waiting—for something to come together, for something to happen. My scholarly interests were spaces where waiting takes place in language—in politics, in journalistic portraits, in story and verse. These were spaces where possibility is made in writing, though not in some utopian, fixed sense of an inscription that makes something tangible or something *real*; object and objectified. They were spaces of possibility where "actual lines of potential that a something coming together calls to mind and sets in motion" (Stewart, 2007, p. 3). Mine was a waiting in language as "becoming, difference, encounter, motion, creativity" (LeVan, 2007, p. 50). Process, rather than product, to use the cliché, though I didn't know it then. I was waiting.

Narrative: Writer, Feminist, Performer, Scholar; Am I that Name?

Writer

I see the invitation, written in red: *Please see me.* Never mind his comments on my short story. Never mind his encouragement, his gentle prodding, his attention to my work in words. I was being summoned to his office. I was in *trouble*, though at the time I didn't think of trouble as something positive, something affectively *good* in the sense of subversion of whatever norms I might have violated. And, indeed, I know I have violated . . . something. I just don't know what.

I arrive early and lean against the cinderblock wall outside his office. I have never been upstairs to the faculty offices. I spend many of my days in the basement of this building, reading the poetry and short stories of others and offering up my own. Until now, there was no invitation, no reason to go upstairs. The door opens and his head emerges, swiveling around until his gaze lands on me, on my body pushed up against the wall.

"Hi. I didn't know you were here. Come in."

I follow him into the office, which is no bigger than a closet and crammed full with books and a massive desk piled high with paper. He inches around the desk and sits behind the stacks of paper, which rise high on either side of him. I take the chair opposite him, pulling my backpack around my body and hugging it to my chest. "You wrote on my paper that I should come and see you."

"Yes. I wanted to talk to you about something."

"I know my story wasn't finished. I didn't quite get where I wanted to go, but I didn't want to hand it in late."

"Your paper is fine. Quite inventive, really. I've made what I think are some good suggestions for revision. That's not what I wanted to see you about, though."

"Oh?"

"No. I want to talk to you about graduate school. Have you thought about it?"

"Graduate school? Um, no. I haven't thought about it."

"Well, you should. You're a wonderful writer, very smart."

"I am?"

"Yes. Didn't you know that?"

"No."

"Well, you are. And you should know."

He said more that day, about graduate programs he thought would be a good fit with my interests and my work, about how to prepare for the GRE and request letters of recommendation, about ordering transcripts and meeting deadlines, though I don't recall any of these details. What struck me then, what strikes me now, was what *happened* in our conversation. In a moment, in the movement of his pen on the page and in our brief conversation, he waltzed me an imaginative *what if*. What if I was a writer? What if that is my name?

Feminist

I think about what the professor said many times over the next few weeks. What if I did go to graduate school? What if I did become a writer? I carry those names, those identities—graduate student, writer—home. I keep them close, not wanting to say them out loud. But why? I suppose I am afraid of their becoming: desired, within reach, true. I keep quiet. Though being there—being home—is not a silent space. It is filled with music and voices, boisterous arguments over who we are, what we are doing, who we want to become. The man I am living with struggles over whether to be a college student or a musician or a small-time criminal. I struggle over my attachments to ideas and to words and to him.

We struggle over nearly everything—friends, the dishes, whose music will dominate the soundtrack of our life together. He plays his music—the Specials, R.E.M., and the Grateful Dead—*loudly*, unapologetically. I play my music—Prince, Sting, and Billie Holiday—quietly, reasonably. He teaches himself how to play the guitar. I teach myself how to write. He sings. I compose.

One day he says, "I learned how to play 'Ship of Fools.' It's your song."

I ask him to play it for me. As he sings, he stares at me. His gaze and his words cut right through me. "I would slave to learn the way to sink your ship of fools."[1]

One day I say, "I want to go to graduate school."

He looks up from the music spread out in front of him and says, "What for?"

"It's something I've been thinking about for a while. One of my professors told me I was a writer. I want to see if that's true."

He looked away and began to play that song, again. Ship of fools.[2] I don't remember what I thought or what I did just then. I do know that I stayed in a home full of noise and struggle, full of scorn and jealousy, full of biting words and blows, rather than set off on my own, alone and adrift. I also know that it was months and then years before I thought of graduate school, and of writing, again.

And when I finally begin graduate school, I spend years writing through that painful and failed relationship, trying to understand why I stayed when I knew I should have left. Why I continued to desire someone who wanted me hurt, small, and bruised. Why I continued to listen to someone who took me for a fool.

One day, Mary, a woman who also waited to go to graduate school, a woman who was also working to understand the choices she had made, hands me a journal article. She says, "Read this."[3]

I look at her, my gaze asking the question I do not utter.

"You'll know. When you read it, you'll know."

The essay, "Numbering the Hairs of Our Heads: Male Social Control and the All-Seeing Male God" by Anne Marie Hunter, was inspired by the author's experience working with battered women and Michel Foucault's writing about surveillance. I underline Hunter's words about how women are watched—what they wear, what they eat, the shapes their bodies take. They are visually vulnerable, both in their own homes and in a social world that looks at, around, and right through them (Hunter, 1992, p. 8). And then I get to Hunter's explication of Foucault's Panopticon. I underline one whole paragraph and part of a second:

> The Panopticon is a nineteenth-century model for a prison designed by Jeremy Bentham. The prison comprises a central guard tower surrounded by a circle of one-person cells. The cells have windows in both the outside and inside walls that allow light to pass through the cell from back to front. The guards in the central tower can thus see every action of each prisoner in silhouette at all times. The inmates do not know when they are being watched, but they know that they can be watched at any moment. The visibility of the inmates and the invisibility of the guards is key to the functioning of the system as a whole.
>
> In the Panopticon, Foucault found a model for his concept of disciplinary power, a way to illustrate how social control has been embodied and carried out in the modern era, a "mechanism of power reduced to an ideal form." (p. 14)

I read the paragraphs again. The air in the room changes. I am pulsing with recognition. I hadn't thought about women's visibility in precisely this way before, though I know now I will never think about sight again without wondering how women are visions, surfaces, sites always already looked at (Hunter, 1992, p. 22). I also know that I will never think about sound—about music—again without wondering how women are speaking, singing, and calling out as subjects always already known and (mis)understood. Already named and dismissed: woman, mother, feminist. As Desdemona, branded a whore and doomed to fall asks, as women in their indeterminate, impossible categorization have been asking for centuries: *Am I that name?* (Shakespeare, 4.2.181; Riley, 2003, p. 114). In my work in graduate school, in my work as a writer, I begin to story how the visual and aural surveillance and self-policing, how the faulty foundational subjugation, how the misunderstanding and underestimation of women, might be *otherwise*.

Performer

When I finally do begin graduate school, I enroll in an MA program in Communication. Although I am becoming a writer, I am not ready to call myself that name. In my MA program, where I study organizational culture and qualitative methods, my advisor tells me over and over: "You are a writer." I begin to believe him. I also tell myself over and over: "You are a feminist." And because I believe this, I begin to live differently.

I decide to pursue my doctorate in organizational studies and enroll in a top program in that field.[4] When I look through the course offerings my first semester, I keep coming back, over and over again, to a course in the performance studies curriculum titled, "Reading and Performing." I am intrigued. I want to learn about performance studies and about theories and practices of reading (which necessarily imply writing). But performing? I am not ready for that. And yet, curious, I attend the first class meeting and I am hooked.

I ask to meet with the professor to discuss the performance question. I arrive at his office and raise my hand to knock on the door. I sigh and drop my arm. I press my forehead against the cool cinderblock wall next to the doorframe. "What did I get myself into?" I wonder. "Too late," I mutter to myself. I knock.

I enter and slump in the chair next to his desk, piled high with books and paper. "I'm not sure what to do for my first performance," I say. "I'm not sure what a performance even *is*. The only performance I've ever been in involved me 'playing' the baby Jesus in the church Christmas pageant."

"That's an auspicious beginning," he says, his laugh warming the room.

I say, "Maybe I should've given up performing then," and this time we both laugh.

We discuss my choice of text, William Carpenter's (1993) "Girl Writing a Letter," a smart and funny poem that contains the lines, "The thief knows what he's doing/He has a PhD" (p. 125). I leave the professor's office with some good ideas and a small measure of confidence. And then, at home, the noisy collision of voices has me feeling defeated and afraid. There are too many characters, too many stories, too many attitudes to perform all at once. And then there are the voices in my head: "You can't do this. You don't know what you want. You're no performer."

On the day of the performance, I sit at the seminar table, palms sticky and throat tight. I wait my turn, watching each of my colleagues deliver thoughtful, artful performances. My vision begins to blur and fear and criticisms are ringing in my ears. And then the professor calls my name. I stand, steady myself, and begin.

I don't remember the rest of the performance or returning to my seat. I don't remember the rest of the class session, at least not clearly. I go home, silent, questioning. Was my performance any good? Was it a performance at all? I am not sure. I don't know. I am restless for the rest of the week. When I sleep, I dream I am standing behind a curtain, waiting to perform. I wait and wait and wait, but the curtain never opens.

On Friday afternoon, I see the professor in the hallway outside of his office. He says, "Nice work the other day. Great poem. Great performance. I thought you said you weren't a performer."

"I'm not."

He laughs, and the music of his voice bounces down the hallway. "Oh you—*you*—are a performer."

Scholar

I perform my writing at a scholarly conference. I am participating in a panel representing ethnographic investigations. After each panelist reports on research conducted in the "field"—barbershops, women's quilting bees, and beauty pageants—I share a story I've written about my becoming as a feminist in song, literature, and writing. I share what these experiences might teach me—teach us, a community of scholars—about doing ethnography.[5] I elect to do this: focus on the story, the personal narrative instead of the analysis clumsily tacked on to the end of my essay. I say my work is autoethnography, though I don't know if that term gets at what I'm doing, at what my writing is doing. If autoethnography seeks to "extract meaning from experience rather than to depict experience exactly as it was lived" (Bochner, 2000, p. 270), if it presents a "visible narrative presence" while "engaging in dialogue with informants beyond the self" in order to improve our "theoretical understandings of broader social phenomena" (Anderson, 2006, p. 375), I don't know if my words are enough. It's not that extracting meaning from experience or generating theoretical understandings of social phenomena aren't important. They are. It's just that I don't know what I know about my work. It seems more in process, more liminal and up for grabs, than some kind of knowledge-generating machine. It seems more a performance—more emergent, more artistic and experimental (Gingrich-Philbrook, 2005, p. 301)—than a pronouncement. If, though, autoethnography is an orientation to *writing* scholarship, a relational and perspectival *approach*, rather than a method, specific set of procedures, or mode of representation (Gingrich-Philbrook, 2005, p. 298), I think what I've said is right, true. It *is* autoethnography in that it works on the politics of knowledge and experience; pays attention to the performative embodiment of identities, discourses, and subject positions; and enacts "a way of seeing and being [that] challenges, contests, or endorses the official, hegemonic ways of seeing and representing the other" (Denzin, 2006, p. 422). But I don't say any of these things. I say that my writing is autoethnographic and I tell my story and I sit down.

When she gets to me, the respondent says, "Lovely writing, just lovely. Beyond that, I'm not sure I have anything to offer. I'm not sure how what you've done contributes to our scholarly conversation." She "couldn't, or wouldn't comment" (Pollock, 2007, p. 241). Perhaps she assumed my use of first-person narrative was a power play: that it made my writing exempt from critique, from engagement and dialogue, from being considered scholarship (Pollock, 2007, pp. 241–242). I wanted to say, that the respondent "chicken[ed] out, refusing to be part of the relational drama initiated in [my] breach in scholarly decorum, scared off in part by the proximity of the body"—my body—that "emerges into the breach" (Pollock, 2007, p. 242). But I didn't know this then. Performance binds bodies and words in space and time, throwing into motion a relational becoming that, while bounded and bonded by power and attempts to control meaning, enacts identities in process, full of possibilities. I didn't know then that the words and the worlds I was making weren't founded in an evidentiary logic of experience or in an appeal for generating and documenting certain knowledge of or on a subject (Gingrich-Philbrook, 2005, p. 304). I don't know that now.

After the panel, after my failed performance of scholar, I thought a lot about what I wanted to call myself and what kinds of relationships I wanted to have. I thought and I wrote and I searched for my people—other thinkers and writers and performers and feminists and scholars who were putting language to becoming and enacting the unforeseen (Pollock, 2007, p. 247; Gingrich-Philbrook, 2005, p. 305). I don't always know whether I've succeeded in my efforts, though these days when I go to a conference and perform my writing, I am no longer afraid, no longer feeling beaten and bruised, no longer wondering, am I that name?

Commentary: Waiting to Know

I don't remember my first performance—the one in which I was the baby Jesus in the Christmas pageant at my church. I don't remember when I first wrote about that performance as a way into the performances that have followed. Such searches for origins are, ultimately, unsatisfying, unbecoming to my narrative on becoming. Still, I search for knowledge about how that performance shapes me, how it helps me on the way to naming who I am, even if such names are shimmering and volatile markers of difference in the spaces of possibility. And in my search for that story, I came upon another story, one as shifting and changing as my own, no matter how much I want that story to hold still. It is the story of how God says, "I am that I am," to Moses when asked for his name. This translates from Hebrew, which doesn't confine language to a past-present-future logic, but instead asks us to think and know in terms of what is possible, in the process of becoming ("I am that I am," 2008, para. 1). A very different sort of movement and ending than that of the unfortunate Desdemona, than that of the ship of fools set adrift, than that of the thief stealing what he believes belongs to him. Does performance in the Christmas pageant and the many performances and stories that followed move me any closer to being, to the divine, or to knowledge? Do my performances and stories take me closer to making a name I can call my own? I don't know what I don't know. I am in process and I am still waiting , though I no longer wait to know who I will be or become. I am on my way, simultaneously process and passage (LeVan, 2007, p. 63). My language, both in learning and in use, is a movement of becomings (LeVan , 2007, p. 64).

Notes

1 "Ship of Fools," lyrics by Robert Hunter, music by Jerry Garcia, recorded and performed by the Grateful Dead.
2 A ship of fools references Sebastian Brant's 1494 *Das Narrenschiff,* a moralistic poem in which 110 sins and vices are undertaken by a series of individual fools ("Stulifera Navis (The Ship of Fools)," 2008, para. 1). A recurring theme in Brant's text is a ship that transports these sinners to Narragonia, the island of fools ("Stultifera Navis," 2008, para. 2). Michel Foucault references the ship of fools (with attention to a Hieronymus Bosch painting (c. 1490–1500) in his book *Madness and civilization,* in which the insane—the unknowing, the unable to learn and to be called by a civilized name—were pushed to the edges of society, tucked behind walls, and set adrift in boats ("Madness and Civilization," 2008, para. 2).
3 This story is based on one that I included in my 2007 book, *Torch singing: Performing resistance and desire from Billie Holiday to Edith Piaf.*
4 This story is based on one included in my 2005 essay, "Autoethnography: Making the personal political."
5 This story suggests my 2002 essay, "The way we were, are, and might be: torch singing as autoethnography."

References

Anderson, L. (2006). Analytic autoethnography. *Journal of Contemporary Ethnography, 35*(4), 373–395.

Bartky, S.L. (1991). Foucault, femininity, and the modernization of patriarchal power. *Femininity and domination: Studies in the phenomenology of oppression* (63–82). New York: Routledge, 1991.

Bochner, A.P. (2000). Criteria against ourselves. *Qualitative Inquiry, 6*(2), 266–272.

Carpenter, W. (1993) Girl writing a letter. *Iowa Review* 23(2), 125.

Denzin, N.K. (2006). Analytic autoethnography, or déjà vu all over again. *Journal of Contemporary Ethnography, 35*(4), 419–428.

Foucault, M. (1988). *Madness and civilization: A history of insanity in the age of reason.* (R. Howard, Trans.). New York: Vintage.

Gingrich–Philbrook, C. (2005). Autoethnography's family values: Easy access to compulsory experiences. *Text and Performance Quarterly* 25(4), 297–314.

Holman Jones, S. (2002). The way we were, are, and might be: Torch singing as autoethnography. In A.P. Bochner & C. Ellis (Eds.), *Ethnographically speaking* (44–56). Walnut Creek, CA: AltaMira Press.

——. (2005). Autoethnography: Making the personal political. In N.K. Denzin & Y.S. Lincoln (Eds.), *The SAGE handbook of qualitative research* (3rd ed.) (763–791). Thousand Oaks, CA: Sage.

——. (2007). *Torch singing: Performing resistance and desire from Billie Holiday to Edith Piaf.* Lanham, MD: AltaMira Press.

Hunter, A.M. (1992). Numbering the hairs of our heads: Male social control and the all-seeing male God. *Journal of Feminist Studies in Religion* 8(2), 7–23.

Hunter, R. & Garcia, J.J. (1995) Ship of fools. *From the Mars hotel.* New York: Arista.

"I am that I am." (2009, January 29). In *Wikipedia, the free encyclopedia.* Retrieved February 2, 2009 from http://en.wikipedia.org/wiki/I_am_that_I_am

LeVan, M. (2007). Aesthetics of encounter: Variations on translation in Deleuze. *International Journal of Translation.* 19(1), 51–66.

"Madness and civilization." (2009, January 29). In *Wikipedia, the free encyclopedia.* Retrieved February 2, 2009 from http://en.wikipedia.org/wiki/Madness_and_Civilization

Pollock, D. (2007). The performative "I." *Cultural Studies (Critical Methodologies)* 7, 239–255.

Riley, D. (2003). *Am I that name? Feminism and the category of women in history.* Minneapolis: University of Minnesota Press.

Shakespeare, W. (2003). *Othello* (2nd ed.) (N. Sanders, Ed.). New York: Cambridge. (Original work published 1622.)

Stewart, K. (2007). *Ordinary affects.* Durham, NC: Duke University Press.

"Stultifera Navis (The Ship of Fools): The Medieval Satire of Sebastian Brant." (2002). Retrieved February 2, 2009 from http://info.lib.uh.edu/sca/digital/ship/introduction.html

Chapter 16

English and Me

My Language Learning Journey

Angel Lin
City University of Hong Kong

As far as my memory goes, the earliest scenario I can remember of English and me is a four-year-old kindergarten girl learning the alphabet by heart—she rote-memorized the order of the letters by rehearsing aloud the letters in the alphabetic order again and again. Growing up in a very poor family in the 1970s of Hong Kong, she and her three elder brothers and one elder sister didn't have any toys. The first toy she got was a small red model car that her father gave her when she came first in her school exam.

English in the kindergarten years wasn't too difficult for her—she spent time memorizing the spellings of words and the alphabet and could reproduce them in the exam. English was just one of the subjects she needed to do (and to do well) in school. She didn't particularly like it or dislike it—she held a similar attitude towards other school subjects. All these were just tasks to finish to get a good grade in the exam to report back to her parents to get their praise and rewards. She could do most of the school tasks well as she applied herself to them seriously and diligently both at school and at home—treating them as her duties and work. What she enjoyed most, as far as she can remember now, seemed to be the moment when she could look at her parents' approving and praising smiles when she got a good exam result to report to them.

I grew up in a home and community where few had the linguistic resources to use English at all, and even if anyone had, she/he would find it extremely socially inappropriate to speak English. My chances for learning and using English thus hinged entirely on the school. However, I lived in a poor government-subsidized apartment-building complex (called "public housing estate") in the rural area (the New Territories) in Hong Kong, where schools were mostly newly put up in the 1960s and they neither had adequate English resources (e.g., staff well-versed in English) nor a well-established English-speaking and English-teaching-and-learning tradition or school culture.

My parents were manual workers. In the 1960s–1970s in Hong Kong, although they labored long hours every day, their salaries were still so small that they had difficulties putting food on the table for their five children. For an extended period of time, we had to depend on the small amount of "relief rice" rationed out monthly from the government's social welfare department. My parents, therefore, put all their hopes and expectations in their children: illiterate in English as they were, they did not fail to be keenly aware of the fact that their children's future (e.g., a better-paying job) depends on doing well in school, and doing well in school depends on mastering the English language in the Hong Kong schooling system.

They have passed on this work ethic to their children. We were urged day and night to "study hard" and especially to study English hard though they themselves did not have the slightest idea as to how one could learn English well! I remember that when I was in

Primary 3 (Grade 3), I was very frustrated by my English "story book" which was full of difficult English words that I did not understand. My teacher then typically read the story once and I could not remember how to pronounce those words afterwards. The whole page was opaque and frustrating to me! I was very frightened then because small as I was (eight years old), I did not fail to realize that I was not going to do well in English. At that time, school teachers generally appeared to be rather formal and distant from students and I did not dare to bother them: for there were far too many difficult words (well, "difficult" to me), at least three or four of them in one line, and I felt too ashamed to ask. And even if they had told me how to pronounce the words, and what the words meant, I would have soon forgotten about them as there were just far too many new things to memorize, especially the difficult sounds of the words.

At Primary 4 (Grade 4), there came a fresh graduate from the College of Education to our school, and he became our English teacher. His teaching methods were very different from our former teachers. He was friendly and approachable and talked to us explicitly about our need to increase our English vocabulary. He asked us to keep a "rough work book" where we put down all new words or new sentences exemplifying a new grammatical point. He gave us ample practice with word pronunciations and meanings. He explained everything clearly. He also taught us how to use an English dictionary. I have started to pick up some confidence and interest in learning English since then.

At Primary 6 (Grade 6), another recent College of Education graduate, Miss Law, came to our school and took up our English classes. She taught us those funny symbols that they use in the dictionaries to indicate the words' pronunciations. I learnt that these funny symbols were called "international phonetic symbols," and I took a strong interest in them. This interest was, however, not shared by most of my classmates. They found them difficult and boring to learn and did not quite learn any of them at all. It might have been luck on my part, as I seemed to have a special aptitude for these things. I listened carefully to everything the teacher said in lesson and wrote down all her examples in my notebook. At home, I started to play around with different combinations of these symbols and to try to pronounce new words in the dictionary by sounding out these symbols. I began to have a new tool to learn English on my own: the English dictionary can help me to learn new words (my parents had squeezed out some money to buy me an English dictionary as I had told them it would help my English learning). I started to go to the public library to borrow English story books and I conscientiously looked up all the new words and practiced pronouncing them. I kept a vocabulary book where I wrote down the meanings, pronunciations (recorded in phonetic symbols) and example sentences of the words (copied from the dictionary) and I read it whenever I had time. During that time, I wished my friends would do the same because I found myself very odd and lonely doing these things all by myself, but they found it too boring and too much work and jokingly said that I was a "jyu-syu-chuhng" (i.e., a "book-worm," a nerd). I often had to beg my best friend many times before she would go with me to the public library.

Before 1978, all children in Hong Kong were required to sit for a series of standardized tests on English, Chinese and Math at the end of their primary school career (i.e., at the end of Grade 6). These tests together were called "the Secondary School Entrance Examination" (SSEE). It would determine whether a child could continue to study in a government-funded public secondary school as well as which secondary school she/he could enter (e.g., English-medium or Chinese-medium schools; well-established, prestigious schools in the urban area or new schools in the rural area). My eldest brother did not get good results in this public examination (especially in the subject of English) and our family was too poor to pay the expensive tuition fees of private secondary schools, and so, he had to go to the urban area to find work at the age of 12. I could still remember the sadness he had on his face the day he got his examination results. For all I knew, he had always "studied hard" though he was often busy helping out with household chores and looking after us. Without any secondary school education, the kind of work he got was harsh and minimal-paying. However, he never gave up learning English. He went to work during the day and saved up money to go to a private evening school which specially taught English. When he came home on weekends, my parents would ask us to bring to him anything we did not understand at school and ask him to tutor us. To me, he was a superb brother and mentor.

During primary 5 and 6 (the last two years before SSEE), our school asked us to purchase thick supplementary exercise books for the three subjects examined in SSEE: Chinese, English and Math. We did a lot of drills/exercises in these books to prepare ourselves for the exam format and content of SSEE. I remember that every time before we did an exercise or a group of exercises on a grammatical topic/structure, Miss Law would first write on the blackboard the grammatical rule and explained the rule with several sentences as examples. Then she would ask us to do the exercise on this rule/structure in 270. Each time, I listened carefully to Miss Law's explanation and illustration of the rule and I understood her clear and systematic explanations (by the way, she explained in our mother tongue and I could fully understand her grammatical explanations). Then as I did the exercises in 270, I would think of the rule and applied it when I did the exercise (i.e., I didn't just mindlessly or blindly follow a pattern in order to finish an exercise, but I consciously thought of the rule as I was doing the exercise). Although these exercises must appear to be quite mechanical and non-communicative nowadays, I could benefit from them at that time because, I guess, I was a good deductive learner—I could start from rules and apply them in exercises and I didn't find them boring. Those drills in the basic grammar of English had laid in me a firm foundation in the grammar of English, which has been very important for the rest of my learning and teaching career.

When it came to my turn to take the SSEE, I got very good results. My class teacher had urged me to choose a well-established, prestigious English secondary school in the urban area and tried to contact my parents to persuade them about this. However, my parents decided that for a young girl of 12 to commute four hours daily between our home and the urban area in order to attend one of those prestigious schools was too much of a worry to them, and they refused to come to school to talk to my class teacher. They decided to choose the best school available in our area.

I adapted to secondary school life quite smoothly. The first day in school with the school assembly addressed by the Principal in English in the big school hall was a bit scary to me as I struggled to follow what the principal said. But in the classrooms, teachers readily used Cantonese and my reading and writing skills in English were good and I had no problems following the lessons and textbooks except the History textbook, which was full of difficult vocabulary. However, unlike when I was in Primary 3, I didn't despair and I would spend hours looking up all the new words in the dictionary and write down their pronunciations (in phonetic symbols), meanings and examples in a vocabulary notebook and read them whenever I had time. My history textbook had become a rich source of vocabulary learning and soon I could catch up with the history lessons and assignments. In particular, I enjoyed reading the history and civilization of the Greeks, the Spartans, the Romans and so on. I often wondered what life was like in those times in those places, and when I looked at the drawings of castles and soldiers in the history book, they seemed to have brought me to another land full of adventures and discoveries.

My classmates were generally school-oriented and the classroom learning atmosphere was generally good. I had made friends with some girls—they were keen learners and we would discuss our homework and also joined extra-curricular activities together, e.g., the photography club, the guitar class, the girl guides, and the bridge club. Some time in our first year of secondary school, the girls in my circle began to develop a hobby of writing to pen-pals both in Hong Kong and overseas. I had pen-pals from all over the world: England, Canada, the US, Austria and Germany. In my circle of girl-friends, having pen-pals had become a topic and practice of common interest and we would talk about our pen-pals and shared our excitement about trading letters, postcards, photos, and small gifts with our pen-pals; we'd also show one another pictures of our pen-pals. We'll share things like different kinds of beautiful letter pads and envelopes, and about what to write to our pen-pals, etc. Although there wasn't a pen-pal club, we had in a way formed our own informal circle of pen-pal-interest group (without having such a name and formal structure, of course). It's a spontaneous "community of practice" (Lave & Wenger, 1991) that had emerged from our own activities and interests. One interesting feature about our practice, now that I'm thinking about it, is that we write in English to our pen-pals, even to those in Hong Kong (who were, like us, Chinese students). We seemed to frown upon writing *in Chinese* to pen-pals in Hong Kong as that would make our activity less "high-level"—we didn't actually say or use those words but there seemed to be a kind of tacit understanding among us that writing to pen-pals in English was a healthy, good hobby that's acceptable to parents and teachers, that we would take pride in when talking about it, and that would improve our English proficiency while we're having excitement and fun getting to know new friends in different places.

I also started to write my own private diary in English every day about that time. I started this habit when a pen-pal sent me a diary book as my birthday present and suggested writing diary as a worthwhile activity to me. I chose to write my diary in English because someone had told me that finding a chance to use English daily would improve one's English. Although I had started off this habit with an instrumental motivation, later on I found that I could write my diary faster and more comfortably in English than in Chinese—for one thing, the Chinese characters are more complicated and take longer to write; but more importantly, I felt that I could write my feelings more freely when I wrote in English—less inhibition and reservation—I seemed to have found a tool that gave me more freedom to express my innermost fears, worries, anger, conflicts or excitement, hopes, expectations, likes and dislikes (e.g., anger with parents or teachers, or a troubling quarrel with a friend at times) without constraint or inhibition—as if this foreign language had opened up a new, personal space (a "third space," so to speak), for me to more freely express all those difficult emotions and experiences (typical?) of an adolescent growing up, without feeling the sanctions of the adult world (in my analysis now: I guess these adult sanctions were very much intertwined with my first language, which was largely the language of my daily world at that time). I guess I was creating an expanded self in English, and English seemed to provide me with the additional resources I need to explore myself in a somewhat different manner, in a somewhat different value system, one that appeared to be less prohibiting than my native language in some areas, for instance, in the area of explicitly articulating one's emotions like anger.

At that time, I had also developed a very strong and close friendship with Gretchen, my pen-pal in Milwaukee, U.S.A. I would write and share with her most of my innermost feelings, troubles, worries, hopes and fears that I wouldn't tell even my best friend in school. She would do the same. We pledged that we would be true friends to each other "forever." We pledged to each other that we would write a letter to each other every day.

English, it seems, had opened up a totally new space for me to express and entrust my secrets and innermost feelings—I felt safe to confide in Gretchen, and to my diary. I also felt that English had provided me with a tool to broaden myself, to reach out to new friends in new lands, to invent and recreate for myself a somewhat different self from the one my parents know. It gave me excitement when new and lasting (lasting it seemed at least at that time) friendships across cultural and geographical boundaries were formed, and it gave me satisfying feelings like those that an adventurer would have exploring into a new land and new culture.

Critical Reflection

However, when I think of all that had happened, I realize that my own chances for socioeconomic advancement seem to have hinged largely on a certain exceptional re-patterning of social and institutional arrangements. Although individual hard work is necessary, individual hard work and sacrifice alone do not count much. For all the hard work in the world, I would not have been able to develop my interest in and ability to learn English, had there not been some well-trained and English-conversant teachers who were willing to teach in a rural school, and provided me with access to some English linguistic capital. For all my hard work, I did not manage to attend one of those well-established, prestigious English-speaking schools in the urban area because of the extremely prohibitive distance constraint imposed by my rural residential location. My own personal history has led me to realize that certain social and institutional structures impose strong constraints on a child's opportunities for bettering her/his life quite independent of her/his efforts and industry. For someone coming from a background like mine, the chances for socioeconomic advancement are slim even with lots of individual hard work. These social and institutional arrangements constrain the child's opportunities for socioeconomic advancement by denying or limiting their access to English linguistic and cultural resources.

It would not be too much of an exaggeration to say that success in learning and mastering English for a school child in Hong Kong impacts significantly on her/his academic success and social mobility, and very often the student's own self-worth directly or indirectly depends on it. We may be justified to call it the "language of self-worth." Notwithstanding its being the mother tongue of only a minority in Hong Kong, English is both the language of power and the language of educational and socio-economic advancement. It constitutes the dominant symbolic resource in the symbolic market (Bourdieu, 1991) in Hong Kong.

The symbolic market is embodied and enacted in the many key situations (e.g., educational settings, job settings) in which symbolic resources (e.g., certain types of linguistic skills, cultural knowledge, specialized knowledge and skills, etc.) are demanded of social actors if they want to gain access to valuable social, educational and eventually material resources (Bourdieu, 1991). For instance, a Hong Kong student must have adequate English resources, in addition to subject matter knowledge and skills, to enter and succeed in the English-medium professional training programmers of medicine, architecture, legal studies, etc. in order to earn the English-accredited credentials to enter these high-income professions. The symbolic market is therefore not a metaphor, but one with transactions that have material and social consequences for individuals.

Where do I stand now? A lot has happened. From 1991–1996 I got the Commonwealth scholarship to study for a Ph.D. in education at the Ontario Institute for Studies in Education (OISE), University of Toronto. Living and studying in Canada had broadened my horizons and I had made friends with people from different places. Everything had become "real"—I was really there, making friends in English with people, crossing cultural and national boundaries, and I felt good about this—it was, in a sense, a material realization of my pen-pal paper world I built and created for myself in my adolescence—all with the help of, and in, English. I felt that I was not just an "Asian," a "Chinese or a "Hongkongese" (though people in general will still identify and classify me with such labels). I felt that I had been able to develop an identity that's broader than just being Hongkongese or Chinese, but as a human being reaching out to other fellow human beings, forming friendships above and across cultural and ethnic lines; different, yet not an OTHER. I also began to love reading poems and literature in English (and even ventured to write some poems in English). Yes, I speak English with an accent, but I promise myself that I'll resist it when occasions arise where some people might try to make me feel ashamed of my accent, to feel that I'm an OTHER. And I'll say to them: I am like you, but I'm not really you, or: No, I'm not you, but I am like you (Trinh T. Min-ha, 1990). Like what Trinh Min-ha says: there's an OTHER within every I; and perhaps I can also say this too: there's an English OTHER within a Chinese I, or equally true, a Chinese OTHER within an English I.

Coda

Now back in Hong Kong as a university teacher, I have lived a hectic life of work—not much time left for the use and enjoyment of English in leisure. But whenever I hear my students express worries about their English proficiency, I also notice that they have had a very different relationship with English than that I have developed with English over the years. I am still trying to find ways to help them stop seeing English as only a subject and a barrier, but as a friend who would open up new spaces, new challenges and new lands for them, both socioculturally and intellectually. Yet I know I had been privileged with some good teachers in my primary and secondary schools, and fortunate to have joined in a circle of friends where the practice of writing in English to pen-pals emerged during my adolescent years. Yet, today, I'm agonized, seeing that many students have such an unpleasant experience with English. Perhaps it's like how I felt when I was frustrated by the difficult English vocabulary in my textbook in Primary 3. Perhaps they need some skills and strategies to break it through. But perhaps, more importantly, they need to develop a new relationship with English, and find new identities for themselves that are more than just "Hong Kong Chinese who need English for exams." English, as I have known it for years, is not and should not be seen as the language of only those people living in or coming from "English-speaking countries."

English, in its diverse accents, should be accessible to anyone who wants to use it. English should also allow itself to be enriched, hybridized, and inter-penetrated and inter-illuminated by people living in different parts of the world.

How do I help my students to turn English from an enemy to a friend, to make use of this medium to express, expand and, possibly, enrich their lives, to transform or hybridize their current identities, to enter into a new world of possibilities as well as relationships with other cultures and peoples in the world? To me, this is a life-long research and practice question to embark on. English, it seems, has to become a friend first, to become a friend to think with, a friend to feel with, and a life-long friend, or else it'll become an insurmountable barrier and enemy in life, because like it or not, we're living in a world where the socioeconomic and political forces have made English important to our life chances, and where our relationship with English to a great extent influences our position and place in this world. We have to be fully aware of the power of English and its gate-keeping functions, fully aware of *how* it gets its power over us, and yet re-appropriating it, hybridizing it, with our own accents, and ultimately to own it. Perhaps the cyber age in the new millennium presents new spaces, new media, and new possibilities for experimenting with new forms of English, new hybridized identities, and new hybridized communities; and perhaps we can work towards helping ourselves to develop and engage in new practices whereby learning and speaking another language is not a continuation of the processes of OTHERING, so much of which we have already witnessed in this world.

References

Bourdieu, P. (1991). *Language and symbolic power.* Cambridge, Mass.: Cambridge University Press.

Lave, J., & Wenger, E. (1991). *Situated learning: Legitimate peripheral participation.* Cambridge: Cambridge University Press.

Chapter 17

Adaptive Cultural Transformation

Quest for Dual Social Identities

Jun Liu
University of Arizona

Background

I was born in a family of four in a small town close to Shanghai, China. I grew up during the Great Cultural Revolution, a critical historical period in China. All the intellectuals were compelled to work in the countryside to experience the "hard life" of farmers and peasants. Criticism and self-criticism were the regular practice to show good will, and the intensive study and memorization of political slogans and quotations from Chairman Mao was a daily routine. Anything related to Western culture had to be abandoned, and anything coming from abroad had to be confiscated. A sense of security was always missing while sleeping at home, as once in a while the Red Guards would stop by without notice for revolutionary inspection.

As an English teacher, my father was one of the people being "poisoned" by Western thoughts and was in possession of Western books. I remember helping him remove from our bookshelves dozens of English novels and short stories he purchased in second-hand bookstores in the late 1940s in Shanghai when he was a university student. We strategically wrapped these books and hid them underneath our beds amidst piles of newspapers. I also remember how much fun my sister and I had displaying on the bookshelves as conspicuously as possible all sorts of works by Marx, Lenin, and Chairman Mao—almost all in red and golden colors. I seldom played truant, but I enjoyed the days when I was excused from school due to sickness. This was particularly because I could be left alone at home with the doors locked, and thus concentrate for hours and hours on going through all the books underneath our beds, looking for the portraits of long-bearded Westerners like William Shakespeare, John Milton, and Charles Dickens. I began to be acquainted with the names of Lord Byron, Percy Shelley, Nathaniel Hawthorne, and Jack London.

One day in a family conversation, a few of these names in Chinglish slipped out of my mouth, and my father was genuinely surprised. While warning me of the "danger" of these books, my father encouraged my sister and me to start reading "Rip van Winkle" from Washington Irving's *SketchBook* word by word, and I remember marking all the pages with Chinese translations and semi-International Phonetic Symbols only I could understand. It was indeed a challenge as it was so different from what my sister and I were taught through the radio or in school slogans, such as "Long live Chairman *Mao*," "A long, long life to the Communist Party," and quotations from *Mao Zedong* translated from Chinese into English. My father was very patient, and used to tell us that even though the story was a challenge for us to read, once we understood it and committed it to memory, our school English would become much easier. After spending lots of time consulting dictionaries, marking phonetic transcriptions and Chinese characters, and reading aloud, my sister and I enjoyed the story of the Cascade Mountains, and had competitions in spelling as well as recitation. My sister always beat me in spelling, but I seemed to be more dramatic in reading aloud.

In fact, during my school days, I was often sidetracked by the temptation to become an artist, a singer, and an actor. Maybe because I naturally had a good voice, I was trained to be a Beijing Opera singer when I was in primary school. Because of my extensive absences in classes due to regular performances, my Chinese teacher had a severe argument with my music teacher one day, demanding that I concentrate on school work. The music teacher, on the other hand, believed that my talent should be fully explored, as I had the potential to be an excellent performer. This kind of dilemma was also echoed at home between my father and mother. While my father strongly believes in solid study without any distractions, my mother would encourage me to do what she believed I was most good at—singing, performing and perhaps becoming a movie star one day. I had to play neutral in order to live up to the expectations of both my parents. Therefore, every morning, I would get up very early and run 5 miles in the mountain. I basically did three things for many years. I would do 100 push-ups to train my will. I would bring an English book to read aloud and recite poems, and also I would practice singing among the trees without being noticed so that I could shout, yell, and scream to the fullest extent possible. I pretty much indulged in this daily routine. Although the chances of being discovered or selected to become a professional artist were slim due to my poor family background, I believed that one day I would do something that would tap on my musical talent, vocal quality, public performance skills, and strong will.

An opportunity came a year after my high school graduation. China restored the college entrance examination system that had been suspended over a ten-year period due to the Great Cultural Revolution, and all those who had graduated over the ten years from high schools would have equal opportunities to take part in the national examination and start college life. I took a chance, and passed the written exams. During the oral interview, however, I was too nervous to do it well. Seeing that the interviewers were not so impressed by my impromptu speeches, I volunteered to sing an English song, which dramatically changed their attitudes. They took an interest in me immediately, thinking that I would be a good asset to the English Department at university-level singing competitions. As a result, I was lucky enough to be admitted to a provincial normal university.

I always remember the days when I was a freshman at a teachers' college majoring in English language and literature in the late 1970s. I had intensive English classes every day, focusing on grammar and word studies of model essays and excerpts from classics. I spent a lot of time deciphering selected readings from eighteenth-century British literature with the help of dictionaries and grammar books. At that time, speaking English with native English speakers, so-called "foreign experts," was something I could only dream about. The small auditorium in which weekly thematic lectures were alternately given by a couple of foreign experts was always packed. I did not know how much I could digest out of an hour-long lecture, but the feeling of exposure to authentic English was great. Sometimes I laughed while others were laughing without knowing why. However, I always made the effort to tape-record the lecture and then spent hours listening to the tape until I found out why I laughed with others during the lecture. Like some of my classmates, I was curious to see whether and how the pattern drills we practiced in listening and speaking courses and the vocabulary we learned from the textbooks could be used in real communication.

Fortunately, *Suzhou*, the city where my university was located, was known as *Venice of the East*, full of beautiful gardens and pavilions open for tourists. They were usually packed with visitors from China and abroad. Whenever there was a chance, I would go to one of those gardens either by myself or with my friends to seek opportunities to speak English with foreign visitors. I worked very hard to commit into memory English versions of introductions to and descriptions of the gardens with the hope of using them in real communication. I wanted to make sure that I sounded British, so I constantly listened to and mimicked BBC and Linguaphone tapes. My eagerness to gain communicative competence in English was sometimes responded to less than enthusiastically, as the very people I wanted to speak English with were busy enjoying the scenery under time pressure. However, I felt encouraged even with a mere exchange of greetings.

I was obsessed with English, and I resumed my habit of morning exercise and recitation. I set up very high standards for myself and buried myself in practicing the four language skills, and I trod every corner of the campus whenever I had time, reading aloud whatever I had learned in class. I refused to give up until I had a full grasp of the text, be it an essay, a poem, or a dialogue. I was bumped from a mediocre student to one of the top candidates, asked to join the faculty upon graduation.

Incident

In 1991, I came to the United States to pursue my Ph.D. in second and foreign language education at the Ohio State University, which marked the beginning of my professional career. With a decade of experience in teaching English as a Foreign Language (EFL) in a college in China, I was very confident in my English upon my arrival in the US. But on many occasions, I felt very uncomfortable, as I did not yet know the rules of communicative competence in America.

When I first arrived at the airport in Columbus, Ohio, a would-be friend who kindly took me to his house for dinner that evening picked me up. As soon as we reached his house, his wife asked me if I wanted something to drink. Out of my Chinese sense of politeness, I said "No, thanks," feeling very thirsty, but expecting her to ask me again. To my surprise, however, she served herself a drink and started talking with me while preparing dinner. About half an hour later dinner was ready, and this time she asked me directly whether I cared for a glass of root beer. Although I did not quite catch the modifier of the word "beer," I accepted her offer without hesitation, thinking that a glass of beer, whatever kind it was, would help me relax after a 17-hour stressful flight. No sooner had I had the first sip than I realized that American beer had a very special taste. But such a different flavor quickly became too unique to appreciate. To please my hosts, I kept drinking, pretending that I had really enjoyed the beer while waiting for the chance to request something else to drink. What I did not expect was that the hostess, impressed by my speed of drinking, happily took my glass, saying, "So you like the taste, and I bet you can't find it in China, eh?" "Yes, well, you see . . ." I tried to search for words polite enough to show my dislike of the taste. But my hesitation was understood as approval, even though the word "yes" in my reply did not exactly mean "yes" in this context in Chinese culture. Sure enough, my empty glass was soon filled up with the liquid of the same color. This time, however, I did not finish it, being afraid of having the glass refilled again. I used my Chinese strategy of implicit polite refusal by sipping it a little bit at a time. Half an hour later, the glass was still full.

Commentary

Deeply embedded in the above incident is the Chinese concept of face saving. I was not straightforward, so I suffered from drinking something I did not like. However, I would rather suffer than upset my hostess as I "saved" my Chinese face and her American face at the same time. There are two concepts of face in Chinese: Lian and Mianzi (Liu, 2001b). While Mianzi refers to prestige and reputation, Lian represents the confidence of society "in the integrity of ego's moral character, the loss of which makes it impossible for him to function properly within the community" (Hu, 1944, p.45). In Chinese culture, Lian carries much more weight than Mianzi. For instance, the loss of Lian is considered more serious than the loss of Mianzi in that the former refers to a condemnation by the community for socially distasteful or immoral behavior or judgment (Hu, 194, p. 45), and the latter indicates the loss of one's reputation and good image. In the incident described above, if I showed my dislike of the taste of root beer to someone whom I had just met, I would embarrass the hostess, and thus cause her to lose her face. In order to protect her face in public (the family situation), I had to endure the taste and pretend that I enjoyed what was offered. In my Chinese mindset, I would rather suffer temporarily from the endurance of bad taste than to upset someone who was innocently generous to offer me the drink. This kind of logic might not be perceived in the same way as Western concepts of face (Brown & Levinson, 1987). Admittedly, some differences exist between Brown and Levinson's universality of face and the Chinese dual conceptualization of face. Central to Brown and Levinson's definition of face as "the public self-image that every member wants to claim for himself" (1987, p. 61) is their emphasis on the individual, rather than the communal aspect of face. Thus, face becomes a self-image, and the self is "public" only to the extent that it is dependent on the other's face being maintained (Brown & Levinson, 1987, p. 61). The overall composition of this self-image, as stated by Mao (1994), is not "susceptible to external pressure or interactional dynamics, and it only concerns the individual's 'wants' and 'desires'"(p. 459). One of the key characteristics of Chinese face, however, is that it does not place itself in the most important position as Brown and Levinson's concept of face does. Rather, Chinese face "encodes a reputable image that individuals can claim for themselves as they interact with others in a given community" (Mao, 1994, p. 460). Chinese face is within the purview of the community and depends on how individuals think their character or behavior is being judged or perceived by the people around them, such as my incident indicated.

Symbolically, what happened above marked the beginning of my Chinese identity loss in a totally new environment. A couple of months into the first quarter at Ohio State, I began to realize the difference between how people spoke in daily communication and what I had learned from eighteenth- and nineteenth-century British and American literature. The idiomatic expressions I had picked up from books and tapes sometimes caused confusion in communication; the canned proverbs, jokes or tongue twisters I consciously carried into conversation were not received as humorous. What was worse, some British poems I proudly inserted in conversation to reveal my solid literature background sometimes made me look comical. Oftentimes, I was dissatisfied with my conversational English, and I began to wonder how I had learned and taught English in China. Pragmatic incompetence apart, my lack of cultural experience on many occasions aggravated my frustration in communication. I felt ashamed that my knowledge of English, which was mainly obtained from books, did not give me much help in feeling natural in daily communication.

In essence, what was taken for granted by Americans was completely new to me. It was not the language per se, though I could tell the difference between the language I used and the language spoken by Americans, but it was American culture that overshadowed my linguistic abilities. I came from a different culture where the beliefs, values, and norms that governed my social behavior no longer seemed to function well in this new environment. What I needed then, and what I later benefited from, was my desire and courage to embark on the journey of cultural adaptive transformation (Liu, 2001a).

Embedded in this early experience of mine was a passion for learning and using English. This passion affected my choice to major in English at college, to become an English teacher upon college graduation, and to study abroad after ten years of teaching experience in China, and eventually affected my decision to take a tenure-track position in the United States. However, my cultural adaptive transformation in the target culture did not come easily. Perhaps the biggest challenge I encountered in this process was how to strike a balance between my Chinese cultural background and the American cultural environment I am in, and between my identity in Chinese communities and in American communities. I was highly motivated both instrumentally and integratively to adapt myself to American culture—to gain new cultural experiences in order to understand and appreciate the target culture. But my Chinese-self characterized in Chinese beliefs, values, customs, and habits, as illustrated with my earlier experiences in the United States, often presented conflicts in the process of my communicating across cultures (Ting-Toomey, 1999).

Cultural adaptive transformation requires determination and willingness to recognize our own culture and to understand and respect the target culture. In my journey of cultural adaptive transformation, I gradually perceived my Chinese cultural boundaries as permeable and flexible (Liu, 2002). Instead of letting my Chinese culture and my well-established L1 social identity become a shield blocking me from constructing my L2 identity in American culture, I became open-minded, and was willing to participate in various social activities to give myself opportunities to experience and understand the target culture.

Like many Chinese students in the US, I underwent quite an adjustment period in my cultural adaptive transformation. But the biggest challenge for me was what I should do upon graduation. Many friends and relatives constantly reminded me over the years that I should change my major and be prepared for the simple fact that I would not be able to find a job in the field I was trained in. "Why would anyone hire you to teach English as a Chinese in the US?" "Are you out of your mind to teach in a US university as a nonnative English speaker?" Given the intense competition in the job market in TESOL in US academia which I had set my mind to, I was prepared to open "Chef Jun's restaurant offering organic Chinese food" or perhaps to team up with my friends to open a private language institute or cram school in China to make a lot of money. But really, the ambition to remain in US academia to inspire thousands of Nonnative English speaking students like me in my career has never been out of my vision. I was determined (and rightly so!) that I would be able to realize my dream, and I was prepared that it might take time to reach that level, as I envisioned a lot of challenges and difficulties. So what? If we want to do something meaningful for the profession of teaching English to speakers of other languages, no matter how much cost and investment we have to put into it, we will, sooner or later, get it.

Fortunately, I got a job as an academic program specialist, teaching English composition to nonnative English speaking students, at Ohio State University upon confirming my doctorate, and I was able to inspire hundreds of students who considered me as their role model among nonnative English speaking teachers. I later took a tenure-track position in the English Department in the College of Humanities at the University of Arizona. Now I am a professor and, ironically, as the only Chinese in the English Department, I am the Head, and fully perceived as a Chinese American (who still prefers Chinese food on a daily basis).

I would like to end my chapter by telling another story, which somewhat reflects the gist of what I am talking about—the challenges in my adaptive cultural transformation. It was my experience the first day of class, teaching an introductory course in Linguistics to undergraduate students.

I was sitting among the students when the bell rang. All the classmates started looking around and complained that their professor was late. I stood up and slowly positioned myself in front of the class, looking around. I told the class my name and that I was their instructor. They looked at me, dumbfounded, and surprised. "How could this Chinese dude be my teacher?" many of them thought. There was a moment of dead silence before I started the class. "I speak Chinese much better than English, but I know about English much better than Chinese. I started learning English grammar before most of you were born." "What? What is this crazy Chinese talking about?" Students began to exchange whispers. "But," I raised my voice, "Can you tell me about the meaning of the subjunctive mood in English? Have you heard the term Transformational Grammar?" I did not need to ask further. The students repositioned themselves, and they were all ears when I briefly introduced the syllabus. Later in the semester when I introduced the Chinese writing system, my office hours were packed for weeks. Standing in line to get their names translated into Chinese with beautiful Chinese calligraphy, my students were surprised that their English names actually had very deep and symbolic meanings in Chinese.

References

Brown, P., & Levinson, S.D. (1987). *Politeness: Some universals in language usage*, Cambridge: Cambridge University Press.

Hu, H. C. (1944). The Chinese concept of "face." *American Anthropologist, 46*, 45–64.

Liu, J. (2001a). *Asian students' classroom communication patterns in US universities: An emic perspective.* Westport, CT: Ablex Publishing.

Liu, J. (2001b). Constructing Chinese faces in American classrooms. *Asian Journal of English Language Teaching, 11*, 1–18.

Liu, J. (2002). Negotiating silence in American classrooms. *Language and Intercultural Communication, 2* (1), 37–54.

Mao, L. M. (1994). Beyond politeness theory: "Face" revisited and renewed. *Journal of Pragmatics, 21*, 451–486.

Ting-Toomey, S. (1999). *Communicating across cultures.* New York: The Guilford Press.

Chapter 18

On this Writing

An Autotheoretic Account

Allan Luke
Queensland University of Technology

> There is a crack in everything. That's how the light gets in.
> (Leonard Cohen, *Anthem* 1993)

The invitation to write for this volume just might be a critical incident. I've never thought of myself as a 'writer'. Teacher, perhaps, academic, researcher, scholar and public intellectual, but not as a 'writer'. After many years of learning and practicing the craft of third person, expository social scientific prose – the invitation to tell a story about critical incidents in my writing and about *this* writing is like a crack in the door. I'm writing this in three sittings over two days, each time going back over bits before I start again to figure out what I've done. I made one major block cut/paste move, moving the narrative to the middle. But I'm hoping I can work without the usual staging and rewriting. I say this not as apology or invitation, but as an initial standpoint, as a promissory note for an unplanned writing on writing. Anything could happen. But then, who am I as author to know what you might do with this?

Writing about Writing

Where does writing come from? This is at once a question about the technology and about each instance of use, of history and everyday practice, of phylogeny and ontogeny. The origins of writing are ambiguous and multilayered. We know that writing developed from gesture and speech as a technology of representation – a 'cognitive amplifier' (Bruner & Olson, 1977) enabling new lexicogrammatical choices, genres and semiotic conventions (Halliday & Martin, 1994), new social relations of exchange and hierarchical knowledge/power relations (Bourdieu, 1990). We know also that it makes messages recoverable and transportable, so that they can be read – as this text is being read – by readers in lived contexts wholly beyond those imagined and anticipated by authors (Goody, 1980). All writings, even those produced digitally, are generated within material cultural contexts. Writers and their machineries of inscription make agentive choices and live in idiosyncratic though not wholly individuated possible worlds – 'conditions of production' (Fairclough, 1990) – as readily as their readers. And I know not where you live or what 'conditions of reception', cultural schemata or presumptions might shape your reading of this text, this year or whenever you or somebody long after us might run into it in a library or on a bookshelf. Further: whether, how and in what ways writing might enable and shape, mediate and construct particular political economic and material conditions is a subject of a half century of theoretical speculation and empirical scrutiny (Innis, 1951; McLuhan, 1962). But we can discuss that elsewhere.

Even as I write this text – working a keyboard from my own temporal and physical location (very hot and humid veranda, February Southern Hemisphere summer, Brisbane, Australia) – from what for me are specific material conditions and speaking positions (as a Chinese, Australian, Canadian, once American, heterosexual male, middle class, privileged academic with a previously published available body of text that I am said to have written, working comfortably and relatively unconstrained by economic need, cultural tension or political censorship or surveillance) – I write with no certainty of the uptake, of whether and for whom any of this will see the light of day. No matter how I try to interpellate your readership, modalise this or modulate that, use imperatives or interrogatives to try to shape your reading position (Luke, 1989), I have no control over how and what you might take from it, interpretively or otherwise – or for that matter whether you might reckon, perhaps already by now, 'This is all too much, on to the next chapter'. If so, I've thickened my skin sufficiently to understand that this would be a reflection neither on me nor you. Stuff happens to texts. Sometimes they are recirculated and recycled, but inevitably they are pulped.

Where, after all, does *this* writing come from? And with what language might we describe it and its writer? The answers just might be as much theoretical as biographical. Some of the features that roll out across the page might be accounted for by intrinsic features of the *techne* of writing, word processing and publication (font, binding, costs and accessibility, intertextual connections to the editors' introduction, their own stories of writing and those of other writers here).[1] Others might be attributed to my training, history, disposition or 'culture'. But neither you nor I will ultimately know, with any certainty, about what 'determines' this writing or its readings. Writing, Derrida (1980) reminds us, is always indeterminate, unfinished, and deferred. Writing creates polysemous and contingent worlds (Eco, 1980) – no matter how we try to sandwich it and ourselves into a universe of linear causality or structural determination.

But let's assume provisionally that writing comes from 'inside' the writer – whatever that might mean. This is a solid Eurocentric adage, probably dating to post-Enlightenment Romanticism: writing as the externalization of the self. It is me here, behind my eyes and with my idiosyncratic history, material conditions, and semiotic resources, who is making choices and decisions on the keyboard. I'll decide what to 'show and tell' about myself, my context, and my history. About which 'self' to craft and represent, about which cards to show and which to hold. I could present 'another ethnic autobiography' (Luke, 2009a) of writing from the margins, of writing against the odds, of writing in spite of and to spite institutions. But that too would be another selective account, however heroic, tragic or clichéd. This isn't Barack's story.

In these ways, I control the coding, the lexicogrammatical choice, whether this is a deliberative text, whether this is the product of multiple revisions and premeditations or, indeed, whether this might be something more akin to the 'spontaneous' overflow of powerful emotions that Wordsworth and Coleridge described in *Preface to Lyrical Ballads* (1789).

Writing From this Body

My favourite 'writings' (McHoul, 1991) this week is from Montreal songwriter and poet Leonard Cohen (*Anthem*) and American novelist Annie Proulx (*On Close Range*). In another time, they might have been Stuart Hall or Amitir Ghosh or Dominique Dunne or Georg Hegel. Echoing through my head this past week has been Cohen's metaphor:

'There is a crack in everything. That's how the light gets in.' Yet these authors and texts cannot be models for this writing. Different genres – different personae, media, context, and indeed, a different craft.

This writing is overdue. I've procrastinated it, made excuses to the editors, and failed to meet deadlines. I hope they take it. It's another piece of academic writing in the queue of six unfinished short pieces and one overdue book. It could be just another piece in the production line, another brick in the wall. At the same time, I turn to it now because it interests me: the opportunity to narrate in a self-reflexive, tautological way about writing, rather than the distanced exposition of data or the rhetorical structure of the essay – staples of the craft. Narrative and what American poet HD called 'automatic writing' (Scott, 2007) can be undertaken alert or tired, drunk or stoned, fuelled by seratonin or noradrenalin, nicotine or caffeine, in religious ecstasy or political rage – a different kind of indiscipline. Certainly, nobody explained how to do this in graduate school or the APA handbook. Let's see where it leads.

I grew up in Echo Park and, later, Silverlake just outside of Los Angeles Chinatown in the 1950s. We didn't have a lot, but we didn't know that we didn't have a lot and we were comfortable. We experienced racism before we could see it – living and playing behind our own eyes (Luke, 2009b). I learnt to read and write with Dick and Jane (Luke, 1988),[2] in reading groups where we would subvocalise and chant in unison lines of dialogue from Dick, Jane, Sally and Spot (yes, Spot would occasionally produce statements, or perhaps that was my imagination). We went to Chinese school afternoons and on weekends, making characters with ink and brushes, filling in copybooks and following tracing lines. There were books in our home – but no kids' lit bedtime stories. I went to school knowing little about Grimm or Hans Christian Andersen, or Confucius, for that matter, but an awful lot about John Wayne and Hank Aaron.

My father left a similar Chinese copybook book he used in the 1920s in Seattle Chinatown. My father had been a writer, but I rarely saw him write. He had a 1930s journalism degree from the University of Washington, one of their first Chinese-American graduates. But he had lost his vocation because nobody at the time would even consider hiring a Chinese writer, especially the Hearst Press that had invented *yellow journalism.* So he worked as a linotyper (producing hot lead slugs for the presses of local newspapers – I used to crawl around the pressroom floor and, yes, put lead slugs in my mouth), a proofreader (checking the texts of people who might not write as well as him) and as an actor (reciting the words of Others) (Luke, 2009a). Part of the folk narrative of success bequeathed to me by my parents was the mythology or fact that my Guanzho grandfather who I never met had been a 'scholar', which I later learnt meant he was a peasant who could read and write. At any rate, this writing stuff was a gift with reciprocal obligations (Luke, 2008). It was non-negotiable, and poor marks caused a real hassle in our home. And it came with the warning from my Father and my stolid year six teacher, Herbert Leong: that in a racist society you had to be twice as good as Whites.

In school we filled in blanks, circled answers, and wrote stories and diary entries with our number five pencils. Sometimes there were rules about what kinds of erasures were allowed, what kinds of *writing over* we could do. These had to be fulfilled before we could move onto using ball point pens (BICs used to explode in your pockets on hot LA days) to write reports on animals, countries and people (usually copied in large slabs from one of three authoritative sources in the school library: the *World Book*, the *Britannica*, and back editions of *National Geographic* that hadn't had the maps ripped out by kids who weren't patient enough to use the tracing paper, the reproductive technology of the day). By the end of year six, we were allowed – those of us who had access to them – to use typewriters, mostly *Royal*, long before the advent of erasable bond or the invention of whiteout by Mike Nesmith's mother.

I was an above average student in a mixed-race and social class environment, usually ending up in the 'second group' behind some of my brilliant classmates. In year three, Lance Ito (later, well-known LA Superior Court Judge) and Shelley Wong (current President of TESOL) were mysteriously promoted a year ahead of our cohort. I imagine it was their Iowa or Binet test scores, since we were tested at least twice a year. So my work would come back with red marks on it, but I was pretty steadily getting B's in English by the time I finished grade school.

I guess I learnt to produce text. My father would proofread my homework. But this burden associated with having to write became second nature. I got it done, but it was always a matter of putting it off until the last minute, and then, pulling teeth and making words. This presented practical technological problems in those days, since the aim was to produce 'correct' writing – with revision and alteration before computers nothing less than Sisyphus pushing text uphill. We would handwrite the report over and over in cursive script until it was more or less how we wanted it. I remember seeing *Looney Toons* portrayals of writing as authors throwing wadded paper into trash cans. That was a good description of getting through high school: crumpled spiral notebook paper in trash cans. I think it still is, despite all the slick technology that enables endless pastiche, paste and glue.

I started university in 1968, studying English literature and philosophy, but I was really interested in playing the guitar, counterculture lifestyle and anti-war protest. Though I took poetry-writing from the American poet Kenneth Rexroth, and listened rapt to teachers like M. Scott Momaday, H.D.F. Kitto, Thomas Steiner and, most importantly, Walter A. Davis,[3] much of my experience was mastering the third person academic essay. It still entailed, long before computers, tossing lots of paper into the trash, procrastination, and long overnight sessions producing overdue texts. But I had some hints of what might be. In my last year in university I was hired to copyedit a manuscript by poet and critic Frederick Turner[4] – and as I worked with his raw text, full of gaps and rough sketches, and partly baked ideas, I realized that this was handicraft, not the work of genius or lightning bolts.

After teaching school for several years, starting a family and fiddling more with the guitar – I returned to graduate school with a particular goal from working with rural, poor and migrant ESL students: to study and develop critical, politically engaged approaches to teaching reading and writing. Though I had taught writing at primary, secondary, technical college and university in Canada in the 1970s, I struggled to write in the academic registers of the social sciences. My mastery consisted of about four sentence structures that I repeated endlessly, adding lots of complex words. This sure wasn't like writing poetry or songs, and it definitely wasn't English lit. The more I read, the less I felt I knew. And as I read the writing of accomplished scholars, many of whom two decades later became colleagues and friends – I was stunned into silence. I could never write with such fluidity and confidence. My pedigree and training weren't theirs.

In the apprenticeship of doctoral studies, my writing began to develop. For better and worse, the gaps between thought, speech and text began to close. My first refereed coauthored text appeared in 1981, with my supervisor Suzanne De Castell and another graduate student, Dave MacLennan (De Castell, Luke & MacLennan, 1981). They were generous. I probably contributed all of five paragraphs to the article, adding words and occasional sentences to the bulk of the text, trying to edit their academic prose into something this reformed English teacher could grasp. Their words flowed through me. I could actually see how I could have written like Suzanne or David. It's like jamming instrumentally with musicians who are far better than you – you imitate their licks and runs, you watch them play, you add a note here and there, you stop them and ask how on earth they did that.

This was my first experience of *acting as if*: of overcoming feelings of displacement and fraud in the academy. Writing still requires this of me: a kind of wilful suspension of disbelief in one's own incapacity. It is a game of creative pouseurship, of mistaken identity deliberately fashioned. I recently played bass with an excellent drummer and turned to her and said, 'For five minutes we are the best rhythm section in the world.' And indeed, for that five minutes, in that place, we were.

The next critical juncture occurred a decade later, after I had published 50 or so decent pieces. My Australian colleagues Mary Kalantzis and Bill Cope invited me out to a public event on multicultural policy in Townsville, a provincial town in North Queensland where I held my first academic job. I begged off, saying that I had to stay home and finish another overdue article (I have a terrible reputation with editors, but nobody has yet to say it to my face). As they left the house, Bill said to me something to the effect of: 'Do you really think writing another article on literacy will make a difference to anybody?' I asked Mary if she had any better ideas about what was to be done. Without batting an eye, she said, 'Change Australian history.'

This was why I started academic writing in the first place: the purpose of philosophy was not to describe the world but to change it. What Mary and Bill did was remind me that this wasn't about writing, or about getting published, but it was an overall project, in the broadest existential and political sense. It forced me to ask, again and again: Why are we doing this 'scholarship' in the first place? This helped me to consider how the capital, indeed the literacy, that I'd acquired – whether through work, gifting or inheritance – could be enlisted for public intellectual work.

The third 'moment' for me as a writer came from my partner, Carmen Luke, whose fluid writing and truly unique understanding of the world have shaped everything I've done. She has always written by flow, by instinct, through intuition – her writing is a dense packing of associations and generative ideas. She does not plan and draft carefully, but just thinks, reads and then produces text on time with great physical and temporal discipline. At one point she was reading something I had written and said: 'You need to quit citing everybody every time you make a claim. You've been at this for a while. Just say something that's yours for once.' I asked to explain how she did it and she said: 'You need to start trusting what you know and start making up new ideas.'

In the early 1990s, I started putting together new theories, making up explanations rather than finding and reciting someone else's explanation – and 'making things up'. This isn't a case of fraud, but the unleashing of what C. Wright Mills (1959/2000) termed 'a sociological imagination': of seeing the social in the world. For the first time, I felt at home in the academy.

Autotheory

How do we account for writing? This depends on how we theorize the various discursive, linguistic, and cultural resources that we might call into play. Somehow they seem to be in this body (Luke, 1992). That is, as my fingers cross the keyboard, there is a making material of something 'inside' of me. Yes, we have lots of available explanations: that the writing is a product of inspiration, that, indeed, others' voices might be speaking through me (My parents? In Cantonese? My teachers, in unspoken I/R/E classroom exchanges long past?), that I am a self-same product of a particular generation, a particular cultural formation and experience (journalists in Australia stick the generational labels of 'postmodern', 'Marxist', and 'politically correct' on my writing). Or indeed, that this text is the construct of the peculiar longitudinal pathway I've described here. Alternatively, we might explain it as a neurological process, produced through a set of synaptic firings, or that I and this text are merely produced by 'dominant' scaffolds, genres and ideologies. Or we could speculate that this piece of writing is an idiosyncratic moment in a universe of uncontrollable discourse. Or perhaps this is merely an intertextual 'revoicing' of things I have written across 30 years of published text: one big exophoric cohesive tie.

I view writing as a learned craft, at times a form of satisfying unalienated labour, as a tool using activity in a field of social relations. At other times it is sheer drudgery. It is kin to whittling and woodworking, continuous reshaping and redesigning. In other instances, it is like playing a musical instrument, where you can recombine and augment tones and notes, scales and chords. I doubt that anything is original, including this text. Writing is a reassembly of what we've heard and read, subvocalised and spoken and written to ourselves and Others. I do different kinds of writing: lots of email and occasional written texts to friends and family, and sometimes, to people who I wouldn't know from a bar of soap. I write music with the limited vocabulary, technique and structure of a frustrated grade school student. But mostly I write as professional labour, as the labour of professing.

Academic writing is lonely. I never know what the uptake will be. I'm often convinced, as with this chapter, that very few people will actually read the stuff. This can make the writing a bit easier. Yet while my partner, a writer for 30 years, can seem to detach herself from text – seeing it neither as an embodiment of identity or value, but as something she just 'does' for work – I still get caught up in those self-serving and self-destructive games of putting the self on the line, of second guessing what I've done, wondering what so and so will think of it, whether it meets imaginary benchmarks of what might count as good scholarship. Perhaps this is gendered. But I've learnt over the years to drop it in the mail and try to forget about it. I wish they had never invented Google Scholar. It turns a mystery into a game show.

No matter how much I write – it always brings with it a particular set of psychological and cultural obstacles. This is in part a matter of multimodality and synesthesia. I see the task as one of closing a gap between what I can experience, feel and think, what I can say, and what I can manage to get down on paper. At times, I've been able to think new and interesting things but my linguistic repertoire on the page has been unable to capture this. At the same time, as a scholar, I've had to learn to 'talk like a book': to speak without conversational deixis, in grammatically complete sentences, with nominalizations, parenthetical phrases and logical connectors taken from academic prose. In this elaborated code it is easy to sound like we know more than we do, as Labov (1971) pointed out. And after 30 years I can now sometimes write authoritatively with the appearance of coherence even when I have little or nothing to say.

In academic writing, I often 'feel like a fraud' – as if I'm not really supposed to be here, as if I really know nothing and that by committing words to the page, that all and sundry will be able to see through this. This is common for many of us – particularly those whose class, cultural linguistic and gendered histories make us 'minorities' in what is still predominantly a White, male-dominated and scientifically hierarchical academic culture. This is well documented in the feminist and critical race theory work on standpoint (C. Luke, 1996). Academic writing has the veneer of 'naturalness' only for those who might feel born into it, those who have an intuitive sense of its language games, or, alternatively, those committed to a kind of logical positivism that denies standpoint, militates against position, and views subjectivity as epistemological flaw and methodological failure.[5]

For the rest of us, for those of us whose ancestors weren't supposed to be in the Western academy, writing hurts. Perhaps we are the light that the cracks let in.

Writing and scholarship are forms of semiotic self-representation. If *professing* is about embodying and performing a field – and not about possessing its facts, axioms and wisdom per se – then writing is the recoverable and sustainable trace of that profession (Derrida, 2002). The production of written artifact is the tangible evidence of our research, scholarship, reflection, and whatever else winds up on the page. This is intrinsically fraught with a kind of self-cantered drive to 'produce the self in text for others' – a galling experience when one can't control who gets the text, its readership, much less what they might make of the text.[6]

This feature of writing, it strikes me, is an empirical fact – not an artefact either of Romantic literary theories of genius, or of psychoanalytic theories of ego identity, though they may indeed be spot on. It's unsurprising, then, that for many of us writing is intrinsically fraught, insecure and always contingent. Academic writing entails risk, insecurity, and immanent hurt. When the printers' galleys come back, I often read them over and cringe, spotting every gaping hole in the argument and data, every rhetorical trick. This could indeed be the contingency of writing, the eccentricity of discourse (Foucault, 1982). Even exact copying, Borges' (2007) imaginary author Pierre Menard knows, will not produce equivalent texts in voice and meaning, history and effect.

No summary, no grand narrative on offer here. No overarching theoretical schemata or claims. It's a record of my writing, over two days, in this place, with this history. These are some of the critical junctures in my work as a writer. I don't assign any determining effects to them. As I close down this file and send it to the editors for their consideration, I have no choice but to leave it to you to make of it what you may. If it ever gets to you. Feel free to rewrite it.

Acknowledgments

This piece is dedicated to Patrick Wong. James Ladwig introduced me to Thomas King's (2003) CBC Massey Lectures, 'The Truth About Stories: A Native Narrative', inspiring and inspired work.

Notes

1 It an axiom of the field of 'reading hygiene', which predated reading psychology, that font, layout, page size and binding provide different stimuli for reading behaviour (Huey, 1916). These, Huey argued, condition the reader's foveal fixation points and saccades.

2 I'm of the opinion that all scholarship is autobiographical and narrative: this applies both to classic ethnographic narratives that are about the author as much as about the subjects

she described (e.g. *Ways with Words* (Heath, 1982)) as it does to the ostensibly dry science of, for instance, a graduate student investigating inclusive education or communications disorders. There is invariably a link between life history and choice of research question and topic.

3 http://www.walteradavis.com/, retrieved 15/2/09.
4 See http://benturner.com/genesis/bio.html, retrieved 12/2/09.
5 This was the goal of Thomas Spratt and the architects of 'Royal Society Prose', which at the height of British empiricism sought a one-to-one correspondence between word and object, signified and signifier, subsequently lampooned by Swift in *Gulliver's Travels* (Kenner, 1985).
6 When playing live music, the audience response, depending on their degree of inebriation, is never commensurate to the quality or depth of the performance.

References

Borges, J.L. (2007) *Labyrinths.* New York: New Directions.

Bourdieu, P. (1990) *Outline of a Theory of Practice.* R. Nice, trans. Cambridge: Cambridge University Press.

Bruner, J. & Olson, D. (1977) Symbols and texts as tools of intellect. *Interchange* 8(4), 1–15.

Cohen, L. (1993) *Stranger Music.* London: Jonathan Cape.

De Castell, S.C., Luke, A. & MacLennan, D. (1981) On defining literacy. *Canadian Journal of Education* 6(3), 7–18.

Derrida, J. (1980) *Writing and Difference.* A. Bass, trans. Chicago: University of Chicago Press.

Derrida, J. (2002) *Without Alibi.* P. Kamuf, trans. Palo Alto: Stanford University Press.

Eco, U. (1980) *The Role of the Reader.* Bloomington: Indiana University Press.

Fairclough, N. (1989) *Language and Power.* London: Longman.

Foucault, M. (1982) *The Archeology of Knowledge and the Discourse on Language.* A. Sheridan-Smith, trans. New York: Harper Collins.

Goody, J. (1980) *Domestication of the Savage Mind.* Cambridge: Cambridge University Press.

Halliday, M.A.K. & Martin, J.R. (1996) *Writing Science.* London: Taylor & Francis.

Heath, S.B. (1982) *Ways with Words.* Cambridge: Cambridge University Press.

Huey, E.B. (1906) *The Psychology and Pedagogy of Reading.* New York: Macmillan.

Innis, H. (1949) *The Bias of Communications.* Toronto: University of Toronto Press.

Kenner, H. (1985) *The Counterfeiters.* Baltimore: John Hopkins University Press.

King, T. (2003) The truth about stories: A native narrative. *Canadian Broadcasting Corporation Massey Lectures.* Retrieved from: http://www.cbc.ca/ideas/massey/massey2003.html.

Labov, W. (1971) The logic of nonstandard English. In Pier Paolo Giglioli (Ed.), *Language and Social Context.* Harmondsworth: Penguin.

Luke, A. (1988) *Literacy, Textbooks and Ideology.* London: Falmer Press.

Luke, A. (1989) Open and closed texts: The ideological/semantic analysis of textbook narratives. *Journal of Pragmatics* 13, 53–80.

Luke, A. (1992) The body literate: Discourse and inscription in early literacy instruction. *Linguistics and Education* 4(1): 107–29

Luke, A. (2008) Pedagogy as gift. In J. Albright & A. Luke (Eds.), *Pierre Bourdieu and Literacy Education* (pp. 61–97). New York: Routledge.

Luke, A. (2009a) Another ethnic autobiography? Childhood and the cultural economy of looking. In R. Hammer & D. Kellner (Eds.), *Media/Cultural Studies: Critical Approaches* (pp. 482–500). New York: Peter Lang.

Luke, A., (2009b) Race and language as capital in school: A sociological template for language education reform. In R. Kubota & A. Lin (Eds.), *Race, Culture and Identities in Second Language Education* (pp. 286–309). London: Routledge.

Luke, C. (Ed.) (1996) *Feminism and Pedagogies of Everyday Life.* Albany: State University of New York Press.

McHoul, A.W. (1991) ReadingS. In C.D. Baker & A. Luke (Eds.), *Towards a Critical Sociology of Reading* (pp. 15–22). Amsterdam: John Benjamins.

McLuhan, M. (1969. *The Gutenberg Galaxy.* New York: New American Library.

Mills, C.W. (1959/2000) *The Sociological Imagination.* Oxford: Oxford University Press.

Proulx, A. (1999) *On Close Range.* New York: Scribner.

Scott, B.K. (2007) *Gender in Modernism.* Chicago: University of Illinois Press.

Wordsworth, W. & Coleridge, S. (1789/2000) *Lyrical Ballads.* Harmondsworth: Penguin.

Chapter 19

The *Festival* Incident

Michael McCarthy
University of Nottingham

Autobiographical Statement

I began teaching English as a foreign language in 1966, a long time before many of the readers of this volume will have been born. Far too young for the job (just 19 years old), I left my home in the UK for Spain, armed only with secondary-school Spanish, a suitcase and some money. I had answered an advertisement for a job in a Berlitz language school (they must have been desperate!). That year was my baptism of fire. I learnt a lot about teaching simply by teaching (there was no EFL teacher training available in those days). I had a great time socially, and, most usefully of all, I learnt a lot of Spanish. I took that skill home with me to the UK and subsequently studied Spanish at university, where I acquired not only a better and deeper knowledge of grammar and vocabulary, but a life-enhancing familiarity with Spanish and Latin American history and culture through the vast amounts of Hispanic literature we devoured as part of our course. I loved the bright, light-filled, rainbow-coloured world of Spain and Latin America, seen through rosy spectacles no doubt from my grey, chilly, northern European student room. I loved meeting Hispanic people; they seemed to have an energy, a love of socializing and partying, a zest for friendly but heated and passionate discussion that contrasted so greatly with the glum reticence of the English. Cultural stereotypes I hear you say. Yes. I was young and believed in them.

While doing my PhD, I took a job in a local language school, to earn what we used to call in those days 'pin money', money to support myself at a basic level while completing my dissertation. By now I had reached the ripe old age of 26 and thought I knew it all and had seen it all in the classroom. I had slipped into a comfort zone of teaching grammar and vocabulary and getting my students to do bits of writing. The notions of integrated four-skills work had yet to be invented, and the notion of 'discourse' was only just emerging in the academic world. My students were mixed nationalities of young people who were in the UK to improve their English. They were from all over the world, including Spain. I prided myself on being able to handle and understand any problem a Spanish speaker might have in English. After all, I knew their language and culture, their way of thinking, did I not, and I could surely use that to their and my advantage. In those days, we didn't worry if we used a student's L1 in class – we were very pragmatic: if it helps, use it, and we would have been bemused by the sort of interesting debate that the question of leaning on L1 in class has generated in recent years (e.g. Stanley, 2002). The other factor was that I was a native speaker of English, and my authority was unquestioned. Native speaker teachers still today occupy a privileged position in the job market, but at least a healthy debate has been well underway for some time now as to whether they are necessarily the best and most authoritative voices for the classroom (Medgyes, 1994; Leung *et al.*, 1997). It was while teaching in that unruffled situation that an event happened that helped to change my perspective on what I taught, how I taught and on my own language awareness.

Narrative

One day, my intermediate, mixed-nationality class were doing their usual task of writing a short composition for me on a worthy topic. That day it was 'If I ruled the world'. Composition time was usually a welcome respite for me from teaching, a time to sit at my desk at the front of the class and mark their homework, read a magazine or perhaps just daydream. That day I took it upon myself to walk around the class and look over people's shoulders. I glanced over the shoulder of a young Spanish man and saw the title I had set, neatly underlined at the top of the page, *If I ruled the world*, and then on a new line, just one word: *Festival*.

My student was looking thoughtful, hesitant, pen poised above the paper. He needed my help, the help of an expert, of one who knew his language and English, and could get him moving with his composition. I gazed at the word *Festival* and pondered: what is he going to say or trying to say? My cultural knowledge kicked in. Aha! Of course, as an ebullient, warm-blooded Mediterranean Latin, and as ruler of the world, he would want to throw a huge, global celebration, a party to end all parties, to make everyone feel happy, even if we cold-blooded, boring, unfriendly, gloomy and splenetic northern Europeans would hate it. A party, *una fiesta*, or *un festival*, or maybe a carnival to eclipse the carnival of Rio de Janeiro, a festival for the whole world and all its people.

He looked thoughtful. I wanted to help.

'What sort of festival are you thinking of, Carlos? An international one? A festival for young people?'

He looked completely confused and dumbfounded.

'Sorry? Ex- excuse me?' he stuttered.

'A festival,' I said, '*una fiesta, un festival*? What kind?'

'What kind?' he repeated, puzzled. '*Fiesta*?' His brow furrowed deeper and deeper. 'No,' he said, 'not fiesta. This is what English people say all the time when they want to give their opinion. I hear it all the time. They say "Festival, I think it is important . . ." etc.'

It dawned on me: what he wanted to say was *First of all, . . .* I corrected his spelling and wrote it on the board, and told him he should pay more attention when reading.

Commentary

What Carlos had done was to hear a ready-made chunk of language, and he had clearly heard it often. He had figured out that (a) this was something people commonly used to preface their opinions and arguments and/or to organize their thoughts, (b) that they used it right at the beginning of a series of points, and (c) that it was perhaps a homophone of another word he'd seen or knew, *festival*. And why should it not be? English was full of homophones: a *bank* could be somewhere where you put money or part of a river, a *bat* could be a flying creature or something you hit a ball with, *well* could mean being healthy, doing something skilfully, a place to get water or a way of prefacing a comment, and so on. So why shouldn't *festival* mean a public event and something for organizing your thoughts, or even a type of sausage or a handle for opening a window? That's what English was like – anything was possible. Or maybe he had diligently searched in his dictionary till he found a good match under 'F' for what he was hearing.

As his teacher, what I had done was to interpret his English in the way I always interpreted my students' English: what word were they trying to use, and was it the right one? What meanings did they want to convey, and how could I help them express themselves properly? Could I use my knowledge of their L1 (if I had any) and its culture(s) to help them? So far, so good. 'No, you do not mean festival – festival means *una fiesta* or *un festival* in Spanish – you mean *first of all*. It's a completely different thing.'

The incident stayed in my memory for a long time, and was often brought out in those social gatherings where teachers exchange funny stories of things their students have said or written, and it certainly always got a laugh. Such funny stories are the social currency that language teachers dine out on. At that time, my general language awareness was pretty poor – remember, my generation did not have the advantage of training courses and TESOL conferences, and, anyway, who had ever heard of 'language awareness'? And the idea of a global party fitted well with my cultural stereotype of the all-dancing, all-partying Hispanic. Over the years, though, I came to see the *festival* incident as more than just a good laugh, and began to see it more and more as a parable for the way students (and teachers like me) typically approach the language learning task, and it taught me something about language and the cultural gap between learner and native user. But let us first briefly consider Carlos's problem: it will help to explicate mine, and why I needed a greater awareness.

When you are first immersed into a second- or foreign-language environment, the speech-stream is just that: a stream of sounds. One of your tasks is to segment those sounds into meaningful portions (just as many anthropological linguists have done when faced with new and, for them, exotic languages in tribes and communities that have lacked contact with other languages). This is not easy. I myself lived in Sweden in the late 1970s for a couple of years before I realized that a word I used every day, and which I thought was a single word (something like *justé*, pronounced like *you-stay*, and meaning *right* or *exactly*), was in fact two Swedish words, *just det*. Not a huge problem if all I ever wanted to do was to speak Swedish, but clearly a problem if I wanted to write. I was doing exactly what Carlos had done a few years before with *first of all*. I had heard the stream, got the meaning, but had no idea how it corresponded to the words and phrases of the target language. One conclusion we might possibly draw from this is that words often may not penetrate our consciousness fully and properly until we have seen them written as well as heard them in speech. As teachers, we often throw out new words and phrases orally in class and expect our students to be able to process them on the hoof, as it were.

But another, more complex reason may underlie the problem of processing new words. Separating words from the speech stream is something all infants have to do in learning their mother tongue, and the process is seen by cognitive psychologists and first-language acquisition researchers as subtle and complex, involving the processing of multiple cues and strategic actions (e.g. Davis, 2003). In the case of the first language, the skills are typically acquired in the target culture environment, and acquisition is much more than just acquiring words; we acquire them as badges of membership of our L1 culture too, so that they become part of our cultural identity, just as much as our diet does, our home décor, our tastes in music, and so on. The more we as teachers understand just how complex and difficult the processing of new language is, the more we can show sensitivity to learners and devise ways of integrating visual and audio material to support this vital learning process. Supporting listening dialogues with visual material, harnessing technology to slow down the speech stream so that students can listen without too much stress and cognitive processing load, along with other learning aids, are all things that never even touched my consciousness, let alone were very practical in those distant days, but which are, fortunately, more readily available today.

So what were the problems for me as a teacher? What could I learn from this to transform my professional situation? Most of all, I was a product of those times, ill-trained, blasé in my confidence as a native speaker and therefore so-called 'expert' in English, and unaware of just what it meant to grapple with the complexities of a foreign language and to enter a new culture, to begin to clothe oneself in a new cultural identity.

Let us return, briefly, to my biography. In the 1980s, I got a job as a lecturer at the University of Birmingham, UK. I worked with the late Professor John Sinclair. Sinclair inspired us all to look at language with fresh eyes, unprejudiced by the conceit that, as native speakers, we knew it all. We clearly didn't. What emerged most strongly from Sinclair's work was that meaning in language resided in more than just single words, and not just propositional meaning, but interpersonal meaning, connotation and cultural meaning. Everywhere one looked, there seemed to be repeated patterns and frozen 'chunks' of meaning. One such chunk, unsurprisingly, is *first of all*, which occurs 380 times in the 10-million word spoken segment of the British National Corpus (BNC), more often than many single words in the same corpus, including the word *festival*, which occurs just under 100 times. The fact that language, especially spoken language, occurs in chunks, and that there are so many chunks, and that they had developed specialized pragmatic, discoursal and cultural meanings, was new and profoundly significant for me. It changed the way I taught my international student classes, influenced the class texts and books for teachers that I was beginning to write, and it changed my language awareness fundamentally.

Now, 25 years on, it is axiomatic for academics like me and for highly professionalized teachers around the world that the business of learning a language has as much to do with learning and using chunks as it has to do with learning single words. Chunks go by different names (see O'Keeffe *et al.*, 2007, Chapter 3 for an overview), but whatever term is used, the phenomenon linguists recognize is that there are thousands of relatively fixed, recurring strings of language which are stored in memory and which can be retrieved whole, off-the-peg, as it were. Chunks are available for use at any moment of communication and are not put together afresh each time they are needed. Native speakers of languages know and use thousands of such chunks automatically, so automatically that they operate at a subliminal level and we are hardly aware of them. For the native speaker, the ability to use chunks is part of their identity, a badge of their membership of the speech community (Prodromou, 2008), an aspect of their 'enduring selves' (Spindler and Spindler, 1994), a point we return to later. As part of the user's linguistic (and hence cultural) identity, their use gives out the signal 'I am one of you'.

For the language learner, chunks may be something to avoid, or else something very low on the radar of all the tasks they have to accomplish to become proficient in the target language. The most idiomatic chunks, even where there are similar idioms in the L1, may be avoided because learners have a suspicion that such idiosyncracies of their language and culture probably cannot be transferred to the L2. The evidence presented in Kellerman (1986) gives some credence to this. Learners may be more sensitive to the 'badge of membership' issues than we think. Equally, their text books may pay only scant attention to all those thousands of chunks, comfortable in the tradition of pumping as many single words as possible into the learner's consciousness, and their teachers, if they are like I was, may see little to be gained by devoting scarce and valuable classroom time to the learning of chunks or to raising language awareness. I, for one, had little idea all those years ago of the delicate threads our learners weave in trying to create an identity for themselves in the L2 culture.

But let us consider another aspect of chunks. Chunks such as *first of all* are not only very frequent but, as we have said, are instantly retrievable for the native speaker or expert user. Their contribution to any discourse, whether spoken or written, is to make it able to flow in a steady stream, rather than dripping out single word by single word. Indeed it seems obvious that such a flow, for which we use the Latin-derived word *fluency*, would be virtually impossible without chunked output. In other words, the fluent speaker or writer is one who, amongst other abilities, can use chunks (McCarthy, 2008). But what is the relationship between fluency and cultural identity? This is a question with no simple answer. However, studies with a more sociological bent, outside of language teaching research, often show that cultural capital, in Bourdieu's (1992) sense, among incoming groups in societies, can be linked to perceptions of fluency or lack of it. Success or otherwise in integration and problems of cultural stress among international students living and studying in L2 environments have been linked to perceptions of fluency (Yeh and Inose, 2003), and the economic fortunes of immigrant workers have also been seen as related to their perceived fluency levels (Shields and Wheatley Price, 2002).

It thus seems that chunks are by no means innocent bystanders in the struggle for the learner to harness a new language and culture. Kramsch (1993) presents a memorable view of the learner as a person making a long and difficult journey from one cultural context (the classroom) to another (the target culture). If we as teachers do not understand that this is what is happening in our classrooms and just see the learning enterprise as a question of vocabulary, grammar and pronunciation, we are doing less than our whole job. But Kramsch says more: the learner seeks a third place in between the two cultural contexts, where a transformed cultural identity can be forged. The texts we expose our learners to, whether spoken or written, are voices of the target culture, and their words and chunks are potential tokens of entry into that culture. There are echoes here of Spindler and Spindler (1994) and their model of the three dimensions of the self, which include famously the enduring self, the situated self and the endangered self. In the enduring self lies the feeling of continuity that a person has with the past (and, in our case particularly, the L1 cultural identity) which forges their social identity. In the situated self we see the individual in a continuous, goal-oriented adaptation to their environment and to new environments. The situated self is an instrumentally-oriented entity. It is there we find the language learner. For teachers, this is the locus where we must develop the maximum degree of awareness and sensitivity. What we should not do is endanger that self, push it into a zone of confusion and a feeling of being threatened, for it is then that the individual withdraws.

Such apparently banal and, at the time, insignificant moments as the central narrative of this chapter are eruptions in the fault-lines between the various identities, which can either be healed or harmed. Making a student feel they are inadequate or silly, or simply blanketing an incident with one's own cultural stereotypes may prove disastrous. Exploring the moment and transforming it into an exploration of what the student is trying to do (or who they are trying to be) is the lesson I needed to learn at that point in time.

On this central question of identity, Prodromou (2008) argues, with convincing empirical evidence, that everyday chunks locate speakers within cultural communities and signal a 'deep commonality' amongst speakers which the learner may not necessarily wish to exercise. So, a note of caution has to be exercised before we rush headlong into the force-feeding of chunks into our learners' lexical repertoires. Ideally, we should let learners learn and use those chunks with which they feel most comfortable, with which *they* can identify, and which may grant them the cultural capital that is so necessary if they ever wish to or need to integrate into any layer of the target culture, for example, as international students studying through English, or as migrants wishing to integrate in L2 communities. In terms of social integration it would certainly seem that those who integrate more successfully are likely to learn and use chunks more naturally, for which Adolphs and Durow (2004) present some evidence. Carlos, contrary to my initial interpretation, did not wish to project his identity as the laughing and dancing Latino who just wanted a big party. He wanted to present a sophisticated image in presenting his argument, and had been listening carefully to find out how it was done by native speakers. This was the key piece of the puzzle that I was missing in those days, because of my lack of awareness of just how deeply the currents run between language and culture. The danger for many teachers is that we still think of language, on the one hand, as a lexico-grammatical system, and culture, on the other, as the more public manifestations of difference, variety, behaviour and belief.

The literature suggests that it may be unwise to analyse chunks, since they are, by their very nature, fused lumps of language which have developed pragmatically specialized meanings over long periods of use. On the other hand, the classroom is the very place where time and space are created for reflection, analysis and awareness of a kind not possible in the hurly-burly of real-time language use outside of the school walls. Indeed, the more students we have in our classes who have picked up chunks here and there, the more opportunities we are given, not just to correct mishearing and misunderstanding from the privileged authority of the teacher's chair, but to see moments like Carlos's use of *festival* as learning opportunities. He may have apprehended the wrong (written form), but Carlos had clearly taken *first of all* as his own and reacted strongly when I misunderstood it in his composition. *He* knew what he wanted to say and he knew who and what he wanted to be; I didn't. I was straying into the dangerous territory of endangering his situated self. I needed a new kind of awareness, not least an ability to see my own language as 'exotic' and above all to understand better how language and the cultural aspects of language use are intertwined, and it took me a decade and the inspiration of a giant on whose shoulders I stand (John Sinclair) to achieve that.

References

Adolphs, S. and Durow, V. (2004). Social-Cultural integration and the development of formulaics. In Schmitt, N. (Ed.), *Formulaic Sequences*. Amsterdam: John Benjamins, 107–126.

Bourdieu, P. (1992). *Language and Symbolic Power.* Translated by G. Raymond and M. Adamson. Cambridge: Polity Press.

Davis, M. H. (2003). Connectionist modelling of lexical segmentation and vocabulary acquisition. In P. Quinlan (Ed.), *Connectionist models of development: Developmental processes in real and artificial neural networks.* Hove, UK: Psychology Press.

Kamhi-Stein, L. D. (Ed.). (2004). *Learning and teaching from experience: Perspectives on Nonnative English-speaking professionals.* Ann Arbor, MI: University of Michigan Press.

Kellerman, E. (1986). An eye for an eye: Crosslinguistic constraints on the development of the L2 lexicon. In E. Kellerman and M. Sharwood Smith (Eds.), *Crosslinguistic Influence in Second Language Acquisition.* Oxford: Pergamon Press, 35–48.

Kramsch, C. (1993). *Context and Culture in Language Teaching.* Oxford: Oxford University Press.

Leung, C., Harris, R. and Rampton, B. (1997). The idealised native speaker, reified ethnicities, and classroom realities. *TESOL Quarterly, 31* (3), 543–558.

McCarthy, M. J. (2008). Profiling spoken fluency. *The Language Teacher, 32* (7), 32–34.

Medgyes, P. (1994). *The Non-native Teacher.* London: Macmillan Publishers.

O'Keeffe, A., McCarthy, M. J. and Carter, R. A. (2007). *From Corpus to Classroom.* Cambridge: Cambridge University Press.

Prodromou, L. (2008). *English as a Lingua Franca : A Corpus-based Analysis.* New York: Continuum International Publishing Group Ltd.

Shields, M. and Wheatley Price, S. (2002). The English language fluency and occupational success of ethnic minority immigrant men living in English metropolitan areas. *Journal of Population Economics, 15* (1), 137–160.

Spindler, G. and Spindler, L. (Eds.). (1994). *Pathways to Cultural Awareness: Cultural Therapy with Teachers and Students.* Thousand Oaks, CA: Sage Publications.

Stanley, K. (Ed.). (2002). Using the first language in second language instruction: If, when, why and how much? *TESL-EJ, 5* (4). Available at: http://tesl-ej.org/ej20/f1.html.

Yeh, C. J. and Inose, M. (2003). International students' reported English fluency, social support satisfaction, and social connectedness as predictors of acculturative stress. *Counselling Psychology Quarterly, 16* (1), 15–28.

Chapter 20

Changing Identities in Japanese–English Bicultural Names

From Parents to Children

Steve Marshall and Tim Mossman
Simon Fraser University

Steve

I'm married to Miyuki. Miyuki changed her name to Miki in the UK for the sake of easier pronunciation. Miki's family belongs to a tiny historical minority in Japan: Japanese Catholics from Nagasaki. As a child in post-war Nagasaki, people would throw stones at Miki's mother as she walked in the street, shouting '*gaijin*!' (foreigner!). She looked foreign. Her grandchildren also look foreign. In the UK they look Asian, and in Japan they look Western.

Just before my sixth birthday, my parents took the unusual step of emigrating from Canada to the UK. I grew up as a foreigner in a small town in the west of England. We became known locally as 'the Americans', even though we came from Ontario, Canada. I now describe myself as English. Just before my elder son's sixth birthday, history repeated itself in reverse: we moved from London to Vancouver.

Living between languages and cultures is an integral part of our story and our lives. Today, we live in Vancouver with our two bilingual boys, in a one-parent one-language home environment. I have learnt Japanese 'naturalistically' at home, listening to my wife and two boys. At home we eat a lot of Japanese food, as well as less common Nagasaki dishes: *saraudon, champon, kakuni donburi*. At my son's school one day, the kids wrote down their favourite food: he wrote *cacoonee manjoo* (*kakuni manju* – a kind of steamed pork bun). This made me laugh as I used to do 'kakuni manju attacks' on my boys, shouting out the words in an evil tone '*kakuni manju*!!!', samurai style, as I pretended that I was about to tuck into their chubby legs. We gave our children bicultural names (English first then Japanese): Joseph Joji (now 10 and called Joey), and James Shouta (now 8 and called Jamie).

Tim

I was born and raised in Vancouver, BC. I'm married to Eiko from Saganoseki, Oita, Japan. I went to Oita soon after graduating from university to teach English conversation. I had planned to stay two years. I ended up staying three. Before I left home, my knowledge of Japan was limited to a few maps, a book called 'Top Shopping in Japan', and several visits to an *Ichibankan* Japanese restaurant on Robson Street. My Japanese language ability was virtually non-existent. Awed by the sights, sounds, and tastes of my new home, I soon immersed myself in all things Japanese. I ate rice with *furikake*. I joined a *kyokushin karate* club and learned how to yell in Japanese from 1–10, grunt, meditate, and show respect. I started bowing a lot. Even on the phone. I actually began to enjoy raw fish. I slept on a futon. I acquired my Japanese informally at first, picking up words and phrases here and there. Watching TV, especially 'Kato chan, Ken chan', proved to be a wonderful source of slang which I couldn't wait to try out on my bewildered neighbours and students. I soon was living up to the '*hen na gaijin*' (strange foreigner) representation that some Japanese have come to expect of foreigners. In 1987, Eiko and I '*musubi awasarerta*' (literally, 'to make a knot') in Chapel Noah, a quaint, little white church in Oita. Shortly after we were married, we moved back to Canada to start a new chapter in our lives.

Eiko and I now live in Vancouver, BC, with our two bilingual sons. When our boys were preschoolers, we lived in a non-dominant home language environment, both of us speaking to our boys in Japanese. However, our home has since morphed into a mixture of Japanese and English language and culture. My love for Japan and my wife's Japanese background were the main reasons we gave our boys bicultural names (Japanese first then English): 優介 Yusuke Timothy, who is now 20) and 平 Taira Micah, who is 16.

We (the authors) have both chosen bicultural names for our sons. Yet, how and why did we choose these names? Our wives described in informal conversations their reasons for the names:

Miki: When we decided their name the most important thing was that the English name has to be easy to pronounce for Japanese, not including the 'r' or 'l' sound, which is difficult for us to pronounce. I was always thinking about my parents because my parents cannot speak any English at all, so they could use this name really freely or without struggling.

Eiko: Yusuke was a popular name in Japan when he was born. The 'Yu' in Yusuke means 'gentle/excellent'. It also has a good sound. Taira is written with a single Chinese character, and means calm and peaceful. I liked the simplicity and uniqueness of the single Chinese character. I was also influenced a little by a Japanese manga (cartoon) artist named Taira Hara who frequently appeared on quiz shows in Japan. I admired him and thought he was smart.

We chose names that were pronounceable for parents, meaningful to family tradition and ethos, with appropriate Chinese characters for representation in Japanese, and names that sounded right. Our intention was to give our boys a bi-cultural grounding, or core, through binominal identification. Yet, how often do we as parents consider the effects that a name, in particular a bicultural one, will have on our children's daily lives and processes of identity formation? Have our children constructed the same meanings around *their* names that we intended their names to carry: *our* attitudes and desires regarding *their* languages, cultures, and identities?

'I'm Not Shouta! I'm Not Shouta!'

Things were going very well with the one-parent one-language home environment that we both strictly followed. In an act of self-indulgence, I never corrected my boys' mistakes for the first four years. I also took notes and recorded their language use as it developed. In fact, Joey understood, but spoke little or no English until the age of three, even though we lived in London. Jamie developed spoken English and Japanese simultaneously. During these years, I noted a range of forms of codeswitching, borrowing of words, and syntactic calque.

As I was about to make Joey's fruit puree in the blender one day, he told me at the age of two: '*not guru guru suru doing yetto*' [*guru guru* = woosh woosh; *suru* = do]. At the age of four, Joey told us about his first French class at school: '*Mummy, boku ipai remember de kiru*' [*boku* = I; ipai = a lot; *de kiru* = can]. The same year, Joey was watching his mum put on make-up: '*Boys not do, girls dake suru*' [*dake suru* = only do]. He would ask: '*Nani doing? Nani looking? Nani eating?*' [*nani* = what]. When Jamie was three, he developed a taste for cheddar cheese and grapes: '*Because when I do cheese dake it's so karai*' [*dake* = only; *karai* = salty]. At the same age, he would call me over by saying '*Daddy, little bit come*', a translation of the Japanese '*chotto kite*'.

I also liked to try out my Japanese at home in London, breaking the one-parent one-language norm, yet Jamie frequently became hysterical, screaming and crying if I spoke to him in Japanese: '*Don't speak Japanese!!!*' We soon noticed that he began to feel uncomfortable with his middle name, Shouta. Shouta is pronounced like the English 'show' and 'ta'. One problem is that it sounds like 'shorter' in British English, and it reads like someone who shouts a lot, a 'shouter'. And here arose my critical moment, when one morning, half out of experimental curiosity and half for fun I called him Shouta-kun (kun is added to boys' names in Japan). Jamie ran at me with venom screaming at the top of his lungs, enraged, '*I'm not Shouta! I'm not Shouta*!' kicking me hard in the legs on arrival. His rage turned to inconsolable crying. Bemused, I reflected on his rejection of the bicultural name that we had given him with all of the positive intentions in the world.

I've always remembered this event but avoided reflecting on it in any depth until now. I thought I'd ask Jamie what he thought. Asking my 8-year-old boy to reflect on his bicultural name was always going to be a long-shot, but I was sure that Jamie would, in some ways, be knowledgeable enough to reflect. After all, he goes to an International Baccalaureate school where reflection is big. Yet, I was wondering how interviewing your own 8-year-old child would fit with Giddens' (1984) view that all agents are knowledgeable. In fact, Jamie's answers show no direct memory of the event, but enough knowledge and reflection to give some emic perspective to this event. In an informal conversation, I asked Jamie about his name and the event.

S: Why do you think we gave you two names, one English and one Japanese?
J: Because my dad's from Canada and mum's from Japan so we wanted to have both.
S: And what about your other name Shouta? How do you feel about that name?
J: I like it, it's not my favourite name.
S: Why not?
J: Because I don't have a clue.
S: When you were little I used to call you Shouta and you'd start punching me and kicking me (Jamie laughs). Remember?
J: No.
S: Don't call me Shouta!! (Jamie laughs) Why do you think you did that?
J: I haven't got a clue. Because it wasn't my favourite name.

Joey also offered some insight into his brother Jamie's critical moment, citing European identity and difference as the factors that he interprets as being behind Jamie's reaction to being named Shouta:

J: I think he didn't like that name because he, I think he likes to be European and doesn't want to have any Japanese in him, he wants to be a European person. Well that was the same with me before. Well, I thought because there were a lot of people who were English and stuff, I wanted to be like them because I don't like being different. And I think that was the same with Jamie, but now I'm getting used to it, it's fine to be different.

I asked Miki her views about the same critical incident. She refers to perceived expectations on the part of Jamie about language use and self/other identification, which relate perhaps to the rigid one-parent one-language home environment:

M: It was not really natural for you to say Shouta, because I think he thought, because you are British in his mind, he thought you have to use, the father has to use his British name, not Japanese, and he didn't like it when you would use Japanese language. He got the idea that Japanese does not belongs to you.

I ended up with the idea that the bicultural names that we gave the boys represented parental attempts to attach or fix a sense of belonging to two cultures, two countries, two languages, to them, and that carrying both names would facilitate their ability to belong in two cultures. Although Jamie shows a lack of memory regarding the event in question, and unfamiliarity with reflecting on something as essential as his names (*I don't have a clue*), he does show a clear understanding of a link between each name and each country/culture. As we were in Europe, and his first name was European, and used almost exclusively in Japan and the UK, he associated Shouta with the other place, the other self within him.

'Dad, Can You Call the College and Tell Them I Want to Switch my First Name to Tim? I Hate it When They Mess Up'.

When Japanese star pitcher *Daisuke Matsuzaka* signed a $52 million, six-year contract with the Boston Red Sox on December 14, 2006, Red Sox nation was ecstatic. Despite his prowess on the mound, his name presented a major phonemic hurdle for his English speaking fans. The nickname 'DICE-K' soon caught on with the media. It wasn't long before T-shirts printed with 'DICE- K' and a pair of dice, number 1 and number 8 (18- his jersey number) were quickly marketed. Ingenious. Unfortunately, no such clever mnemonic exists for my son, Yusuke.

Yusuke and Daisuke share something more than just Japanese blood. They share a name that is hard to pronounce. Yusuke, like Daisuke, is a very common name in Japan, but in Vancouver, a rarity. Written in Chinese characters as 優介, Yusuke can also be represented in the Japanese phonetic script *hiragana* as the four syllables ゆうすけ. The first two syllables – the *Yu* in *Yu*suke, written ゆう in hiragana – sound similar to the English pronoun 'you'. When pronounced in Japanese, the う (*u*) after ゆ (*Yu*) is elongated. The real difficulty lies in the last two syllables, すけ (*suke*), a feature Yusuke shares with Daisuke. Japanese speakers often pronounce the vowel う (*u*) very faintly or drop it entirely at the end of the syllable す (*su*). And the syllable け (*ke*) sounds like the English letter 'K' when pronounced in Japanese. So Daisuke sounds just like 'DICE-K' and Yusuke, like 'YUSE-K'. Here's the problem: English speakers will typically *stress* the す (*su*) and/or pronounce け (*ke*) as 'KEY'. Yusuke, then, often gets called 'YuSUke', 'YuSUKEY', or some other deviant variety.

The above quote reveals a critical moment in Yusuke's life. Yusuke has had to put up with people mispronouncing his name most of his life. What prompted Yusuke to ask me to call the college to switch his name around before the beginning of classes? Was it fear? Could he still hear the voices of his elementary and high school teachers reading through the class list in alphabetical order on that first day of class every September? As his teachers slowly worked their way alphabetically to the Ms, what went through his mind? If we had named him *Timothy* Yusuke, would he still be the person he is today? In Canada, *Yusuke* is marked. It sets him apart. It defines him as different. And it's tough to say. By asking me to switch his name around, was Yusuke making a claim on his inherited *Canadian* identity in a desperate attempt to move out of this marked foreign identity that has followed him around all these years? There can be no doubt that certain languages and accents carry greater cultural capital weight than others. But what about names? In Yusuke's eyes, does *Tim* have greater cultural capital?

Yet, the naturalness of being *Yusuke in Japan* seemed to play a positive role in his identity formation as an adolescent. At age 13, upon returning from a summer spent at his grandma's in Oita, it was obvious to me that he had changed. Not only was he much more confident and fluent in Japanese, but it was like he had discovered a part of his Japanese self that he was very proud of. What followed was equally intriguing. When school began that fall, Yusuke was drawn (instinctively?) to the many Asian international students attending his high school. With a foreign name and half Asian looks, he was even mistaken for an international student as was evident on the page in the yearbook that year devoted to the international students at his school – there was Yusuke smiling for the camera posing with his best friends from Korea. His closest friends were, and still are, Korean.

The mispronunciation of his name has not gone away. But Yusuke seems to have developed some strategies for dealing with it, as was revealed during an informal interview for this story:

Y: It still happens. When people would first meet me they wouldn't know how to pronounce my name. Ummmm, so they would have to ask me a couple of times how to pronounce it and like even later on they would be like, 'Oh, what was your name again?' And when I talk to new people. When I meet people, they say, 'What?' I just say, 'It's Japanese.' And then they understand.

Wanting to better understand how Yusuke felt about being bicultural, I asked him a few more questions:

T: Are there times when you feel more Japanese than Canadian?
Y: Uh, yep.
T: When do you feel that?
Y: Umm, when I hang out with Asian friends.
T: You have a lot of Asian friends?
Y: Ya.
T: How come you have so many Asian friends?
Y: How come? Because . . . I don't know, I connect with them more. I like Asia better than North America.

T: Why is that?
Y: I don't know. It's just the way I am. I like their culture.

The above interview sheds some interesting light on Yusuke's competing identities. Admittedly, there are times when Yusuke connects more with his Japanese side when he is in the company of his Asian friends to whom he feels close. However, what is particularly revealing is that his Canadian-ness seems to occupy a prominent space in his psyche as revealed in his use of the pronouns *them* and *their* to refer to his Asian friends. Why this distinction even though he himself is part Asian?

What, then, can we bring from academic literature to the discussion? The answer is not a lot in terms of building upon studies that look at naming strategies, or specifically, bicultural names in bicultural families. In his 1984 discussion paper, Lieberson highlights the void in the systematic study of first or given names. He suggests that the choices that parents make in naming children relate to conditions of the society and that 'the choice of names may be viewed as involving an interaction between the images that the names held for the parents and the expectations, hopes and visions they have about their children at the time of birth' (1984, p.86). He hypothesizes that names indicate 'the disposition of parents toward the child in the socialization process and this disposition in turn will affect the child's eventual adult position' (1984, p.86). Li (1997) studies naming conventions in Hong Kong, in particular the adoption of a western name as a facilitating strategy in inter- and intra-cultural encounters. The bilingual, bicultural, and binominal identities of 1.5 Generation Korean Americans are analysed in Thompson (2006), specifically the role of Korean and American names in Korean Americans' struggles for identity. Thompson draws on data from one participant who changed her name during school years as a result of difficult pronunciation and teasing, and another who plans to give her children two names in the belief that they will derive benefits from having an American and a Korean name.

Li and Thompson both suggest that the selection of a name from one *language/culture* can play a part in the evolution or conscious construction of a *social identity*, which carries cultural capital (Bourdieu, 1994). The *language* and associated *culture* of the name is thus linked to an aspired-to *identity*, as was the case in our own bicultural naming aspirations, although in a different context. Any theoretical understanding, therefore, must recognize a close link between language and identity: English (British and Canadian) and Japanese names as a grounding or core for a bicultural identity. The common view in the literature on sociolinguistics is that language and identity are indeed closely linked, with language seen as playing a range of roles: a fundamental role in identity (Joseph, 2004, p.3); a symbolic association, not one that can directly predict actual usage (Gumperz, 1982); 'a contingent marker of ethnic identity', and in some cases, a key factor (May, 2000, p.373); language as 'constitutive of and constituted by a language learner's identity' (Norton, 2000, pp.4–5); and identity construction within a relationship between language and culture, and thus meaning making (Hall, 1997, in Phan, 2008). Our children's bicultural, bilingual names thus form a two-way bridge: they constitute and are constituted by social, linguistic and cultural identities.

Our naming choices were about first who *we were* and second who we wanted *our children to become*. In his 2004 work on language and identity, Joseph defines identity in its most simple terms: identity as *who you are*. In this essential sense of 'being someone', a grounded self, the names that we gave our children were an attempt to provide an essential binominal core or anchor with which our children could navigate their bilingual, bicultural worlds. Yet our stories also illustrate that the identities in question are also about who our children were and still are becoming: *what they might become* (Hall, 1996). While the names stay the same, the identities evolve over time, changing with ongoing reflection, and changing senses of self; in this way, they can be understood as reflexive and ongoing narratives of the self as defined in Giddens (1996). Equally, changing social context plays a part, as the example of Yusuke's discovery of his Japanese self and his subsequent desire to switch from Yusuke to Tim illustrates. The bicultural names are thus also linked to socialization and cultural discourses (Benwell and Stokoe, 2006), that is, the socialization processes of our sons, before, during, and after their critical moments. The contexts of this evolution could also be understood as transnational, located in a third space (Bhabha, 1994) somewhere between Japan and the West. Yet we would question whether this makes the identities in question totally non-essential, hybrid, and unfixed in a third space. Instead, we would suggest that a core bicultural sense of self grounds our sons, not only through their names but also through the contexts of their daily lives, and through adapting according to context: their identities are thus 'multiple, dynamic and hybrid' (Phan, 2008). According to Phan, identity can be understood as something like a 'core', a 'root' on which new values are constructed (Phan, 2008, pp.12–13). Their bicultural names are a core that can be understood as being both Japanese and 'Western', *both* rather than one or the other, or neither.

I Don't Like Being Different . . . But Now I'm Getting Used To It, It's Fine To Be Different.

Kumaravadivelu argues that difference is a key determiner in identity, and that 'identity can be understood in a meaningful way only by understanding others and by recognizing and highlighting one's difference in relation to others' (Kumaravadivelu, 2008, p.145). Yet difference in this case is less about 'being Japanese as opposed to being Western', or vice versa. It is more about movement within a bicultural core. Where the English name comes before the Japanese name, the difference is less marked in English-speaking countries; when the Japanese name comes first, the difference is more marked. Through our choice of name order, we marked and formed our sons' identities. And through the choice of having two names, our boys can reject, temporarily move aside, or bring forward a name and an associated identity: '*I'm not Shouta!*'; '*I want to switch my name to Tim.*'

Concluding Points

We have presented our microethnography as a form of ethnography: a means to record and interpret our daily social practices and their reproduction within the socio-cultural contexts of our lives (Bourdieu, 1977; Geertz, 1973). Our ideologies and aspirations as parents were passed on, yet they have evolved through time, space, generation, and social practice. In giving bicultural names to our children, we were searching for something essential, a core identity that would ground our children in our, and hopefully their, bicultural worlds.

Our discussion has offered our personal stories, reflections and a search for meaning in academic theory. Our theoretical understanding centres on a close link between language and identity: English and Japanese names as a grounding, or core, for a bicultural identity, and bicultural, bilingual names as a two-way bridge: constituting and constituted by social, linguistic and cultural identities. These identities are about who you are, and what you might become. And finally, as identities, they are also transnational, ongoing narratives of the self, linked simultaneously to socialization and sociolinguistic discourses.

References

Benwell, B. and Stokoe, E. (2006). *Discourse and identity.* Edinburgh: Edinburgh University Press.

Bhabha, H. (1994). *The location of culture.* London: Routledge.

Bourdieu, P. (1977). *Outlines for a theory of practice.* Cambridge: Cambridge University Press.

Bourdieu, P. (1994). *Language and symbolic power.* Cambridge, Mass.: Harvard University Press.

Geertz, C. (1973). *The interpretation of culture.* New York: Basic Books.

Giddens, A. (1984). *The constitution of society: Outline of the theory of structuration.* Cambridge: Polity Press.

Giddens, A. (1996). *Modernity and self-identity: Self and society in the late modern age.* Cambridge: Polity Press.

Gumperz, J. J. (1982). *Discourse strategies.* Cambridge: Cambridge University Press.

Hall, S. (1996). Introduction: Who needs 'identity'? In S. Hall and P. Du Gay (eds.), *Questions of cultural identity*, pp. 1–17. London: Sage Publications.

Hall, S. (1997). Cultural identity and diaspora. In K. Woodward (ed.), *Identity and difference*, pp. 51–59. London: Sage Publications.

Joseph. J. E. (2004). *Language and identity: National, ethnic, religious.* Houndsmill Basingstoke: Palgrave Macmillan.

Kumaravadivelu, B. (2008). Cultural hybridity and its discontents. In *Cultural globalization and language education*, pp. 118–140. New Haven and London: Yale University Press.

Li, D.C.S. (1997). Borrowed identity: Signaling involvement with a Western name. *Journal of Pragmatics 28*, pp. 489–513.

Lieberson, S. (1984). What's in a name? . . . some sociolinguistic possibilities. *International Journal of the Sociology of Language 45*, pp. 77–87.

May, S. (2000). Uncommon languages: The challenges and possibilities of minority languages. *Journal of Multilingual and Multicultural Development, 21* (5), pp. 366–385.

Norton, B. (2000). *Identity and language learning: Gender, ethnicity and educational change.* Harlow: Pearson Education Limited.

Phan, L. H. (2008). *Teaching English as an international language: Identity, resistance and negotiation.* Clevedon: Multilingual Matters.

Thompson, R. (2006). Bilingual, bicultural, and binominal identities: Personal name investment and the imagination in the lives of Korean immigrants. *Journal of Language, Identity and Education, 5* (3), pp. 179–208.

Chapter 21

Berlin Babylon

Stephen Muecke
University of New South Wales

Berlin. Here I'm a stranger and yet it is all so familiar. You can't get lost, you always end up at the Wall. I'm waiting for my photo at the machine and it comes out with another face. That could be the beginning of a story . . .

(Marion, in her caravan, in Wim Wenders' *Wings of Desire* [*Der Himmel über Berlin*])

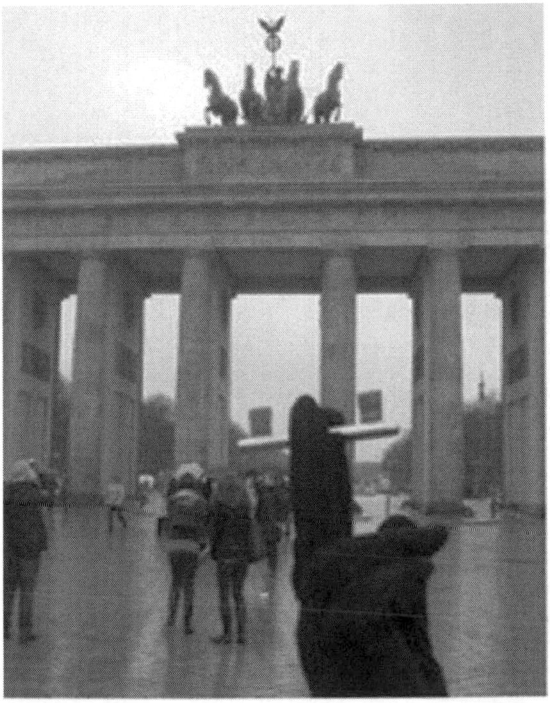

I had never been to Berlin, and I knew there would be no Wall. I knew language would present no great barrier either. Yet I spent six weeks going to evening classes at the Goethe Institute in Sydney to prepare myself for a five-month visiting professorship at the Freie Universität in Berlin. It was more out of a feeling of the need to be polite than any sense of the absolute need to acquire German, for, as everyone says, the Berliners all speak English, and in any case I would be teaching my Australian Studies courses in English.

It is polite, I thought, to have a few words; to make the linguistic gesture from time to time. So, by the time I arrived I indeed had a few words, and could come up with reasonable sentences given a little time to formulate them. In any case I like to learn languages because of my long-standing interest in that particular medium, whatever it is. *Whatever it is?* No, I still don't know, despite years of training in linguistics, learning French and then Spanish, acquiring enough Italian to get by, learning Australian Aboriginal English in the course of field trips in the Kimberley region of Northern Australia.

The vibrations of language are the noise of our social body; we produce these noises individually and collectively. They are essentially part of social reproducibility. Yes, our major human task seems to be *reproduction*, one way or the other, and language is a means to reproduce the sense and sensibility that goes into creation. Through sexual reproduction we create other beings in our own form, and we also, more mechanically, reproduce texts according to a pattern that is still not fully comprehended. Whatever it is, language is not just *structural* or *functional*, nor divided up into Phonetics, Syntax and Semantics. It is also vibration, noise and music; it also attracts and repulses. In this essay I want to explore some of the most intimate attractions of language (at the word, the sentence level) and also its capacity for spinning out into myths and stories.

You need a partner to reproduce, to keep things alive, even to keep a work in progress like learning German alive, so I sought out a *Tandempartner* in my early days in Berlin, someone for conversational exchange. I met Evelyn Boho through the university, so she became my *Tandempartnerin,* writing to me saying: *Lieber Herr Muecke, ich freue mich, Ihnen mitteilen zu können, dass wir für Sie eine Tandempartnerin für Deutsch-Englisch gefunden haben.* We met at the Balzac Kaffeehaus in Steglitz, near where I lived. She was wearing a cute linguistic T-shirt: *I'M SO ADJECTIVE, I VERB NOUNS.* It quickly became clear that her English was nearly perfect, while my German was still at the *kindergarten* stage, as we say in English-German. What could I offer? I gave her advice on improving her accent: 'Just fake it,' I said,

> like, there's no point in trying to be *yourself* if you want to improve your accent in English, you have to *perform* the kind of English accent you like. Actors do it all the time. So the more you practise performing the English-speaking version of yourself, the more it becomes second nature and, and hence, nature. No one could tell anymore if you are faking it. In any case, its *sexier.* Sorry, what I mean to say is, you sound more confident.

Our social order which we reproduce, among other things, via language, is something that is *performed* and *maintained* rather than given in advance. Evelyn and I danced around and negotiated our awkwardnesses over language, but more importantly attraction/repulsion, whether there was a hidden agenda or whether this partnership would last, and so on. I find out she is unemployed, that she came from Prague as a young girl in that famous 1968 Spring. Three sessions later I'm showing her family photos on my laptop and after that the partnership lapses. Too much information and not enough reproduction?

For me it is not a question of language representing the world, as if we (and our language) are *over here* waiting to intervene in the already-real *over there,* rather each intervention is into a negotiable reality and these realities are multiple. Different kinds of practice, even different styles and performances, constitute different worlds. It is in this spirit of engagement with the multiple real, where each engagement furthermore engenders some kind of reproduction, that I venture into a major international exhibition at the Pergamon museum, 'Babylon: Myth and Truth'.

Visitors pause in front of the marvellous image of the Striding Lion in turquoise and orange baked tiles. It was brought from Iraq in the early twentieth century, part of the Processional Way which led out of the ancient city of idolaters through a massive gate named for the Mesopotamian goddess of love and war, Ishtar, whose symbol was the lion. Each year, during the celebration of the great New Year Festival, the images of the city's deities were carried out through the Ishtar Gate and along the Processional Way past some 120 guardian lions such as this one to a special festival house north of the city.

This was all part of the accumulation of treasures brought to Europe by cultures newly obsessed with antiquities. While some scholars worked on artefacts, others investigated, and then mythologized via comparative philology, the origins of the European languages back down the Indo-European tree to Sanskrit. Babylon was one of the crossroads of this linguistic history, and here in the museum the roads cross again as the ancient is layered with the contemporary, literally on two levels: 'Myth' and 'Truth'. The floor above presents various creative departures on the Babylonian mythologies: *Myth* begins with a video installation Zid/Wall by Danica Dakic from Sarajevo. Sixty-four close-up shots of lips moving feverishly, telling different stories in as many languages. The cumulative, and fitting, result was babble-on. 'The talking wall', the caption noted rather prosaically, 'reflects the linguistic condition of our time'.

Two of the major ideas of this Babylon exhibition are that our civilization is currently going through a Babylonian moment, and that it is haunted by Babylonian themes. Dakic's piece turned on this first idea, while the second came across strongly in a video installation entitled 'Black and White (Babylon)' by Douglas Gordon, famous for another film about Zinedine Zidane. Gordon's piece depicts a buxom 1950s stripper, hypnotically swaying in black and white slow-motion. She looks like the Mother Of All Strippers; I'm thinking her style *keeps reproducing* Ishtar, Goddess of Love or Babylonian whore, depending on whether you follow the pagan or the Christian nomination.

Dash Snow, New York Graffiti artist turned bad boy sculptor, had a piece which was *NY Times* front pages featuring Saddam Hussein decorated with his own semen. The decadence and waste of the contemporary world, resonating back down the ages! Yet 'Truth' is represented by archaeology, by the whole lower floor of the exhibition, by the magnificent Ishtar Gate, as if it were not already replete with Myth. Why is it so easy to draw that fictional line between fiction and non-fiction, as if there were only two levels for the real to occupy, or one really: Truth and its distortions?

A quotation from Wittgenstein is spinning in my head, 'A whole mythology is deposited in our language' (1979: 10). I find I cannot look at a word without feeling the capillary roots of mythology extending down into its history. I can't read the word 'salary' without wondering if I am 'worth my salt' [a. AF. *salarie* = OF. *salaire,* It. *salario,*

Sp., Pg. *salario*, ad. L. *salarium*, orig. money allowed to Roman soldiers for the purchase of salt, hence, their pay]. *We must plough over the whole of language*, Wittgenstein went on, in his 'Remarks on Frazer's *Golden Bough*'.

Key Story

I had arranged to get an apartment in Prinzlauerberg, where else? Met the agent in her office on Eberswalder Strasse. When she handed me the set of keys, the largest of the bunch was an extraordinary key that I had never seen before.

> 'What on earth is this?' – showing her the double-headed key.
>
> '*Also*,' she said. And, as she explained, I realized that this was a Berlin story.

In a city, surrounded on all sides, you can begin wherever you like. You can begin telling a story right here and now, about any little thing, or big thing. Where you begin is contingent and arbitrary. But having begun, the constraints fall into step beside you, like comrades joining the march. Yes, the constraints are allies! By constraints, I mean the formal limits that are set; could be objectivism, could be something as formal as a text organized as an *A–Z*. Constraints are also set by practices, because each observation is a selection, each word enchains a syntax, and you are committed to following the experience through to the end, following it through its chain of transformations. This is the logic of the story, as opposed to fictions. Fictions, having encapsulated the experience, lift themselves out of places. They have *Aufhebung*. Fictions are defined by a transcendent and cosmic being; they create their own imaginative worlds that float off somewhere.

But here in Berlin, with Brecht and Benjamin, we feel the pull to follow the thread of experience as it forms that transformative chain of mediations. Berlin is the city also of Simmel, Kracauer and Hessel – all were inspired by living in a city which tried out its identities with and against others, a 'performing . . . unfinished city [which] does not seem merely to perform but to *show itself* performing' (Whybrow, 2005: 16) says Nicolas Whybrow, usefully citing Christine Boyer:

> As the distinction between reality and fiction becomes an artifice, just one manner of constructing a series of things, 'we depart from the Euclidean universe of unity, identity, centre, and enter the non-Euclidean universe of pattern, superimposition and differential function. Instead of continuity we have leaps in space, instead of linear time we have time warps that 'superimpose one part of the pattern on another.'
>
> (Boyer, 1998: 492)

'Leaps in space' I'm not so interested in. I'm getting on a bit; it is too strenuous a metaphor for me. Rather I want to *follow* the everyday experience and *reproduce* it so that is has something of the stickiness of that which is memorable. The only way I know how to do that is with storytelling.

And just what is this experience? It is not always the same kind of thing. Each bit of experience, each contingency, potentially has a life of its own, a mode of existence (Latour, 2000). It is not all sitting there at the same level, the same substance, objective reality or whatever you want to call it: waiting for the human subject to come along and give it an interpretation. A world of only two poles, subject and object, would be a fearsome reduction: 'stuff' on the one hand and the mystery of human subjectivity on the other?

'So this Berlin Key', explains the agent letting the apartment, 'we call it *der Schließzwangschlüssel* or "close constraint key". It is a design that forces people to close and lock their doors, typically the front door of an apartment block, so the same key is shared by that community – kind of socialist', she jokes. 'Now, look, it has two business ends, see? After you unlock the door, the key must be retrieved on the other side of the door after it has been locked again. The mechanism makes the retrieval of the key impossible until the door has been locked again from the other side. A Berliner locksmith, Johann Schweiger, invented it in 1912, and it was produced by Albert Kerfin & Co; the company still exists, I believe. That was about the time that big avenues were being built out from the central part of the city, with lots of apartment blocks. It saves on having a concierge keeping an eye out for undesirables. Today of course it is being replaced by the electronic keypad.'

I'm thinking this little bit of technology, this clever invention, also builds a morality, by imposing its formal constraint. It is impossible to be irresponsible and leave the door open so any passing tramp can come in out of the snow and sleep in the *hof*. It is impossible to take your key from the lock until you have bolted the door from the inside. Bruno Latour was so engaged by this key that he called a little book *La Clef de Berlin*, and included a chapter discussing it in his lively fashion. He is imagining an archaeologist of the future finding this strange object and trying to interpret it:

> . . . Without a demonstration, with directions, she would certainly have an attack of hysterics. These keys that pass through walls are too reminiscent of ghosts not to frighten us. This gesture is so unhabitual [sic] that one can only learn it from someone else, a Berliner, who has in turn learned it from another Berliner, who in turn . . . and so on and so forth by degrees all the way back to the inspired inventor . . .
>
> If our friend were fond of symbolic anthropology, she would have consoled herself for not being able to go in by endowing this key with a 'symbolic dimension': in West Berlin, before the wall fell, the people supposedly feel so locked in that they double the number of bits on their keys . . .
>
> There, that's it, a repetition compulsion, a mass psychosis of the besieged, a Berlin-Vienna axis; hm hm. I can already see myself writing a nice article on the hidden meaning of German technological objects. That is certainly worth spending a cold night in Berlin. But our friend, thank God, is only a good archaeologist devoted to the harsh constraints and exigencies of objects.
>
> (Latour, 2000: 332)

I too am tempted by the symbolic: the double key that opens up the double city, a key that 'goes both ways', being symmetrical, that is, more about diplomacy and negotiation than it is about dialectics. But Latour's satire notwithstanding, he has given me three intellectual tools for my ethnography: *objects* that are indispensable to storytelling based on a singular *experience*, and the necessary *contiguity* (or contagion) of the story ('one can only learn it from someone else, a Berliner, who has in turn learned it from another Berliner'). And third there is the *democratization* of humans and things. Stories don't just circulate among humans, for humans; they are a technical-social-moral-metaphysical complex. As Benjamin said about storytelling, 'with these words, soul, hand and eye are brought into connection' (1968: 106–7); stories are rhythmed with tools and labour, or emerge out of boredom ('the dream bird that hatches the egg of experience' (90)), and the connection with memory: '*Memory* creates the chain of tradition which passes a happening on from generation to generation . . . it starts the web which all stories together form in the end. One ties on to the next, as the great storytellers, particularly to Oriental ones, have always readily shown' (97).

So once installed in my apartment in Prinzlauerberg, I have had a lot of fun going in and out to get stuff, just so I can use the *Schließzwangschlüssel* as often as possible, while 'freedom in constraint' has become a little refrain in my mind that amuses me. After a couple of days I hear that my friend the Australian novelist Gail Jones is passing through town, so I arrange to meet her at the Buchhandlung Café in Tucholsky Strasse, in Mitte; I thought this would appeal to her literary tastes, since the name means 'bookshop'. I had arrived early and had a chance to look around the neighbourhood and make a couple of interesting discoveries before opting for a drink at the Buchhandlung while I waited. I tried a Berliner Weisser beer, and was informed that this was indeed colourless beer and should be coloured with green or red cordial.

There were no books to speak of in the Buchhandlung, though a couple of youths were sprawled on raised platforms and reading trendy magazines. Above the bar, a mechanical contraption made of conveyor belts moved the oars of toy galleons uselessly. Watching this gave me something to do, apart from listening to the conversation of the American couple next to me, who seemed irritated by the world in general.

Gail arrived before I had managed to dispose of the embarrassing sweetly coloured local specialty. I whisked her out of there: come on, I want to show you a couple of things. Just up here on Oranienburger Strasse, not far from the Neue Synagogue, this old building has been preserved in its half-bombed state: It used to be the Tacheles Department store (Tacheles is Yiddish for 'plain speaking', 'or in German *Klartext*', adds Nicolas Whybrow, who quips that 'the only thing that's clear about this text though is that the story it would tell is by no means over' (96)). The exposed walls make the street-scape gap-toothed, where walls are opened up to a gaze inviting new planes of composition, like a canvas, or inviting the cinematography of Wim Wenders in *Wings of Desire*. But the building, occupied by squatters in the early 1990s, has an interrupted or fragmented structure; stairwells leading to health and safety nightmares for the authorities. Downstairs on the street they sell T-shirts and avant-garde *schmuck*, and there are nightclubs and bars thick with graffiti and stencilling. The rear, much of it missing, has been repaired in a gaudiesque style, and there is a workshop in the back yard where clunky steel sculpture is welded together.

Now, let's head back down this way along August Strasse, I found this other place that might be good for dinner. In my first couple of days in Berlin, I have discovered, all by myself, an old *Ballhaus* dating from the 1920s. But having made this discovery it will turn out that everyone knows about this place, and its story will keep cropping up, strangely contagious. But at this early stage, I have this sense of unmediated contact. Here are Gail and myself, standing inside the doorway of Clärchen's Ballhaus, the maître d' is trying to tell us about the place, but we need translation from another couple, a young Berliner with his Brazilian girlfriend. She is radiating southern-hemisphere sunshine in this northern winter; we get chatting. They are thinking of coming back later for dinner and a dance, so are we. And we do, a pizza, *Tchechische bier*, the music that evening is a DJ spinning rock classics.

So what are these stories you are collecting? Gail is asking me. Well, I already have one. My next door neighbours from Sydney took me to dinner last night, and their friend from Munich was there. Günther was a chief engineer at a major German firm. On his retirement he decided to go back to Burma where he had done some work and spent a few years. He wanted to help children from the Hills tribes, located in that country rising towards the Himalayas, with their education. So he set up a foundation, very low key so that it would not draw the fire of the Myanmar authorities. About 120 friends contribute their own funds that are channelled through Franciscan monks in Burma, who then build dormitories and schools so that these kids can continue their education. Günther was advised by a Buddhist friend, 'Don't give your money to the Buddhist monks; they will only use it to gild their pagodas; the kids won't see a penny!' So that's how he ended up in a good working relationship with the Catholics.

Meanwhile, for the last 30 years, he has been walking the Alps. Every year he takes a couple of weeks off, and, having started in the far west of the mountain chain, walks a calculated stretch, climbing peaks on the way. Different people join him in different years, guys who know how to rock climb. Günther says he has the wrong physique to be an extreme climber, too lanky. Short stocky people make strong climbers. He has timed it so that he will walk into Vienna for his seventieth birthday, at the end of his journey, and all his friends will be there to celebrate.

Tobias Sunday, November 2, 2008

The next week, I meet Tobias, friend of a friend, who was *captured* by the kind of speech we call a *spiel* in English, borrowed from 'play' in German. Tobias recounted over a beer that he didn't know he could get so involved in a performance that it would kidnap him. It could have been the dope, but that induces caution rather than recklessness. Very late, one night in the street in Prinzlauerberg, an old guy, long greasy hair, a baseball cap, says, '*Komme*! It's a performance we put on. *Komme*! Down here.' What, into a hole? Tobias didn't want this Faustian invitation into a dirty cellar, dirt floor. But there's a conversation and because he's a student and into all that *Intellektualismus*, the guy is saying *yes!* Adorno! He was the last; all the philosophers after that are just DJs spinning quotations. Now Tobias is hooked, and when they descend, they lock the door behind them. There is only one candle in the corner on a wooden crate. And the performance begins with another weird person who enters the cellar with a computer and crashes it to the floor; the pieces fly dangerously everywhere. Scary, very scary. The atmosphere thickens and there is no escape. Now the baseball cap pulls a gun, or something that looks very real, and is pointing at one, then another, saying this is not what it seems, you were wrong, no, right, or wrong? Make up your mind NOW! Who will rise again . . . long pause . . . after the death I can instantaneously induce? The terror persists long after, but the baseball cap is saying now, almost pleasantly, so how did you like it, OK?

The Horsetrough

I walked past *Zur Pferdetränke* many times on my way home before working up the courage to go in. It is a narrow bar with a spider-web crack low on the dirty front window, just where someone might have landed a kick after being refused credit yet again. Or maybe a more respectable local resident got tough, couldn't control their outrage any longer. The window has remained unrepaired for months. *Zur Pferdetränke* wears it proudly like the clientele wears their tats and piercings. Fuck *you* if I'm going to participate in *your* order of things! Ordinary feelings pool up and burst their banks. It might be the same in any city, especially a national capital. These high-density dwellers can be arrogant or proud, and condescending towards provincials. It's like an assertion of presence. You live alone, you haven't spoken to anyone all weekend, and she gives you the wrong bread rolls in the bakery: 'No! those two, them there!' You realize you have barked. Her lips go to set position. Eyes flash. You get your change, *Ruckgeld*, without a word. But that was a little bit of street theatre that you created; it will return to you throughout the rest of the day, lapping in diminishing circles of intensity. It is necessary to create, any way you can, does she realize that? Now service people are being trained to say, 'Have a nice day', 'See you next time', '*Shön Abend*'. The Berliners are not fooled: they go away muttering, *Klishee! Klishee!* Originality is necessary too.

The Storyteller

The great Berliner Walter Benjamin wrote about storytelling like it was a dying art: 'The art of storytelling its reaching its end', he wrote, 'because the epic side of truth, wisdom, is dying out . . . And nothing would be more fatuous than to want to see in it merely a "symptom of decay", let alone a "modern" symptom. It is rather, only a concomitant symptom of the secular productive forces of history . . .' (86). Secular capitalist society, the novel, information, are what replaces the craft of the storyteller for Benjamin, but I would like him to be wrong. Benjamin says

> What differentiates the novel from all other forms of prose literature – the fairy tale, the legend, even the novella – is that it neither comes from oral traditions nor goes into it. This distinguishes it from storytelling in particular. The storyteller takes what he tells from experience – his own or that reported by others. And he in turn makes it the experience of those who are listening to his tale. The novelist has isolated himself. The birthplace of the novel is the solitary individual, who is no longer able to express himself by giving examples of his most important concerns . . .
>
> (87)

This is why I would argue that the novel, even fiction writing in general, is a confidence trick, but a good one. It takes our eyes off the ball, the ball being what we can learn from experience. It breaks the chain of experience. It repackages experience as illusion, and puts it on the production line to sell as if the literary product itself were so much ore. Non-fiction is outselling fiction because people want real stories again, not the pretty pictures or imaginings of isolated artists.

In 'The Work of Art in the Age of Mechanical Reproduction' (1968) Benjamin seems to have overstated the modernist break with the primitivist past, for reproduction is and was always in place, with or without mechanical assistance. In arguing that language is 'generative' (in a reproductive rather than a Chomskian sense), I have suggested that each language operation works through the attraction of partners, that language works through such alliances at both micro levels and at the level of the genres we might label Myth or Truth. These stories about being in Berlin have rather suggested a multiplicity of ways language can exist in the spaces of a city. Only if we conceive such a context as nurturing can mythologies continue to hatch from our words.

References

Benjamin, W. 1968 [1935]. The Storyteller. In *Illuminations*, New York: Shocken Books.

Benjamin, W. 1968 [1935]. The Work of Art in the Age of Mechanical Reproduction. In *Illuminations*, New York: Shocken Books.

Boyer, C. 1998. *The City of Collective Memory: Its Historical Imagery and Architectural Entertainments*, Cambridge, MA: MIT Press.

Latour, B. 2000. The Berlin Key or How to Do Words with Things. In P. Graves-Brown (ed.), *Matter, Materiality and Modern Culture*, London: Routledge.

Wenders, W. 1987. dir. *Wings of Desire* [*Der Himmel über Berlin*].

Whybrow N. 2005. *Street Scenes: Brecht, Benjamin and Berlin*, Bristol: Intellect.

Wittgenstein, L. 1979. Remarks on Frazer's *Golden Bough*. in C.G. Luckhardt (ed.), *Wittgenstein: Sources and Perspectives*, Hassocks: Harvester Press.

Chapter 22

Changing Stripes – Chameleon or Tiger?

Denise E. Murray
Macquarie University

Background

I grew up in a small Australian city, one with a small, but diverse ethnic population – Aboriginals, Papua-New Guineans, European refugees from the aftermath of World War II, descendents of Chinese gold miners, British immigrants trying to improve their economic lot, and Greek and Italian coffee shop and restaurant owners. Not that I knew any of these people. I lived in white lower middle class suburbia. But, somehow, I had an affinity for difference. I read travel adventure books voraciously and lived other lives vicariously. I imagined myself as a patrol officer in New Guinea, a medical doctor in India, or an intrepid traveller in Europe; I identified with girls in British boarding schools or young women growing up on the East Coast of the USA or Canada.

Two books from my childhood in particular stand out – and, despite several moves around the world, have remained in my library (along with the classics such as *Little Women*). One, *The Young Traveller in Switzerland* (Meier, 1951) started me off reading most of the 'young traveller' series. While the 'plot' is contrived and not very engaging, I was entranced by the descriptions of life in the various countries. The Switzerland book especially intrigued me because it described the different languages (French, Italian, Romansh and Schwyzerdütsch) and dialects used there. This was my first exposure to a truly multilingual country and to the idea that even within one language there are varieties. I loved reading the glossary and trying to pronounce the Schwyzerdütsch words (the books provide a helpful pronunciation guide). The other book that has followed me around the world is *Danger Patrol*, an adventure story of the life of a new patrol officer in New Guinea. Here I was amazed, not only by the languages and exotic scenery and lives of the local people, but by the way law was administered by Australians in a locally relevant way. At such a young age I discovered that laws are sociocultural and sociopolitical artefacts – not that I could have articulated such an understanding. But, it started me on a life journey of both questioning the status quo and tolerating ambiguity.

In my sixth grade, my primary school enrolled its first non-British-origin student – a young Dutch girl. I was entranced. She was ignored by my classmates, but I latched onto her. We tried to communicate – she had no English and I certainly had no Dutch. We became fast friends until after a few months, her parents moved to another suburb and Patsy to another school. I still wonder where she is and how her identity was fashioned as a New Australian (as immigrants were called officially in those days).

In primary school, I loved mathematics, grammar and especially Greek and Latin roots! I was intrigued by patterns and how Greek and Latin had influenced English. In high school, I was taught both Latin and French. While I found I was not a natural language learner, I was fascinated by the structures of language – the differences and similarities. Speaking French was another matter. As in my 'conversations' with Patsy, I was frustrated by my inability to communicate ideas and feelings accurately and fluently. I became a high school maths and English teacher, even being asked to teach the grammar sections for other teachers! I taught in country schools and city schools and had several non-English speaking students in my classes over the years.

Like many Australians, I planned a trip to Europe and a working holiday in England. Since airfares were far too expensive, my friends and I decided to go by ship – a long journey, made longer (five weeks) by the closing of the Suez Canal after the Six-day (Arab-Israeli) War. We chose a Greek ship – because of cost and in the hopes of a different experience. The ship we travelled on was not a cruise ship – it brought Greek immigrants to Australia and on its return trip took Greek families back to Greece to visit family. Only a handful of passengers were not Greek. Therefore, for the year prior to our trip, I decided to learn Greek (no, not ancient Greek – modern Greek). The only possible teacher was the local Greek priest, whose only English was an enthusiastic and often-repeated, 'Greek is such a rich language'. Since he also taught Greek Saturday school to children of Greek-Australian families, I had to use children's books and sentences he made up to translate. Greek was intimidating – lots of declensions and lots of conjugations, and three genders for nouns. The possible combinations were infinite. But, I moved in the local Greek community, attending weddings, church services and events, and even dating some Greek men. My infantile attempts at speaking Greek were greeted with great enthusiasm, tolerance, and an outpouring of gratitude that a non-Greek Australian would take the trouble to learn Greek. Once I got on the ship and then to Greece itself, I found the same acceptance. I knew my Greek was grammatically flawed – but it didn't seem to matter to my Greek interlocutors. This changed my view of language. So, I didn't have to be accurate to pass a test; I could muddle along and, as long as my conversational partners were welcoming, we could communicate. More proof that tolerating ambiguity was acceptable. In Greek I had conversations that went from banal 'Where's . . .' to discussions of philosophy, literature, and politics.

From then on, my modus operandi when in any non-English speaking country was to try to use the language, even if it was a string of nouns and verbs with no grammatical morphemes – and, it mostly worked. I knew I was a foreigner. I never tried to assimilate. I just wanted to communicate.

What Variety to Use?

Rather than relate one particular incident, I want to list a string of incidents all on the same theme of language variety.

In my twenties, I lived in London. After a frustrating stint as a supply teacher, which was more baby-sitting than teaching, I tried unsuccessfully several times to get positions teaching high school English in private schools. I did eventually get a position, but teaching maths! The school had several Japanese girls, whose fathers worked for Japanese banks, airlines, or the Embassy. Their fathers wanted them to get extra coaching in English and also for their mothers. The two English teachers at the school were not interested in additional work, and so they asked me if I was interested, knowing I had been an English teacher (as well as a maths teacher). I was more than happy to earn extra money to help finance trips to Europe, theatre tickets, and so on (teachers were very poorly paid in the UK at the time). I loved the work and enjoyed meeting the girls' families. In fact, I became good friends with several families and we have stayed in touch to this day. I realized fairly quickly that ESL was different from teaching grammar and literature to native speakers and so took a training course at International House. I fell in love with ESL/EFL teaching. So, I tried to get teaching positions in Europe during the summers – primarily to have more experience and to live in Europe. For many positions, I never even got to interview. Twice I did get an interview, but was told 'We don't accept teachers with an Australian accent. We want to teach British English.' As a very stubborn Aussie, I thought 'I'm going to sound just like the Queen and see if they refuse me then!'

So, I worked on my accent and vocabulary. I was indistinguishable from a well educated English woman. I constantly confused people. I was at a cocktail party given by the Victoria League, a society that provided social events for visitors from the British Commonwealth. Guests were from a variety of different Commonwealth countries. The hosts were upper class English men and women doing their bit for Commonwealth visitors. A well-dressed older woman approached me and we started to talk . . . the usual cocktail party small talk about the weather, theatre etc. During the conversation, I mentioned the school I was teaching at (quite prestigious). She commented that she hadn't seen me at any other functions or committee meetings. I said, 'But, I'm not here as a host. I'm a guest. I'm from Australia.' She looked horrified. 'But, you don't sound like an Australian,' she said as she stalked off.

Fast forward several years. I return to Australia and begin teaching in an intensive English programme for international students. I'm at one of the large Australian department stores, buying make-up. The Australian shop assistant is very friendly and talkative. During the transaction, she asks, 'Do you like it here?' I'm confused and so tell her I think it's a good department store. But, I'm thinking, 'What a weird question to ask!' She clarifies, 'No, sorry. I meant do you like living in Australia?' She has assumed I'm a British immigrant and is trying to be hospitable.

Fast forward several more years. I marry, arrive in California and look for work. I apply at the local adult education centre, where a very friendly American reviews my qualifications (by this time I have a master's, more than seven years' ESL/EFL teaching experience, and some teacher training experience) and informs me, 'Well, you're certainly well qualified. In fact, overqualified. And, we need a teacher to start straight away. But, you'll have to do something about your accent. Do you think you can learn an American accent?' she says tongue-in-cheek.

I'm standing in line at the supermarket and talking with my husband. We get to the checker, who says to me, 'Where are you from? I love the way you sound.' And, this is repeated over and over again – at restaurants, in department stores, and so on. I'm teaching undergraduate and post-graduate students at San José State University. Students fill out evaluation forms. One student writes at the bottom, 'I love your enthusiasm for the subject AND YOUR ACCENT.' Over the next two decades, I receive numerous paraphrases such as 'I love to hear you talk'. I wonder, 'Do they ever listen to the content of what I say?'

My husband and I are on a visit to family in Australia. We strike up a conversation with an Australian couple at a waterfall in North Queensland. They ask how we're enjoying the trip and then, sensitive to Canadians who don't want to be assumed to be American, they ask, 'What part of North America are you from?' 'San José,' I say. 'But, I'm originally Australian.' 'You've sure picked up the lingo,' they comment.

Why Be a Chameleon or a Tiger?

So, why did I change my variety of English so completely in Britain that I was assumed to be native and yet, after almost three decades living in the US, I have a blended variety that is neither Australian nor American? The answer lies in the rather opaque title I gave this chapter. In some situations, I'm a chameleon; in others, like the tiger, I can't and don't change my stripes. I prefer to be different.

As we construct our own identities, identities are imposed on us – by society at large and by those we interact with. In Britain, my variety of English was looked down on; I was refused work because of it. But, we are not without agency. We may assimilate, adapt, or reject various identities available to us. Language is central to this identity construction. Through language we position ourselves – we let others know who we are and how we want to be perceived. In my case in Britain, I chose to adapt – acquire the local variety and appear to assimilate through language. I say 'appear' deliberately, as I never rejected my Australian identity. I was in fact a chameleon. In contrast, in the US, my variety has some prestige. In fact, as I was writing this chapter, my local newspaper reported on a survey conducted in the US. The survey asked people in the US to respond to questions about their accent. While 47 per cent said they were happy with their particular regional accent, 36 per cent also said they would like to speak like the Queen of England, while speaking like Australian actor Hugh Jackman was ranked second (SpinVox, 2008). So, in the US, I adapted by keeping various features of my Australian/British variety, thus retaining my identity as Australian through language. Like a tiger, I kept (some of) my stripes! However, I adopted sufficient North American linguistic features for people outside North America to assume I was North American. Chameleon-like, I changed some of my stripes. There is also a subtle irony in the story line of *The Young Traveller in Switzerland.* The hero was a young English boy of 14! So, when I enjoyed his adventures, as I identified with John, I was constructing an identity with a different gender, age (I was only 11) and nationality – I'd learnt from a very early age that being a chameleon was quite an adventure.

My husband and I recently spent six years in Australia and we have visited often over the past three decades. During our time living there, I noticed that Bill consciously chose Australian vocabulary, while I retained US terms. He'd use *lift,* while I'd use *elevator.* He changed some of his pronunciation, sometimes saying 'nyu' rather than 'noo'. He even tried to adopt the Aussie term of solidarity, *mate* (sometimes astonishing the locals). His identity as an American was never in doubt to anyone he interacted with, but he wanted to accommodate to Australia and demonstrated this accommodation through his choice of language. I, on the other hand, wanted to be different. By using American vocabulary and maintaining the salient pronunciation features I'd acquired in the US, I was identified as being American. My American friends and colleagues find it hilarious that Australians (and other non-North Americans) think I'm from North America.

Defining oneself within one's larger social context is fundamental to human life. 'The development of a personal identity includes the meaningful integration of basic notions of space, time, and social relations' (Fantino & Colak, 2001, p. 591). It is generally agreed that identity is the view that we have of ourselves and of our place(s) in the world in the past, now and in the future. However, our places in the world are multiple, changing, sometimes conflicting, and influenced by the power relations in individual interactions and in society more widely. My life experiences have profoundly affected my view of myself. But, I don't have just one view; I have many views of myself. I am a chameleon.

Research shows that essential to our self-identity is our cultural identity (Wakholi, 2005). So, moving from one set of cultural norms to another can lead to disruption in identity formation. One such cultural context is national identification. When we move from our country of origin, we lose daily contact with the interactions that characterized the cultural values, beliefs, and behaviours that had defined our identity. So, moving from our country of origin can be a dehumanizing experience (Coker, 2004). People who move to another nation must therefore (re)define themselves in terms of their new national context. Yet, nationality is not only a political construct, but also a sociological construct, as I found the first time I lived outside my country of birth.

While living in England, I was particularly struck by the ongoing debate about 'U' and 'non-U' language, which began with the publication in 1954 by Alan S.C. Ross of 'Linguistic class-indicators in present-day English' in the Finnish philological periodical *Neuphilologische Mitteilungen.* I read with interest *Noblesse Oblige* edited by Nancy Mitford and containing a condensed version of Ross' paper, along with witty and satirical articles by Mitford and Evelyn Waugh, among others. U referred to Upper Class and Ross gave lots of instruction about what language U speakers use, from address terms to vocabulary to pronunciation. Thus, to be considered upper class, I needed to say looking glass, jam, table-napkin rather than mirror, serviette, and preserve; and not sound the /l/ in gold, Ralph, or solder. But, according to Ross, a non-U speaker adult can never become a U speaker! Mitford humorously claims that it is only through their speech that the upper class can be recognized 'since they are neither cleaner, richer, nor better educated than anybody else' (Mitford, 1961, pp. 37–38). So, while I may have 'passed' as upper class British, I never could BE one – at least once they learnt I was born in the colonies!

So much of the literature on identity formation or identity dissonance has been conducted with refugee and immigrant populations. Further, the effect of language on identity construction is mostly around languages, rather than varieties. While I recognize that delimiting language and dialect is essentially a sociopolitical act (see, for example Hudson, 1980), it is a useful distinction for my discussion here. While there is a considerable body of research on the characteristics of and attitudes towards dialects (Pakir, 1991), especially as related to standard language ideology (see, for example Cameron, 1995; Kachru & Nelson, 1996; Pennycook, 1998) very little attention has been paid to code-switching across dialects, to multidialectalism or the effect of dialect choice on identity formation. Lippi-Green (1997), however, shows how we appropriate different varieties to 'position ourselves in the world' differently (p. 30); how we use different varieties to mark our associations and identities. Can a tiger change its stripes? Only if it's a chameleon disguised as a tiger.

References

Cameron, D. (1995). *Verbal hygiene.* London: Routledge.

Coker, E. M. (2004). Dislocated identity and the fragmented body: Discourses of resistance among Southern Sudanese refugees in Cairo. *Journal of Refugee Studies, 17*(4), 401–419.

Fantino, A. M., & Colak, A. (2001). Refugee children in Canada: Searching for identity. *Child Welfare, 53*(5), 587–597.

Hudson, R. A. (1980). *Sociolinguistics.* Cambridge: Cambridge University Press.
Kachru, B. B., & Nelson, C. L. (1996). World Englishes. In S. L. McKay (Ed.), *Sociolinguistics and language teaching* (pp. 71–102). Cambridge: Cambridge University Press.
Lippi-Green, R. (1997). *English with an accent: Language, ideology, and discrimination in the United States.* London: Routledge.
Meier, M. (1951). *The young traveller in Switzerland.* London: Phoenix House.
Mitford, N. (Ed.). (1961). *Noblesse oblige.* Harmondsworth: Penguin Books.
Pakir, A. (1991). The range and depth of English-knowing bilinguals in Singapore. *World Englishes, 10,* 167–180.
Pennycook, A. (1998). *English and the discourses of colonialism.* London: Routledge.
SpinVox. (2008). Hugh Jackman's strine and Bono's brogue also rank high, but when it comes to James Gandolfini . . . fuhgeddaboutit! [Electronic Version]. *SpinVox.* Retrieved September 22, 2008, from http://www.spinvox.com/americans-love-their-accents-but-wouldnt-mind-queen-of-englands-stately-tongue.html
Wakholi, P. (2005). *African cultural education: A dialogue with African migrant youth in Western Australia.* Unpublished MEd Thesis, Murdoch University, Perth.

Chapter 23

Vanishing Acts

Cynthia D. Nelson
The University of Sydney

With a sudden surge of determination, I recently purchased instruction books, short stories and a dictionary in Italian, a language that I grew up with but never mastered. After a period of studying on my own, it became clear that to improve my fluency I would need to actually converse with others, so I spent some time investigating all of the different Italian classes on offer here in the cosmopolitan city of Sydney. I never did sign up; I lost my nerve. Despite a love of all things language-related, a career in language teaching and research, and a visceral longing for the sounds and feel of my childhood language, the thought of taking a language class as a student fills me with dread.

On the Move

My family never stayed in one place for long. Born in the United States to a family with mixed European ancestry, by the age of seven I had lived in three US states and three European countries. My father was in the Air Force, so I attended mostly American-run schools on military bases. While we were living in Italy I did pick up a bit of the language—not in school, not a single Italian lesson there, but on the streets and balconies of the neighborhood: playing with the neighbor kids (and chickens) in the alley, making a game of writing out English-Italian vocabulary lists, engaging in the intricate bargaining required at the local markets in order to buy anything from boots to blood oranges, or listening to the smooth radio hits of Sergio Endrigo, heartthrob of the Puglia region.

When we returned to the US, this time Texas, I befriended some Latina girls in the lunchroom. They'd chat away in Spanish, I'd interject in Italian, and we'd generally understand each other—if not the specifics, then at least the gist. When my family moved north I studied high-school French, since neither Italian nor Spanish were on offer at the new school. (My French teacher was fluent in Italian but adamantly refused to tutor me in it, which I gathered had something to do with the Italian occupation of her native Yugoslavia during World War II.) At university I took a course in Italian, but this, I soon discovered, was a far cry from Ostunese, the local dialect I had spoken as a kid. Standard Italian soon got left behind in the swirl of university life, where I studied English and world literature, acted in plays, and began to dabble in the joys and despairs of love (or what looked like love at the time).

During and after university I worked in a multitude of jobs that did not interest me in the slightest—pulling espresso, raking leaves, typing legal briefs. These jobs allowed me to pursue both an education and unpaid work that did interest me (peace activism, street theatre), but I longed to pay the rent doing something I actually liked. One day

I saw an ad for a weekend workshop on teaching English to refugees. I signed up immediately, plunking down my last $20 for the training book. True, I was broke and my stomach was growling. But it was in that church basement, teaching American greetings to a Laotian man who had only been in the country for a matter of days, that I found my calling.

As a graduate student in a Master of Arts in Teaching English as a Second Language (ESL) program, meeting fascinating people who shared my life-long passion for words and the world's cultures, and standing in front of my own classes for the first time, I experienced a joyful integration of heart and mind, humor and spirit; I felt at home, in my element.

Except that in the foreign language classes I was taking as a student, just the opposite was occurring. It didn't seem to matter which teacher I had or whether the class was at the university or at my local neighborhood center (in desperation I tried them all), sitting in class day after day I felt myself quietly disappearing.

Unwanted Lessons

Sprawled diagonally across my bed, I am writing Spanish answers into a spiral notebook while my enormous orange tabby looks on. I know the drill: answer each yes/no question with a complete sentence, even though the resulting "dialogue" is more peculiar and stilted than any conversation I can imagine having. One question gives me pause: *¿Fue usted al cine con su novio anoche?* Did you go to the movies with your boyfriend last night?

I have a rule, which is that I never lie in a foreign language. I never say things that are not true just for the sake of getting through a language exercise. This rule is surprisingly difficult to uphold, but I make a point of it, not just to maintain my own sense of integrity but also because I am convinced it will help me to learn the language, make it my own. I consult my bilingual dictionary and, after some deliberation, answer the question as best I can.

After a few days our assignments are returned, graded. Two points have been taken off for one answer: *No, fui al cine con mi novia anoche.* The teacher has circled the words "No" and "novia," perceiving these to be in error. Where I had written "No" she wrote "Sí"; where I had written "novia," she "corrected" the final "a" by putting a slash through it and writing an "o" over it. In other words, she changed my answer from "No, I went to the movies with my girlfriend" to "Yes, I went to the movies with my boyfriend."

I imagine going up to the teacher's desk after class to discuss my homework, explaining that, actually, what I had meant to say was that I'd gone to the movies with my girlfriend, my partner, my lover, and I had looked up a few options in the dictionary and settled on "novia," which I had thought wasn't quite the right word as it sounded too "married up" . . . I mean, my girlfriend and I didn't live together, and we each dated other women, but it was sort of a serious relationship; but then it wasn't like we were *engaged* or anything. So what should I refer to her as in Spanish?

I never raise it with the teacher. What I do instead: start sitting in the back row, sink down low in my seat, try to avoid her eyes. Keep the wrongness of those missing points completely to myself, tucked deep.

***

I'm basking in the pleasure of hearing my own words wash over me, but in perfect-sounding Spanish, without the impediment of my own fumbling accent. We were asked to write a page about someone we admire, and today my work has been chosen by the teacher to be read aloud. I think I detect a few corrections she's made to my verb tenses, but I'll have a chance to pore over her written comments later, when our papers are returned.

I chose Lily Tomlin. I wrote a few paragraphs about seeing her perform live: how much I laughed at her comic routine, how my mother liked her too, how the woman who wrote much of her material, Jane Wagner, was her partner in life as well. The class is applauding (just part of the routine) and the teacher is handing back my paper before I realize what has happened. She read out my tribute, but skipped over the part about Lily Tomlin's female scriptwriter being her life partner. As the teacher places the paper in my hand, her eyes meet mine with a look that seems to say "Sorry, but I'm not that brave . . . and *don't* pull that again."

I am stunned. Completely deflated.

I could catch her after class—ask why she had censored those particular sentences, tell her how that made me feel. What I do instead: finish out that language class. Never take another.

***

We're having lunch at an outdoor café in New York City, chatting with the couple at the next table. Turns out they too flew in for yesterday's lesbian and gay rights march, which drew over 1 million people from far and wide. It is the twenty-fifth anniversary of the Stonewall riots: the streets are chock-a-block with queers, and sheer exhilaration is in the air. My honey and I have had an entire week of hand holding without being stared at, glared at, cursed, or spat upon; instead, we've been met with nods, friendly greetings, all-out grins. This change is affecting me like a healing balm; I am becoming jubilant, carefree.

These two men are from Berlin, where the gay scene is very lively, they tell us; both are out to their families and in their workplaces; everyone's happy, life is good. Our conversation turns to work, and when I mention that I teach ESL, one man's face turns suddenly dour.

The year before, he tells us, he had gone to California for a few months seeking to improve his English. In the first few days the class was asked to describe their perfect partner: "I am lucky, I already found mine," he answered, and went on to describe the man he'd been sharing his life with for seven happy years. From that point on, the class became a nightmare. He'd walk in, and the whispering, giggling, and pointing would begin. Nobody would sit near him for pair or group work. I ask him what the teacher did about it. Nothing, he says; she seemed as horrified as his classmates at the thought of interacting with a gay man. So he dropped out of that program and transferred to another.

In the new class, he tells us, he did things differently: his Hansel became a Gretel. With great care and vigilance, he'd make sure to speak of "she" and "her" when asked about life back home; he'd get phone calls from Berlin and say it was his girlfriend calling. This daily charade kept him from being harangued or isolated—in fact, he became quite popular; but at the same time, he says, it left him feeling deceitful, distracted and exhausted. "On the outside I was happy, but on the inside—." He shakes his head, turns his gaze to the street.

Disallowed, Disengaged

When asked to contribute to this book, I knew immediately what I wanted to write about. Of the hundreds of thousands of faces in New York that week, it is that Berliner's that I vividly recall, some fifteen years on. Of all the hours I spent in foreign language classrooms, it is the slow-motion memories of feeling silenced and shamed that stay fixed in my mind. For me, the events I've described carry a potent emotional charge that hasn't diminished with time.

Despite some trepidation, I am putting these narratives into the public domain because, unfortunately, the experiences they relay are not unusual. Over the years I have heard many similar tales from friends, colleagues, and students, yet stories like these rarely, if ever, make it into print in the highly mono-sexualized literature of language education.

Mi Novia

In my first narrative, I was essentially recast as being in a straight relationship instead of a lesbian one, when a sentence (which seemed to me perfectly grammatical) in my homework was marked wrong and "corrected" by the teacher. Why didn't my teacher simply explain that "novia" refers to a woman, and that if that was what I meant then my sentence was fine? However, if I had intended to refer to a man, here was the way to do it . . .

Language learners are highly likely to make linguistic errors related to gender, which means that when references are made to same-sex relationships it will not necessarily be clear whether the wrong pronoun or word-ending was used inadvertently, or whether a gay identity or relationship was disclosed intentionally (De Vincenti, Giovanangeli & Ward, 2007; Nelson, 2009). Nonetheless, potentially ambiguous communications do need to be addressed in ways that will not simply alienate those students who may, unbeknownst to the teacher, be gay.

It seems that learning environments are often dominated by heteronormative thinking, which involves "creating, sustaining, and perpetuating the erasure, marginalization, disempowerment, and oppression of sexual others"—that is, anyone who is not heterosexual (Yep, 2003, p. 18). Telling a female student that she did not go to the movies with her girlfriend (as she had indicated) but with her boyfriend may not constitute a *deliberate* act of erasure or marginalization, but it does perpetuate the erasure and disempowerment of lesbians—especially since many of us are quite used to having our love lives and desires denigrated or denied.

The "severe prohibition against naming queerness" (de Castell & Bryson, 1998, p. 233) that continues to pervade education settings and discourses often relies upon "a kind of *studied* ignorance" that makes it possible "*not* to see or to acknowledge, nor, therefore, to *act* upon the complexities and contradictions staring you straight in the face" (p. 237). Morrison (1989) refers to "willful oblivion" (p. 12), Sedgwick (1990) to "ignorance effects" (p. 415). Did my teacher not even canvass the possibility that my answer was, in fact, plausible? If so, was she willfully "acting ignorant"?

In any case, as a fledgling language learner and a newly out lesbian, incidents like these diminished my confidence, and made it seem less and less possible that, with perseverance and practice, I could one day inhabit this new language, and make it mine.

Lily Tomlin

In my second narrative, the teacher censored the lesbian content of my writing when she read it out to the class. Just naming a well-known entertainer as a lesbian was apparently transgressive; in doing so I broke an unspoken rule of the classroom—that same-sex relationships and realities were unmentionable in that space. Why didn't this teacher simply read out what I'd written? Or, if she thought I might not want that, why not simply check with me?

"Heteronormativity is ubiquitous in all spheres of social life yet remains largely invisible and elusive" (Yep, 2003, p. 18), which can make it difficult to challenge.

Even when the task at hand would seem to open the door for a discussion of homosexuality, the topic can still be forcefully silenced, as illustrated in a study by Moita-Lopes (2006) of a fifth-grade literacy class in Brazil. During a unit of work on the theme "respecting difference," the students were instructed to write a report on "a situation in which someone has acted in a biased way," as the teacher put it (Moita-Lopes, 2006, p. 37). When one boy, Juca, asked whether he could write about prejudice associated with homosexuality, the teacher seemed to find that topic completely unacceptable. She responded by reprimanding the boy for being disrespectful: "If we are going to be disrespectful, I am going to put my books away and go home, we are wasting time here." Another boy, Rico, immediately reinforced the teacher's reprimanding of Juca for raising homosexuality as a possible topic. Rico said to Juca: "You're such a brat. Why are you talking about this now?" Rico received no reprimand from the teacher for his remarks (Moita-Lopes, 2006, p. 38; see also Dalley & Campbell, 2006).

What lessons did the fifth-graders take away from this classroom interaction? How does the experience of being censored or reprimanded for just raising gay themes affect student engagement and learning? In my case, the recurring pattern that I witnessed in my foreign language classes—the heteronormative silencing of any mention of lesbian or gay existence—had the effect of directly impeding my own learning, by making me feel that in just speaking *about* a lesbian, let alone *as* a lesbian, I was unwelcome, insignificant, in the wrong.

Gretel

My third narrative relays the challenges faced by a German man trying to study English in the US. Finding it impossible to be openly gay in the language classroom, thanks to the behavior of his classmates and teacher, he deliberately constructed a straight persona in order to make that restrictive environment tolerable.

Unfortunately, the language learning experiences and classroom dilemmas of gay men, bisexuals, lesbians, transgender people, those questioning their sexual identity, and those whose sexual subjectivity is fluid or ambiguous, remain largely under-researched. This remains the case even though recent studies suggest that a number of students learning a language are doing so for reasons directly connected to their sexual identities or relationships: for example, having migrated with the aim of fleeing anti-gay persecution or violence (Beebe, 2002; Nelson, 2009); or seeking to meet, or to better communicate with, a partner from another part of the world who speaks a different language (Ellwood, 2006; King, 2008).

One of the teacher educators I interviewed for my investigation of sexual identities in language education spoke poignantly of witnessing young gay men and lesbians in his classes who had a "sense of dissociation from themselves . . . That sense of I'm here . . . but I've left my sexuality outside the classroom . . . You can . . . see it in their eyes" (Nelson, 2009, p. 99). Something of this sort occurred for my acquaintance from Berlin, who in order to be part of the class felt he had to dissociate from himself and craft a heterosexual persona that required constant linguistic vigilance, rather than being able to simply focus on his studies.

Trying Again

As a young woman trying to broaden my linguistic horizons, what I was seeking seemed so simple: a classroom in which I was "allowed" to be a language student and an out lesbian at the same time, so that I could use the new language to speak freely about my daily life. The German man I met in New York was seeking something similar. Yet for each of us this proved impossible.

The experiences recounted in this chapter, which took place well over a decade ago, have fuelled, haunted, and guided my own efforts to promote linguistic diversity and language learning by investigating language education as a multi-sexual space. Through my research, I have found that many language teachers (gay and straight) are eager to engage rather than alienate the queer students in their classes, and are experimenting with ways of teaching multi-sexual cohorts and curricula (e.g., De Vincenti et al., 2007; Moita-Lopes, 2006; Nelson, 2009). I have also found that students (straight and gay) from around the world say they benefit from open class discussions about the ways in which sexual identities and inequities feature in their day-to-day communication and intercultural interactions (Nelson, 2009).

Narratives may prove useful prompts for such discussions, as they can help to unpack the ways in which identities (sexual and otherwise) are variously enacted, interpreted, denied, misunderstood, embraced, and disavowed during the processes of language learning, language teaching, and language use.

***

While I was finishing this chapter, my partner was searching for a French class. She found a downtown language school that sounded good, and asked me if I wanted to study Italian at the same place, since it too was on offer there.

Why not, I thought. I've changed. The times have changed.

She rang the school and spoke with one of the teachers. Their conversation, she told me later, went something like this:

"I want to take a French class and my partner wants to take Italian."

"What level are you?"

"Probably Beginner 2."

"And your partner, what's he?"

"She's intermediate, I think."

"Well, he will need to be assessed."

"So, can she ring you to do that?"

"Yes, just have him call us."

"Right."

How much have the times changed, I wonder.

References

Beebe, J.D. (2002). Unfinished business: Identity formation and rejection through language learning. *The Language Teacher (JALT), 22*(6), 17–21.

Dalley, P. & Campbell, M.D. (2006). Constructing and contesting discourses of heteronormativity: An ethnographic study of youth in a Francophone high school in Canada. *Journal of Language, Identity, and Education, 5*(1),11–29.

de Castell, S. & Bryson, M. (1998). Don't ask; don't tell: "Sniffing out queers" in education. In W.F. Pinar (Ed.), *Curriculum: Toward new identities.* (pp. 233–252). New York: Taylor & Francis.

De Vincenti, G., Giovanangeli, A. & Ward, R. (2007). The queer stopover: How queer travels in the language classroom. *Electronic Journal of Foreign Language Teaching, 4*(Suppl.1), 58–72.

Ellwood, C. (2006). On coming out and coming undone: Sexualities and reflexivities in language education research. *Journal of Language, Identity, and Education, 5*(1):67–84.

King, B.W. (2008). "Being gay guy, that is the advantage": Queer Korean language learning and identity construction. *Journal of Language, Identity, and Education, 7*(3/4), 230–252.

Moita-Lopes, L.P. (2006). Queering literacy teaching: Analyzing gay-themed discourses in a fifth-grade class in Brazil. *Journal of Language, Identity, and Education, 5*(1), 31–50.

Morrison, T. (1989). Unspeakable things unspoken: The Afro-American presence in American literature. *Michigan Quarterly Review, 28*(1), 1–34.

Nelson, C. (1999). Sexual identities in ESL: Queer theory and classroom inquiry. *TESOL Quarterly*, 33(3), 371–391.

Nelson, C.D. (2005). Transnational/Queer: Narratives from the contact zone. *Journal of Curriculum Theorizing, 21*(2), 109–117.

Nelson, C.D. (2008). The class is asked what they think of when they hear the words "United States" (poem). *Multicultural Education, 16*(1), 30.

Nelson, C.D. (2009). *Sexual identities in English language education: Classroom conversations.* New York: Routledge.

Sedgwick, E.K. (1990). *Epistemology of the closet.* London: Penguin.

Yep, G.A. (2003). The violence of heteronormativity in communication studies: Notes on injury, healing, and queer world-making. In G.A. Yep, K.E. Lovaas & J.P. Elia (Eds.), *Queer theory and communication: From disciplining queers to queering the discipline(s).* (pp. 11–59). New York: Harrington Park.

Chapter 24

Dog Rice and Cultural Dissonance

David Nunan
University of Hong Kong/Anaheim University

The first foreign language that I was ever taught was Latin. I attended the local Catholic boys' school in a mining town in the semi-arid interior of Australia. After my mother's death, I was going through her rather meager possessions and came across my school report cards. I have no idea why she kept these. They did not paint a particularly flattering portrait of me as a young student. ("David is a distraction to himself and all those around him.") One fact that did surprise me however was the number of students in the class—86. It never struck me or, as far as I know it, any of my classmates that this was at all unusual. We did not consider ourselves to be victims of "the large class" syndrome. Class sizes of 80 to 90 students were the norm, although they must have been hell for our teacher, the Marist Brothers and lay teachers. I realize now why we were mostly addressed as "boy" or "you"—they simply didn't have the head space to remember all of our names.

We were taught Latin, because it was the firm conviction of the Brothers that all 86 of us should aspire to join a religious order. To qualify for the seminary, we would need Latin. It was the firm conviction of most of us that we should get the hell out of the school as soon as the law allowed and join our fathers, uncles and brothers on one of the mines. By the end of junior high school, the number of students in the class had plummeted to 14. By then, however, the Brothers had long given up on us and switched us from Latin to Geography. I was extremely disappointed. Most of my classmates couldn't care less either way, although a previous owner of my dog-eared Latin primer would have been pleased. On the inside of the cover, he had written:

"Latin is a language as dead as dead can be
It killed the mighty Romans.
And now it's killing me."

Latin stood me in good stead when it came to my next attempt at learning a foreign language—Italian. Or so I thought during the first few lessons. I started studying Italian for fun just after I had graduated from university. Also I had met the person who taught the course at a social event and she convinced me it would be fun. After the first few lessons, as the learning load increased exponentially, it became somewhat less than fun. Despite my experience with Latin, a considerable number of years ago now, Italian grammar trips me up at every twist and turn. And do I really care whether or not Mrs. Bruni finds her way to the post office? She's a native speaker of Italian, after all. If she can't find her way there, what hope do I have? It isn't until I go to Italy the following year and attempt to activate my "book learning" that the language begins to fall into place.

My third attempt at being rescued from the disease of monolingualism (which bumper stickers assure me is curable) occurs when I take a position as an assistant professor at Chulalongkorn University in Bangkok. I find myself living in a neighborhood where no-one speaks any English. (As this is the late 1970s–early 1980s this could be practically anywhere in Bangkok.) I throw myself into the task of learning what, in those days, was an exotic tonal language—these days of course thousands of foreigners are totally fluent in the language. When I tell my Thai acquaintances that I plan to learn Thai, they applaud my ambition, but then pour cold water on it by telling me that Thai is an impossible language to learn. My Western friends just laugh and give a "been there, failed at that" roll of the eyes.

My narrative is an account of a single incident that occurred at a point where I had acquired a reasonable degree of proficiency in the language. In the next section of the piece, I present the narrative. In the section that follows I try to make sense of the incident in terms of the theme of this collection: language, culture and identity in contact. Although the narrative presented in the following section might appear to be somewhat pedestrian, if not trivial, it was critical to my identity as a second language user in ways that I explore in the discussion section of the chapter.

I live at the end of a very deep soi in Bangkok. Sois are lanes that snake their way off the main arterial roads in Bangkok. It takes about fifteen minutes to make my way to the main road. Sometimes I take a tuk-tuk, or three-wheel taxi. I do this relatively infrequently—when I'm not feeling well, or when I have a heavy load of shopping—because it costs two baht and on my (local) salary, this is extravagant. Despite the heat, today I decide to walk. By the time I get to the mouth of the soi my shirt is sticking to my back. It's a Saturday afternoon, and I'm on a shopping expedition. I go to the wet market on the opposite side of the main road for fruit, vegetables, fish and pork, and then cross back to buy a bag of rice at the rice store. That is all they sell—rice. There are five grades of rice. The top grade is eaten by the Thai royal family, corporate CEOs and foreigners (otherwise known as "farang"). It is comparatively expensive. Not surprisingly, the bottom grade is the cheapest. It is eaten by dogs and by me. Unlike most foreigners working in Bangkok, I am not wealthy. In fact, as a teacher working on local terms, I struggle to make ends meet. I am paid the same salary as Thai teachers, but have to pay foreign prices for most things. The assumption is that all foreigners earn whacking great salaries and should therefore pass a little of this largesse back to the Thais. This has given rise to the two-tier system of charges, something of which most foreigners are blissfully unaware. Only those who have learned to read Thai can decipher the squiggles on the admissions counter at Dusit Zoo announcing that the entry fee for Thais is ten baht, while the rest of humanity will have to pay twenty-five.

I don't eat dog rice out of extreme poverty. Despite my modest salary, even I can afford the grade that is enjoyed by nobility. I eat dog rice because I actually prefer it to the fancier and more expensive stuff. It has a chewy, almost meaty texture that I really like. This admission will probably annoy my family and embarrass my friends, but it's out there now. And I am not alone. This shameful preference for the cheapest variety of rice has been admitted to me (often after one or two Beer Singhas), not only by foreigners, but also by Thais.

The rice shop is about as basic as any shop can be. It is long and narrow, with a counter and five big bins of rice. It is dark inside the shop, a nice relief from the relentless glare of the sun outdoors. There is a musty smell, and the countertop and floor are dusted with fine powder from the rice bags.

The woman who runs the rice store has her back to me as I enter. She is pouring rice into bags, weighting them, and then sealing them up. I bid her a good morning in Thai.

She replies, and asks what I would like. I ask for a bag of dog rice. Continuing to pour rice into bags, she asks me what kind of dog I have.

"Oh, I don't have a dog," I reply.

"So what do you plan to do with the rice?" she asks.

"I plan to eat it."

At this she turns around.

Registering me as a farang, a look of horror flashes across her face. She drops the bag of rice she is holding onto the counter and says to me in Thai "Phut pasa Angrit mai dai." (I don't speak English.)

"I wasn't speaking English," I reply to her in Thai.

"Phom paasa angrit mai dai." "I don't speak English," she repeats.

"I'm not speaking English." It does no good. The linguistic shutters have gone up. I point to a bag of dog rice and push some coins across the counter.

I worked hard at becoming fluent in Thai, the first tonal language I had attempted to learn. I did this for two reasons. First, I lived in a neighborhood where no one spoke English. To meet my basic daily needs, I had to learn Thai. Second, and this sounds rather mealy mouthed but it happens to be true, I wanted to show my respect for the country and the culture in which I was living. I wanted to identify with Thai language and culture. I liked the language and the people. I loved the food and would often wander around the covered wet market near my home even when I had nothing in particular to buy. (Although there was *always* something to buy in the wet markets!) I even enjoyed the weather. About the only thing I did not enjoy was the traffic.

Before proceeding with an interpretation of the narrative, I should make a brief comment on how I am using "culture" in this piece. As we noted in our framing chapter to the collection, there are well over 100 definitions of culture in the literature (Gudykunst and Kim, 2003). I rather like Judd's characterization. Judd suggests that culture can be defined as ". . . the system of shared objects, activities and beliefs of a given group of people" (Judd, 2002: 10). While the definition may appear simple, and even simplistic, it captures the three essential variables that differentiate a given culture from other cultures: the artifacts or tools that members of the culture possess, the ways they behave, and the beliefs they hold. In my narrative, the artifacts were language and the Thai classification system of rice. The behavior was the interaction between me and the rice-seller, and the beliefs had to do with what was considered possible in terms of foreigner use of the Thai language.

Attempting to define identity is just as tricky as trying to define culture. I think one reason for this is that capturing the essence of any given culture can only be done in terms of "the other." Just as a fish is unaware of water (until it is removed from the stream), so we are unaware of our own culture until we rub up against another culture. I should modify this from "culture" to "cultures" as we all simultaneously belong to multiple cultures or subcultures, although we may not be consciously aware of the fact. At its simplest, identity is the recognition of membership of a particular culture or subculture. I find it impossible to talk about identity without considering culture, and I wonder whether, in fact, the constructs are separable. For me they are not.

How does this speak to the dog rice incident? Most SLA research into the construct of identity is based on the assumption that an individual's identity is derived from his or her membership of one or more social groups (see, for example, Tajfel, 1981). The dog rice incident (and this was just one of many that occurred to me in my time in Thailand) reinforced the fact that there was never any possibility that I could identify with the target culture in the sense of becoming a member of that culture, and, in fact, it would have been a form of cultural arrogance to expect that I should be accepted. What I did want, however, was to be acknowledged and accepted as a competent speaker of the language and someone who was sensitive to and appreciative of the culture. In some ways, the dog rice incident served to push me away. Alienation would be too strong a word, but such incidents (and, as I say, there were many during my time in Thailand) did engender a sense of social distance—a rather childish attitude of "if you don't want me, then I don't want you."

According to Schumann's Acculturation model, the greater the distance between two cultures, the greater the difficulty in learning the language of the culture. My experience of living and working in Thailand and attempting to learn the language certainly supports this notion. Once it became apparent to me that attempting to narrow the gap between my culture and my adopted culture were futile, indeed contradictory, my motivation declined. Having developed a comfortable working knowledge of the language, I was no longer motivated, as I had been in the beginning, to become a highly proficient user of the language. I was able to "get by" quite comfortably with my current level of proficiency, and my inability to "close the gap" between my own cultural space and that of my host culture acted as a disincentive to further effort. (For a detailed review of current considerations of identity in L2 learning, see Ricento, 2005.)

In thinking about the intersection between language and culture, I recalled Halliday's (1993: 11) comment that

> Language neither drives culture nor is driven by it: the old question about which determines which can be set aside as irrelevant, because the relation is not one of cause and effect but rather (as Firth saw it, though not in these words) one of realization: that is, culture and language co-evolve in the same relationship as that in which, within language, meaning and expression co-evolve. Thus, above and beyond the random, local variation between languages that was the subject matter of earlier topological studies, we may expect to find nonrandom variation realizing different construals of reality across major alterations in the human condition.

Earlier I hinted at the difficulty of separating culture and identity. Indeed, I suggested that one can only be defined in terms of the other. Halliday has now thrown language into the mix. Halliday, of course was speaking phylogenically about the evolution of language and culture in general. My experience was ontological, and concerned the individual experience of acquiring a second language. The experience of learning another language does, however, drive home the complex interrelationships between language and culture, in this case a four way interrelationship between my first language, my home cultures, the target language and the target culture. In interactions with native speakers of Thai, a set of reciprocal relationships and assumptions had also to be taken into account—that is, the attitudes and frames of reference of my interlocutor about his or her home language and culture as well as assumptions about my first language and culture. The number of variables therefore grows to eight. (The literature on "host culture" and "host custom" is pertinent here. See, for example Cushner and Brislin, 1996; Gudykunst and Kim, 2003.)

In other words, I had assumptions and beliefs about:

- my first language and the way it is used to get things done;
- my home culture and the norms and rules in that culture that have to be followed to get things done;
- the Thai language and the way it is used to get things done;
- the Thai culture and the norms and rules in that culture that have to be followed to get things done.

However, there is also, and always, "the other," in this case the dog rice lady and her assumptions and beliefs about:

- her first language and the way it is used to get things done;
- her home culture and the norms and rules in that culture that have to be followed to get things done;
- the *farang's* language and the way it is used to get things done;
- the *farang's* culture and the norms and rules in that culture that have to be followed to get things done.

Getting something done, even something as simple as buying a bag of rice, will call into play these eight sets of assumptions and beliefs. I'm not suggesting that these will be well-formed or even consciously held but they will frame the interaction nonetheless. The success or otherwise of an interaction will hinge on the crucible into which these eight variables are thrown. In most intercultural interactions, stereotypes and misperceptions are the norm. (Regrettably, in many Asian cultures, some Westerners get away with bad behavior because they know they are expected to behave badly.) However, roadblocks on the road to effective communication can be dealt with if there is good-will and a willingness to negotiate, as Block (this volume) so powerfully attests. Vitachi (this volume) also has some interesting things to say on this issue.

When I was moving to Thailand, I made an initial foray into the language and also attempted to find out what I could about the culture. I found that "outsider" descriptions of Thai culture tended to be grossly oversimplified. Kramsch (1991:218) calls this the "four Fs" in which culture is reduced to "foods, fairs, folklore and statistical facts." In my case, prior to moving to Thailand, my cultural sensitivity training consisted mainly of practical tips such as "Don't pat small children on the head" and "Don't point the soles of your feet at others when sitting down." Underlying these practical tips was the complex panoply of Buddhist cosmology of which, at the time, I was blissfully unaware. Most cultural sensitivity and awareness can only be picked up as one makes mistakes and confronts cultural and linguistic dilemmas in situ. It is one thing to learn the different form of address to use to those of higher and lower status (one's work colleagues and landlady versus servants, waiters and small children). I had no trouble in knowing how to address my landlady, a very wealthy member of the Thai establishment and President of the Bangkok Bank of Commerce, but how did I address her grandsons. Did I use the high status "khun" form, or the diminutive "nou" (meaning mouse)? It was as bad to use the high status form inappropriately as it was to use the low status form. When greeting people with a "wai," palms held together as though praying, how high should one hold one's hands. The only way to learn was to get it wrong, and then learn from the mistake.

The incident with the dog rice lady, trivial as it was on the surface, triggered in me a chain reaction of thoughts, emotions and reactions. I was in the process of forming my identity as a *farang* in Thailand, and desperately wanted to avoid being stereotyped as "one of those overbearing strangers with big noses who are badly behaved." I wanted to become fluent in the language and get close to the culture, realizing that I could not have one without the other.

In my struggle to make sense of the dog rice incident, I had to confront the issue of identity. I quickly came to the realization that identity is a troublesome construct. One could say it is the slipperiest of notions in a pantheon of troublesome constructs. "Who am I?" is a question that lurks at the back of most people's minds once they reach the stage of abstract conceptualization. But, as we intimated in our introductory chapter, there is no single answer to the question.

> Keith Richards was once asked "Who is Mick Jagger?"
>
> "Oh, he's a great bunch of blokes," Richards replied.

And this is the numb of the identity problem. It is not a unitary construct. We are not unitary creatures. Identity is therefore not a monolithic entity, a sort of psychological Stonehenge (Lin, 2008). Like all slippery creatures, identity won't stand still. Our identity shifts according to the company we keep and the languages we speak. My identity is partly constructed by my perception of you. It is also partly constructed by my perception of your perception of me, which may be accurate or way off the mark.

The radical psychotherapist R.D. Laing put his finger on the problem, capturing the linguistic knots that men and women get tied into in a series of Jack and Jill poems. Here is a selective example:

JACK: The trouble with you is that you are envious of me.
JILL: The trouble with you is that's what you think.
JACK: You never give me credit for anything. You can't bear to admit that I've got it.
JILL: That's where you go wrong. You can't bear to admit I don't care.
JACK: You are a pain in the neck. To stop *you* giving me a pain in the neck I protect my neck by tightening my neck muscles, which gives me the pain in the neck you are.
JILL: My head aches through trying to stop you giving me a headache.

(Laing, 1970:10)

And perhaps linguistics is the numb of the problem. The philosopher Wittgenstein argued that all philosophical problems are linguistic at heart. How can linguistics help inform the debate on identity? The linguist Michael Halliday argues that our propensity for nominalization is the root of a great many linguistic evils. Nominalization is a process of turning processes into things. The result is a kind of metaphor. When we identify with a particular cultural or social group, we see ourselves as belonging, in part at least, to that group. When we nominalize the process by talking about our identity, we are turning a process, a happening into a thing. But perhaps the thing itself does not exist. It is a concretization of a process, freezing a set of shifting processes into a thing in the same way as the molten lava from Mount Vesuvius turned the living breathing inhabitants of Pompeii into stone.

There is considerable evidence that the ability to connect with the target culture and community outside of the classroom significantly enhances the language learning experience. Take for instance Campbell's (1996) diary study of her experience as a language learner of Spanish in Mexico. Halfway through her intensive language course she began dating one of her teachers (Tito). This gave her an entrée into rich language learning and cultural experiences such as parties, family gatherings and weddings. In one of her diary entries, she notes:

> Week 5: There were plenty of positive aspects to the evening at the Piano Bar in terms of language learning. I heard a lot of slang and fillers that I haven't gotten anywhere else. Maybe I could pick some up if I had more of the input. I did have to talk a lot in Spanish, like to Alberto and Mari's brother. And with Tito I spoke Spanish and he often spoke English, but not all the time. I spoke English only when I had a difficult verb structure coming up—past modals, counterfactual conditionals, etc. I commented at one point how I was speaking Spanish and he English, and he said it was fun. And it's true, it *was* fun.
>
> (Campbell, 1996: 211)

There is also evidence that an inability to connect with the target culture can have a seriously damaging effect on one's ability to climb beyond the foothills of a foreign language. The classic story of the dissonance between attempts to learn language and attitudes towards the culture in which the language is embedded is told by Schumann who documents the failure of a Puerto Rican immigrant into the United States. Carlos failed to learn English despite repeated attempts to do so. Schumann concluded that his informant's failure to learn English could be traced to his inability or unwillingness to identify with the culture of the United States. Out of his case study, Schumann developed the acculturation model. (See Schumann, 1978a, 1978b.)

It was my inability to tap into rich linguistic, cultural and social experiences that led to considerable frustration on my part. Perhaps like Cherry Campbell, I should have found myself a Thai girlfriend! (Actually, the thesis I am pursuing here is that even this would probably not have helped me cross the cultural divide to the extent that I wanted.) Peck (1996) makes the point that cultural sensitivity is a two-way process, and we can't mandate sensitivity when it comes to the host culture. The thesis I am advancing in this piece is that it is much more than that: that it is a complex, multi-layered process involving at least eight interacting variables between interlocutors.

Another issue, which I will touch on here, but will not elaborate upon as my word count is rapidly running out, concerns the status of the languages involved in the interaction. Block (this volume) makes the point that the use of English can place native speakers of other languages at a considerable disadvantage even though they are communicating within their own culture. I chose to speak in Thai, not because I wanted to excise linguistic hegemony, but because I knew the dog rice lady simply wouldn't understand English. In fact I could have used the "point and grunt" technique to get what I wanted. However, in addition to getting my bag of dog rice, I wanted to send a message. "Solidarity" is too strong and too smug a word. I wanted the dog rice lady to feel that, through using her language, I was trying to get closer to her culture. Eventually, I came away from the rice shop with a bag of dog rice and an acute sense of failure.

I discussed my experience of attempting to use Thai with other foreigners who had lived and worked in Thailand much longer than I had done, and most reported similar experiences. Several took their inability to reach their desired level of intimacy with the culture badly, and became cynical and critical. Their attitude appeared to be "If they won't accept me, then I'm going to reject them." This sometimes led to hypercritical complaining sessions in which every shortcoming of life in Thailand was criticized no matter how trivial or imaginary it might be.

On the other side of the ledger, there were a great many Thais who seemed genuinely pleased at my attempts to master the language. They would go out of their way to act as my informant, cheerleader, practice partner and to fulfill various other roles.

Conclusion

In this piece, I have tried to argue that even a simple transaction in another culture such as buying a bag of rice can raise complex and problematic issues of language, culture and identity. I have also suggested that this complexity arises from a complex eight-way interplay between the assumptions and beliefs of the interlocutors about their own language and culture and the language and culture of "the other." This interplay is complex, subtle, and not always conscious. It plays out in situations where success often crucially depends on a considerable degree of good-will on the part of the interlocutors.

I guess the moral of a story that takes its departure from a single, seemingly simple intercultural encounter, is that our own foreign language identities are co-constructed by our interlocutors through a complex, multilayered process. This process involves the interaction of self and other beliefs about language and culture. When we dig beneath the surface, even the simplest transactional encounter can bring us face to face with the question: who are we, when we use a language other than our first?

References

Bailey, K. and Nunan, D. (eds.) 1996. *Voices from the Language Classroom.* Cambridge: Cambridge University Press.

Benson, P. and Nunan, D. (eds.) 2004. *Learners' Voices.* Cambridge: Cambridge University Press.

Block, D. 2010. Speaking *Romance-esque.* In D. Nunan & J. Choi (eds.). *Language and Culture: Reflective Narratives and the Emergence of Identity.* New York, Routledge.

Campbell, C. 1996. Socializing with the teachers and prior language learning experience: A diary study. In K. Bailey and D. Nunan (eds.). *Voices from the Language Classroom.* Cambridge: Cambridge University Press.

Cushner, K. and Brislin, R. W. 1996. *Intercultural Interactions: A Practical Guide.* London: Sage Publications.

Gudykunst, W. and Kim, Y. Y. 2003. *Communicating with Strangers: An Approach to Intercultural Communication.* New York: McGraw-Hill.

Halliday, M.A.K. 1993. The act of meaning. In J. Alatis (ed.). *Language, Communication and Social Meaning.* (pp. 7–21). Washington DC: Georgetown University Press.

Judd, E. 2002. *Cross-Cultural Communication. An ESL Training Module.* Chicago: Office of Language and Cultural Education.

Kramsch, C. 1991. Culture in language learning: A view from the States. In K. de Bot, R.B. Ginsberg and C. Kramsch (eds.). *Foreign Language Research in Cross-Cultural Perspective.* (pp. 217–240). Amsterdam: John Benjamins.

Laing, R.D. 1970. *Knots.* London: Longman.

Lave, J. and Wenger, E. 1991. *Situated Learning. Legitimate Peripheral Participation.* Cambridge: Cambridge University Press.

Lin, A. 2008. *Problematizing Identity: Everyday Struggles in Language, Culture and Identity.* New York: Lawrence Erlbaum and Associates.

Peck, S. 1996. Language learning diaries as mirrors of cultural sensitivity. In K. Bailey and D. Nunan (eds.). 1996. *Voices from the Language Classroom.* Cambridge: Cambridge University Press.

Ricento, T. 2005. Considerations of identity in L2 learning. In E. Hinkel (ed.). *Handbook of Research in Second Language Teaching and Learning.* Mahwah NJ: Erlbaum.

Schumann, J. 1978a. The acculturation model for second language acquisition. In R. Gingras (ed.). *Second Language Acquisition and Foreign Language Teaching.* Arlington VA: Center for Applied Linguistics.

Schumann, J. 1978b. *The Pidginization Process: A Model for Second Language Acquisition.* Rowley Mass.: Newbury House.

Tajfel, H. 1981. *Human Groups and Social Categories.* Cambridge: Cambridge University Press.

Vittachi, N. 2010. A short course in Globalese. In D. Nunan and J. Choi (eds.). *Language and Culture: Reflective Narratives and the Emergence of Identity.* New York: Routledge.

Chapter 25

'Where Am I From'

Performative and 'Metro' Perspectives of Origin[1]

Emi Otsuji
University of Technology, Sydney

> This past is not a 'what', but a 'how', indeed the authentic 'how' of my Dasein.
> (Heidegger 1992)

I am sitting at a desk in 'my' room in Tokyo. It is the desk which was passed on to me from my father. Next to the desk, a doll that was bought on one of the family trips to Italy when I was a primary school student is sitting on top of an old upright piano. I open the lid of the piano and I touch the scratches on the space beside the piano keys. I can hear my piano teacher's voice: 'Play ten times for each piece every day.' The scratches must have been from ten yen coins when I transferred them from one side of the piano to the other each time I practiced a piece. An old fashioned bookshelf is half opened and *First Love* by Ivan Turgenev, *The Great Gatsby* by Scott Fitzgerald, and *Golden Pavilion* by Yukio Mishima are peeking out. As I further open the bookshelf, the smell of old papers tingles my nose. On the wall, there is my oil painting of Queens Park in Edinburgh, the view from my window when I was living there at the age of twelve, with five sheep of identical size between the top and the bottom of the hill; I also see the picture of Shwedagon Pagoda that was given to me when I was backpacking in Burma at the age of twenty. This is the room where I stayed up all night struggling to write an essay on Martin Heidegger's *Being and Time* regretting that I started at the last minute. I used to belong to and played a big role in constructing this culturally 'schizophrenic' space twenty years ago when I was a university student. Now this room is used as a guest room and I also have been an occasional sojourner for almost twenty years. Theoretically, I do not 'own' this room anymore, but whenever I find any traces from my past, I feel as if I have found a precious shiny marble in the bottom of my drawer. I write in this room in 2008 back from Sydney visiting my mother to spend Christmas and New Year.

Today, I saw an old lady in the craft shop near Sasazuka station knitting frantically in the back corner in the same ways she did eighteen years ago. She must be in her eighties by now. When I saw her, I grinned and was satisfied. On my way to Sasazuka station, the smell of soy sauce was coming from the old wooden ramen shop. I used to love this smell as a primary school child visiting grandparents during holidays. It has been my ritual to turn into a cat in the first few days of my return to this house: I sniff and patrol around the house and the neighbourhood and try to find any traces of things which are still the 'same'. I am overwhelmed with the sense of connection when I smell, hear, see and touch something very familiar. But I know that as the days go by, the 'pure' nostalgic feelings will be eroded and taken over by the ambivalence and incommensurability of a sense of connection to this room, to the neighbourhood and more broadly to 'Japanese' cultural practices. The unfamiliar sounds, sensations, smells and practices alienate me and confuse me. I feel as if I am a free floating entity with a ghostly connection to Japan. The sense of alienation and the sense of connection within me co-exist and yet do not co-exist: they present an expected-unexpected, commensurable-incommensurable, paradoxical-orthodox, resonant-disruptive interplay. Immersed in unidentifiable feelings, I wonder where to compromise and negotiate my position between 'where I came from', 'where I am' and 'where I am going'.

This house stands on the land my grandfather bought. My mother was born and grew up on this very spot. Even though it is only one station away from Shinjuku, she could see Mt. Fuji from her balcony when she was small. My mother returned to this house after my father passed away and she decided to move back to Tokyo in her mid-fifties from Fukuoka. When we were living in Osaka, Fukuoka or Edinburgh, without hesitation my mother told other people that she was from Tokyo. But how many people have overlaps between the places where they were born, grew up, live now, want to live and eventually want to die? I had drinks with my high school friends from Fukuoka last week in Shinbashi, a business district in Tokyo. They have moved to Tokyo to work and are living away from where they spent their adolescence. Many of them are married to someone from a different part of Japan and eat varieties of *Ozouni*[2] at New Year, different from what their mothers made. What happens if one engages iteratively in different and initially (perhaps always) unusual practices for a number of years? Can these practices ever become part of 'where you come from'? Is, therefore, one's 'origin' fluid, dependent and relative to the context in which the question was asked as well as to one's biographical pathway? Or is the 'origin' exclusively where one was born or grew up and thus is exclusively a static and irreversible point of departure?

Identity fluidity and hybridisation are often associated with globalisation where information, people and commodities move globally (Appadurai 1990; Featherstone 1990; Featherstone and Lash 1999; Hannerz 2001; Kraidy 1999). This phenomenon, however, is not exclusively the property of globalisation and in fact what constitutes local and global may just be relative. As the example of my high school friends demonstrates, identity fluidity and hybridisation can also be observed on every level of society and inevitably makes people tackle questions about how to come to terms with their future and life trajectory including their 'origin'.

Narrative

Throughout my life, I have experienced an ambivalent and unstable sense of origin. Within me, the sense of connection and alienation co-exist and yet compete against each other. What is the implication of this as it relates to the definition and the constitution of the notion of 'origin'?

I was born in Philadelphia. My family returned to Japan when I was about three years of age. Within Japan, we lived in Tokyo, Osaka and Fukuoka, and Fukuoka is the place where I spent most of my adolescence. I lived in Scotland for approximately one year in my early teens; four years in Singapore; six months in Holland; and this is my fifteenth year in Sydney, Australia, the longest I have lived in the same city in my life.

Every so often at an initial encounter with a Japanese person at a social event in Sydney, the conversation starts like this:

Japanese person (J): *Goshusshin wa dochira desu ka?* (Where are you from in Japan? Literally, where were you born?)

This question normally means that someone wants to know where in Japan your hometown is. I always have a problem answering this question. So I normally hesitate and answer:

Emi: *Ano . . . e . . . to . . . Soo desune . . . chotto wakari masen . . .*
(aah . . . ummm . . . well . . . I don't really know)

When I say this, people look startled as if I am mad. They continue:

J: *Ja, O-umare wa?* (then, where were you born?)

E: *Amerika desuga 3-sai de Nihon ni modottanode . . . Chichi wa Osaka de, haha wa Tokyo no Shusshin nandesu ga . . . demo . . .*
(I was born in the US but I returned to Japan when I was three . . . so . . ., my father is from Osaka and my mother is from Tokyo but . . .)

Before I begin to tell my completed life story, they interrupt either by changing the topic or jokingly saying:

J: *Ja, Nihon jin ja nai ne* (Then you are not Japanese)

Such topics as 'home town', 'the university one went to', 'the length of stay in Sydney' and 'the suburb one lives in Sydney' are the most common questions to ask at an initial encounter in the Japanese community. This type of information provides a point of reference and enables people to find out how to relate to each other, including language choice (whether to speak in honorific language or not). Interestingly, notwithstanding the fact that there are many people whose father or spouse had/has a job which required or requires moving around Japan and changing school every three years or so, almost always one of the first questions is 'where do you come from in Japan?' as if people should have one static particular origin or point of reference in life. However, how valid is this question especially to people who have no overlaps between where they were born, grew up, lived before they came to Sydney or with where their parents are based and also for those who grew up moving around Japan every three years? How about children of immigrants who grew up in Sydney?

Asking one's origin at the initial encounter, of course, is not only a Japanese cultural practice. On various occasions, I am often asked which country I came from by 'non-Japanese' people. I have been asked if I am a Filipina, Thai, Indonesian, South American, or even Spanish, Mexican or North African! I immensely enjoy being identified as someone with a variety of ethnicities and cultural backgrounds. I often take advantage of this and answer jokingly that I am 'Filipina' or 'Mexican' to find their reaction and also to see how long I can get away with these answers. And if I do say that I am from Japan, people say 'No, you are not Japanese! You do not look, behave or think like a Japanese.' This also makes me wonder what it means to say I am from 'Mexico' or from 'Japan' and how multivalent the meaning of this statement is.

Regardless, despite being critical about the validity of this question, I often find myself trying to categorise people by their nationalities or ethnic background and assume that they have one identifiable origin. I realised that I was doing this when I was teaching Japanese the other day. My students are of diverse backgrounds and have ethnic, linguistic or cultural associations with such countries as Korea, Hong Kong, mainland China, Indonesia, England or Greece. I try to make the most of this ethnic and cultural diversity in classroom activities and carry out critical discussions to break down stereotypes about Japanese language and culture. I often ask students to consider factors such as culture, age, institutions, personality and gender to deconstruct the language. The following exchange happened when I was trying to group students in an intermediate Japanese class to discuss 'Hataraku Josei' (working women):

Emi: *Chigau kuni kara kita gakusei to guruupu wo tsukutte kudasaine. Tan-san wa dochira kara desuka?*
(Please form a group with people from different countries. Tan-san, where are you from?)
Student: *E . . . to Chugoku kana? Demo ryooshin wa Shanghai kara kitakedo, Chuugoku nokotowa amari wakarani desu. Kocchi de sodatta kara . . .*
(Well, maybe China . . . my parents are from Shanghai but I don't know much about China. 'Cause I grew up here)

Another time:

Emi: *Paul-san, Indonesia dewa dou desuka?* (Paul, how is it in Indonesia?)
Student: *Watashi wa Australia-jin desu* (I am an Australian)

I feel very embarrassed assuming that students are from a particular country only because their family name sounds Chinese, or because they can speak Cantonese. I am trying to teach students how they should not stereotype Japan and that the relationship between language, nation state, cultural identity and ethnicity is fluid (Luke 2002; Otsuji 2008; Pennycook 2003; Pennycook 2004). Nonetheless, it is ironic that I am categorising and fixing the students' cultural and ethnic backgrounds in a context where we are aiming to deconstruct Japanese cultural practices. These exchanges disclose my unconscious assumptions that the students have a monolithic fixed origin. Moreover, it indicates not only how invalid it is to think that people belong to one particular culture and language group but also how easy it is to fall into the trap of essentialising cultural background and origin. This also relates to my aforementioned dilemma regarding the difficult compromise between 'where I came from', 'where I am' and 'where I am going' as well as the question regarding the epistemological underpinnings of origin. The tension between contrasting perceptions – fixed origins versus fluid origins – may make it difficult to answer the question 'where are you from'.

Commentary

I am now writing this commentary section sitting in 'my' room on a sunny summer afternoon in Sydney after my Christmas and New Year holidays in Tokyo. I can hear my neighbour's children playing in the pool. My cat is sun bathing on the porch. I feel peaceful and comfortable. When I was coming back from Sydney airport and saw the Sydney Harbour Bridge, I thought 'I am back'. But what does 'back' mean? People often say that it is nice to be back after overseas trips. I say this twice: when I go back to Japan and when I come back to Sydney.

My sense of self can be traced back to soy sauce ramen noodles, the old upright piano and shops around Sasazuka station: these practices and experiences around my grandfather's house are etched into me. Correspondingly, my origin is also attributable to my adolescence in Fukuoka: a bicycle I rode to go everywhere while thinking about Ivan Turgenev and a pork-rib ramen I had with my high school friends. On paper, I can be both American and Japanese. I am also partially the sedimented product of experiences associated with Queens Park and sheep in Edinburgh, a monastery I stayed in in Sagaing in northern Burma and Jurassic fish head curries in Holland village in Singapore. It is also true that my current life in Sydney is contributing to how I perceive my origin and sense of connection and alienation. All these factors (such as 'where am I from' and 'where am I now') affect my future decisions and this in turn may rewrite how I perceive these questions. In other words, this whole process of past, present and future is organically intertwined and reconstitutes itself. This accordingly allows my 'origin' to be multivalent, ambivalent and in flux as well as to be constituted by and beyond the logic sequential time.

How flexible is the act of rewriting one's origin? What are the limits and possibilities of teasing these borders? How can we reconcile fixed and fluid origins? Transgressing time may provide an opportunity for flexibility and creative links between language, ethnicity, nation state and notions of 'origin'.

Pennycook (2003, 2004) argues that language is performative. His idea of 'performativity' draws on the work of Butler (1997, 1999a, 1999b, 2004) in her query into the ontology of gender. The main argument of her notion of performativity is that gender is not pre-given but is the sedimentation of iterative performances; in other words, gender is 'a set of repeated acts within a highly rigid regulatory frame' (Butler, 1999b: 43). Following this thread, Pennycook challenges the foundational notion of languages as normative pre-given entities and proposes to develop an anti-foundationalist view which is based on the conception that language is an emergent property in the process of its repetitive use and is a sedimentation of the communicative act. On this note, he conceives that language is not a prior system tied to ethnicity, territory, or nation. Along the same line, in my study on the transcultural workplace, I suggested that ethnic and cultural labels such as 'Japanese' and 'Australian' are also performative and the borders between discrete labels are not fixed but are performatively constructed (Otsuji, 2008).

We might, then, be able to extend these performative claims to the notion of origin. My daily drive to work past the Harbour Bridge in Sydney overlooking the Opera House and my yearly visit to my culturally 'schizophrenic' room supersaturated with my 'past' in Japan reassure me that origin is explicable from the anti-foundational view rather than conceivable as static and pre-given with a simple one-to-one link to a particular ethnicity, nation, territory and birth. 'Where I am from' to me is not pre-given but is an ambivalent, transgressive and dynamic discursive construct that manifests itself through repeated acts (including the answers I provide to the question 'where are you from?'). And these acts perpetually continue to sediment, re/de-sediment alongside my sense of connection versus alienation, inclusion versus exclusion and resonance versus disruption to write, rewrite, claim and reclaim my (discursive) origin. In this sense, the epistemology of 'origin', then, is not an a priori concrete point of departure or place but is a *posteriori* discursive construct in and through the ongoing repeated *interactions* between past, present and future.

To this effect, we can say that this performative, discursive and posteriori nature of 'origin' gives new meaning to what constitutes 'someone from Japan' or 'someone of a particular ethnic background'. 'Metroethnicity' as proposed by Maher (2005) provides insights into this. In his paper on 'Metroethnicity, language, and the principle of Cool', Maher challenges the orthodox notion of ethnicity by looking into post-ethnicity. His example is of a young *Ainu*,[3] whose sense of being *Ainu* has a different meaning from that of his father. 'You are a residual ethnic code that is becoming a new, emergent code,' Maher writes (2005: 98). The young man conceives that being *Ainu* in current society is cool and he is assured that he is *Ainu* without being able to speak the language. Thus, instead of being a conventional *Ainu*-speaking *Ainu*, he is aligning himself as a cool Italian-speaking *Ainu*. Maher (2005: 84), accordingly, defines metroethnicity as 'an exercise in emancipatory politics. It is an individual's self-assertion on his own terms and that will inevitably challenge the orthodoxy of "language loyalty".' The implication here is two-fold. First, metroethnicity allows the self-reconstruction of ethnicity and an alternative way of being and becoming in relation to one's origin. This may in turn reconstitute the concept and the discursive content of origin. This is in line with the previous discussion on the discourse of 'origin' as an emergent property. Second, metroethnicity is about an emancipatory power that enables people to disassociate legitimised links between language, ethnicity and nation state. This corresponds to the arguments made by Pennycook (2003, 2004) and Luke (2002) on the subject of the creative link between language, ethnicity, nation state and birth. My aforementioned students – who speak 'Indonesian'[4] better than 'English' but claim to be 'Australian' or who think they are from 'China' (while not knowing much about 'China') – are good examples of this. This performative and metroethnic nature of 'origin', therefore, not only avoids reductive thinking but also provides an alternative link between language ethnicity, and nation state. Yet, the degree to which the re-constitution of 'origin' and the reconfiguration of these links is attainable needs to be scrutinised in light of Butler's important claim that iterative acts are operational 'within a highly rigid regulatory frame' (Butler, 1999b: 43). In that case, a performative, 'metro' origin is a discursive practice of limits as well as possibilities.

...

I started to write this chapter in Tokyo. I thought it was a great idea to write about this theme in Japan. The theme was relentlessly on my mind: when I was squeezed in a crowded train, when I was drinking Japanese vodka (*Shochu*) with my high school friends talking about our school days, when I was on a hot spring trip to Hakone overlooking Mt. Fuji, and when I was cleaning my grandfather's and my father's graves. I was obviously struggling. I could not write further than the description of the room and the story about the house. I simply could not see my origin clearly and easily say 'yes, I know where I came from'. But when I came back to Sydney, I realised that I was not able to write because I was only immersing myself in the past. I was only looking at the oil painting of Queens Park, smelling old books and touching the piano keys. I was not thinking about the Sydney Harbour Bridge, conversations with my friends from various parts of the world in a pub in Sydney, my cat sitting in the sunny garden as well as my desires and prospective plans. I also could not write because I did not allow my origin to be an ambivalent, unstable, flexible and transgressive discourse sedimented through my iterative acts including the various ways in which I deal with and express the sense of origin across places and time. People might say that I am cosmopolitan. But I know that what I am struggling with cannot be reduced to this. Cosmopolitan is seen as an open perspective or an aesthetic disposition for differences and for other cultures, experiences and values (Hannerz 1990, 2001; Woodward *et al.* 2008). This limited and abstract notion is illusive, idealistic and uncommitted (Skribis and Woodward 2007). Performatively constructed 'metro-origin', on the other hand, is a discourse concerning the limits and possibilities of emancipation, desire and commitment to being/becoming. This provides the answers as to why some people cling to vestiges of one particular 'origin' while others may have more fluid and multiple origins. It thus tells us why one single person could have different origins synchronically and diachronically in the different stages of their biographical trajectory as well as in different contexts.

A performative metroethnicity offers new discursive options for what it means to be 'Japanese' and what it means to be someone with a Japanese 'origin' and thus calls for a reframing of the concept of 'origin' beyond essentialistic views of a country and people. At the same time, it provides us the freedom (always already within limits) to tease notional borders of space and time related to the definition of one's origin.

I can be someone from Japan with frizzy hair and round eyes while being puzzled in front of the vending machine for 'passmo' cards, a new train pass, at Sasazuka station. I can equally be someone from Australia with a Hello Kitty tattoo as I talk about Japanese and Australian beer to a stranger from Croatia in a London pub.

Notes

1 I would like to thank Alastair Pennycook for his insightful comments when I was finalising this chapter. I owe this paper to George Fogarasi and thank him for his inspiration. This paper is a product of numerous dialogues with him by email between Canada and Australia but it also has roots in the Fish Head curry sessions we had in an alley in Holland village, Singapore in the early 1990s while fighting over eyeballs.

2 *Ozouni* is a soup that Japanese people eat during the New Year.

3 The *Ainu* is an ethnic group in Hokkaido, Northern island of Japan. The Ainu language is distinct from that of Japanese. Ainu people have long been the target of discrimination and only in 2008 were they officially recognised by the Japanese Diet as indigenous to Japanese.

4 I am putting quotation marks around language and countries to indicate that they are not pre-given and discrete but are performatively emergent.

References

Appadurai, A. 1990, 'Disjuncture and difference in the global cultural economy', In *Global Culture: Nationalism globalization and modernity* (Ed., Featherstone, M.) Sage, London.

Butler, J. 1997, *Excitable speech: A politics of the performative,* Routledge, London.

Butler, J. 1999a, *Gender trouble: Feminism and the subversion of identity (10th anniversary edition),* Routledge, New York.

Butler, J. 1999b, 'Performativity's social magic', In *Bourdieu: A critical reader* (Ed., Shusterman, R.) Blackwell, Oxford, pp. 113–128.

Butler, J. 2004, *Undoing gender,* Routledge, New York.

Featherstone, M. (Ed.) 1990, *Global culture: Nationalism, globalization and modernity,* Sage, London.

Featherstone, M. and Lash, S. (Eds.) 1999, *Space of culture: City, nation, world,* Sage, London.

Hannerz, U. 1990, 'Cosmopolitans and locals in world culture', In *Global culture: Nationalism, globalisation and modernity* (Ed., Featherstone, M.) Sage, London.

Hannerz, U. 2001, 'Thinking about culture in a global ecumene', In *Culture in the communication age* (Ed., Lulle, J.) Routledge, London.

Heidegger, M. 1992, *The concept of time,* Blackwell, Oxford, UK; Cambridge, Mass.

Kraidy, M. M. 1999, 'The global, the local, and the hybrid: A native ethnography of glocalization', *Critical Studies in Mass Communication,* 16, 456–476.

Luke, A. 2002, 'Beyond science and ideology critique: Developments in critical discourse analysis', *Annual Review of Applied Linguistics,* 22, 96–110.

Maher, J. 2005, 'Metroethnicity, language, and the principle of Cool', *International Journal of the Sociology of Language,* 11, 83–102.

Otsuji, E. 2008, In *Education* University of Technology, Sydney, Sydney, pp. 392.

Pennycook, A. 2003, 'Global Englishes, rip slyme, and performativity', *Journal of Sociolinguistics,* 7, 513–533.

Pennycook, A. 2004, 'Performativity and language studies', *Critical Inquiry in Language Studies,* 1, 1–26.

Skribis, Z. and Woodward, I. 2007, 'The ambivalence of ordinary cosmopolitanism: Investigating the limits of cosmopolitan openness', 55, 730–747.

Woodward, I., Skribis, Z. and Bean, C. 2008, 'Attitudes towards globalization and cosmopolitanism: Cultural diversity, personal consumption and the national economy', *The British Journal of Sociology,* 59, 207–226.

Chapter 26

Sweating Cheese and Thinking Otherwise

Alastair Pennycook
University of Technology, Sydney

The cheese, sitting on a plate in the middle of the round table in the senior staff dining hall, starts to sweat. It's that time after lunch when the campus clears, all but mad dogs and English teachers sliding away from the heat behind mosquito-curtained beds. For several hours, until the afternoon heat recedes, screeching cicadas are the only creatures active across the shimmering campus. Hunan at this time of year is red and hot: stifling, humid summer days stretching on into thick, sweaty, mosquito-humming nights. The iron-rich red earth burns rustily in the heat, yet still nurtures two crops of rice through this long summer. Water buffaloes, knee deep in mud, turn the thick soil over, mixing in pungent nightsoil that has been scooped up from behind the student dormitories and carried across the campus in buckets swinging on poles slung form thin shoulders. The rice here is fresh, succulent, local, though scattered with teeth-threatening stones gathered up from farm courtyards where the husks are laid out to dry.

This is peasant country, red and hot. Down the road is ShaoShan, Mao Ze Dong's birth place, a small village with a vast railway station, a remnant of the years during the cultural revolution when red guards would pour into the Hunan countryside to visit the great helmsman's birthplace. Now it's another sleepy, Hunan village, a bicycle-ride away, where we go now and then, pilgrim-like, clutching an old copy of the Little Red Book. This university, a concrete and brick sprawl across rice fields, was supposed to be Mao Ze Dong University, but changing politics had it renamed in the end after the nearest town, Xiangtan. But this is still Mao country, where the memories of all that was brought through land reforms stays fresh, where old cadres come back to eat in the university dining hall, in their high-collared jackets and caps, eyeing foreign nouveau-Maoists with suspicion. The Autumn Harvest Uprising, the start of the Long March, Mao's returns to his hometown and hillside retreat, the land reforms, the cultural revolution, all came from and have come back to the hot, red soil of Hunan.

And with the rice, there is always chilli, red and hot. Not the hot sauces of Szechuan, but simpler, hotter. There's pork and chilli. You can always hear when a pig, kept in pens by peasants' houses, is being slaughtered. Often first the sound of a squealing pig roped down on a simple wooden wheelbarrow being pushed along the narrow, winding paths between the rice fields, a jolting, wailing ride across the valley; then, as if an advertisement to the community across the fields, the pig screeching towards its silence. Fresh pork to be had across the fields. With chilli. Chicken and chilli, squawking poultry chased down across the farmyard, or brought clucking from the market, feet tied over the handles of a bicycle. With chilli. Sometimes fish, big, heavy grey-meated fish from the muddy ponds between the fields. In winter, dog meat, good for keeping you warm. With chilli. Or that summer treat, frogs, plucked from the pond-sides at night in mid-croak, skinned and served up whole next day. With chilli. And when the meat is low and the vegetables are running out, just chilli. With chilli.

And the cheese is sitting uncomfortable, sweaty, out of place. Like Wallace Stevens' jar in Tennessee – round it was, upon a table/it made the slovenly dining hall/ surround that table . . .[1] – it starts not only to fill the dining hall with its unlikely presence, but to make the dining hall surround it. One of our old colleagues, visiting China from North America, has brought it with her. 'I've got something for you', she says, after lunch, bringing this round of blue cheese on a plate borrowed from the coal-smoky kitchen. We don't get many visitors here in the Hunan countryside, and even fewer exotic tastes from the outside world. The cheese has been brought as a present, but also as something we probably miss. Other foreigners in China often talk of things they miss, and that they think we, so far from everything, ought to miss. But don't you miss television, chocolate, music, salad, strawberries, wine, . . .? people ask. These lists of tastes and sounds and sights thought so necessary to our lives. No, we have frogs, mudfish, dog, chilli. But don't you feel cut off? There are 60 million people in Hunan. 'Cut off' has very particular assumptions behind it that don't seem to describe life well here.

Fu Shifu, the head cook, comes over to have a look. We know him well – a gentle, congenial man, with sadness in his recent past. He likes to talk about food and life, to sit down with us and share a drink. He is a man of many sympathies. We always call him *shifu* – (師父) master – like the drivers. There is a great respect in this term, an acknowledgment that cooks (not chefs) are crucial members of society. The drivers, who drive the cars from each unit's car pool, are also *shifu*, and always eat with those they drive. So when professors and vice-chancellors from other universities come to visit, and eat in this dining hall, the drivers always sit at the table too. Fu shifu runs a good dining hall. But lactose products are not something he deals with. There are virtually no cows in Hunan. There is no milk (only powdered milk for nursing mothers). And cheese? He looks at it suspiciously. We start to explain, grasping for suitable terms in Chinese. Well it's sort of old milk, left to go mouldy. A bit like *choudofu* – stinky, fermented tofu. He sniffs, and wrinkles his nose. We urge him to taste a bit, and cut a narrow slice. He holds it between thumb and forefinger, sniffs again. Finally he tries it on his tongue. The wrinkle on his nose spreads across his face. The sides of his mouth turn downwards. He shakes his head. And walks away.

We might start to make sense of this moment in terms of the smallness of all our cultural worlds. For many people other tastes always remain other, if not downright unpalatable. For many, the hot chilli-laden food of Hunan, the frogs, the dogs, the endless rice and vegetable from a wok, was either too boring or too spicy. For our students, by contrast, a trip down south into the better-known gastronomic zones of Guangdong (Cantonese food) meant sweet, bland food that could only be improved with a few spoonfuls of chilli, carried lovingly in jars from home to turn otherness into comfort. Australians have been known to travel with Vegemite (that strange, dark bitter paste made from malt extract, apparently deeply different from its British cousin Marmite). Argentineans may have a packet of *mate* with them; Dutch may be on the lookout for pickled herring. The cheese too was meant this way: here is a piece of home, of taste and texture that will transport you back to where you belong, that will remind you of what you miss. For Fu Shifu, a man who lived with tastes and smells and food preparation, this was just too different, too alien.

We might, then, invoke a notion of culture to enlighten us about this moment. This might be an encounter between Western and Chinese food and tastes. But these clumsy categories, as if cultures were easily nameable entities, only take us a short way and fall down. What is cheese eating as a cultural practice? And what is this moment of rejection? Chinese? Hunanese? Xiangtanese? Or just a cook's sense of what food should be like. We might also want to look at this moment in terms of context: While for some, travel or living elsewhere becomes simply the recreation of a similar living space, for many this becomes far more contextual. Things have their place, and cheese may taste fine in some places, but in others it just does not work. And this is not just a question of what goes with what (certain tastes accompany each other well) but that contextual arrangements – weather, furniture, smells, sounds – reconfigure space to the extent that things are no longer the same. What is excellent, rich, tangy, cheese in one place is simply no longer so in another. Thus, rather than seeing this only in contextual terms, it might be useful to consider it within a richer set of spatial relations (e.g. Crang and Thrift, 2000).

Yet the question I want to explore here is a far broader one of how we engage with otherness. For in that moment something else happened. As I sat there watching Fu Shifu taste and reject his sliver of cheese, I felt for a moment that I saw myself through his eyes. Instead of looking at a Hunanese cook trying to come to terms with exotic lactose products, I started to see the cheese not as part of my northern European lactose-oriented culture, but as his otherness. This cheese, and those of us round the table were not part of this world. I saw my own strangeness, my being out of context, my incompatibility. And when I too am offered a slice of cheese, brought as a gift to old friends, carried on crowded trains and buses across China, offered as something that will connect us, something from home, I too turn it down. Cheese has become other to me. And at that moment it's not just the cheese that has become other but I that have become other to myself. We are located, constructed by our practices, and to reject the cheese-eating is to reconstruct myself. 'Je', as Rimbaud famously announced, 'est un autre'.[2]

Of course to claim that I saw myself through an other's eyes immediately needs to be challenged. It implies not only a capacity to step outside oneself, to think outside one's own locus of enunciation, but also to enter the position of another, to know how a cultural other is framing the world, and in addition to know how this other is framing you. There are too many leaps of unlikely interpretation here to make this plausible. And yet, I saw something here which was more than a mere awareness of myself, more than just an ability to see that others might think differently about me and my cultural artefacts than do I. Travel writing and books on intercultural communication may endeavour to make the unfamiliar familiar, to render the strangeness of other languages, cultures and tastes, assimilable into our own frameworks. We have long known, too, that travel, our encounters with difference, may be a journey into ourselves as much as journey elsewhere. My interest, here however, is in the moment when the familiar becomes unfamiliar, when what we think we know, and like, and do becomes unfamiliar to us. If we consider seriously the difficulty of engaging with the Other, of the incommensurabilities of cultural difference, what then can it mean to assume the double distinction of both knowing the other and knowing the other's reading of oneself? This a moment not only of otherness, but of double otherness.

The 'Through Other Eyes' (TOE) project developed by de Souza and Andreotti (forthcoming) brings a pedagogical focus to this question. Developed as an educational orientation to enable teachers and students 'to reflect on their own knowledge systems and to engage with other knowledge systems in different ways, in their own learning and in their classrooms', this work emphasizes the importance not of learning to learn but rather of 'learning to unlearn', of becoming aware both of one's own ways of thinking and of other possibilities. Drawing on the work of Benhabib (2002), Brown (2006), Butler (2005) and others, de Souza and Andreotti ask how we can escape the post-essentialist relativism of views of culture that fail to locate their own location. The point here is that in moving beyond those limited framings of culture that have now been largely decried as essentialist, we cannot simply fall back on a cultural relativism that apparently acknowledges difference without locating itself. This, then, has to be a process of unlearning, of questioning the familiarity of one's own location. As Fabian (2007) reminds us, we must constantly ask ourselves how we engage with alterity.

Rather than assuming, therefore, that this is a moment of seeing through others' eyes, I would rather reframe it as a moment of thinking otherwise – *penser autrement*, as Foucault (1984) called it. As Foucault argued towards the end of his life, it becomes indispensable at a certain point in life to try to think otherwise if we want to continue to think and reflect usefully. If philosophy is to do anything other than continue to rethink the already-thought, we have to ask how and how far we can start to think otherwise. For Hoy (2004), the line of critical thinking that can be followed back through Derrida and Foucault to Nietzsche, may best be described as a form of critical resistance. Many forms of resistance to power and domination, and many 'utopian imaginings of freedom may not be aware of the extent to which they presuppose the patterns of oppression that they are resisting' (p.3). In order to develop a form of critical resistance, he argues, we need a form of freedom that 'is tied conceptually to the openness to possibility'. Critical resistance, in other words, needs ways of thinking otherwise, of seeing other possibilities.

At this moment in rural Hunan, not far from Mao's birthplace, I was deeply engaged with these questions about how we do our politics. I had also started to read Foucault, to engage in this different lineage of critical resistance that asked harder questions about the categories we used for thinking about politics. While I was convinced (and still am) of the importance, for example, of the post-revolutionary land reforms for Chinese peasants (and frustrated by the revisioning of Chinese history that has started to efface this as part of the background to China's ascendancy), and while I was also convinced of the importance of the opening of markets for the peasantry (you only had to step over the campus wall and talk to the peasants to confirm either of these), I was also starting to wonder whether a critical politics also needed to move beyond some of these assumptions about politics and the economy. Perhaps we needed to start asking different epistemological questions about the cultural and philosophical assumptions we brought to any analysis. Critical resistance required an openness to possibility, and seeing cheese through others' eyes, or acknowledging the importance, yet the impossibility, of doing so, was one such moment of possibility.

This moment of believing that I can see myself through the eyes of another, then, is better thought of as a moment of not knowing, of radical decentring. As Butler (2005) puts it at the end of her discussion of what it means to 'give an account of oneself',

> we must recognize that ethics requires us to risk ourselves precisely at moments of unknowingness, when what forms us diverges from what lies before us, when our willingness to become undone in relation to others constitutes our chance of becoming human.
>
> (p.136)

It is this that is ultimately important here. As the cheese sits sweatily unconsumed on the table, this is far more than a moment of going off cheese, of opting for chilli frog over lactose products. At that moment when I feel what Fu Shifu signals with his wrinkled nose, I have understood more than the relativity and contextuality of taste. There has been a moment where the possibility and then the unfeasibility of seeing oneself through others' eyes has presented itself. It is a moment of impossibility, of vulnerability, of unknowingness, when a willingness to become undone constitutes a moment of humanity. And it starts a whole new way of thinking, of searching always for ways of thinking otherwise. For what else is worth doing in this world?

Notes

1 Adapted from Wallace Stevens' (1967) Anecdote of the Jar. 'I placed a jar in Tennessee/ and round it was, upon a hill. It made the slovenly wilderness/ surround that hill.'

2 In a letter to Paul Demeny, May 15th, 1871. This idea has been taken up by many French thinkers, from Lacan to Derrida and Deleuze.

References

Benhabib, S. (2002). *The claims of culture: Equality and diversity in the global era*, Princeton, Princeton University Press.

Brown, W. (2006). *Regulating aversion: Tolerance in the age of identity and empire*, Princeton, Princeton University Press.

Butler, J. (2005). *Giving an account of oneself.* New York: Fordham University Press.

Crang, M. and Thrift, N. (Eds.) (2000). *Thinking space.* London: Routledge.

Fabian, J. (2007). *Memory against culture: Arguments and reminders.* London: Duke University Press.

Foucault, M. (1984). *Histoire de la sexualité II: L'usage des plaisirs.* Paris: Gallimard.

Hoy, D. (2004). *Critical resistance: From poststructuralism to post-critique.* Cambridge, Mass: MIT Press.

Souza, L. and Andreotti, V. (2009). Challenges and tensions in the culturalist debate: The predation of difference and the resistance to resistance in post colonial-indigenous Brazil. In J. Lavia (Ed.), *Cross-cultural perspectives on policy and practice: Decolonizing community contexts.* London: Routledge.

Stevens, W. (1967). Anecdote of the Jar. *The palm at the end of the mind: Selected poems and a play.* New York: Vintage Books.

Chapter 27

Multilingual Couple Talk

Romance, Identity and the Political Economy of Language[1]

Kimie Takahashi
Macquarie University

'The Special Day'

English was the language spoken by my first object of romantic infatuation – the Hollywood actor, Tom Cruise. When I saw *Top Gun* for the first time, I could not believe that someone like him existed. I remember madly screaming '*Kakkoiii, kakkoiii*!!' with my equally hysterical friend in the cinema. Maybe one day, as I used to believe so firmly, I'd get a chance to meet him in person. I would tell him how I dreamed about him, day after day, night after night. For this special day, I needed to know English.

Unfortunately, this dreamy passion did not translate into learning English at school. In fact, I *hated* English as a school subject. As thousands of fellow Japanese from my generation would agree, it was the teaching method – grammar translation – that killed my interest. In all honesty, it was not just English classes that I dreaded attending. School work in general did not mean much to me back then. The reason: I grew up in a working class suburb of Yokohama and my parents had little interest in their daughter's education. English? What for? There was simply no connection between my English classroom in my hometown, Tsurumi and the English speaking, glamorous world of Hollywood, to which my 'Maverick' belonged. Unsurprisingly, I finished high school with little knowledge of English (and all other subjects, to be more exact). I was perfectly happy to continue my carefree lifestyle into early adulthood with a part-time job in an *izakaya* (a pub) in Tokyo. Life was good – for a while.

When I turned 20, anxiety set in. Somehow it started to bother me that I had no tertiary education, no specialized skills, no specific direction or passion in my life. I can't recall exactly how, but I figured that studying English might improve my prospects. In the mind of a naïve 20-year-old girl, it happened something like the equation of 'English' = 'Tom speaks it' = 'international' = 'flight attendant as a career?' = 'cool!' I enrolled myself in a two-year college of English in Tokyo, which was known for its English-only approach, Spartan work ethic and their business motto: we take anyone as long as they pay the school fee. It suited me fine.

My two years there turned out to be the most rewarding learning experience. There I learnt English from scratch through immersion – all classes and conversation with teachers and fellow students had to be in English and we were fined 1,000 yen if we were caught speaking Japanese on the school site (my total contribution – 12,000 yen). We produced everything in English, essays, group reports, speeches and graduate theses. Periodically we presented English drama productions, and I happily volunteered to sing *Danger Zone* and *Take My Breath Away* as a solo performance. As a school policy, all these writings and presentations had to be checked and approved by native speaker teachers from the UK, the US, Canada or Australia. Through this 'native speaker check' system, however, we developed a somewhat problematic belief about English language learning and use. It was a belief that made us think we 'need' a native speaker's assurance in all things English. It was not our language, hence we had no authority.

This belief powerfully informed my romantic life, too. Everyone has certain preferences for their partner. Mine had to do with linguistic identity, that is, being a native speaker of English. Since my arrival in Australia in 1992, all my romantic partners were native speakers of English, although their cultural and racial backgrounds varied widely. Living in a predominantly English-speaking Western country, I saw my identity as a second language speaker of English and being Asian as a disadvantage. Thus I wanted my partner to be 'perfect', to be someone from whom I could get assurance in all things English, and Western. It *never ever* occurred to me that I would get romantically involved with someone whose first language was not English, let alone get married to one. Until I met Marcin.

'My Lucky Night' and Beyond

The Three Wise Monkeys was quite busy that night. It was the final day of the 2005 Australian Open and I was watching the men's final match on the pub's big screen with my research participants, Eika and Ichi.[2] At that time, I was conducting fieldwork for my PhD research on Japanese women learning English in Sydney (Piller & Takahashi, 2006; Takahashi, forthcoming). Some of my participants were frequent visitors to the Three Wise Monkeys, a popular pub in George Street, Sydney, which was, and still is, regarded as a cheesy pick-up joint by many locals. While my main intention was data collection that night, I was also enjoying drinks with 'friends'.

When the tennis match was over, we decided to go upstairs for more drinks and live music. As soon as we found a table, two young Irish men approached us. As an ethnographer-researcher, I'd consciously observe their interaction. I quickly gathered that Eika and Ichi were not interested in talking to them – they were not good-looking enough and their accent was a major put-off as it made their conversation impossible to understand. To show their lack of interest, the women left for the dance floor, but the Irish men did not get the message. They followed the women, trying hard to dance with them.

Looking at the men's attempt from the table, I was thinking to myself, 'boys, you don't have a chance', and wrote this observation into a little notebook. During my fieldwork in Sydney, I often observed this kind of gendered L2 interaction, where young Japanese women had the upper-hand to decide who could talk to them, how long and about what. I found this really interesting as it challenges the essentialist assumption that non-native speakers of English are powerless, lacking confidence and thus disadvantaged. Many of my participants were often powerful, confident and took advantage of the discourse of the desired Asian *other* – they ruled, quite brutally sometimes, in a romantically charged social context in Sydney (Piller & Takahashi, 2006).

Left alone, I was surveying the crowd in the pub and suddenly noticed a Caucasian man drinking with his friends near our table. I noticed him because he was exceptionally good-looking, well-built and had a gorgeous smile. After we exchanged a polite, non-verbal hello, I made a quick gesture, inviting him for a chat (so much so for my interest being 'strictly research only'). When he arrived at my table, I was pleasantly surprised that not only was he even more handsome up close, but he was also surprisingly well-mannered for someone hanging out at a pub 'like this'. 'I'm Marcin, nice to meet you', he introduced himself and politely thanked me for the unexpected invitation.

As we talked on, however, I was beginning to feel puzzled. Umm? he sounds 'different'. Based on his Caucasian look, I simply assumed that he was Australian or American, or at least some variety of native English speaker (Piller, 2002b). As I started to hear his L2 'accent' more clearly, I felt slightly disappointed. The inevitable question came to mind: 'Where are you from?' It's a tricky question in a country like Australia – it immediately positions people in an identity category of 'outsiders' (Farrell, 2008) and I myself feel awkward, if not resentful, every time someone asks me the very question (see Otsuji's chapter for more discussion on this issue). Nevertheless, it was perhaps because of the few drinks I had had earlier, or his friendliness, or my hope to find that he was from some 'cool' European country, or my ego to position myself as a 'local', I asked him anyway. 'I'm from Poland', he said, with an even more gorgeous smile on his face. I was repeating 'Poland . . .' several times in my mind trying to retrieve any relevant (and possibly glamorous) information about his country in my mental drawers. No. Nothing. I knew absolutely nothing about Poland. Now, he is not only a non-native speaker of English, but also someone from a country I know nothing about. It would have been the end of my flirting escapade.

But that night, I kept on talking to him. Not even a single moment of losing interest throughout the night. The more I listened to him, the less I heard his accent. The more I learnt about him, the less I cared about where he was from (or not knowing anything at all about Poland). I was just so completely mesmerized by his amazing looks – beautiful blue eyes, long eye lashes, gorgeous smiles, large chest and big arms – and his sweetness and gentlemanly manners, that my initial unease with his linguistic and national identities took a backseat, and then, a complete exit. 'If I can just spend one night looking at this gorgeous guy', I thought to myself, 'Who cares if he's not a native speaker or where he comes from?' At that time, I was not interested in a long-term relationship (my relationship of eight years had ended a few months earlier). Nothing else mattered to me but to finish my doctoral thesis. I couldn't care less whether he was going to ask me for my phone number or if he was going to call me the next day, let alone whether or not an L2 romance would work. It was my 'lucky night'. Look at him, he is gorgeous. I'll just enjoy the 'view', for tonight.

***

'*Ohayo~! Pankeeki tabetai*?' Once a week or so, my husband wakes me up by asking me if I want pancakes for breakfast, in his fluent Japanese. As I drag myself out of bed and wash my face in slow motion, he yells out from the kitchen, '*Hayakuuu, hayakuuu*!' with a pretend annoyance. '*Hai, hai . . .*,' I respond grudgingly, and by the time I sit down at our dining table, my first pancake arrives. '*Hai, dooozo*!' says Marcin with beaming smiles. It was exactly four years ago when these gorgeous smiles captured my heart. Perhaps he's gained a few extra kilos (more places to kiss, as a Polish saying goes), but his beautiful blue eyes, big chest, muscular arms, sweetness, and of course his accented English, are still intact.

Between my lucky night at the Three Wise Monkeys and this morning in our Sydney apartment, many things have happened – a week after that night, he 'officially' asked me to be his girlfriend; after submitting my PhD thesis, I dragged him to Japan and lived there for a year and half, where he learnt many Japanese words and phrases including 'Please allow me to have your daughter as my wife'; after coming back to Sydney for my work, we exchanged our marriage vows in my second and his third language in August 2008; in the following month, we went to Lodz, his hometown in Poland, for a wedding party organized by his ecstatic, loving parents, whose next dream is to become live-in caretakers of their future grandchild. I'm so proud that Marcin is fluent in Japanese. My Polish is nowhere near as good as his second, or third or even his fourth language. 'It's not a competition,' he smiles. I say 'Yes, it is' as I frown. When our first child finally arrives, her first language will be Polish. For that special day, I want to know Polish.

Multilingual Couple Talk

My years of infatuation with Tom Cruise have been over for quite some time. Instead, the list of people I idolize today include quite different faces. They are researchers, activists, and journalists whose work and insights have broadened my mind and inspire me to explore the relationship between language and identity in our lives. On the top of the list is Ingrid Piller (2002a, 2002b, 2007, 2008, 2009). This paper was inspired by, and titled after, her research on *Bilingual Couples Talk* (2002a), in which she explores the discursive construction of bilingual couplehood between linguistic and national border-crossers, namely L1 speakers of English and L1 speakers of German. Piller argues that our identity is not a matter of labels and categories, but rather an 'act of doing'. Most of this ongoing construction of identity is done linguistically, in other words, 'language and social identity are mutually constitutive' (p. 12). Taking the social constructionist approach, Piller illuminates complex ways in which her participants 'do' their bilingual and cross-cultural couplehood in their private talks, and highlights how their private practices are in turn informed by wider public discourses such as gender, nationality, immigration and international marriage. Obviously her participants' linguistic, cultural and racial backgrounds are different from ours. Yet I've never learnt so much about my own romantic relationship from an academic book as I did from her book. On this note, I'll begin this commentary section by drawing on her work in order to interpret my lucky night and beyond. In particular I will address the questions of 'language desire', language use and shift, and proficiency, which embody our identity as a multilingual couple.

First of all, central to my lucky night narrative is the 'slight' disappointment with Marcin's linguistic identity, a non-native speaker of English. Piller's conceptualization of 'language desire' sheds light on this (2002a, p. 100). She found that many of her participants, female partners who were L2 English speakers, reported a great deal of emotional attachments to the English language and embraced the widely circulating masculine discourses, such as Wild West America or English gentlemen, *before* they met their partners, i.e. US or UK native speakers of English. As one participant, Natalie, points out, she studied English because 'I always wanted to marry a cowboy' and 'I've always liked English', and her marriage to her US-American husband was 'not at all coincidental' (Piller, 2002a, p. 101). I can wholeheartedly empathize with Natalie, except that her cowboy was my Top Gun pilot. But both were still US native speakers of English, our shared romantic attraction. The flipside of language desire for English was at work all my life, i.e. I never ever considered romance with non-native speakers of English, no matter how attractive or popular they were. In an English-speaking (heterosexual) romantic market, Hollywood films and the world of advertising alike, there is an on-going discursive construction and promotion of certain European men, French men in particular, as romantic and their accent as sexy (Piller, 2003). As a second language speaker of English myself, I found 'accented English', not as sexy, but an obstacle to proper communication and also a sign of these men's inability to provide emotional (and linguistic) assurance. This clearly explains my 'slight' disappointment on that particular night.

In fact, Marcin's linguistic identity did become an issue later on and it continues to play a major role in our relationship to date. For instance, as a 'traditional' man that Marcin was, he asked me, 'would you please consider becoming my girlfriend', one week after we met. I was ecstatic, but also anxious inside. When we were just 'dating' without such an official declaration, it was not a problem. But this official pledge for a commitment as a couple brought back my initial concern regarding his language background. Do you think it'd work? English is my second language and it's his third! I even consulted with my friends, who rolled their eyes at my concern as trivial and just wanted to meet my new boyfriend. It was not trivial at all, however. Because I knew that I could no longer ask my partner to edit my PhD thesis, draft my emails to officials, improve my pronunciation, or finish my sentence in a conversation, in English.

Most of these things listed above are what I do for him now. And such discursive practices are often a site of contestation over power. We both know that neither of us is 'perfect' in English, but we also know that I have more developed linguistic skills than he does. 'Correct me if I mispronounce something.' As requested, I do so every now and then, but obviously this hurts his pride as a competent speaker of English. Instead of accepting my suggestion, he sticks to his original pronunciation on purpose, which, if I'm not in the best mood, drives me crazy. 'Very often, the person one feels the deepest love and affection for is also likely to be the most irritating person in one's life' (Piller, 2002a, p. 3). Nothing captures ongoing negotiation of identity between Marcin and me better than this.

Another issue that Piller wanted to find out was language choice and use among the bilingual couples. She was not convinced about the prevalent assumption that language shift to the majority language is a 'done deal' resulting from linguistic intermarriage (2002a). Her study indeed reveals how it was often not the case among the German-English bilingual couples and their language use and choice was a fluid, but highly contested practice which intersected with their identities, symbolic value of the two languages and communities of practice in which they participated. In our early days, Marcin and I predominantly used English as a couple language. It was the only language we used to communicate with each other, because Polish (or let alone his second language, Russian) was unknown to me as much as Japanese was to him. As our morning conversation above shows, however, there is an emerging shift towards an increased use of Japanese in our relationship, which is clearly a minority language in Australia. As I will show below, our increasing use of Japanese in both private and public space is 'an act of doing' our multilingual couple and cross-cultural couplehood (Piller, 2002a, p. 2). Let me expand on this by first looking at how it all began.

When we moved to Japan in 2006, Marcin immediately took on board a new challenge of learning Japanese as his fourth language. He bought (very expensive) Japanese textbooks, attended Japanese classes at a local community centre, watched TV, mingled with my family and Japanese friends and constantly nagged me to teach him useful words – day and night. Of course, he made many mistakes in the beginning. When my mother asked him if he would like more rice during our dinner, he beamed at this opportunity to show off his newly learnt phrase, '*Onaka ippai desu* (I'm full)', but actually told her, '*Onanii ippai desu*! (I masturbate a lot!)' I kept eating in silence. No matter how embarrassing his mistakes like this may be, we are in fact very fond of these because they form part of our shared, cherished narrative – a discursive resource in performing and creating our identity as a multilingual couple. It signals, not how deficient he was as a language learner, but how far he has come. 'Remember what you said to mum?'; such a simple conversational cue, yet it powerfully brings up a warm memory of our time in Yokohama.

To him, however, I was not a proactive teacher in Japan. He was actually right. At that time I didn't see any benefit in his increased fluency in Japanese. I had L2 Japanese speaking partners in my early years in Australia, but I was never willing to use Japanese as couple language. Just like many new migrants do (Colic-Peisker, 2009; Norton, 2000), I had so much social and emotional investment in establishing an identity as a competent L2 speaker of English – I needed to compensate for my Asian identity by achieving 'native-like' fluency. At the same time, I was secretly worried that I'd be seen as a Japanese woman who blindly goes for a Japanese speaking Western man because she has a Western fetish but can't speak English – a prevalent misogynistic criticism in the 1980s, aka the 'Yellow Cab' discourse (Kelsky, 2001). Thanks to support from my family and friends in Japan, his Japanese improved considerably. But I thought he'd lose interest in learning Japanese once we moved back to Australia. How useful could it be there? I couldn't have been more wrong.

Back in Sydney in 2007, he became an instant celebrity. He was no longer just an ordinary L2 English speaking migrant, but rather, a rare breed – a L2 English and L3 Japanese speaking Polish man. His Japanese can be best understood as linguistic capital, which, in his case, immediately transfers into tremendous social capital (Bourdieu, 1991). This transfer is necessarily a performative act, achieved in interaction with others who evaluate and respond to his performance; every time he 'happens to' disclose his rare linguistic identity, he receives the 'Wooow, you can speak Japanese!' kinds of instant social gratification, admiration and respect. He is definitely out with his friends if he answers my call on his mobile phone, '*Moshi moshiii*?' and tries to converse entirely in Japanese. Since the 1990s, Japanese has emerged as one of the most prestigious foreign languages, widely taught in Australia. Surely many Japanese speaking Aussies are around? In this country haunted by the monolingual mindset (Clyne, 2005), however, a white man speaking Japanese as a fourth language still remains as wow material.

As the good partner that I am, I often go along with him, even when I am not entirely sure what he is talking about. Our use of Japanese no longer worries me – I have rewritten my negative narrative, and gained enough self-assurance in my identity as a competent user of English and as a mature woman. Now I draw tremendous joy from seeing Marcin receive the special attention. This is my most favourite 'act of doing' our multilingual couplehood.

When there is no one else to impress, our use of Japanese functions differently. Piller (2002a, p. 154) discusses, for instance, that some of the bilingual couples she worked with had a preferred 'conflict language'. In their case, English is often perceived as 'easier, simpler, and quicker' for a row, but this inevitably disadvantages L2 English speaking partners. As Marcin asked me to stress, we do not fight, very often. But when we do, English is the main language, together with Marcin's occasional outbursts in Polish (supposedly 'self-directed' swearwords). In my view, fighting is relatively easier than dealing with the aftermath, which often requires us to swallow our pride and reaffirm our love for our partner. For us, Japanese has become our 'make-up language'. He not only learnt the linguistic skills from me and my female Japanese friends, but he also mastered the performative repertory of acting 'cute', in a typical Japanese feminine way. Thus, it makes it easier for him to apologize because, I quote, 'I don't feel so sorry when I say it in Japanese – it's too cute to be serious'. Indeed, even if he insists on an apology by saying, '*gomennasai wa*! (say sorry!)', his use of Japanese and well executed performance of cuteness soften the possible harshness of such demand. Every time Marcin so demurely utters '*gomennasaaai* . . .' with his head down and hands on his lap, my anger quickly melts away – this, of course, inevitably disadvantages me, the L1 Japanese speaking partner.

So far, it may sound as if he is the only one trying to learn his partner's L1. I do speak Polish, to an extent. However, the question of 'how well' is a difficult one to answer because one's proficiency is often an ongoing co-construction between partners, and a 'product of performance' (Pennycook, 2007, p. 59). For instance, Piller (2002a) found that the bilingual couples' L2 proficiency or linguistic knowledge in their partners' L1 is 'interactively' assessed and constructed in private discourses. It certainly applies to our case, too. Thanks to Marcin's unyielding positive remarks about my Polish, I quickly gained confidence, and began claiming ownership over the language – even publicly (the Modesty Maxim out of the window) (Leech, 1983). For instance, when I met his Polish friends in Sydney, I'd confidently declare, 'I speak Polish' and expect thunderous applause. This delusional linguistic identity, however, came to a crisis when I finally found myself surrounded by his parents, relatives and friends – monolingual Polish speakers – during our 2008 wedding visit to Poland. What I gained from this experience is (1) a renewed confidence in humankind that even without a common language, we can truly communicate and embrace each other's company *if* there is a real willingness to share the communicative burden in understanding each other, and (2) a more realistic view of my fluency in Polish. Quite a shift it was – from being a (over)confident owner to a humble L3 'learner' of Polish.

Epilogue

Research on 'private' conversations presents very unique methodological issues. As Piller (2001, 2002a) shares hers with us, I too encountered a number of ethical and methodological dilemmas during my first attempt at microethnography of multilingual couple talk. My first concern was whether or not it was necessary to get a formal ethics approval from my institution and official consent from Marcin in collecting and presenting 'data' for an academic publication. I emailed this concern to my trusted colleague and her advice read: 'Don't tell me you didn't include this in your pre-nuptial ;-)'. Since we didn't even think about writing one, I resolved that I'd just ask for his personal permission. He was happy to 'participate' – initially. As I showered him with questions about our first meeting, our linguistic practices, future parenthood and so on, and on, for the last one month, he became increasingly reluctant to talk about our 'private' thoughts and practices. When I took out my IC tape-recorder from my bag and began taping our conversation one day, he groaned, 'Forget it'. So I just listened, tried to remember his every single comment and understand and interpret what it means for him, me, and us vis-à-vis wider discourses of second language learning, multilingualism and identity. The result is this paper – polyphony of our voices as a multilingual couple in love, multilingual parents-to-be. I thank David and Julie for giving us this opportunity to revisit the very special night in our lives and expand our imagination for our next special day, which is still in its making.

Notes

1 I'd like to extend my sincere *arigato* to Nick Dungey, Emi Otsuji, Emily Farrell and Louisa O'Kelly for their encouragement and helpful comments on my earlier draft. My special thanks go to Ingrid Piller for her thoughtful comments on my earlier draft and introducing me to the fascinating research topic of bilingual/multilingual couplehood through her book, *Bilingual Couples Talk* (Piller, 2002a) in the first place.
2 All the participants in my research were given pseudonyms.

Bibliography

Bourdieu, P. (1991). *Language and symbolic power.* Cambridge, England: Polity Press.

Clyne, M. (2005). *Australia's language potential.* Sydney: UNSW Press.

Colic-Peisker, V. (2009). *Migration, class, and transnational identities: Croatians in Australia and America,* Chicago: University of Illinois Press.

Farrell, E. (2008). *Negotiating identity: Discourses of migration and belonging.* Unpublished doctoral thesis, Macquarie University, Sydney.

Jackson, R. L. (2007). Reconsidering public discourse on private language planning: a case study of a flexible one-parent-one-language model. *The Japan Journal of Multilingualism and Multiculturalism, 13*(1), 1–11.

Kelsky, K. (2001). *Women on the verge: Japanese women, western dreams.* Durham, NC: Duke University Press.

Leech, G. N. (1983). *Principles of pragmatics.* London: Longman.

Norton, B. (2000). *Identity and language learning: Gender, ethnicity and educational change.* Harlow, UK: Longman.

Okita, T. (2002). *Invisible work: Bilingualism, language choice and childrearing in intermarried families.* Amsterdam, Philadelphia: John Benjamins Publishing Company.

Pennycook, A. (2007). *Global Englishes and transnational flows.* London, New York: Routledge.

Piller, I. (2001). Linguistic intermarriage: Language choice and negotiation of identity. In A. Pavlenko, A. Blackledge, I. Piller & M. Teutsch-Dwyer (Eds.), *Multilingualism, second language learning, and gender* (pp. 199–230). Berlin, New York: Mouton de Gruyter.

Piller, I. (2002a). *Bilingual couples talk: The discursive construction of hybridity.* Amsterdam: Benjamins.

Piller, I. (2002b). Passing for a native speaker: Identity and success in second language learning. *Journal of Sociolinguistics, 6,* 179–208.

Piller, I. (2003). Advertising as a site of language contact. *Annual Review of Applied Linguistics, 23,* 170–183.

Piller, I. (2007). Cross-cultural communication in intimate relationships. In H. Kotthoff & H. Spencer-Oatey (Eds.), *Handbook of Intercultural Communication (Handbook of Applied Linguistics 7)* (pp. 341–359). Berlin and New York: Mouton de Gruyter.

Piller, I. (2008). 'I always wanted to marry a cowboy': Bilingual couples, language and desire. In T. A. Karis & D. K. Killian (Eds.), *Intercultural couples: Exploring diversity in intimate relationships.* London: Routledge.

Piller, I. (2009). *Language training and settlement success: Are they related?* Retrieved Thursday, 29 October 2009, from http://www.ameprc.mq.edu.au/research_projects/2008/language_training_and_settlement_success

Piller, I., & Pavlenko, A. (2009). Globalization, multilingualism, and gender: Looking into the future. In L. Wei & V. Cook (Eds.), *Continuum contemporary applied linguistics, vol. 2 (Linguistics for the Real World)*. London: Continuum.

Piller, I., & Takahashi, K. (2006). A passion for English: Desire and the language market. In A. Pavlenko (Ed.), *Bilingual minds: Emotional experience, expression and representation* (pp. 59–83). Clevedon, UK: Multilingual Matters.

Takahashi, K. (forthcoming). *Language desire: Gender, sexuality and second language learning,* Clevedon, UK: Multilingual Matters.

Chapter 28

Transforming Identities In and Through Narrative

Sumiko Taniguchi
Chuo University

'Am I the only Asian-looking person in the whole auditorium?' I ask Richard, a friend of mine, sitting next to me at the Wollongong Entertainment Centre, about 80 kilometres south of Sydney. We are waiting for the start of the Long Way to the Top concert, featuring Australian rock legends of the late 1950s, 1960s, and 1970s. 'A once in a lifetime musical event', according to the advertisement. The auditorium is full of people over the age of forty. It could be easily mistaken that this is the venue of the senior citizen's trivia night, or their thirtieth or fortieth high school reunion. I can easily blend in the audience age-wise, I thought.

However, once being seated in the auditorium and looking around, I suddenly noticed that the audience is predominantly white Australians. Richard and I started looking carefully at the appearance of the audience, and finally found one possible Asian-looking person in a distance. Well, two is bigger than one, but still a small number. Having stayed in a multicultural city, Sydney, for some time for my graduate study, I realized that I have almost forgotten the sense of being a visible minority.

I am a minority in another sense, music-wise. While the audience here is to listen to the music they used to listen to in their teens, I am new to the Australian rock music. Popular music is the backdrop for many aspects of daily life for teenagers (Elder, 2002). 'They danced to it, chatted up the opposite sex to it, drank to it, partied to it' (Elder, 2002). They must have listened to a number of songs from the car radio. I can imagine that their music memories must have been closely connected with what kind of car they were driving, and with whom they were listening to the particular song. In fact, Richard told me, during the concert, 'I started to go out with Jill [his wife], when this song was on the hit chart.' Thus, for them, this concert is a nostalgic event, something like a journey to the past. On the contrary, having grown up in Japan, I was not immersed in the same music in my teens. Or, to be honest, I hadn't even known that Australia had their own rock stars and rock festivals until I watched the TV programme, Long Way to the Top on ABC (Australian Broadcasting Corporation). One night when I turned on the TV, the scene of the rock festival appeared on the screen. Although I am a great fan of British and American rock music, to my surprise, I didn't know any of the songs that were played, or any musicians that were playing. All sorts of questions suddenly popped up. Who are they? What are they playing? When and Where was it? Why don't I know them? It took me some time to realize that the rock festival that I was watching on TV took place somewhere in Australia in the early 1970s. I felt ashamed of my ignorance. Even though a comprehensive rock and roll history by BBC-TV did not cover Australian music scenes, it didn't mean that there was no original music down under other than 'Waltzing Matilda'. Since then my interest in Australian rock music started to grow. I bought a book *Long way to the top: Stories of Australian rock & roll* (Cockington, 2001), double CDs (original soundtrack from the ABC-TV series), and finally the concert tickets. I am excited at the idea of being able to listen to the live music, and see the live performances for the first time in my life.

When the music started, the audience seems to be travelling back to their teens. A couple of women started dancing in the aisle, and Richard is singing along with all the songs in a low voice. On a big screen, images of the musicians' original performance are shown. I can't help comparing these images with how they look now. Obviously the lapse of time is visible in their appearances. Perhaps this applies to the audience, too (including myself). Although I don't share the context in which the music was first played, it doesn't stop me loving the music. I lack the concrete association between the particular song and the particular life events. Nevertheless, I don't feel alienated in the middle of the crowd who shares a similar ethnic and music background. This is partly because I am not alone but with an ex-Australian-teenager. It might be different if I was sitting here just by myself. Also it is partly because of the demographic change of the larger sociocultural context. If this concert took place in the 1960s, would I still enjoy it without being conscious of my difference? I wonder. While the audience is reminiscing of their bitter and sweet memories, I am also travelling back to my teens, to my memories of my first sojourn in America.

Some of my music memories in my teens are closely associated with the landscape of corn fields stretching almost to the horizon in Illinois. The song, *Born to be Wild* by Steppenwolf, for instance, always reminds me of two things. One is a movie, *Easy Rider,* and the other is a stretch of corn fields through which I was travelling in a car with the music from the car radio. As I was always quiet in a car, music was indispensable to fill the space in place of the chat.

In 1970–1971, when I was 18 years old, I spent one year in the United States as an AFS exchange student. It was my first overseas experience and also my first time living away from my family. I stayed in a suburb of Chicago, Illinois, with a population of 30,000 people almost all white middle-class. There was only a handful of visible minorities. I must have been the only Asian background student in a high school. I could not project the image of melting pot or salad bowl to this community. Nor could I hardly believe that this community was a part of the US, which was still fighting in Vietnam. Although I was not a strong activist, anti-war movement and demonstrations had been part of my everyday life in Tokyo. To my surprise, this middle class suburban community looked so peaceful and quiet. I felt the gap and wondered, 'Where is America?'

Soon after I moved into this community, I became self-conscious about my difference. My physical appearance looked different, my language sounded different. I felt that I was displaying my difference all the time, and then I felt I was being observed. Or on the contrary, sometimes I felt that I was invisible to people's eyes, being not worthy of attention.

I felt the sense of loss in many ways. First, I lost words. Though I had spent five years in studying English at school, it was useless. In spite of the loss of words, I was expected to tell people around me what kind of person I was through words because I was a total stranger. People kept telling me 'Say something', when I was sitting quietly in a car, at the dinner table, or in the classroom. I was expected to make a decision instantly, or to tell my preferences immediately, when being asked. I thought that I had something to say, but when I tried to open my mouth, I found that I had nothing to say. Although I was physically close to the American people, I felt that I did not get to know them, as I thought that English proficiency determined one's place in the new community. I had neither competence nor confidence in my English proficiency. Thus, it was only natural that I was placed as an outsider. I could not gain membership to fit into the US High School. Instead of striving for acceptance, I slipped into silence and non-participation.

In conjunction with the loss of words, I experienced an identity crisis. I felt that I lost a grasp of who I was in a different culture. Having lived for 17 years in Japan, I thought I created a kind of self-image, and people around me had some sense of what kind of person I was, although their image might not have been the same as my self-image. I believed that there must be something stable, unchangeable in my identity across time and place. If I brought myself to a new environment, people around me would take me as I was. However, in the States I found my presupposition totally groundless. I felt that I had nothing to tell about myself. 'Be yourself.' I was told this many times from different people. However, if I didn't know who I was, how could I be myself? I considered my personality as sociable, outgoing and friendly in Japan, but where had that sunny side of myself gone, the self I wanted to believe as the real me? I lost self-confidence all together.

To illustrate my self-image at that time, I quote from my self-evaluation sheet submitted to an AFS office at the end of the program in July 1971. (Original spelling and grammar have been preserved here.)

> Personal experience: How have you, as an individual, been influenced by this year's experience?
>
> *'This is the year of real experience. I didn't expect only happy experience. And it was true. I had a very hard time, too. I have become more aware of myself. I found so many bad points. I hated myself. I could not be 100% myself in this country. I don't want to be said Americanized. I tried not to change myself. I tried too much, sometime.'*

My answer above presented a rather negative self-image as an exchange student. The possible interpretation is as follows. I had a kind of image of an ideal international exchange student: a self-assertive person with flexibility trying to understand an unfamiliar language and culture, overcoming one culture shock after another until gaining a membership to the new community, and becoming happy. However, I thought that I did not meet these criteria, because I failed to participate in the new communities (such as family and school). This sense of failure created negative effects on my self-perception. I considered my silence and non-participation as my personal fault. I wrote elsewhere, '*We (my host sister and I) didn't get along too well. That is my fault. I just could not be myself.*'

I attributed my failure of being a good international exchange student to various factors. At an early stage, I attributed my discomfort to my language problems, which created communication breakdowns. Gradually, I added other factors to my list: race, ethnicity, and culture. When I observed other international students from different parts of the world, some of them appeared to be happier and better adjusted to American life. Most of them were from Europe, Oceania and South America. I considered that the determining factor was their proximity to the mainstream American culture, although I was unable to define precisely what the mainstream culture was. I thought that their Caucasian appearance did count to place them closer to the mainstream and to make them blend well. However, as a counter example, I also found some Japanese or Asian students who were excellent exchange students, despite their language and cultural background. Thus, I concluded to attribute my failure to my own inadequacy. It was my personal problem, and it was my failure.

The AFS website says, 'Students return home with improved abilities to navigate across cultural boundaries' (AFS intercultural programs, 2008). I did not think that I did. I did not return home with an understanding of myself. Rather, I felt that I came back with a huge assignment. I started exploring who I was, and whether I was basically the same or easily became different when I moved into a new culture.

Commentary

My AFS experience has not finished. It is still ongoing. After returning home, I worked as a volunteer for AFS Japan office as a university student, and later as a liaison person. We hosted a Thai student for a month in our family. My daughter also went to Australia as an AFS student and stayed with a host family, whose mother and one of her host sisters went overseas as AFS students. Actually, Richard, with whom I went to the Australian rock concert, is my daughter's Australian father.

After all these years and experiences, I looked at international students from many different angles: as a returnee, a mother, a host family, and an official support person, and I kept thinking back and rewriting my AFS story. Obviously what happened in 1970–1971 cannot be changed. However, the meaning and interpretation of experience have been constantly in revision (Polkinghorne, 1988).

First, I came to understand that the age factor plays a critical role in intercultural student exchange at high school level. In one's high teens, one tries to search for who she is, and this search is accelerated in a different culture. The intensity of search for self is an age specific phenomenon that happens whether she is at home or overseas. However, the difficulty increases when she is in a different culture, where the vague image she has of herself does not work. She has to create or re-invent one. Thus, high school exchange students have to cope with difficulties that go with developmental stage, and acculturation.

Second, I started to view the social factors in identity construction more seriously, as the impact of social interaction, or lack thereof, is significant upon my sense of identity. Social interaction with target language speakers is not necessarily easily available to language learners/users. In my case, despite the proximity to the target language speakers, my opportunities to gain access to social interactions were limited.

In recent years, when I have read research articles about ESL students' and minority students' experiences in a host community and a host school (such as Cummins, 1996; Kanno, 2003; McKay & Wong, 1996; Toohey, 2000), I began to identify myself as one of them. This is a new re-storying of my experience. For instance, in Kanno's (2003) longitudinal study of Japanese returnees from Canada, one of the research participants' comments on being an ESL student echo my voice. This person regarded herself and other ESL students as 'second-rate citizens who had no place, no say in their adopted society' (Kanno, 2003: 36). She viewed English as the key to success. From her point of view, 'whether or not one arrived in a new school already equipped with full English proficiency determined one's place in the community: if you did, you were bound for the centre; if you didn't, you were forever on the margins' (ibid.). For her, race and language were 'so inextricably intertwined as to be almost indistinguishable' (ibid.). 'At the core of this group were Anglo-Saxon Canadians, who owned the language and culture of Canadian society. All the rest were allowed in by virtue of their cultural and linguistic proximity to them' (ibid.). The way in which this ex-ESL student describes her place in Canada is similar to my sense of positioning in the hierarchy of the United States. I started to view success and failure of acculturation not as attributes solely of individuals, but 'as specialized social and institutional arrangements' (Lave, 1993: 10). I could have tried harder to participate, but I stopped blaming myself.

Third, my understanding of the conceptions of self and identity has also undergone considerable change. As evidenced in my AFS story, my conceptions of self and identity were rather static. My assumptions were that there was a unified, integrated self within me that was stable across time, and that features of social identity, including race and ethnicity, were the fixed property of the individual. However, the notions of identity, which I take in this chapter at present, are more dynamic and closely related to the notion of narrative.

Researchers in narrative studies acknowledge the close link between narrative and identity, and argue that people can construct and reconstruct their identities through the process of self-narration. Narrative approaches to identity highlight the constructive role of language in the formation and transformation of identity (Crossley, 2000). It recognizes that 'individuals understand themselves through the medium of language, through talking and writing, and it is through these processes that individuals are constantly engaged in the process of creating themselves' (ibid.: 10). Thus, in short, the act of narrating is considered an act of constructing identity.

Important to note here is that people's identities are not solely represented in narrative; they are in fact 'something to be imagined and constructed' (Brady, 1990: 43) through narrative. This is because people construct stories that 'support their interpretation of themselves, excluding experiences and events that undermine the identities they currently claim' (Bell, 2002: 209). Also social discourse shapes what is sayable and what is not (Riessman, 1993). Thus, narrative does not show people just as they were, rather 'it expresses what they believe themselves to have been and to be' (Brady, 1990: 43). It is this 'self-formative power'(Rosenwald & Ochberg, 1992: 1) of narrative that makes it important. Narrative can thus be seen as a 'mediating artefact' (Lantolf, 2000: 23) which people use to make sense of themselves and the world, and also to transform selves.

Lastly, along with these changes, another important change took place. Although I felt the sense of loss in many ways such as loss of words and subjectivity, I came to realize that there was also a sense of gain. The skills and knowledge that I acquired then, and I still use often, are typing and academic writing. I received explicit instructions of how to write academic papers at US high school, which assisted my further study in higher education. Furthermore, my first overseas experience led me to explore the relations among language, culture, and identity, which I am still engaging. In this way, gradually I was able to rewrite my AFS story from 'the story of loss and non-participation' to 'the story of loss and gain'. Thus, it is in the power of telling and re-telling my AFS story that I have re-created the meaning and interpretation of my lived experience, and, in so doing, transformed my identity from 'a failed international student' to 'a struggling teenager'. Human beings have the capacity to reflect on the past to alter the present, and also 'to alter the past in the light of the present' (Bruner, 1990: 109) with the mediation of narrative.

During the Long Way to the Top concert, I have been travelling back and forth across time and space to make meaning of my experience of being a visible minority. My telling and re-telling of AFS experience illustrates the personal, social, and historical levels of change, and the ways in which they interact. Compared to my first sojourn, my second sojourn as a mature student in Sydney is more socially engaged, partly because of my age and life experience, and partly because of sociocultural and socio-historical context of a multicultural city, Sydney in the 2000s, which has a very different demographic profile compared to the suburbia of Chicago in the 1970s. These internal and external factors strongly influence the ways in which I learn and use the second language, my social interaction with people, my affective state, and my identity (trans)formation. Thus, the significance of re-storying past experience is one of the contributions of narrative to an understanding of my own trajectory as a language learner/user.

It is time to bring my story back to the present moment and project to the future, since linking past, present and future is the central role of narrative (Polkinghorne, 1988). On our way home from the concert, we are chatting in a car while listening to the car radio, 101.7 WS-FM, Sydney's great classic hits. 'At first, I felt a bit strange at the concert, but I didn't feel uncomfortable at all. I enjoyed it,' I tell Richard. As a consequence of re-writing my self-narrative, my identities have been and will be constantly in revision. Probably what I'm creating in and through narrative at this particular time and place is my identity as a middle-aged music lover.

References

AFS intercultural programs. (2008). Retrieved 20 December, 2008, from http://www.afs.org

Bell, J. S. (2002). Narrative inquiry: More than just telling stories. *TESOL Quarterly, 36*(2), 207–212.

Brady, E. M. (1990). Redeemed from time: Learning through autobiography. *Adult Education Quarterly, 41*(1), 43–52.

Bruner, J. S. (1990). *Acts of meaning.* Cambridge, MA: Harvard University Press.

Cockington, J. (2001). *Long way to the top: Stories of Australian rock & roll.* Sydney: ABC Books.

Crossley, M. L. (2000). *Introducing narrative psychology: Self, trauma and the construction of meaning.* Buckingham: Open University Press.

Cummins, J. (1996). *Negotiating identities: Education for empowerment in a diverse society.* Ontario, CA: California Association for Bilingual Education.

Elder, B. (2002, 13 September). Most people I know . . . think that I'm almost past it. *Sydney Morning Herald.*

Kanno, Y. (2003). *Negotiating bilingual and bicultural identities: Japanese returnees betwixt two worlds.* Mahwah, NJ: Lawrence Erlbaum.

Lantolf, J. P. (Ed.). (2000). *Sociocultural theory and second language learning.* Oxford: Oxford University Press.

Lave, J. (1993). The practice of learning. In S. Chaiklin & J. Lave (Eds.), *Understanding practice: Perspectives on activity and context* (pp. 3–32). Cambridge: Cambridge University Press.

McKay, S. L., & Wong, S.-L. C. (1996). Multiple discourses, multiple identities: Investment and agency in second-language learning among Chinese adolescent immigrant students. *Harvard Educational Review, 66*(3), 577–608.

Polkinghorne, D. E. (1988). *Narrative knowing and the human sciences.* Albany, NY: State University of New York Press.

Riessman, C. K. (1993). *Narrative analysis.* Newbury Park, California: Sage.

Rosenwald, G. C., & Ochberg, R. L. (1992). *Storied lives: The cultural politics of self-understanding.* New Haven, CT: Yale University Press.

Toohey, K. (2000). *Learning English at school: Identity, social relations and classroom practice.* Clevedon: Multilingual Matters.

Chapter 29

A Short Course in Globalese

Nury Vittachi
Hong Kong Polytechnic University

Summary

People across planet Earth have started talking to each other. Hermit kingdoms sell tours. Internet chat-rooms stretch from Katmandu to Caracas. Individuals travel like never before, trying on each other's clothes and grimacing over each other's foods. What do they speak? English, one of the most complex major languages on the planet, is routinely identified as 'the world language'. But this paper posits that many cross-cultural conversations occur *not* in any sort of formal English, but in a mixed-code tongue using elements from a variety of sources. English vocabulary, Asian grammar, and fashionable terms associated with technology and commerce feature highly. In the first part of this essay, the writer shows how peripatetic groups can deeply infiltrate the vocabulary of the places they visit, particularly if they take significant roles in the socio-political discourse of their destinations. The example given is from Hong Kong, a Cantonese-speaking community influenced by speakers of other languages for historical reasons. In the second part, the writer argues that a similar process is happening on a global scale. As the population-heavy, fast-growing economies of Asia take a higher profile role in global discourse, and as Asia's people travel more, their mother tongues alter the language of international communication. Blended with contributory streams from the old/new media and from advertising, this is leading to the emergence of a new language which could be called Globalese.

Part One: The Case of the Invisible Men

Where's my red pencil? The present writer often acts as middleman between Asian authors and English-speaking book editors. On one occasion, a Hong Kong Chinese author wrote about Mrs Wan who bought 'a five-catty bag of rice with which to make congee'. The English-speaking editor wanted to change 'congee' to 'rice-gruel' and said he'd definitely have to explain 'catty', which he thought was an obscure Chinese measure of weight. The Chinese author was totally mystified by his response. From her point of view, she had already made the translations. The Cantonese word for rice-soup is 'juk', which she had replaced with what she thought was the correct English word, 'congee'; and she bought her groceries by the 'kan', a word she had replaced with the English equivalent, 'catty'. Intrigued by their mutual bafflement, this started me on an odd quest: to compile a list of words which English speakers believed were Chinese, and Chinese speakers believed were English.

Before that day was out, a third item was added to my list. I overheard a tourist ask about the word 'Shroff' on a car park wall in Hong Kong. 'It's Chinese for "cashier",' replied an English speaker. I knew a Cantonese speaker would have said the word was *English* for 'cashier'. The list grew rapidly. Some of the terms were surprisingly high profile. For example, The Bund is the name given to the waterside road/ promenade in the heart of Shanghai, glorified in a thousand postcards. My Shanghainese hosts explained that it was the colonial English name for the place, but the Western visitors in my party said it sounded Asian.

By this time, you will have guessed the origin of the words on the list. Most are from India. Some are from elsewhere in South Asia, particularly the Malay-speaking countries. Just as South Asians have always played quiet but pivotal roles as import-export specialists facilitating trade and communications between East and West, so their vocabulary has slipped into discreet go-between positions.

Here's my list, lightly annotated. Shoppers across East Asia, from Taiwan to Thailand, buy their groceries by the *catty*, a weight of just over 600 grams (about a pound and a third). Each community has its own name for it: 'jin' in Mandarin, 'kin' in Japanese and 'kan' in Cantonese. But all translate it in English to 'catty', because that's what early European travellers called it, having picked up the word *kati* (a unit of weight) when they passed through Malay-speaking regions on the way to the South China coast. Also on my list was the word *tael*, a tiny bar of gold. Chinese assume this is English, since their own word is 'liang', and English speakers assume it is Chinese, since it isn't used in the West. It comes from the Malay *tahil*, a one-sixteenth of a catty measure. Rice-gruel is 'juk' in Cantonese, as mentioned above. The word *congee* is believed to come from Dravidian roots. *Shroff* is an Indian word, originally 'saraf', meaning banker or money changer.

The word *coolie* conjures up images of porters wearing Chinese conical straw hats. Type it into Google and it literally conjures up such pictures. While there is a similar sounding term in Chinese ('koo li' can mean 'suffer labour') most authorities trace the term back to the Hindi term 'quli', meaning 'hired servant'. What could be more Chinese than the *palanquin*, the stately box on poles used to hand-carry the wealthy? The word is derived from 'palyanka-s', a Sanskrit term literally meaning 'that which bends around the body' but generally used to refer to a bed. The word *pagoda* is also neither English nor Chinese. It is believed to come either from the Persian 'butkada' ('idol dwelling') or the Tamil 'pagavadi' ('deity's house').

Also on my list was *mandarin*, which comes from the Hindi term *mantri*, or councillor. It was first used for Chinese officials by visitors from India and Europe, and its meaning spread from there. It is recorded as referring to the speech of Chinese people in 1604, and became the name of a fruit by 1771. (The fruit was a deep orange in colour, similar to that of the robes worn by Chinese officials.) The name of The Bund, the waterside promenade in Shanghai, neatly shows the South Asian role as the invisible middleman holding East and West together. While the early residents of the swamp on the River Pu were Chinese, the colonialists setting up the infrastructure were mostly British. But the workers pulling the barges along the riverbank were Indian, and used the Hindi word *bund*, meaning 'water enclosure'.

While the words given above are familiar in East Asia today, they hark back to a specific period in the early history of the region, from about 1590 to 1850. The population of Hong Kong was Chinese, but many socio-economic decision-makers were European sailors fresh from Malay-speaking lands, and other expatriate communities, with Indians playing a key role. Hong Kong's iconic Star Ferry was started by an Indian. Indian investors played major roles in setting up the University of

Hong Kong, the Ruttonjee Hospital, and even the Hong Kong and Shanghai Banking Corporation.

Today, the discourse in Hong Kong's media is almost entirely in Chinese, the Indian community is largely invisible, and we no longer see Indian words taking key positions in the daily language of its inhabitants.

Part Two: The Emergence of Globalese

I was puzzled: something didn't ring true. As a journalist with an interest in the English language, I would often travel through Asia with books about its history in my bag. One message I read over and over again baffled me, because it clashed so dramatically with what was right in front of my eyes. It was this.

English is one of the most complex major languages in the world. It has an unusually large number of irregular verbs. It has an extremely large vocabulary. There is a problematically wide gulf between how words are spelt and how they are pronounced, which makes learning to read and write the language difficult. The language is bedevilled by a huge number of arbitrary rules which can only be learnt by listening to native speakers.

There's no doubt these statements are accurate. The evidence is plain in the sheer thickness of books which parse English grammar or list the words in the language.

Yet this clearly was not the whole story. In almost every place I visited, from rural Laos, to bustling Taipei, to sleepy Vietnam, to baking Kerala, I found a different story. I had no problem communicating with visitor-friendly locals, even children. We spoke a language that contained stripped-down English and many other things too. While shopkeepers in Vientiane or Xiamen would use their vernacular language with each other, they would slip into this other tongue for travellers. Two things need to be noted. First, this language was *not* reserved purely for communications between locals and visiting English-speakers, but for exchanges between any two parties who did not share a tongue. In other words, Nepalese owners of Internet cafés use it to talk to visitors from Holland or South America or (in my case) Sri Lanka. Different communities of Chinese use it when their dialects are mutually unintelligible and there's no opportunity to write Chinese characters. And, I was curious to note, within the visiting groups themselves (often clusters of tourists or journalists), people from, say, Norway would use something very similar to talk to their counterparts from, say, Italy or Spain. Second, this tongue was not just a form of simplified English. While that language was the biggest contributor to the vocabulary bank, it was not the only source. High up in the list of core terms were Japanese ones such as 'karaoke' and 'Nintendo' and Indian words such as 'curry' and 'masala'. Furthermore, most of the grammar and syntax was not English: Chinese or related languages appeared to be major contributors. There were technical terms ('Internet' and 'mobile' are widely known) and brand names, too: in Vietnam, you may be offered a choice of 'Coca-Cola Coke or Pepsi-Cola Coke' or offered a 'DVD' or a 'Nokia'.

This is not a tongue limited to simple exchanges, but one which can be employed for relatively complex discussions. It is not a children's language, nor is it a creole, although it may have something in common with pidgins. It is not *Taxi*, the nickname of a miniature dialect in which Western expatriates learn only the vernacular phrases needed to talk to taxi drivers. So what is this tongue? I suggest it is the basis of what is already becoming an informal world language: it could be called Globalese.

What exactly is this, and why is it emerging now? On the south coast of China 200 years ago, the active shapers of society operated in Chinese, English, Indian and Malay. And we can clearly see signs of this tucked away in the vocabulary generated at that time, as shown in the opening part of this chapter. The same principle is at work on a larger scale today. International discourse for the past century has been dominated by the activities and interests of the West, and English has become the world language. But the focus of international discourse is moving to the interests of the world's most populous countries: China is number one now and India will be from around 2025. Already the country with the largest number of speakers of English is India, followed by China. Add to this the fact that a hundred million Asians have joined the ranks of globetrotters and we can see that change is not just likely, but inevitable.

The best way to explain what Globalese is might be to provide a sample conversation. Consider the following scene, which took place in a café in Malaysia. A pair of customers approached an open air canteen. The proprietor ushered them to a table and had an exchange with one of them.

Proprietor: Hullo, how you? Long time no see. Sit sit. Beer you wan? Coca-Cola?
Customer: Doe wan. Coffee have?
Proprietor: Kopi have. Two dollar only. Latte? Cap?
Customer: Latte, how much?
Proprietor: Same-same, two dollar. You wan eat? French fry?
Customer: No need. McDonald already breakfast.
Proprietor: You wan look-see menu?
Customer: No need, too fat already, aiyeeah.

Although this conversation was recorded in shorthand by the present writer in Kuala Lumpur, I have overhead similar conversations at similar establishments throughout the Asia region – and not dissimilar ones further afield. As you can see, there is no need to provide an English translation of the exchange. It is readily understandable as it is. Indeed, one might be tempted to think of it as a conversation in 'bastardized English'.

But closer examination reveals that it owes as much to Chinese as it does to English. 'Long time no see' is a classic English idiom borrowed from Chinese, a direct translation of the four characters in the Cantonese phrase 'ho loy mm geen' – literally, 'great time no see'. The restaurateur says: 'Sit sit', and 'same-same'. Repeating a term to add emphasis or insistence is characteristic of many Asian languages, but not a significant characteristic of English.

The simplification of the speech is also very East Asian. Plurals are ignored: 'Two dollar only', 'french fry'. Possessives are dispensed with, so 'McDonald's' becomes simply 'McDonald'. The word-order is also non-English: 'Beer you wan?', 'Coffee have?' And the use of 'no need' instead of 'no' as a negative response is a direct translation from conversational Chinese. The snipping-off of endings on occasions when words end in two consonants makes the English words conform to the traditional form of individual Chinese syllables. Thus, 'Don't want' becomes 'doe wan'. So we can see that the conversation above, although it looks ostensibly as if it is in English, is thoroughly informed by Asian syntactical structures, mostly Chinese.

Also, the influence of international business can be seen in that conversation. Breakfast was 'McDonald' and the coffee styles are those popularized by Starbucks: latte and cappuccino.

But here's the kicker: neither of the two participants in the English-Chinese conversation above were English or Chinese. The proprietor was Malay, and the visitor was a Bangladeshi who had been in Asia for several years. Both parties had learnt through trial and error that English vocabulary and Chinese grammar form a new dialect that facilitates quick and easy communication in most situations they will encounter in Asia.

Anyone who moves around Asia will be familiar with conversations such as that above. But is it not a step too far to call this 'Globalese' and suggest that this is becoming a world language? Perhaps. But before making that judgement, consider the following.

As Asians start to travel more, and the region's culture takes a higher profile in international discourse, Asian forms of speech will inevitably spread. A simple statistic indicates how likely this is: Asians presently make up about 62 per cent of the world's population. If a language really belongs to its speakers, English is arguably *predominantly* an Asian tongue. Given the high birthrates in Asia, compared to the low rates in many Western countries, the 62 per cent figure is more likely to rise than fall in the near future. And these travellers are mixing more. Thirty years ago, few mainland Chinese people were able to leave their country. Today, they are the single biggest group of tourists in many of the holiday destinations in the region. India is also producing globetrotters in large numbers.

These vast numbers of people will ensure that Asian English will be spoken increasingly often around the world. Many go to Europe, Australia and the Americas. Some will be able to use formal English, but most will need a simpler brand. They will use words and phrases such as 'same-same' and 'McDonald' and will find communication easy enough. Non-English-speaking communities in the West also often use English vocabulary with their own simpler-than-English grammatical structures – this is evidenced by each community's possession of lists of half-and-half phrases: look up 'Spanglish' on the Internet as proof of this. These simplified English systems overlap in many areas with Asian versions of English and each will reinforce the other.

The present writer, on a recent visit to The Hague in continental Europe with a group of authors, used both English and Globalese and found the second more useful at street level. For example, a typical English negative response runs as follows.

Waiter: Another coffee?
Customer: It's okay, thanks.

The customer is saying that he is content with his coffee intake, and is not in need of more. However, were he to give a positive response in English, his words could be almost identical:

Waiter: Another coffee?
Customer: Okay, thanks.

The difference between the negative and the affirmative responses is extremely hard to hear, and it is likely that the waiter will have to look for non-verbal signals to work out which is intended. If the customer holds up his cup, he is probably asking for a refill.

In contrast, Asians at this same gathering tended to use Globalese responses.

Waiter: Another coffee?
Customer: No need.
Waiter: Snack menu?
Customer: Yes-yes, bring, thank you.

The simplicity ('bring'), directness ('no need') and built-in redundancy ('yes-yes') of Globalese makes the intended meaning extremely clear.

The posited existence of Globalese serves to solve another mystery, mentioned in passing above. There are many sub-categories of English listed in books and on websites. Singaporeans are said to speak Singlish, Spanish speakers talk in Spanglish, Chinese speakers use Chinglish and so on. Yet when we look at these, we find enormous amounts of overlap. In most cases, the lists consist of English phrases stripped of their complex tangle of auxiliary elements, inverted word-order and unpredictable suffixes, and placed in a simpler grammatical structure. For example, the English phrase 'Is it feasible?' becomes 'Can or not?' in Singapore English. But it becomes the *same thing* in Chinglish *and* in Malglish (Malaysian English). These 'glishes' may eventually come to be seen as what I believe they really are: regional subcategories of the evolving world language, Globalese.

Is this essay an attempt to sell a language system? No. There are many constructed languages based on one or other form of simplified English. These include Basic English, Simple English, Globish, and so on. This paper is not an attempt to launch a new one. Globalese is not a lab-constructed language, but merely an attempt to identify a form of speech that is already observed to be in use across Asia and which may be on its way to wider status.

Just picture yourself in a straw-roofed beach hotel, practically anywhere in Asia, and you can almost hear the staff speaking to you in Globalese rather than English:

Yes. = Can.
No. = Cannot.
Yes, definitely. = No problem.

This is the briefest of essays, and there is no space to provide a phalanx of arguments backed by requisite reams of data. Rather, this can be seen as little more than the sharing of an observation from a working journalist. But if Globalese does exist, anecdotal evidence suggests that core items of vocabulary would include the following, in random order. This list was compiled by the distinctly unscientific method of jotting down commonly used English words in conversations of a mixed group of non-English speakers at a hotel in Bali, Indonesia.

karaoke	Chinese	come
hotel	Indian	house
taxi	English	you like?
trouble	jiggy-jig	bus
plenty big trouble	talk-talk	double
mobile	honey	coffee/kopi

very nice	beautiful lady	tea
same-same	curry-chicken	Starbuck
look-see	gay man	chicken-rice
Nokia	Nintendo	new one
burger	latte	old one
salad	Jesus Christ	big one
McDonald	Internet	small one
ice cream	TV	big boss
chocolate	ice-water	mother-father
Coca-Cola	doe wan	DS (short for Nintendo Dual Screen)
Nike	okay	movie
America	friend	download

A curiosity in this area is that Asian forms of English are widely mocked, yet it seems likely that users will have the last word by sheer force of numbers. It is ironic that the most energetic attacks on Asian English have come from the Singapore government, which banned the use of Singlish in television drama, for example. Their action was misguided. The people of Singapore have developed one of the most flexible and complex sub-categories of Globalese on the planet. It is a lively language that can be learnt at a fraction of the time it takes to learn formal English. And that's the key. The factor that makes it most likely that Globalese rather than formal English will grow to be the world language is this: as mentioned at the start of this essay, English is an extremely complex language with a huge number of arbitrary rules. To achieve fluency takes years of study. In contrast, Globalese is easy and straightforward and can be picked up in weeks by talking to tourists and watching movies. People who travel a great deal and spend time talking to marginal English-speakers will find themselves slipping into Globalese automatically. To show how easy it is, here are two well-known pieces of formal English translated into Globalese.

Original:

> To be, or not to be: that is the question:
> Whether 'tis nobler in the mind to suffer
> The slings and arrows of outrageous fortune,
> Or to take arms against a sea of troubles,
> And by opposing end them? To die: to sleep;
> No more.

Globalese:

> To be: Can or not ah?
> That question I asking.
> Is it more good to be hit
> By plenty big trouble?
> Or to fight back and finish all quick-quick?
> I dead; I sleep;
> Enough already.

Original:

In the beginning God created the heaven and the earth. And the earth was without form and void; and darkness was upon the face of the deep. And the Spirit of God moved upon the face of the waters. And God said, Let there be light: and there was light.

Globalese:

Number one, God make heaven and earth. Earth not very nice, nothing there. Also too dark. God make avatar go look-see waterfront. God say, Light on. Light on.

References

Crystal, D. (2003). *English as a Global Language.* Cambridge: Cambridge University Press.
White, B. (1994). *Turbans and Traders.* Hong Kong: Oxford University Press.
Wolman, D. (2008). *Righting the Mother Tongue.* New York: HarperCollins.

Afterword

The winter of 1940 was a bittercold winter. The water pump in the yard was frozen stiff, the water jug in the outhouse was a block of ice, the only wood stove in the living room managed with great difficulty to bring the temperature up to a chilly three degrees Celsius but the bedrooms were well below zero. My French grandmother, who had lived through two wars with the Germans, had had the foresight in the 1930s to buy a house in a small village as far as possible from the border, in the Dordogne. "Mes enfants, ces Allemands, on va les revoir!" [Children, these Germans, we're going to see them again!] she used to warn us. And so it was. When the Germans reached Paris in June 1940, we children got evacuated to the Dordogne.

We didn't see any Germans in Badefols before April 1943. I didn't know anything about Germans except for the reports from the front given every evening on the radio, the terrified faces of the neighbors, and the "Achtung! Achtung!" bellowed over the loudspeakers when we crossed the demarcation line in Vierzon. The two words "les Allemands" inspired fear and hatred, and for us children they were the terrors in our dreams. But my grandmother, who had studied the piano with German masters and prided herself on her good command of German, talked with fondness about the German au pair nanny who took care of her children around 1905 and the wonder-filled world of German music and German fairtytales. So while our food rations for the week were warming up on the stove, my grandmother would reach with chilblained fingers for a thick green book of German *Maerchen* (little myths or fairytales) that the nanny had left her as a souvenir in 1909. She would sit down in her wicker armchair, with my sister and me on the Moroccan leather poufs, and she would slowly start to read . . . or rather, translate for us the mysterious gothic hieroglyphics into comprehensible French. Our terrors subsided, we forgot the cold. My grandmother's fingers that would usually play silent arpeggios on her knees, were now carefully cradling the book and turning the pages, her index sliding down the golden letterings and exotic curlicues, spotting the foreign Umlauts and es-zets, transposing the cadences of the German sentences into our French vocabularies. The room suddenly filled with wondrous woods and streams, magic potions, princes and princesses, and wishes come true. "Alors, mémé, raconte!" [go on, Grand'ma, tell us the story!] we would exclaim when suddenly the storyteller stopped because she had to read the German first. "Attendez, mes enfants, il faut bien que je traduise!" [wait children, I have to translate!] and she would read the German aloud just to give us a taste of the difficulty of the translator's task. But all she managed to convey was the seductiveness of the foreign sounds and the beauty of a language we didn't know but were supposed to hate. Later

I fell in love with German. I chose to study German literature and become a teacher of German.

If there were any doubt about the nature of the multilingual imagination, the wonderful collection of essays in this book brings ample evidence of its mythical bent. Already as the titles suggest, tricksters, shape-shifters, chameleons, vanishing acts, grammar games and bilingual blends populate these essays. Indeed, when multilingual academics reveal their personal stripes, the result is exhilarating, inspiring. I have found with delight in this book some of the motifs of the fairytales of my childhood: liminal situations occasioned by the loss of a loved one, the move to a foreign country, displacement or dyslexia, linguistic disownings, exclusions and invisibilities, hyphenated existences, but also the power of names, the magic of transformations and metamorphoses, unexpected encounters and revelations, and through it all the symbolic power of language. This is the stuff that myths are made of, these are the triggers for the personal quest for meaning of the hero with a thousand faces. The storytellers in this volume have had an obvious pleasure at reversing the curse of Babel: playing with words, coining new ones, speaking Spanish while pretending to speak French, animating, ventriloquating someone else's words, wordsmiths playing at being wordsmiths, native and non-native speakers playing at being someone else. The autobiographical genre has revealed the passion behind the trade, the fire behind the expertise. I now feel like re-reading the academic writings of these authors to hear the personal voices behind the research papers, the storytelling behind the academic prose. These deeply personal essays speak volumes about the close link between scientific inquiry and narrative imagination in applied linguistics. We owe them a vow of gratitude.

Claire Kramsch
University of California, Berkeley
July, 2009

Index

An environmentally friendly book printed and bound in England by www.printondemand-worldwide.com

PEFC Certified

This product is from sustainably managed forests and controlled sources

www.pefc.org

PEFC

PEFC/16-33-415

Mixed Sources

Product group from well-managed forests, and other controlled sources

www.fsc.org Cert no. TT-COC-002641

© 1996 Forest Stewardship Council

FSC

This book is made entirely of chain-of-custody materials

#0014 - 151111 - C0 - 229/152/13 - CB